## DATE DUE

| | |
|---|---|
| OCT 3 1 2012 | |
| JUN 1 1 2013 | |
| | |
| | |
| | |
| | |
| | |
| | |
| | |
| | |
| | |
| | |
| | |
| | |
| | |

*Also by David Andress*

The Terror: The Merciless War for
Freedom in Revolutionary France

# 1789

# 1789

The Threshold
of the Modern Age

DAVID ANDRESS

Farrar, Straus and Giroux
New York

Farrar, Straus and Giroux
18 West 18th Street, New York, 10011

Printed in the United States of America
Originally published in 2008 by Little, Brown, Great Britain
Published in the United States by Farrar, Straus and Giroux
First American edition, 2009

Library of Congress Cataloging-in-Publication Data
Andress, David, 1969–
    1789 : the threshold of the modern age / David Andress. —
1st American ed.
        p.   cm.
    Includes bibliographical references and index.
    ISBN-13: 978-0-374-10013-1 (hardcover : alk. paper)
    ISBN-10: 0-374-10013-6 (hardcover : alk. paper)
    1. Europe—History—1789–1815.   2. United States—
History—1783–1815.   I. Title.

D308.A63 2009
909.7—dc22

                                                    2008044697

www.fsgbooks.com

1   3   5   7   9   10   8   6   4   2

# CONTENTS

# ACKNOWLEDGEMENTS
## AND AUTHOR'S NOTE

My thanks go to all those involved in the production of this book, especially my agent, Charlie Viney, for some hard work on its initial shape and direction. Thanks to Tim Whiting at Little, Brown for taking the project on, and Steve Guise and Iain Hunt for work in the latter stages. To all my colleagues at Portsmouth, who continue to create a collegial work environment under pressures only we will ever know, and especially to Brad Beaven, without whom chaos would loom, many thanks. To all the various people who told me they were looking forward to seeing the finished product, I hope it was worth the wait; and to Mike Rapport special thanks for a late read-through and some crucial pointers.

To Hylda and Robert, Sheila and Michael, thanks for being there. To Jessica, with all my love as always, and to my darling girls, Emily and Natalie, for you, with love and hope.

**Note:**
For comparison of the various sums of money mentioned below, at the end of the 1780s one British pound was worth just under five US dollars, and somewhat more than twenty French *livres*. Note also that contemporaries had a habit of referring to 'England' and 'Englishmen' irrespective of the hybrid nature of Great Britain and its population. This is inevitably reflected in the source materials quoted here, but I have tried to keep my own text free of such prejudices.

North
Sea

Great
Britain

*Austrian Netherlands*

THE
EMPIRE

Boulonnais

Artois

Flanders

English Channel

Picardy

Metz and Verdun

Rouen

Île de France

Normandy

Paris
Versailles

Champagne
and Brie

Toul

Alsace

Lorraine

Strasbourg

Brittany

Rennes

Maine

Orléanais

Anjou

Touraine

Saumurois

Dijon

Nivernais

Franche-
Comté

Berry

Burgundy

Poitou

Bourbonnais

Swiss
Confederation

Aunis

Marche

Dombes

Saintonge and
Angoumois

Lyon

*Bay of
Biscay*

Limousin

Auvergne

Lyonnais

Kingdom
of
Sardinia

Bordeaux

Dauphiné

Guyenne and Gascony

Languedoc

Toulouse

Provence

Béarn

Marseille

Papal territory

Foix

Roussillon

N

SPAIN

*Mediterranean
Sea*

W          E

S

0    50    100    150    200 miles

0       100       200       300 kilometres

# France in 1789

———— French frontier 1789

··········· Boundaries of provinces
(military gouvernements)

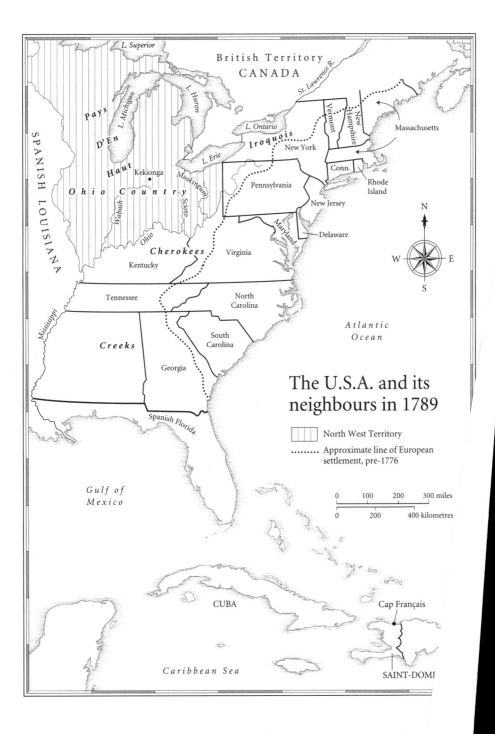

The U.S.A. and its
neighbours in 1789

North West Territory

........ Approximate line of European
settlement, pre-1776

| 0 | 100 | 200 | 300 miles |
| 0 | 200 | | 400 kilometres |

British Territory
CANADA

St. Lawrence R.

L. Superior

L. Michigan

L. Huron

Pays

D'En

Haut

Kekionga

Ohio Country

Muskingum

Wabash

Ohio

Scioto

L. Erie

L. Ontario

Iroquois

New York

Vermont

New Hampshire

Massachusetts

Conn.

Rhode Island

Pennsylvania

New Jersey

Maryland

Delaware

SPANISH LOUISIANA

Cherokees

Virginia

Kentucky

Mississippi

Tennessee

North Carolina

Creeks

South Carolina

Georgia

Spanish Florida

Atlantic Ocean

N
W    E
S

Gulf of Mexico

CUBA

Cap Français

Caribbean Sea

SAINT-DOMI

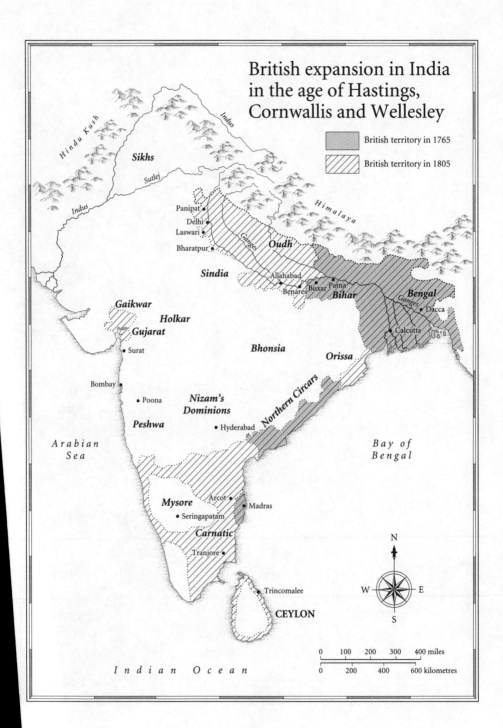

British expansion in India in the age of Hastings, Cornwallis and Wellesley

British territory in 1765
British territory in 1805

# 1789

# INTRODUCTION

'Twas in truth an hour
Of universal ferment; mildest men
Were agitated, and commotions, strife
Of passion and opinion, filled the walls
Of peaceful houses with unquiet sounds.
The soil of common life was, at that time,
Too hot to tread upon.
      William Wordsworth, *The Prelude*, 1805

Winter had come upon Europe like an apocalypse. The frosts had arrived early, and by November 1788 the land was thickly carpeted in snow. Far into the south of France the numbing cold had done its work, shattering the ancient olive trees and withering vines in the stone-hard ground. Nothing moved on the blizzard-buried roads, and rivers were frozen like iron. Cold was not the only portent of doom that had come from the skies. In the high summer a hailstorm had swept in from nowhere, ripping its way through the ripening crops across a huge swath of central France. Peasants had gazed on their ruined fields, well knowing the likely consequence, and by the end of that summer there had already been riots bred from a real fear of hunger. Now the whole of France looked out on the damage done by the awful cold, and could see only disaster ahead.

Late in January 1789, as an early thaw set in, turning the rivers to impassable torrents, the French were summoned from their firesides to meet in every parish in the land, there to answer the call of King Louis XVI to send him delegates for an Estates-General. No one had an inkling of what such an event might produce – the last had happened 175 years earlier. For all that time, the will of the king had been enough to give the country new laws, and to wrestle taxes from its recalcitrant population to fight in Europe's endless succession of wars. Now, by a remarkable twist of historical irony, a war embarked on to help free Britain's American colonists from the imperial grip had left the aristocrats of France fiscally exhausted. The country's coffers were drained by ruinous loans to fund ships and soldiers, and government teetered on the verge of paralysis as age-old institutions locked horns with the king and refused to cede new taxes.

Judges and lawyers had pored over archaic records, deciding that the Estates-General, a meeting of delegates of Clergy, Nobility and Commons, was the only way to produce new laws that might wrest the country from its impasse of bankruptcy and fiscal deadlock. They also knew that to summon the Estates was to invite the grievances of the population, and so the king's official proclamation had been explicit: 'His Majesty wishes that everyone, from the extremities of his realm and from the most remote dwelling places, may be assured that his desires and claims will reach Him.'[1] Thus tens of thousands of nobles, clergymen, lawyers and merchants, hundreds of thousands of townsfolk, and millions of peasants, trudging through slush and mud to their village churches, prepared to unleash upon the Crown of France the weight of their troubles. From their current material suffering, from long reflection on the inequities of an aristocratic society riddled with traces of feudal exactions, from the reverberations of a century of new enlightened thought, and not a little from the echoes of revolutionary events across the Atlantic, the French were about to create the conditions for the traumatic birth of modern Europe.

Far to the north, in comfortable lodgings amid the deep snow of Yorkshire's Pennine Hills, one man knew a great deal about the power of grievances to change history. Thomas Paine was approaching his fifty-second birthday after a life full of incident that was only just about to launch into its most turbulent episode. Paine was from humble roots, the son of a Norfolk stay-maker, and after failed careers as a privateer and excise man had landed in Pennsylvania fifteen years before, just as the fires of American independence were being stoked. Eager to put his pen to work in this new cause, and ever keen to provoke controversy, he gained instant fame with *Common Sense*, a pungent tract in favour of the colonials' liberty. As the conflict unfolded, Thomas Paine had documented it in a series of broadsides he called *The American Crisis*, lambasting both the British enemy and divisions in the rebels' ranks. Summoning new strength with his pen, he was the Americans' most able propagandist, a man who could justly claim to have brought an empire low with his words.

But now, as 1789 dawned, Paine was working to build, not to destroy. A long-nosed seeker after quarrels, his piercing black eyes always questing after dispute, he had a difficult reputation, not helped by a fondness for the bottle that every enemy, past and future, was to harp on. Paine's almost pathological inability to be diplomatic had made him enemies among the new American elite, and he had taken refuge from politics in the realm of engineering. The sharpness of his disputatious intellect was not confined to politics, and modern techniques of forging iron had given him inspiration for a new kind of bridge, a low arch that might be cast across spans of hundreds of feet. Weather such as that now devastating France was common in the northern United States, where bridges built on pilings soon clogged with winter ice. Paine's bridge would soar above such difficulties, but even in a new young land, ripe for innovation, he could not persuade anyone to invest in his scheme, and remarkably, given his radical history, Paine had turned to the monarchies of old Europe for help.

Benjamin Franklin, another man of humble origins who had risen to become one of the sages of the era, had written Paine letters of introduction to France's Royal Academy of Sciences. Just as the republican Franklin had wooed the French grandees into financial and military support for the infant United States in the 1770s, so Paine now hoped to gain royal cash for his upstart scheme. Nor did he confine himself to France. After gaining a favourable technical report from the French experts, and entering his bridge into a competition for a new crossing of the Seine in Paris, Paine took several ideas from his rivals' models, incorporating them shamelessly into a design granted a British patent under the Great Seal of 'His Most Excellent Majesty King George the Third'.[2]

By the logic of our times Paine was an enemy of the British state. But by that of the late 1780s he was a 'citizen of the world', embraced by the international 'Republic of Letters' that united scientists, engineers, doctors and thinkers. Like our own age, the late eighteenth century embraced globalisation and the free circulation of

ideas – at least, those ideas that did not threaten to disturb the
unthinking masses. With the vehement prejudices of militant nation-
alism still only a shadow on the future, Paine and men like him
could surpass the confines of geography. He had no hesitation in
sending a precious, laboriously made model of his bridge to Sir
Joseph Banks, president of the Royal Society in London, who kept
it securely for months, as its owner shuttled between London and
Paris seeking support for his invention.

By early 1788 it was apparent that the French end of this effort
would come to nothing, as the only bridge granted public funding
was the entirely conventional stone design for what is now the Pont
de la Concorde. However, new avenues were opening up for Paine's
project, and by the end of that year he was hard at work in his
Yorkshire fastness, having secured the support of the Thomas Walker
iron foundry, a substantial firm well able to undertake the ambitious
experimental arch Paine had in mind. The course of events seemed
to be disproving the prejudiced note Paine had fired off against his
native country a year earlier: 'While the English boast of the freedom
of their government, that government is the oppressor of freedom in
all other countries, and France its protectress.'³ Paine's American
experience, and sympathies, inclined him to see British politics in
particular with a jaundiced eye, and yet it was on Britain that he
would continue to rest his hopes of commercial success for several
years to come, years in which his revolutionary understanding of the
world would first seem to be validated, before everything he
believed would be called into question.

The world in 1789 stood on the threshold of a great transformation,
one that centred squarely on the three interlocked powers of Great
Britain, France and the United States of America. These states
alone, although pre-eminent in definitions of the 'West' since this
era, do not of course represent global history. Their peoples were,
and are, but a small proportion of the globe's population, and vast
epics of history, even since 1789, have been forged without their
participation. But it is also worth recalling how absolutely significant our three subjects have been in that same era, and that between
them they present the challenge of *a* global history. As soon as one
begins to find the words to justify a focus on the United States,
the task itself seems absurd – the great goal of emigrant hope in

the nineteenth century, accelerating industrial powerhouse, financial motor of Allied victory in 1918, arsenal of democracy in the 1940s and on, ever upwards in wealth, influence and, let it be said, ambition.

Britain too, at least before 1945, commands a reckoning. From a small, damp island to sovereignty over a quarter of the world, and control of over a third of global commerce: this is a story bearing comparison with any epic. France, perhaps, lacks such an easy claim to distinction, though in the eighteenth century, and after, the French were themselves clear that the British, in particular, were engaged in a shameful and mercenary usurpation of a natural Gallic supremacy. However, France in the modern era was the only nation to hold down a multi-continental empire that even began to approach the scope of the British, and the only one to continue to parlay it, into the late twentieth century, into a geopolitical role of similar significance. France in 1789 also gave the world a new political language: the Rights of Man. Simultaneous with the inauguration of the first government under the United States Constitution – and almost to the day with the Americans' drafting of their own Bill of Rights – the French revolutionary declaration marked a true epoch in world history.

The interplay between freedom and subjection, equality and difference, is complex in every historical era. The claims about freedom, equality and rights launched in 1789 were strikingly clear, but also bore with them unexpectedly intricate subtexts and contradictions in practice. If a new language emerged to confront the holders of power within societies, such assertions too often also licensed aggression against those outside the boundaries of constitutions and declarations. A remarkable number of currents converged on 1789, some of which contributed to its humanitarian ethos, and some of which challenged and subverted it. In Britain and France it marked a political birth for anti-slavery campaigning, while in the Caribbean it was a high point in the evolution of slavery, an institution that was to weather attacks, both political and physical, and endure for over a generation to come. In India, a step change took place in relations with European traders, soldiers and administrators, turning them from actors within the shifting confines of South Asian civilisation to overlords, claiming the right to remould a culture they had only just begun to try to understand. Across the Pacific, sailors, convicts, explorers and mutineers were imposing themselves on societies as far removed in space and culture as they could be from the cold shores of Britain, France and America. The new age of federal government for the United States was also about to bring down a new reckoning, rooted in a tangled nexus of fiscal and financial realities, for the American Indian nations that struggled to live alongside the new continental behemoth.

Meanwhile, within these Western societies bent on global expansion, other currents were also at work, beyond the liberalism of the makers of declarations. The new focus on the individual, which in France in particular launched a frontal assault on a society framed by hierarchy and collective distinctions, was matched by new explorations of ways to control that individual. One solution embarked on by the British was to turn convict transportation from the sideline it had been across the Atlantic into a new branch of imperialism in Australia. Other routes, however, looked more closely into controlling society from within, so that the individual became more, rather than less, beholden to the state in the age of rights. Juxtaposed to an ongoing process of industrialisation, which took a major leap forward into steam-powered mechanisation in these years, such changes were yet more foundations for the distinctive modernity that was to be the final gift of this era to the world. The more we look into this moment, the more striking are the convergent lines of evolution that mark a radical shift from a pre-modern past to a contemporary world.

Thomas Paine was among those who foresaw only good from the transformations of the moment. On the one hand, his plans for his own bridge, fruit of the era's advances in metallurgy, saw it as capable of spanning the Seine in Paris, or London's Thames, or being transported in kit form 'to any part of the world to be erected'.[4] He it was, on the other hand, who would cast into his own brand of fervent, demotic English the message of French revolutionary change as *The Rights of Man*, and see himself hounded from his motherland for seditious libel, imprisoned in France as a suspect foreign plotter and shunned in his final retreat to the United States as a drunkard atheist infidel. Not least of the lessons of 1789 is how fast the nations that most eagerly erected ideals into principles retreated from them in practice; and how, even more strikingly, the nation that shunned such effusions, Britain, built a new set of world-spanning imperial claims upon such opposition.

To approach all these topics means seeing 1789 as a culmination of multiple crises, and as the point in time when contingent threads of economic, social and political development were bound together into new patterns, many still coloured by what had gone before, but the whole irresistibly changed nonetheless. It means we must begin with the existing crisis out of which 1789's events would coalesce, and with a trip back to review the deeper currents on which the politics of the 1780s were swirling. Few men can illustrate these better than the one to whom Thomas Paine had gone to gain introduction to the leading minds of Britain and France, who was in his fashion the epitome of all that was positive in the roots of the transformations to come: the homespun sage of the eighteenth century, Benjamin Franklin.

# 'He snatched lightning from the heavens'

*Benjamin Franklin, the Enlightenment and France's crisis of the 1780s*

In 1787 France and the nascent United States both faced crisis from the same cause: their joint triumph four years earlier in securing American independence from the British Empire. Under the pressure of the vast debts incurred in struggling with the world's pre-eminent commercial and naval power, the constitutions of both victors were hamstrung and, from the point of view of their critics, tottering on the brink of collapse. One was a sketchy minimalist agreement wrung from thirteen jealously independent colonies become states; the other a centuries-old accretion of rights, duties, privileges and exceptions. Both lacked the means to raise new taxes without radical change. Out of desperation, both countries' leaders summoned extraordinary meetings to consider such change. The venerable sage Benjamin Franklin, eighty-one years old and almost as revered in France as in America, drew attention to the parallel when he jocularly baptised the gathering that year at Philadelphia with the name of the other at Versailles: it was, he said, 'une assemblée des notables'.[1] From the conflict just ended, with its own complex interweavings of influence across the Atlantic, now came a crisis that would turn the United States, France and Britain, too, towards modernity – each in very particular ways, but none quite able to lose sight of their interconnections.

Franklin can stand as an emblem of the century of dramatic change that had led to this point, and of the turbulent links between young America, aristocratic France and the powerful pull of their common enemy, Britain. Franklin had been a restless innovator all his adult life, gifted with an excess of mischievous personality. Through his energy, and his transformation of a position of utter marginality to one of cultural and social leadership, he could stand as a model, albeit a uniquely successful one, for the new middle classes rising up in these nations. Abandoning the Boston of his birth to settle as a journeyman printer in the more vibrant community of Philadelphia as a youth, and pioneering there new forms of rampantly self-publicising journalism, Franklin spent the early decades of his adult life playing both sides of any number of disputes against the middle; such a middle being, invariably, where he saw his own interests lying. He was not above, for example, stoking a social or political controversy with conflicting pseudonymous letters and articles in his papers, boosting circulation with stylistic exercises that were either refinements of wit or the lowest mendacity, according to taste.

His willingness to court authority was shown in his appointment as postmaster to the colonies by the British Crown in 1753, a post he was to hold for over twenty years, bringing in handsome profits. But even this appointment also revealed Franklin's other, more progressive side: he effectively modernised the whole postal service at his own expense, running up several hundred pounds of personal debt, and he used the newly efficient system to encourage the circulation of ideas throughout the Thirteen Colonies – that congeries of seaboard settlements from Massachusetts to Georgia, erected on an enormous variety of institutional footings, that was creeping slowly towards a sense of itself as a potential whole.[2]

Franklin's devotion to progress may not have been more important to him than his devotion to his own well-being, but it is fair to say that the two ultimately became so entwined, and Franklin himself so publicly identified with progress, that there ceased to be much, if any, conflict between the two goals. Franklin grew up in a world that, compared with our own, was almost empty of real public interchange, of politics as we understand them and of opportunities for individual development. Rebelling in his own ways against both the closed, aristocratic nature of rule and the pinched restrictions on communication it profited from, Franklin throughout his long life surfed a wave of innovation, so that by his twilight years he could look on a near-global vista of claims to popular sovereignty, vibrant public discussion and advancing scientific knowledge. Movement towards the growth of a new, more individualist public had begun much earlier, but so slowly as to be almost imperceptible. The tortuous coils of religious dispute coming out of the sixteenth-century Reformation, the reinvigoration of elite engagement with classical civilisation that the Renaissance had prompted a hundred years before: these fed into an almost-subterranean emergence and dissemination of knowledge, even as Europe and its colonies were racked by religious conflicts for a century up to their exhausted, devastated conclusion at the end of the Thirty Years War in 1648.

Only a few years after Galileo Galilei had been condemned by the Catholic Church for his 'heretical' scientific views in 1633, the French philosopher René Descartes launched a new wave of intellectual reflection, beginning from his 'I think, therefore I am' to try to build a rational conception of existence and meaning. Such thinking crossed with the ferment of the English Civil War of 1642–51 to produce a generation of philosophers prepared to put the institutions of society under the microscope, this device being a new invention of the 'Scientific Revolution' simultaneously under way. While Thomas Hobbes became famous for his *Leviathan* of 1651 (written largely in French exile), in which he argued for strong governments to contain civil strife, he was equally at home disputing both the mathematical and philosophical arguments of Descartes, and his political views emerged from a strikingly 'modern' meditation on humanity as a materialistic and self-interested species.

In the succeeding generation the baton of change was picked up by John Locke, another scientifically trained thinker who produced at the time of the British Glorious Revolution of 1688–9 a body of work absolutely fundamental to the astonishing century that followed. Ranging from the psychology of the senses to the question of the 'natural' state of humanity, and challenging Hobbes's pessimism, Locke offered a view of individuals as free and (at least potentially) rational beings, whose 'natural' rights ought to be respected, and their differences tolerated, in a good society. As Locke's works served as a foundation stone for a new century in which the individual would be liberated from compulsive obedience, so the transcendent genius of Isaac Newton, whose *Principia Mathematica* was published at almost the same time, in 1687, began to free the natural world from the tinkering hand of God, and to expose the working of natural laws in motion, gravitation and the nature of light. If Newton himself, unlike some of his scientific contemporaries, retained an obsessive interest in the religious foundations of existence, the works of the generation of British scholars that he graced offered the chance to exchange the authority of churches and divines for that of reason, reflection and open discussion.

Such discussion was as yet confined to small, elite groups. Newton's works were published in Latin, and while London's Royal Society, which sheltered him and other scientists and 'natural philosophers', had the patronage of kings, it would take wider social change to make such topics the meat and drink of polite society's conversation. One agent of such change was the humble coffee bean. Coffee-houses burst into European life in the second half of the seventeenth century, inspired by Turkish customs, and rapidly developed a new culture all their own. The first coffee-house in England opened in 1650, and before the end of that decade such places were already noted as the haunts of political radicals and freethinkers. New generations of urban dwellers with both business to transact and leisure to pursue broader discussions soon made them their own. Paris, which saw its first café in 1672, had 280 by 1720 and nine hundred in 1789.[3] With coffee providing stimulation, but not inebriation, these institutions rapidly became noted for their freedom of speech. Attempts to ban them in Britain in the 1670s failed, and elsewhere it became more common for authorities to eavesdrop on the conversation for information than to try to halt it. Café debate acquired something quite new in European history: public political legitimacy. While discussion in the majority of such places never veered towards the seditious, it did offer the chance for a growing circle of the urban well-to-do, and those who aspired to rise in the world, to engage with events, even if only by talking publicly about them.

While discussion in cafés could create all sorts of circles and networks – for example, from Lloyds of London there emerged the world of maritime insurance – it could not in itself bind together a 'public'. For that a new step was needed beyond the restricted circles of pre-modern communication, towards a genuine periodical press. Writers and publishers by the early eighteenth century already had a long experience of innovative and polemical productions. Printed broadsides in pamphlet form had inflamed the politics of the English Civil War and Commonwealth, while at the same time across the Channel the vicious printed slanders against the royal minister Mazarin, the *Mazarinades*, had defined a whole era of heated debate bordering on rebellion. But such pamphlets, though they lacked for little in stylistic innovation or imaginative vocabulary, did not possess the solid basis provided by a permanent existence – each one, though part of a series, and sometimes of exchanges between parties and factions, had to stand alone. Government-sponsored news-sheets and gazettes from the mid-1600s began to offer a more regular diet of information, but their official status generally brought with it a requirement to be careful, safe, anodyne on the very topics where the coffee-house publics increasingly wanted meatier stuff.[4]

That such meat need not be in the scurrilous form that political pamphlets continued to peddle was proven by the success of a series of papers produced in London between 1709 and 1714. The *Tatler* and the *Spectator* (which had several incarnations), launched originally by an editor of the official London *Gazette*, offered witty commentary on contemporary events for an audience that felt itself respectable and wanted to be spoken to in a refined style. Moving from manners to art, and diplomacy to religion, and evolving over their short life further towards detailed cultural commentary and observation, away from the mere flow of events, these papers proved that an audience could be engaged, and indeed constructed, by the output of the press. So successful were they that the *Spectator* in particular continued to be printed in book form, and translated into a slew of European languages, for decades to come.[5]

It was this atmosphere of possibility that the young Franklin tapped into in 1720s Philadelphia, using the lower forms of journalistic gossip to drive into debt a competitor (and former employer) who had launched a paper to pre-empt Franklin's own plans, until the rival was forced to sell up to him, leaving Franklin in October 1729 as the proud publisher of the *Pennsylvania Gazette*. Here he combined a low wit suitable to sly interchanges with a lively concern for the public interest (and what interested the public, almost never the same thing), juggling gossip and innuendo with the serious business of coaxing into existence a public from the diverse constituents of a colony of emigrants.

Alongside the *Gazette* Franklin also produced, from 1732, his annual editions of *Poor Richard's Almanack*, in which he offered his wry and witty approach to life – avowing, through the mouthpiece of his fictitious 'author' Richard Saunders, that he wrote not for 'the public good' but because 'I am excessive poor' – but also a set of distinctly innovative virtues for contemplation. He honed a collection of folk sayings and maxims into sharper versions, and preached a concern for material gain and moral rectitude entirely in tune with the changing times, and an audience far removed from the aristocratic elite. As Franklin's life prospered, so increasing numbers of men like him, and their families, were making their mark. The public of the coffee-houses and the newspapers, in Philadelphia, New York and Paris, Bordeaux, Nantes, Bristol and Birmingham, was outpacing the nobles and churchmen who had run the affairs of nations for so long. Cities grew, populations rose and trade and industry flourished, with worldwide avenues of commerce growing stronger and broader decade upon decade, boosting the fortunes of hundreds of thousands and drawing millions into their workforce. Whole regions became dependent on busy middlemen who could supply raw materials for manufacture and shift goods to distant markets, even if most of those who laboured for them still worked industriously in their own cottages and attics.

Still largely shut out of politics, save as audiences and occasional commentators (and, with their rougher brethren, as rioters in turbulent times), the men of the middle classes were nonetheless learning to take an interest, preparatory to taking a place in the affairs of state. The wars of their kings took on a new character, for no longer, as under Louis XIV before 1715, would the religious bigotries and personal glories of a king be enough to drive European conflagration. Wars still came, sometimes overtly about no more than disputed dynastic successions, but they also carried an ever more global charge. The rising power of Atlantic trade and the near-industrial production of the Caribbean slave islands; the vast prospects of North America; and the rich pickings of trade and alliances in India: all these gave a mercantile cast to the eighteenth century's wars. Where once Drake and Hawkins had chased galleons laden with Spanish gold, soldiers and sailors now fought and died for trading rights and slave-tilled soils. Control and monopoly of new horizons for systematic profit, rather than the plunder of the Spanish Main, were the new, less dashing, more prosaic aims of conflicts that France and Britain brought to the seas of the world again and again.

It was those who profited quietly from all this change whom Franklin sought to address. His civic sermons set out the values of a new middle class, for whom religious seriousness was combined with profit-making and a desire for improvement. Even in setting out the principles he saw fit for this new society, his humour persisted: when he assembled many of his moral ideas into a sermon by 'Father Abraham' in his final edition of 1757, he also had 'Poor Richard' report at the end that 'The people heard it, and approved the doctrine, and immediately practiced the contrary.'[6] With such mockery Franklin attacked no one as much as himself. He was throughout his life convinced that society could advance best through the twin means of self-organisation among men of talent and the technological and scientific innovations to which an open society was most receptive. His personal example gave the lead, founding through his own energies in Philadelphia a spectrum of groups ranging from the American Philosophical Society to a volunteer fire-fighting corps.[7]

The bitterest clashes of Franklin's life came with the colonial administration of Pennsylvania, a 'proprietary' colony ultimately owned, quite literally, by the Penn family. The descendants of the original Quaker founder William Penn, safely ensconced in England, proved less interested in their souls than their purses, and persistently vetoed meaningful reforms to the colony's public life through the 1750s and 1760s. Twice in wartime crises Franklin was instrumental in forming militias to ward off French and Indian attacks, only to be coldly repudiated by the colonial governor, jealous of Franklin's popularity and his allies in the colony's elected Assembly. It was this antagonism that in 1757 led to Franklin's appointment as the Assembly's agent in London, to lobby for reforms, there to begin a whole new stage in his life.[8]

For most of the next three decades Franklin lived in Europe, first in London and later, during the Revolutionary War, in Paris. Here he at last became a figure on the world stage. In purely political terms he would rise to become agent in Britain for the colonies at large, and hold talks, as the crisis deepened into the 1770s, with the highest in the land. More broadly, Franklin found himself in a world of philosophical and scientific inquiry that took him to its heart. He had always cultivated his interest in natural phenomena, observing the mysteries of weather and sampling seawater on ocean voyages for evidence of currents, for example. Having retired from his printing business at the end of the 1740s, he used his increased leisure time to expand his experimental interests, and in 1752 he had found international renown with his kite-flying demonstration of the electrical properties of lightning. Already part of a wide circulation of scientific information, he won for this the 1753 Copley Medal of the Royal Society, and in 1756 was inducted as one of its very few non-resident members. Thus upon his arrival in London he found himself among brothers. He conversed with doctors, economists, legislators and experimenters, and involved himself in schemes both practical and theoretical. He was called on to erect lightning rods on St Paul's Cathedral in London, and on royal arsenals in the city. He experimented in epidemiology, diagnosing lead poisoning as the cause of a number of common ailments among trades using the substance, and corresponded with the president of the Royal Society about the effect of displacement on the speed of ships passing along canals.[9] He was an integral part of a scientific ferment, as what was coming to be called the Enlightenment put the human and the natural world to the test of new questions, freed from religious shackles.

Although Franklin felt deeply at home in London (so much so that he formed a comfortable, if platonic, *ménage* there with his amiable landlady, while his wife lived out her last days sadly alone in Philadelphia), he was ultimately unable to reconcile his vision of the colonies' future with the evolving political situation. That vision had been spelled out publicly in one of Franklin's first forays onto the wider political stage, at a conference of colonial delegates at Albany, New York, in June 1754. Called to discuss relations with the Iroquois confederation, who held the balance between French and British interests on the colonies' north-western frontier, and more generally to plan for an equitable management of colonial defence, the conference was both constructive and ultimately pointless. Only seven colonies accepted the original invitation from the British authorities, and most of those ordered their delegates to reject any scheme that threatened their autonomy. Such rejectionists included even the Assembly that appointed Franklin one of Pennsylvania's delegates, but undeterred he helped to impose on the conference an essentially federalist vision – a union for external defence and westward expansion, governed under the Crown, preserving the internal rights of each colony's legislature and constitution. In a deeply ironic reflection of future troubles, the British government rejected the proposal for its democratic overtones in electing a general assembly of the colonies, while every one of the individual colonies spurned the plan as an abridgement of their powers.[10]

As late as 1774 Franklin was to be found in confidential talks with British politicians about plans to reconcile Crown and colonies. A year later, at the First Continental Congress, the meeting of colonial delegates that began to propel the Americans towards independence, he proposed again a form of union, with a strong central government and local autonomy, that would function equally well inside or out of the British Empire. It remained too much of a shift for his newly rebellious colleagues, and the plan was shelved more or less undiscussed, one result being that the United States spent the years of their war for independence still wrangling over Articles of Confederation and staggering from one financial expedient to the next to fund the conflict.[11]

Franklin meanwhile embarked on yet another phase of his already remarkably long life, dispatched to Paris (after a brief period in which he managed both to edit Thomas Jefferson's draft of the Declaration of Independence and join an arduous and futile invasion of Quebec), there to solicit the aid of Europe's pre-eminent absolute monarchy in the liberation of the new Republic. Wise to the bizarre nature of the mission, but also to its crucial importance, Franklin deployed all his charms to woo the sentimental side of the country that claimed the Enlightenment as its own. Such a claim was rather ironic, since the Grand Old Man of French Enlightenment, Voltaire himself, had come to many of his scientific and political views after being dazzled by the works of Isaac Newton, and by political debate he saw in Britain in the late 1720s, while avoiding arrest back home for anti-religious and anti-aristocratic satires. Whereas in Britain the Enlightenment had begun among a serious-minded scientific elite, and subsequently spread to a wider public, encouraging more subversive political and social attitudes, in France it was superficially subversive satire that had provided the first opening for writers who evolved into true *philosophes*, or lovers of knowledge. As with Voltaire, so with the baron de Montesquieu, whose first major publication was the *Persian Letters*, using the device of foreign envoys observing the morals of Paris in the 1710s to poke fun at shallow pretensions, and also at political despotism. He had evolved to produce thirty years later the *Spirit of the Laws*, a comparative anthropology of political authority that was to have a profound influence on both sides of the Atlantic.

By the 1750s innovative thought had become respectable in France: official Academies, regional assemblies of scholars under official patronage, sponsored essay competitions that encouraged reflection on the nature of society without reference to God. Yet at the same time, to insult religion or other powers-that-be openly remained criminal. Indeed much of Voltaire's later career was taken up with challenging the right of the Church to continue persecutions that belonged, he thought, to an earlier, darker age. To be locked away by royal decree for offending civil or religious power became a badge of honour for the authors of France's great age of the Enlightenment, and those who avoided such a fate did so largely by declining to publish their real thoughts, circulating them in manuscript to closed circles of friends.

The great project of the mid-century decades was the *Encyclopédie*, a compendium of knowledge both speculative and useful, that was to make the thinking of the age available to all who could read. Once again paradoxes were legion. If the *Encyclopédie* made much of its claim to diffuse economically useful innovations, and filled volumes of prints with illustrations of machines and industrial techniques, its main readers were the leisured gentlemen, clerics and scholars who could afford this massive multi-volume reference work. And if the *Encyclopédistes* wanted to challenge authority, led by the scurrilous Denis Diderot, who once wrote a political satire in which the secrets of a kingdom were given away by talking vaginas, they had to hide their critique under sly asides and references, most famously when the article on cannibalism, 'Anthropophagy', was cross-referenced to Christianity's Eucharist.

The intellectual ferment that, in the person of Franklin, seemed a logical consequence of social change was rooted in France in a far more paradoxical soil. What made Enlightenment thinking possible there was its patronage by the social elite. In an aristocratic society where boredom always threatened, writers and artists were adopted by nobles to add sparkle to conversation. Outside the closeted world of court ceremonial, a central part of elite sociability took place in *salons*, gatherings in private homes where hostesses regulated the talk of assembled guests and, depending on the interests of those present, anything from poetry to physics might be scrutinised for what was new, interesting or simply strange. Some *salons* dealt in political news, others in culture, others still in science, but all were hubs from which tendrils of protection and publicity extended, binding those who wrote into networks of power, opening doors to sponsorship, royal favours, appointments and endowments. Through the *salons* and their exchanges, and through the gatherings of Freemasonry, where noblemen could rub shoulders with wealthy non-nobles and feel the thrill of apparent equality, those who lived at the very pinnacle of a system of social privilege in eighteenth-century France could also hold themselves to be the supporters of modernity, freedom and justice. And thus they could become deeply attached to the notion that the Thirteen Colonies should be free of their tyrannical British masters.

In furthering this cause, no one was better suited than Franklin. He dazzled the leading lights of society, allowing them to believe, since they seemed to want to, that this religious sceptic was in fact, more romantically, a Quaker. He sported a slightly outlandish fur hat as part of his homespun image, striking echoes of the equally beguiling yet far less sociable Jean-Jacques Rousseau, France's very own cult philosopher of the 1770s. Rousseau's rejection of the outward proprieties led him to sport a long gown and fur hat in what he termed 'Armenian' fashion, though such a rejection never stopped him, like Franklin, accepting the near-idolatrous praise, and generous hospitality, of the wealthy and fashionable. To people who never went out in public without silks, brocades, red heels and tottering wigs, the philosopher who preached self-sacrificing civic virtue was an unlikely hero. Since he also proclaimed the merits of chaste and sentimental love, his reception among an elite that accepted extramarital affairs as a normal means of personal gratification and political manipulation was equally odd. Franklin's image of broadcloth coats and unpowdered straggling hair, and the pithy wisdom of his almanac, long a bestseller in translation, appealed to the same oddly contradictory ideals of this noble, sentimental elite.

But also like Rousseau, Franklin was no buffoon, and unlike him, had a hard political side. Wearying weeks and months of negotiations followed, including bitter disputes with fellow American representatives, and complex games of double-dealing with the British and other spies inserted into the negotiating parties. The end result was both the vital military aid the United States required and a strong emotional attachment among the elite of society that endured after the messy (and, for the French, unprofitable) conclusion of hostilities. Franklin's impact is symbolised by the epigraph composed for him by Anne-Robert-Jacques Turgot, baron de l'Aulne. This man of learning was also one of the most dedicated servants of France's monarchy, yet he could give authentic praise to Franklin's scientific and political achievements in writing: 'He snatched lightning from the heavens and the sceptre from tyrants.'[12] The dilemmas that were to be provoked by the definition of tyranny this implied would change the world forever.

The collections of the Metropolitan Museum of Art in New York and the Musée Carnavalet in Paris both include a white porcelain figurine group that embodies all the paradoxes of France's relationship with America, and its view of its place in the world. Celebrating the treaties of alliance between the two countries signed in 1778, the figures are of Benjamin Franklin, then sixty-two years old, and the young King Louis XVI, still a few months shy of his twenty-fourth birthday. Franklin appears in a calf-length coat trimmed with fur, or possibly velvet, hanging carelessly open over a stout pot belly confined in a plain waistcoat. His age shows clearly on his lined face, and his hair, as in all his most famous images, cascades at liberty down to his collar. He is posed in a half-bow, receiving with open arms the treaties from the king, two scrolls emblazoned in gold letters 'Independence of America' and 'Freedom of the Seas'.[13] The figure of the king is far more extraordinary. While Franklin is rendered almost wholly as a 'natural' man of the age, Louis is transformed into a martial god. Standing on a raised platform to make him more than a head taller than his companion, he puts forward a graceful leg and gestures with an open hand towards the gift of amity he presents. Beneath powdered hair, its side curls tight above his ears, he wears a suit of splendid plate cavalry armour descending to his knees, its scales overlapping on his arms and thighs like the shell of an ornamented lobster, the metal outlining his limbs far tighter than any real armour could have been worn. Around him swirls a vast cloak embellished with fleurs-de-lis, and he is less a man than an image: an idea of kingship rendered in a form obsolete on the battlefield for well over a century.

The real King Louis XVI was far less of an anachronism, and ironically that may have been one of his greatest problems. When he had come to the throne a few years before, he had made a stark contrast with the bloated, pox-rotted sack of his grandfather and predecessor, Louis XV. The latter had grown to maturity in an age when kings still led armies to battle, as he was to do one last time in the 1740s, but also, notoriously, presided over a court where the very worst excesses of sexual and political libertinage held sway. His young successor was an impeccably moral man, raised in the maxims of both religion and enlightened reason, and who, astonishingly, declined to keep a mistress. Setting out on a series of reform programmes, he found himself thwarted and increasingly isolated by the very structures that sustained his rule, and continued to present him to the world, somewhat lumpish and rather shy youth as he was, as both avenging Mars and defender of liberty.

France in the later eighteenth century was caught up in a series of jarring political and cultural clashes, all of which fatally inhibited its ability to profit from a time of notable social and economic expansion. A population that in the seventeenth century had been checked repeatedly by war, famine and epidemics grew relentlessly, from around twenty-one million in 1715 towards twenty-eight million in 1789. The great cities that traded across the Atlantic, such as Bordeaux and Nantes, the Mediterranean, such as Marseille, and the land frontiers to the east, such as Lyon, swelled, doubling or tripling their populations. Even at its lowest imperial ebb, losing Canada at British hands in the 1760s, France retained lucrative trading posts on the shores of India and still drew massive revenues from its Caribbean sugar islands. Hundreds of thousands were employed in textile industries at home at least as advanced as those of their rivals in Britain, while French artisans and craftsmen led the world in the production of luxury goods, charging inevitable premium prices to an international clientele.

The difficulty France had was in translating all this to taxation, and thus to real state power. Such was the size and wealth of the country that for most of the century the underlying problem remained hidden. By schemes and expedients the king's servants raised enough money to fight war after war across the 1700s (such conflicts being still the natural and inevitable way to settle disputes in the turbulent politics of Europe), but as they did so, the finances of the state slipped nearer and nearer to unavoidable disaster. French tax-gathering suffered from problems that were both practical and more deeply structural. The vast size of the country and the broad dispersal of the population were problems in constructing efficient organisations. One response had been to 'farm out' taxes to private concerns – such *fermiers* were consortia of financiers who offered the state a guaranteed level of payment and then planned to make a profit by collecting more than they promised to pay. Tens of thousands of paramilitary private mercenaries battened on the French taxpayer, inserting avarice and corruption into a system that already saw being a 'taxpayer' as something shameful.

This was the deeper problem of the French state. Americans had revolted for 'no taxation without representation', but the motto of the French elite might well have been 'representation means no taxation'. The monarchy's practice for centuries had been to reward status with privilege, and sometimes to sell that privilege for short-term income, compounding the longer-term problem. For what privilege meant, beyond mere social cachet, was the right not to have to pay tax. State office-holders, along with tens of thousands of nobles, the inhabitants of some entire provinces and anyone else with any real social status were effectively outside the regular systems of taxation. The main tax on land and personal wealth, the *taille*, was effectively confined to the peasantry, for to be *taillable* was to be the lowest of the low. Even membership of a town council, an office available for purchase through most of the century, conveyed exemption from some direct and indirect taxes, as did holding office in a guild or being in the employ of a more privileged superior.

Though the privileged classes did pay hefty sums in supposedly 'emergency' property taxes brought in under the pretext of war, such amounts were vastly lower, as a proportion of their wealth, than the burden imposed on the unprivileged, and the powerful could always find ways to beg or bluff their way out of much of what the state claimed they owed.[14] The king's own brothers and cousins, the Princes of the Blood, should have paid almost 2.5 million *livres* a year, but coughed up barely a twelfth of that, thanks to the reluctance of officials to tangle with men whose influence stretched so high. As the duc d'Orléans, a man who owned more land than some countries, remarked, 'I pay more or less what I like.'[15]

French financial affairs were of a complexity dazzling even to experienced contemporaries, taxes flowing through numerous separate offices, their holders often men who had paid good money for their positions and intent on exploiting them for gain. What monies actually belonged to the Crown, as opposed to its various subcontractors, could be profoundly unclear. When reforming ministers did drag figures out of the system, the picture was dire. In 1775, before spending on the American War began, taxes and other revenues brought in some 377 million *livres*. Expenditures totalled 411 million, including 154 million in debt interest and repayments. In a good year, a peacetime year, the French Crown thus had to borrow about thirty-five million *livres* just to cover outgoings, and pay out almost five times that much to service earlier borrowing.[16] To get its finances through the war years, it had turned to a Swiss-born financial wizard, Jacques Necker, installed (thanks to his foreign birth and Protestant religion) in the ambiguous position of Director of Finances, rather than full Finance Minister. Necker's magic, however, allowed things just to keep on getting worse. When he started borrowing, his skills and reputation enabled him to negotiate fairly low interest rates. As he kept coming back for more, the rates crept up. What made things worse was that many of the loans were actually *rentes viagères*, life annuities. Not only was life expectancy rising faster than contemporary accountancy allowed for, but current practice allowed the 'life' for the term of which the funds were offered to be nominated freely by the buyer of the annuity. Canny Swiss financiers nominated young healthy unmarried women, especially those who had already survived smallpox and who could be cloistered as living investments, expanding the scope of the French state's liabilities far beyond what had been calculated for. Necker himself fell from office in a complicated tangle of anger and offence (given and received around the king's council table in equal measure) in 1781, and his successors were able to use the argument of wartime to force through extra taxes. Nonetheless, supporting the freedom of the Americans turned the situation of French finances from a problem to a disaster. Within a few years from the end of hostilities in 1783, French state expenditure was exceeding income not by a mere thirty-five million but by over 160 million, and bankruptcy loomed.

The crowning dilemma of French politics was the absence of any simple chain of fiscal and political responsibility. French ministers were answerable to no one but the king himself. Legislation was the will of the king, articulated in decrees, not Acts of Parliament as in Britain. France had institutions that shared that medieval name, *parlements*, but they were law-courts, staffed by cohorts of hundreds of judges who made up the core of a 'robe nobility' of state servants, ennobled by their roles and by the ownership of their lucrative offices. Unfortunately, while these *parlementaires* were ardent defenders of legitimate power and, for the most part, well-qualified upholders of the law, their view of their place in the unwritten constitution differed from that of kings and ministers. For decrees to become law, they had literally to be inscribed on the statute books held by the various regional *parlements*, as the highest appeal courts. For the Crown, this was an administrative function, an obligation of the judges' role. For the *parlementaires*, however, it was a cornerstone of their claim to safeguard the state against unreasonable innovation, and their right to refuse to register new laws (and especially new taxes) had occasioned bruising political crises.

The paradoxes of privileged resistance to reform, in the supposed home of the Enlightenment, were evident to see. Voltaire's literary talents lifted him from his origins as a notary's son to royal appointments in France, the life of a landed proprietor on the Swiss border, and to correspondence with, and at one point a salary of twenty thousand *livres* from, Frederick the Great of Prussia. Like the earnest correspondence that Diderot kept up with Catherine the Great of Russia, such a relationship marked the intellectual pre-eminence of authors who sought reform. But it turned out to be very hard to make any of this stick in France itself. Enlightened absolutists such as Frederick and Catherine might succeed in imposing rationalising reforms on backward countries, but France was a more complex affair. The very same elites who encouraged reforming authors in the privacy of the *salons* were likely to join in hypocritical public condemnation of ideas that threatened the status quo that underlay their wealth. A vicious circle of association drove reformers to look for authoritarian rulers to be able to implement their ideas, and thus led to such ideas themselves being condemned as 'despotic' and a threat to liberty. Such condemnation often came from another consequence of France's half-hearted approach to publicity – continued censorship of the press gave encouragement to secrecy in publication, and thus to irresponsibility, gossip and slander. Many widely circulated papers came from outside the country's borders, produced by buccaneering exiles; others circulated as manuscript news-sheets to privileged groups before finding their way into print as the *Correspondance secrète* (Secret Correspondence) or *Mémoires secrets* (Secret Memoirs) of unsavoury elite behaviour.

Through the 1760s and early 1770s a generation of government ministers who had learned about rational administration through enlightened discussion failed to apportion taxes more fairly, or to cut back on the political role of men who had inherited or bought their offices and privileges. Such opponents had also learned from the Enlightenment about the value of public opinion, and how to conduct politics through pamphlets and newspapers, including the many illegal and clandestine ones. When the ageing King Louis XV and his Chancellor, René Nicolas de Maupeou, tried to strike decisively at some of the most obstructive members of the privileged elite, they felt the full force of this. Maupeou's *coup* of 1771 disbanded the *parlements*, and for three years the king's ministers fought back a tide of anti-government propaganda from the *parlementaires* and their allies, who included other elite factions, and who were prepared to subsidise even openly pornographic assaults on the intentions and morals of the alleged ministerial 'despots'. The fruits of the Enlightenment, and the consequences of decades of sophisticated discussion in civilised *salons*, turned out to be the blistering political filth of writers prepared to accuse ministers and courtiers of incest, sodomy and rape, and to portray the king himself as a feckless debauchee in thrall to his ex-prostitute mistress, Madame du Barry.

Between and around the obscenities, the anti-Maupeou forces also managed to raise enough of a stir in public opinion about the constitutional issues involved that Louis XV's policy could not survive his death in 1774. The new king, Louis XVI, not yet twenty, had a youthfully idealistic view of kingship, and hoped to govern for his people, not himself. He banned persons not of 'recognised morality' from his court, and had opined years earlier that 'I must always consult public opinion, it is never wrong.' One immediate consequence of this was the recall to office, in November 1774, of the *parlementaires*. 'It seems to me,' the king noted, 'that it is the general will, and I wish to be loved.'[17] But that wish fatally compromised his other desire to rule wisely and rationally. Though he brought in Franklin's eulogist, Turgot, as a Finance Minister with sweeping plans for rational reform in tax-gathering, economic regulation and political representation, Louis XVI also let him fall from office less than two years later as the *parlements* led conservative opposition to his changes. Following this came the rise and fall of Necker, and after more political tergiversations, the appointment as Controller-General of Finances of the man who would call the Assembly of Notables a few years later, Charles Alexandre de Calonne. Such was the state of French affairs in 1783, when he came to office, that a leading minister reported that the difficulty in making such an appointment was not that candidates were unqualified for the job, but that 'only a fool or a knave could want it'.[18]

Calonne was no fool, but opinion would remain resolutely divided on his knavery. He had risen, like Turgot and others before him, through the ranks of *maîtres de requêtes*, junior government administrators used both within ministries and out in the provinces as troubleshooting *intendants*, overseeing tax collection and local government. A smooth-talking charmer, creating an impression of calm and order by giving his full attention to every visitor, and cultivating contacts in all the realms of high society – from the aristocrats of the Court to the financiers who kept the kingdom afloat – he instituted a regime that relied on creating a similar good impression, even while crises bubbled below the surface.

In a kingdom running on credit, image was everything. Both Turgot and Necker had been penny-pinchers, concerned to rein in expenditure on luxury at Court that aristocrats took not only as their due, but as a requirement of their status. It was simply not right for a prince not to live magnificently, and it sent the wrong signals both culturally and financially about the resources of the Crown and the kingdom. Calonne argued openly that France was 'a kingdom where resources are increased by the very act of expenditure'.[19] Thus he encouraged expense, arguing anyway that much of the millions he gave away to the aristocracy would be spent in boosting the luxury manufacturing on which France's trading reputation relied. The financiers who controlled tax revenues were encouraged to invest the contents of their coffers in productive enterprises. Other projects for major public works were undertaken, from the beautifying of large provincial cities to the construction of a new naval base in Cherbourg, a showcase not just for victorious power, but for the talents of state engineers, and a warning to Britain of France's serious global intentions. Projects of real substance, such as this and several major roads and canals, gave the lie to some critics who accused Calonne of actively fostering bankruptcy, allegedly to outflank opposition by creating a crisis insoluble through old means. Calonne was punctilious in establishing confidence in state finances. Unlike almost all his predecessors, he insisted on payments from the state's coffers being made in a prompt and businesslike fashion, and even set up a special fund through which old debts could be rescheduled.

For all this to work, however, required time, and this Calonne did not have. His finances were surviving on loans, guaranteed by their registration by the *parlements* as acts of the state. Late in 1785, in an act of factional hostility that amounted to little more than personal spite, another government minister, the baron de Breteuil, alerted his friends in the *parlement* of Paris to alleged financial improprieties by Calonne. The *parlement*, truculently assertive of its own rights since its abolition and restoration in the 1770s, turned on the Controller-General. The hostility it displayed in reluctantly agreeing to register a new loan revealed that no more funds would be forthcoming in that way. In 1786 the temporary taxes secured in the war years before 1783 were to expire. There was no way, under current arrangements, to produce enough revenue to save the state from bankruptcy. Calonne was forced to take down from the shelf of history all the many attempted reforms of the last generation, and roll them up for one last throw. He had no illusions about his prospects, telling the king: 'I would indeed have no regrets if I were the scapegoat necessary for the success of the enterprise.'[20]

The underlying difficulty Calonne faced was that all parties to the disputed political situation were floundering in the turbulent currents of public opinion. This was a novel concept for an absolutist state, but as we have seen, even Louis XVI was persuaded of the merits of the 'general will' as early as the 1770s. France experienced a unique set of problems in trying to apply the lessons of Enlightenment reason to public affairs. All sides acknowledged public opinion, often called simply 'opinion', as a force, and as a judge of public acts, but no one knew how to define it. Opinion was understood to be in favour of reform, of good governance, of representation, of national prestige and prosperity, but it could be invoked by any side in a dispute over how to achieve those goals. Unlike the Prussia and Russia of the 'Great' Frederick and Catherine, or the Austria of Joseph II, who drove through change more rigorously than either of them in the 1780s, France was not a kingdom where the king knew best. Everyone claimed that it was 'the public' who did so, and everyone claimed that 'the public', when it came down to it, was them.

Thus the *parlements* at once projected themselves as guardians of an ancient constitutional order, and as the representatives of a modern public concern with liberty, even when that meant defending privilege against government levelling. The many others beyond the *parlementaire* judges who paid good money for government posts, so-called venal office-holders for whom their positions represented a step on the road to full ennoblement, had their own arguments for their representative position as stakeholders in both society and government. Individual provinces, some of which had time-honoured regional representative gatherings, or 'Estates', proclaimed their own virtues and particularities against overweening change from above. Nobles and clergy of all kinds looked unfavourably on any plan that would strip them of privilege, always while claiming that such status was both historically justified and functionally essential to a well-ordered society. What anyone out among a real public of the unprivileged thought is less easy to gauge, but such people, increasingly well informed by a press for whom the illegality of political comment had ceased to be a great obstacle, watched and waited for their chance to have a say.

Unable to work through the legislative channel of the *parlements*, Calonne plucked from history the Assembly of Notables. Such a body had last been summoned in 1626, when the near-legendary father of absolutist manipulation, the Cardinal de Richelieu, used it to garner support for a crushing assault on rebellious French Protestants. Whatever its dubious antecedents, the idea of an Assembly of Notables had several merits, in addition to the central one of being the Crown's own idea. Hand-picking an elite membership permitted powerful voices to be brought into the political process while avoiding the risk of allowing in the most determined advocates of opposition. At the same time, reliance on historical precedent outflanked the many criticisms of unjust innovation – raised against virtually every royal reform of the last generation – and allowed for far-reaching change to be given a traditionalist mantle. Getting agreement from the Assembly of Notables would, Calonne felt, give the monarchy sufficient political capital to insist on the registration of laws enacting its programme, even from the most recalcitrant *parlementaires*.

The Assembly of Notables opened at Versailles on 22 February 1787, and in so doing attracted further criticism. Among the splendours of Versailles, that monumental structure designed to reflect and refract the timeless glory of an absolute monarch, the masters of royal ceremonial had decreed that the Assembly must meet in appropriate style. Thus many of its prospective members had been kept waiting since the beginning of the year while a room measuring 100 feet by 120 was redecorated in suitable splendour, and a dozen other auxiliary chambers prepared, for committee meetings and retinues. As a news-sheet of the time had it, 'at the moment when all talk is of the state's distress and the economy necessary to remedy it, they start by throwing several millions out the window on a vain and momentary pomp'.[21] Reports were similarly cynically disposed to the gathering itself, and the same news-sheet gave a run-down of all the Notables, saying of, for example, the marquis de Bouillé, 'Not without knowledge, but haughty, imperious, and devoted to despotism: thus nothing good can be expected from this military man.'[22] In general the view was widespread that the Notables were there to be manipulated into doing Calonne's bidding. In this at least opinion was to be surprised.

One hundred and forty-four men, all but a handful noble, but chosen to represent elites from the Church and law-courts to the heads of provinces and municipalities, brought their attention and expectations to bear on Calonne's case for reform. For most of the preceding year Calonne had been desperately juggling to keep the kingdom's finances afloat, resorting to underhand deals with favoured financiers, complex derivative bonds and rights issues, and old-fashioned sale of offices, against all the principles of reforming ministers over the past generation. This was largely public knowledge, as was the grand expenditure since 1783, and led to a sense among many of the Notables that Calonne was trying to pull the wool over their eyes about a short-term problem of his own making. The Austrian ambassador reported the view that the Assembly was 'no more than a petty trick to raise more money', and one minister told the king more tactfully that the Notables 'fear that the deficit in your revenues has not been sufficiently demonstrated' to require the proposed reforms.[23] The Assembly debated the proposals to broaden and level out the tax burden, creating a new tax on all land, not just commoners' holdings, resurveying the whole kingdom to make it equitable, rolling back archaic customs barriers between provinces, seeking, like Turgot, to free internal trade from petty regulations and, like both him and his successor Necker, planning local and regional elective assemblies to legitimise the distribution of tax.[24] They found practical and principled objections to them all.

The hideous complexity of the mingling of an aristocratic Old Regime and an elite Enlightenment here revealed itself fully. Noble members made free, in all apparent seriousness, with arguments that the arrangements for local gatherings were insufficiently representative and risked establishing a despotism of the wealthy, while at the same time arguing that by guaranteeing a proportion of the seats for nobles and clergy, such a danger could be averted. The Assembly refused to endorse Calonne's proposals, denying both that the ideas had merit in themselves and that their gathering had the necessary legitimacy to create such new permanent structures. One senior judge from Paris asserted that to reject the rights of the privileged classes would create 'a bastard republic within the monarchy, and my sworn loyalty to the constitution compels me to oppose this'. At the same time, another magistrate could also state bluntly the *parlementaire* position on the monarchy's limits: 'the king does not have the competence to institute a percentage tax but only to ask for a fixed sum to meet specific requirements'. To concede the royal right to an inflation-proof tax threatened to strip the *parlements* of their supposed right, and asserted patriotic duty, to oversee the necessity of expenditure. If the Assembly allowed such a move it 'would be dishonoured in the eyes of the nation'.[25]

After over a month, during which his proposals had been blasted beyond recognition, the minister struck back with his own appeal to public opinion, in a text that was distributed to parish clergy to be read from every pulpit. In bitter language Calonne condemned 'those who do not pay enough' for objecting to having to pay more, asserted that 'justice demands and necessity obliges' the sacrifice of privileges, and mocked the 'loud squeals' that would result: 'can one ever act for the general good without ruffling certain individual interests?' Though he ended with a denial that he was accusing the Assembly of 'malevolent opposition', and that there existed anything other than unity of desires between a 'nation' and 'a king whom it cherishes', the barbs went home, and caused outrage among the elite.[26] The truth, of course, was that there was intensely malevolent opposition among the Notables. Necker still had many supporters who believed his account of public finances left in surplus in 1781, and a deficit accrued by mismanagement since. The higher clergy were mounting a fierce corporate defence of their own privileges, while the various *parlementaires* and other judges defended a role in the state diametrically opposed to the view of it held by ministers. But, most of all, the reform programme Calonne proposed was undermined by his fellow ministers of the Crown.

Proving that nothing mattered more in the closed world of the elite than short-term advantage and access to power, Justice Minister Miromesnil worked constantly to defeat Calonne, aiming to promote in his place a man suspected of being his bastard son, and who was an outspoken critic within the Notables. He also kept the various *parlements* informed of Calonne's plans, explicitly so that they might oppose them on a common platform if asked to register them as law, and deviously and dishonestly refused to support Calonne's statements about the long-term state of the finances. His opposition was so evident that Calonne resorted to demanding from the king that one of them should go, and on 8 April 1787 Miromesnil was dismissed.[27] But so too was Calonne. He was forced from office, almost unprecedentedly, not for displeasing the king, but for the level of opposition he had raised among the other ministers, and at Court.

Louis XVI had been poised, some accounts said literally, to sign a letter dismissing one of Calonne's other great enemies, the baron de Breteuil, when Queen Marie-Antoinette intervened. For all of her husband's reforming intentions, her presence in the highest councils of politics was a clear sign that France remained, at present at least, a personal, absolutist monarchy. Marie-Antoinette, youngest daughter of the great Empress Maria Theresa of Austria, had been brought to France in 1770, a scared teenager literally stripped of her Austrian clothes as she crossed the border, married at fourteen to a husband who proved tragically unable to consummate their marriage properly for a further seven bitterly childless years. Schooled to act as an agent of Austrian influence in French affairs by the ambassador who remained her lifelong confidant, the comte de Mercy-Argenteau, the future queen initially took refuge in the frivolities that Court life made possible – extravagant expenditures on clothes, jewels and parties, and the cultivation of favourites. Louis' accession to the throne, and the onset of her childbearing years, somewhat sobered Marie-Antoinette, but not before a thoroughly vicious image of her had become fixed in the minds of the French public. Schooled by the excesses of Louis XV's last years and the pornographic representations of them that had circulated so widely, public opinion was all too willing to believe increasingly outlandish tales of sexual excess that circulated around the young queen, of lesbian affairs with her favourites and of sordid commerce of sexual favours for political ones. By the mid-1780s these stories were such a well-known problem that scurrilous journalists based in London could profit by blackmailing the French government to pay them *not* to circulate them in print.

A bizarre real-life scandal, in which the queen's name and promises of her favour were used to trick a high-ranking nobleman into obtaining a fabulously expensive diamond necklace for a criminal gang, tainted her reputation further. The nobleman, the Cardinal de Rohan, was put on trial for defaming the queen by claiming to act on her behalf, but acquitted by the *parlement* of Paris in 1786 amid widespread speculation that Marie-Antoinette had cooked up the whole affair to frame him. Rohan had been so eager to go along with the gang's plot because he had fallen out with the queen, and was desperate to regain her favour. Such was the queen's public image that thousands were prepared to believe she had both the means and the hate-filled motivation to conjure up connections with known criminals, and with a prostitute who had impersonated her for a night-time rendezvous with Rohan, just to spite him. Many also believed that the necklace, which had disappeared into the illicit international diamond market, had somehow found its way into the queen's hands. This belief symbolised a growing conviction that she and her Court circles enriched themselves at France's expense.

Ironically, by this time Marie-Antoinette was trying to take a more restrained approach to life, cutting back on personal expenditure on clothes, for example, and seeking to act in a more dignified fashion in Court politics. She had begun to take seriously her responsibility to protect the king and to give him counsel, and studied much harder than she had before the political currents swirling around her. Unfortunately she could have no conception of the wider changes in public life that had occurred in recent decades, nor of the trouble brewing in the country at large. Only months before the crisis of the Assembly of Notables, she had ordered the construction of an idealised peasant village at her personal palace of the Petit Trianon near Versailles. It would shortly become a bitter symbol of her detachment from looming real hunger in the countryside. Meanwhile the queen continued her new practice of weighing into the king's decisions, judging matters on the closed calculus of favour that had always sufficed in her world. Breteuil, at the moment, possessed that favour; Calonne did not. Thus Breteuil was saved as Calonne fell.

Breteuil it had been who undermined Calonne's relations with the *parlement* of Paris, and who was also up to his elbows in financial speculations that depended on Calonne's failure. At this moment, the first week of April 1787, he was virtually in hiding at his country château, but the queen's wishes saved him. Other ministers also intervened, and were able to paint Calonne as wishing to reconstruct all the ministries in his own image, leaving him isolated. Marie-Antoinette's view 'that it was essential to dismiss the controller-general' weighed in the balance.[28] Louis hoped that by sacking him, and within a month establishing another of the queen's favourites, Loménie de Brienne, Archbishop of Toulouse, as effective prime minister, the vital reforms could be got through. Brienne showed admirable pliability in converting overnight from a principal opponent of the programme to a ruthless advocate of change, but all that Calonne's fall would ultimately prove was that shooting the messenger did not change the bad news.

# 2

# 'The best model the world has ever produced'

*Governing America and Britain
in the traumatic 1780s*

A mong the disparate grouping that had come together to pioneer the American revolution, none were more different than James Madison and Alexander Hamilton. They came from different worlds, and saw the politics of revolution in very different lights. Eventually they would become, perhaps inevitably, enemies; but before that they became friends, collaborators and architects of a new America.

Madison was the son of Virginia planters, solid members of a gentry elite, with a tradition of public service and social leadership, raised amid propertied respectability. Small, slender and painfully shy, he buried himself in studies, and remained so intensely self-conscious that at twenty in 1771 he could not give the public speech expected of every graduate on leaving the College of New Jersey at Princeton. There he had proved his exceptional qualities by passing a four-year degree in only two, at the cost of a nervous collapse upon returning home.[1] Within a few years he was caught up in the whirl of early revolutionary sentiments, having acquired a republican cast already from Princeton. A new wave of Enlightenment emerging from Britain was avidly studied there, now not from the London of the Royal Society but from the Glasgow and Edinburgh of the philosopher David Hume and the economist Adam Smith. Madison found his niche in the committee rooms and corridors of power, first in Virginia and from 1779 in the Continental Congress. There his vast capacity for diligent work, always entering into discussion more prepared than any opponent, earned him a shaping role. There too he met Hamilton in 1782.

Alexander Hamilton was an outsider who had literally fought his way to the heart of American affairs. Born out of wedlock to a pair of star-crossed lovers among the mercantile classes of the British West Indies, abandoned by his father at the age of ten, his mother dying three years later, Hamilton became perforce a clerk to a merchant firm on the island of St Croix. Having acquired a grounding in both the classics and practical skills of mathematics and literary composition, perhaps from his mother and probably not from any formal schooling, he rose in the estimation of his employers and their fellows to the point that a special fund was subscribed to send him to the mainland at the age of seventeen. Taking remedial courses in classics at an accelerated rate, Hamilton sought out a college that would allow him to continue at such a pace. The College of New Jersey turned him down, perhaps because Madison's collapse only two years earlier (and the death from overwork of another gifted student) had soured them against such hothousing. Hamilton instead went to King's College, New York (the future Columbia University), in 1773, and spent two years, as revolution brewed in America, devouring every aspect of learning that came his way.

Tall, handsome, bold, vigorous and brave, Hamilton dashed into a military role in the fight for liberty, though not before pausing to write a closely argued rebuke to local opponents of independence. Distinguishing himself by initiative, courage and efficiency in the otherwise traumatic early campaigns of the war, when after the Declaration of Independence in 1776 ragged militia-based American forces were harried by growing numbers of British professional soldiers and German mercenaries, Hamilton was appointed a lieutenant colonel on commanding general George Washington's staff in 1777, at a mere twenty-two. Showing no sign of seeing this role as other than his due, he was effectively a chief of staff for the general, while at the same time throwing himself into battle in 'a sort of frenzy of valour', as one less than enthusiastic senior officer observed.[2] So intense was this frenzy that after several years it eventually caused a (temporary) rift with Washington and led to Hamilton's being assigned to an independent command, in which he launched a reckless but dramatically successful assault on British redoubts at the decisive battle of Yorktown in 1781. Following this victory he resigned his commission, passed exams for the New York Bar after a few months' study, and entered politics, serving first as collector of revenues for the state and then being elected to Congress, taking his seat at the end of 1782. Both he and Madison would quit within a year, appalled and disgusted at the course of politics in the victorious republic.

The Thirteen Colonies had never had a central government, nor any real uniformity in their structures, and for many of the prosperous men who led the new states, their individual interests came before any real sense of union. The Continental Congress, which in theory had ruled the states' war effort, had in practice been forced to scuttle from town to town by enemy advances, and plead for funds from reluctant state legislatures at every turn. Emblematically, when a messenger brought word of the crowning victory of Yorktown (a victory made possible only by French troops and generals), the representatives had to take up a collection for his expenses from their own pockets, because the treasury was bare. It remained bare, or almost so, for the next six years, as the Articles of Confederation that governed the former colonies' mutual relations allowed no power of taxation to Congress. The failure of an attempt to alter this arrangement and create a 5 per cent import duty to fund the federal government had driven Madison and Hamilton from Congress; the latter particularly outraged, as it was his own state of New York that had vetoed the plan (though Madison's Virginia, along with Rhode Island, had vetoed a similar proposal two years earlier).[3] Congress was left able only to issue what were termed requisitions, which Madison described as a 'sacred and obligatory' demand for payment but were in practice little more than plaintive requests to the individual states to make some, any, contribution. The last requisition issued in 1786 was for $3.8 million. Congress received $663. Against a notional federal budget of only $450,000, the United States in that year could not even raise $1000 in cash to pay for shipment of ammunition and supplies to its western garrisons.[4]

The individual states lived through the post-war years in circumstances of continual tension and dispute scarcely different from those of the Old World kingdoms their inhabitants had left behind. Freed from the heavy hand of British imperial direction, the commercial interests of the various states had struck out in support of their own goals, dominating local legislatures often chosen on narrow franchises of wealth, and using the real powers of the states to engross and monopolise the two great routes to American prosperity: seaborne trade and landward expansion. The smaller seaboard states, already cut off from expansion by existing geography, found fuel for increasing antagonism in this, and even more in the rapacious application of customs dues and tolls by the larger states, which dominated ocean-going trade through their harbours. No fewer than nine states retained their own, separate naval forces at the conclusion of hostilities, and some soon found cause to use them against the shipping of others. Punitive laws allowed for the confiscation of contraband cargoes to the profit of the state and the informer, and these were turned far more often against the vessels of other states than those of foreign empires. Madison, campaigning ardently for a more harmonious solution to these issues, noted that 'New Jersey, placed between Philadelphia and New York, was likened to a cask tapped at both ends' as her neighbours drained her with their customs charges; North Carolina, similarly caught between two hostile neighbours, was called 'a patient bleeding at both arms'.[5]

'Federalists' such as Madison and Hamilton pushed repeatedly, through the middle years of the 1780s, for a fundamental change in the nature of the United States. The disabling conflict of interests between the states was one reason, while another was the insuperable problem of the debts of war. A bewildering variety of financial instruments, paper money, promissory notes and bonds had financed the conflict. During the war states' failure to raise adequate taxes to cover the issue of paper dollars had seen the $220 million issued fall to 1 per cent of their face value by 1780, and an almost equal quantity of bonds for 'impressments' of goods and services for the military languished with the promised 6 per cent interest unpaid. Debts were due to all parties: $1.7 million in interest and scheduled repayments were owed to the French and to Dutch bankers in 1786, and $1.6 million in interest alone on domestic debts. Congress, pleading repeatedly for money to avoid the 'fatal evils which will inevitably flow from a breach of Public faith', noted the shame involved in not meeting sums owed to soldiers, the 'war-worn veteran whose reward for toils and wounds existed in written promises'.[6]

Only a strong central state, the Federalists argued, would save

America from a chaotic bankruptcy that might see the new nation either reduced to penury or re-engulfed by the colonial powers that still loomed around it. Hamilton and Madison worked to mobilise opinion for better solutions by making efforts to address the other problems posed by Congress's impotence. Plans for improvements to inter-state river navigation were put forward at a gathering at George Washington's own home, Mount Vernon, in 1785, and the following year a 'Convention' at Annapolis, Maryland, brought together delegates from five states to discuss trade and allied concerns. If the hopes that all the states would attend were starkly dashed, Hamilton's report to Congress of the 1786 meeting brought forward in urgent terms the argument for a new Convention to revise the existing arrangements of government. He had been arguing thus since the end of the war in 1783, but looming complete penury, and the outbreak of violence in Massachusetts among indebted farmers and former soldiers, momentarily threatening public authority, finally succeeded in forcing Congress to issue a summons for such a gathering.[7]

The 1780s had been hard years economically for the United States. Fighting a war on inflated credit brought an inevitable slump in its aftermath, redoubled for a society now cut off from many of its traditional export markets and coping with the dislocation of a Loyalist emigration. Almost all the state governments faced debt problems akin to the federal one, and the disposition of that debt brought with it ever greater hardships and tensions. In Virginia, for example, county sheriffs charged with collecting back-taxes faced gunshots, night-time raids by armed bands to retake sequestered property and, more commonly than either, evidence that indebted farmers had simply fled: their notes read laconically 'backwoods', 'over Allegheny', 'run away', 'gone to Kentucky'.[8] Massachusetts, the cradle of insurrection in the 1770s, grew ever more bitterly divided on this question. There was already a fundamental opposition between the inland farming communities, who wanted for the most part nothing but to be left alone, and the dominant mercantile elite of Boston and the coast, whose eyes were set on global trading opportunities and commercial confidence. To uphold that confidence, the debts of the state had to be honoured, but to do so meant piling injustices on the heads of the poorer farmers. Land taxes rose as agricultural prices and wages fell, farms were mortgaged and farmers threatened with foreclosure and dispossession. A fear grew among these communities that their very collective existence as free men was threatened, that they might be reduced to a tenantry at the service of wealthy masters. In one county alone, three thousand men were sued for debts in 1784–6 and, across the back country, increasing numbers were flung in prison. The harsh contemporary view was that it was better to have a man in custody, where his friends might be forced to find money to release him, than have him free and working, from where he might abscond.[9]

The origin of the state's debts, and the farmers' poverty, made the bitter situation burn with irony. Many of the farmers had been soldiers in the revolutionary armies, paid off after years of service with paper certificates that they had had to cash in at great discounts to speculative bankers and merchants. The latter were now insisting that Massachusetts (and other states) honour those debts at face value, and dominated the political assemblies that levied the taxes to do so. Lending this same money to farmers and foreclosing on them when they could not repay closed a vicious circle of unjust greed.

Thus it was that in the autumn of 1786 a brushfire of revolt broke out across Massachusetts's back country, soon christened Shays's Rebellion, after Daniel Shays, a former Revolutionary War captain who emerged to lead the groups of 'Regulators'.[10] Several thousand armed men were soon moving through the countryside, their first objective being to block the court sittings that threatened to foreclose on mortgaged farms, and then to release unjustly imprisoned debtors. They also put forward a wider political programme: notably for an issue of paper money to allow debts to be paid without scarce cash, and for a suspension of the state taxes they saw as an unreasonable burden. These were widespread calls in these critical years – seven states had already yielded to demands for paper money by 1786 – but to back them with armed force against the republican government of the state seemed to call into question the very fibre of American society.[11]

After several months in which the authorities, and prosperous public opinion across the states, were stricken with horror at this assault on legality, the Massachusetts government raised an army of over four thousand men and sent them into the back country in January 1787. Seeking arms to oppose this foe, the Regulators besieged a government arsenal, but were scattered by a sudden, and as they saw it treacherous, volley of cannon fire from the defenders. Descending into sporadic guerrilla activity, the 'Shaysites' were picked off gradually, with over two hundred taken into custody, and five sentenced to hang for treason in April 1787. The last act of the drama was played out on 21 June 1787. New elections had already driven from office the uncompromising Governor and officials who had brought about the conflict, and laws passed late the previous year had eased slightly the position of debtors by, for example, allowing back-taxes to be paid in kind.[12] Widespread cries for pardon were heard, but the authorities felt it necessary to lead the condemned men all the way to the gallows, in full expectation of death, before issuing a dramatic last-minute reprieve.[13] Daniel Shays himself fled to the new territory of Vermont, not yet part of the Union, and survived to be pensioned in later years for his war service.

If the rebellion itself petered out, its wider political consequences did not. Coinciding as it did with Federalist moves to call the Constitutional Convention, it had a profound impact in reinforcing the need for such a body. George Washington himself wrote in the aftermath of the Shaysites: 'What a triumph for the advocates of despotism, to find that we are incapable of governing ourselves, and that systems founded on the basis of equal liberty, are merely ideal and fallacious.'[14] Sustaining such 'equal liberty' without a strong state apparatus seemed impossibly difficult; yet the perils of such a strong state were very real in the minds and hearts of those who answered the call of Congress to form a convention as the Shaysites lingered under sentence of death. Rhode Island boycotted the meeting, and many delegates attended in dread of what they might be expected to agree to, and determined to oppose all manner of pernicious innovations. Landowners, lawyers and merchants, the delegates to the Convention were fine examples of where a Franklinesque drive to surpass the bounds of old aristocratic societies could lead men in the century of Enlightenment. Many had made fortunes in the New World, while some had lost them and made them again. Few were blind to the changes that had been wrought in the past decades, or to the possibilities inherent in their new situation – for wealth, glory, true greatness. But many also feared innovation and threats to their acquired rights, no less than did the haughty noblemen who had met at Versailles a few months earlier and were still wrangling as the American delegates slowly gathered from the four corners of their vast domains. As French provinces had their histories and privileges to safeguard against despotism, in their eyes, so too did the states that had haggled their Confederation close to bankruptcy still have much to fear from the institution of active new powers above them.

The Philadelphia Convention met from May 1787 under the chairmanship of George Washington, whose towering reputation rested as much on his willingness to renounce his military powers at the end of the War of Independence of 1775–83 as on his cautious leadership in that victory. The general himself had faced down discontented officers and men in 1783 when they threatened to impose military force on a Congress that hesitated to pay them their due. All those who gathered in Philadelphia expected that, if a new form of federal government were to emerge, Washington would be its first national leader. But even this assurance of virtuous leadership could not quell anxiety. The general also faced scathing criticism for associating himself with the Order of the Cincinnati, a league of former officers that made its membership hereditary and thereby raised the spectre of aristocracy within the new republic. There was a telling moment of doubt on 1 June 1787, when the issue of an executive for the new nation was debated. The proposal was made that the executive should comprise one man, a president (though that word was not uttered). The response was, in the diary of proceedings that Madison religiously kept, 'a considerable pause', an uncomfortable silence as members digested the possible implications of such a conception.[15] Rule by one man was, in a technical sense at least, 'monarchy' by definition, a condition from which they had just escaped. Did they want to re-subject themselves?

Many among the few dozen men who made up the Convention, sitting in the same room in the Pennsylvania statehouse where the Declaration of Independence had been signed eleven years before, were familiar with the writings of the baron de Montesquieu, who almost four decades earlier had established a benchmark for modern considerations of political power with his work *On the Spirit of the Laws*. This remarkable treatise proposed the virtues of a principle that was ultimately to guide the Convention: the separation of powers. Montesquieu offered the first modern definition of the now commonplace distinction between executive, judicial and legislative functions, and ordained that, for the peace and prosperity of a state, it was better that these should subsist in different hands; that in this way a constitution might be balanced and not slide towards despotism or anarchy. James Madison in particular was an overt student of the baron, whose views may have been coloured by his place as a member of both the French aristocracy and the judiciary, in a century when both sought to challenge the rights of an absolute monarch to hold all the reins of government in his hands.

Perhaps most ironically, however, Montesquieu acquired most of the force of his argument from a consideration of the politics of the British constitution, in which, as he saw it, the three elements of Parliament – King, Lords and Commons – 'check one another by the mutual privilege of rejecting', and can only move out of their thus natural 'state of repose' when sound agreement permits of the 'necessity of movement . . . in concert'.[16] Drawing on the seventeenth-century writings of John Locke, whose arguments for political liberty were a foundation of British (and thus also American) thinking on the subject, as well as on his own imperfect acquaintance with Britain, Montesquieu built a theoretical model of constitutional freedom out of the ragged history of British civil war and factional dispute.

The Americans, who had taken Locke's ideas of natural right and placed them at the heart of the Declaration of Independence, were thus in a quandary. All their positive examples of constitutional power came from a system that many of them too had regarded as the best of all possible worlds, until the struggles of the last genera-tion had forced them to confront its own 'despotism' in intemperate and uncompromising language, and by force of arms. And had not Montesquieu also written, in the very same chapter that embodied his praise of things British, that 'as all human things have an end, the state we are speaking of will lose its liberty, will perish'? The nature of this end, bluntly stated by the baron, was further troubling. It would perish, he said, 'when the legislative power shall be more cor-rupt than the executive'.[17] Corruption and its perils was something about which the Convention delegates knew much and feared more. The fear spilled out from the lips of the sage Franklin himself as they debated two other points about the executive: whether it was to have a legislative veto, and whether its holder should be salaried. Franklin's view of both was 'no'. If, he went on, the British case showed no use of the royal veto for three-quarters of a century, the reason was simple: 'the bribes and emoluments' disbursed by the Crown to the Commons made it unnecessary, since their interest lay so clearly in doing the executive's will. If an American executive were allowed financial recompense, similar practices would surely follow, and 'ambition and avarice' would combine until a president's salary became the privy purse of a king, who might 'follow the example of Pharaoh, get first all the people's money, then all their lands and then make them and their children servants forever'.[18] In the presence of Washington, such talk was, in Madison's words, 'peculiarly embarrassing', and in time the Convention would grant the president both veto and salary, but that the ever-thoughtful Franklin could be led on to such observations says much for the alarmed atmosphere of the time.

At the start of June George Mason, a thoughtful Virginian, had written to his son of the task before the Convention, explaining that the travails of the 1770s were

> nothing compared to the great business now before us ... to view, through the calm sedate medium of reason the influence which the establishment now proposed may have upon the happiness or misery of millions yet unborn, is an object of such magnitude, as absorbs, and in a manner suspends the operations of the human understanding.[19]

A month later such understanding still seemed in suspension, ravaged by partisan interests and fears. Such was the tumult that raged in debate that on 28 June Franklin, sceptic that he was, was moved to propose that the Convention be led in prayer each morning by a clergyman, that they might have 'the assistance of heaven' in reaching resolution. The measure failed – it was felt by some that it would be seen by the public as a token of alarm, while another pointed out that there were no funds to pay such a cleric.[20] On 10 July 1787 two of the three delegates from New York State formally withdrew in protest at the centralising plans being raised. The third New Yorker, Alexander Hamilton, was the recipient of a letter written that night by Washington, reflecting starkly on the weight proceedings were placing upon him: 'I almost *despair* of seeing a favourable issue ... and do therefore repent having had any agency in the business.'[21]

After their initial quailing at the notion of a presidential executive, the members of the Convention had gone on to find fault with almost every other model of government put before them. A proposal that the national legislature might be able to veto individual state laws met the fear that large states might 'crush the small ones whenever they stand in the way of their ambitions', and this, at least as much as the impracticality of the constant process of revision the plan implied, saw it voted out.[22] When attention turned in mid-June to the form and composition of the houses of the legislature, it was not just the virtues of the states that were called into question, but those of the people themselves. Edmund Randolph, Governor of Virginia, and architect of an informal plan drawn up in the Convention's first days, whose clauses, or 'resolves', continued to guide debate, spoke out emphatically:

> The democratic licentiousness of the state legislatures proves the necessity of a firm senate. The object of this second branch is to control the democratic branch of the national legislature . . . A firmness and independence may be the more necessary also in this branch, as it ought to guard the constitution against encroachments of the executive, who will be apt to form combinations with the demagogues of the popular branch.[23]

This notion of a strong and balanced government, though it was ultimately to prevail, leaned evidently on a blunt pessimism about the potential for human self-government. So too, ironically, did the opposition to this form, which was very far from having yielded in June 1787. On the 15th the delegate William Paterson of New Jersey laid out a plan for government very different from the Virginia resolves. It challenged the very notion of a national constitution as it had been set out, and attempted to return to states' sovereignty – no complex bicameral legislature, no overarching federal remit, but a single chamber with limited powers, and in which each state held equal representation. Governor Randolph's response, in closing an angry debate the following day, indicated clearly the plight in which advocates of a robust national system found themselves: 'View our present deplorable situation. France, to whom we are indebted in every motive of gratitude and honour, is left unpaid the large sum she has supplied us with in the day of our necessity.' Funds did not exist to support 'our officers and soldiers', or indeed 'the loaners of money to the public'. Only a well-founded government could hope to recover the situation, and delegates should consider 'that the present is the last moment for establishing one. After this select experiment, the people will yield to despair', and thus, he implied, either dissolve the union altogether, or elevate a ruler, demagogue or despot, with neither check nor balance to restrain him.[24]

When debate resumed the next Monday Alexander Hamilton seized the floor and held it for nearly six hours with a starkly alternative vision of an American future. He proposed a presidency, elective, but held for life, and with an absolute veto on laws; and a senate similarly chosen for life; both to balance a democratic lower chamber chosen by the people at large, dispensing with the states in a bold view of America emergent on the world stage as a confident and united actor. It was an astonishing picture of a democratic monarchy, and in his own notes Hamilton had been even more explicit: the executive 'ought to be hereditary and to have so much power that it will not be in his interest to risk much to acquire more'. Out loud, he had echoed general observations already made, but to very different ends: 'Men love power. Give all power to the many, they will oppress the few. Give all power to the few, they will oppress the many.' Division by wealth and activity into few and many were inevitable, and 'the British government forms the best model the world has ever produced' for balancing their interests.[25] It was perhaps just as well that the Convention had agreed to keep its proceedings secret, for it is doubtful whether even Hamilton's towering merits could have protected his future political career if such views had become public. The robust democracy of the American public sphere, which Franklin had helped to found, would have had little taste for a new republic founded on such imperial lines. High summer in 1787, though, found neither America nor France nearer a solution to the problem of emulating, or competing with, the 'best model the world has ever produced'.

That model, meanwhile, had weathered storms scarcely less severe than those buffeting its erstwhile subjects and foes. Epochal defeat had shaken the political establishment to the core, prompting unprecedented alliances, fostering unrestrained enmities and bringing the constitution closer to dissolution than at any point since the upheavals of a century before. British politics in the 1780s were delineated by two figures, who could have been designed expressly to make life easy for political caricaturists. Each was the son of a politician who found fame and power in the imperial triumph of the 1750s and 1760s, and each claimed to represent the 'Whig' tradition of all that was good in the 'Revolution Settlement' of 1689, yet they could not have been more different. Their detestation of each other was all the greater, as from similar ideological roots their conceptions of political duty carried them in quite opposite directions.

Charles James Fox was the pinnacle of four generations of social and political climbing. His great-grandfather had been a simple yeoman farmer; his grandfather a political factotum for exiled royalists in the 1650s and thereafter a knight and MP, and a holder of assorted lucrative court and government posts; his father, Henry Fox, was a notably corrupt but brilliant parliamentarian who secured a peerage in 1763 for putting the treaty that ended the Seven Years' War through the House of Commons. This had needed careful management, for while affirming British supremacy over France in the quest for domination of North America and India, it also yielded up other gains, and did not satisfy every rapacious interest in the maelstrom of party that was the Commons. Henry had early squandered his share of his father's fortune, and made it back through unscrupulous political machinations of every kind. For example, as Paymaster of the Forces during the war he skimmed significant percentages from the funds passing through his hands. True to form, his offspring, including his third son, Charles James, were the products of an elopement with the much younger Lady Caroline Lennox in 1744.

Charles James Fox would prove his father's son in almost every respect. He was a man notorious for his pleasures. By the age of twenty-five in 1774 he had already accumulated debts of £140,000, spent on gambling, women, drink and sundry debaucheries. Yet the squandering of such sums – enough to have built two 100-gun battleships for the Royal Navy, or to have kept a more frugal man in luxury for a lifetime – did not prevent Fox then and for a generation to come from being one of the most important political figures in the British Empire. His genius for machination and undoubted talent for parliamentary debate saw him rise rapidly in politics after first being elected to the House of Commons in 1768, in blatant defiance of the statutory age requirement of the office. Just two years later he held his first government post, and was only removed from office in the Treasury in 1774 at the personal insistence of King George III, disgusted at his character and offensive views. Yet Fox continued to rise, securing a powerbase among Whig politicians opposed to royal policies against America, and hauling himself to Cabinet rank in 1782, in the disastrous aftermath of British defeat at Yorktown.

In the ferociously slanderous popular prints and caricatures that made this period a high point of the cartoonist's art, Fox's unshaven jowls and massive black eyebrows were a permanent fixture, an icon of principle or corruption, according to taste. In almost open opposition to the Crown he purported to serve, Fox was ousted again after a ferocious fight in 1783–4, and from then on directed his considerable energies to forming and guiding a new and more disciplined form of party organisation, opposing what he unhesitatingly depicted as an unconstitutional, indeed despotic, rule through ministerial prerogative and royal influence. Perhaps unfortunately, such opposition necessarily focused attention on his links with George, Prince of Wales, the feckless and permanently indebted heir to the throne, for whom the king preserved a poisonous contempt.

Against Fox, a truly vast figure of a man, so fat that he could scarcely waddle between the stumps at his favourite sport of cricket, stood William Pitt, whose presence in visual satire was marked by a stick figure, his nose seeming pin-sharp enough to burst the bloated balloons of so many overindulging contemporaries. Reserved, slender, in his later years almost gaunt, and averse to the corrupting pleasures of courtly and society life, Pitt was nonetheless equally the product of a dynasty of climbers. His great-grandfather Thomas had been the son of a clergyman, but had made a fortune in India, trading, near-piratically sometimes, outside the official monopoly of the East India Company. Among his coups was to acquire a 410-carat diamond for £20,000 and later to sell it to the Regent of France, Philippe d'Orléans, for £135,000. This 'Pitt Diamond', which once graced the hilt of Napoleon's sword, is still in the Louvre. Thomas established his family in politics by buying the infamous 'rotten borough' of Old Sarum (a locality which had the right to elect two MPs, but no real population), and in 1735 his grandson William Pitt 'the Elder' began his political career sitting in the Commons for that seat. That career was tempestuous, but by the 1750s he had risen to clear prominence, and to rivalry with Henry Fox, among others. His crowning moments came as effective (though not actual) Prime Minister in 1757–61, when Canada was conquered and India secured against French encroachment. His later career was more chequered, and his last years saw his hopes for making an honourable settlement with the rebellious Americans dashed when he collapsed in the House of Lords in April 1778 and died a month later.

William Pitt the Younger, his seventeen-year-old second son, was with him in his final illness, and held in his person all his father's political hopes. He had been a frail and sickly child, educated at home until the age of fourteen, and then at the University of Cambridge under the close supervision of tutors. Unlike Fox, who was given every indulgence by his doting father, Pitt was treated to a regime of precocious political apprenticeship which left him with a devotion to hard work and a penetrating interest in, and talent for, public affairs. Left effectively penniless by his father's indebted death, he became a lawyer in 1780, and in January of the following year entered the House of Commons, sitting for a borough under the patronage of Sir James Lowther, the friend of a friend. Aligning himself initially with Fox's Whigs, only two years after entering Parliament he secured the post of Chancellor of the Exchequer, charged with the kingdom's finances. In the fluid schemes of politics Fox was now a rival, and brought down this government in less than a year. Before being forced to yield to Fox's claim on government, King George III offered Pitt the chance to be Prime Minister, but he demurred, seeing this as excessively precocious. At the end of 1783, however, the king pressed the offer again, and Pitt accepted. He was twenty-four. One popular verse noted it was 'a sight to make all nations stand and stare: a kingdom trusted to a schoolboy's care'. That care, begun in a time of perilous uncertainty, was to endure for a further seventeen years.

The American War of Independence had unleashed a witches' brew of alarm and ill will in British politics. Not a few in the heart of empire thought that the Americans were suffering the 'most cruel oppression'.[26] Those elements who feared the growth of the monarch's power, among them the Protestant sectarians barred from public life as 'Dissenters', could easily see in the imposition of taxes on the colonies without consultation a bridgehead for more repressive government back home. Some indeed were capable of construing the intransigence of the Crown as evidence of 'popish' designs to install an absolute monarchy. Jacobitism, the loyalty of a minority to the Catholic descendants of James II, ousted in 1688, had sent rebel armies marching into central England from their Scottish fastnesses as recently as 1745, and more extreme Protestants were capable of seeing its shadow almost anywhere. One pamphlet in 1774, addressed to British Dissenters, was clear:

> The *pretence* for such outrageous proceedings, conducted with such indecent and unjust precipitation [the government's various acts against the colonies] is much too slight to account for them. The *true cause* of such violent animosity must have existed much earlier, and deeper. In short, it can be nothing but the Americans (particularly those of New England) being chiefly *dissenters* and *whigs*.[27]

By the same token, those whose Anglican faith verged on Catholicism, known as the 'High Church', and who looked with scorn on those who would resist legitimate authority, made accusations that American resistance was part of a transatlantic plot by dissenting Presbyterians to create a British republic.

The majority of British opinion had been content to follow the Crown's line, that the rebels were a mere faction among the colonists, supported by 'mad enthusiasts and desperate republicans', as the *London Gazette* phrased it in November 1775.[28] There were many among even the mercantile classes, where social sympathy for the Americans might have been greatest, who accepted without reserve that the system of duties and monopolistic Navigation Acts rejected by the Americans was essential to British prosperity. Adam Smith might argue differently in his *Wealth of Nations*, published in 1776, but speculative theories of free trade meant less than well-established patterns of control. The early war years also saw a flood of contracts for military and naval provisioning, and a more unexpected flow of goods from America: the rebels did not block exports for some time, and indeed needed them to continue, to lower their own debts. All this kept public opinion, or at least the opinion of the wealthy and influential, on the side of the Crown for at least the first two years of the conflict.

A notable defeat at Saratoga in the autumn of 1777, with the surrender of an entire column of nine thousand men, and the entry of

France into the war in early 1778, began to turn the tide. While
patriotism deployed against old enemies rallied new regiments of
volunteers, the strains of a global war began to bite. New excise
duties multiplied, existing taxes were raised and loans put out at
ruinous rates of interest. The value of government bonds on the
open market dropped by a third between 1774 and 1778 as confidence in the war's outcome waned.[29] Scathing criticism was used in
the House of Commons against the government's manipulation of
the financial markets, doing backstairs deals with cliques of bankers
and likewise offering contracts for supplies to favoured merchants.
Foreshadowing the opprobrium that would fall on Calonne's parallel
practices a few years later, such acts were easily read, in an atmosphere of growing crisis, as yet more evidence of the Crown's
nefarious and unconstitutional intentions. The ability of the aristocratic elite to launch a war on 'freeborn Englishmen' across the
Atlantic, and to rack up taxes on the prosperous middling sort to pay
for it, while continuing to line their pockets with the rewards of high
office, turned the thoughts of some to far-reaching reform.

In December 1779 at York, seat of England's second archbishop
and effective capital of northern England, a mass meeting of concerned individuals led to the formation of an Association for the
County of Yorkshire. Its membership, dominated by 'gentlemen,
clergy and freeholders', dedicated themselves to agitation for reform,
under the leadership of Christopher Wyvill, himself a wealthy landed
member of the Anglican clergy.[30] The central demand of what soon
became known as the Association Movement, spreading within
months to some forty regional and local organisations, was 'economical reform'. In part a simple objection to profligacy and financial
corruption, the movement also carried a strong political charge.
Freeing the Commons from burdens of patronage and obligation
would liberate the political nation to resist overweening state power,
and on the more advanced wing of the movement were those who
saw further steps, towards a wider and more just distribution of the
suffrage and closer democratic control of elected representatives.

In the early months of 1780 it seemed that the Association
Movement had genuinely captured the mood of the nation, including a substantial number of MPs, and even peers. The Duke of
Richmond joined his nephew Charles James Fox in rousing Whig
support, while even the very young William Pitt was drawn in,

thanks to his uncle, the future Earl of Stanhope, who chaired the Kent Association.[31] On 6 April 1780 John Dunning, a former government minister, moved in the House of Commons that 'the influence of the Crown has increased, is increasing, and ought to be diminished'. Carried on a wave of emotion by 233 votes to 218, this was greeted by Fox as a 'second revolution', after which he might die a happy man.[32] However, in the short term at least, this move was to have infinitely less impact than the events of 1689 to which Fox referred. Many of the country gentry who were the backbone of the respectable end of the movement withdrew once its protests had been voiced at the highest level. MPs backed away from supporting immediate changes, especially as the masters of patronage began to work the levers of power against specific proposals to abolish sinecures and offices. A second motion by Dunning, to prolong the session of Parliament beyond its normal annual dissolution – and thus to threaten a real overturning of affairs – though it garnered 203 votes, lost by a majority of over fifty. Events in early June 1780 sounded the death-knell for any hope of change supported by the majority of prosperous opinion, and also revealed yet another dimension to the extraordinary political culture of Hanoverian Britain.

If opposition to the supposedly absolutist tendencies of Catholicism was the bedrock of that culture, and membership of the established Anglican Church a requirement for public office, the British were on the whole tolerant of other varieties of Christianity in their day-to-day practices. Even the ferocious penal laws against Catholicism that rested on the statute books were unenforced. Occasional scaremongering by prejudiced individuals at a local level did not, through the 1760s and 1770s, secure any response from courts or government. Indeed in 1778 a Catholic Relief Act for England annulled some of the most prejudicial measures, with no apparent reaction, allowing the integration of Catholics into landed and mercantile society, and in the ranks of the wartime military, to continue openly.

Slumbering prejudice was brought to life, however, by a bizarre figure. Lord George Gordon was the younger son of a Scottish duke, who had quit a naval career in his early twenties after being refused a command he did not merit, and who obtained a seat in the Commons in 1774 when his opponent for a county seat bought him one in a rotten borough to remove him from the contest. Eccentric to

the point of instability, and violently prejudiced against Catholicism, Gordon formed a 'Protestant Association' to fight the 1778 Act after further such measures were proposed for Scotland in 1779. Able to present his opposition in the same vein as the wider Association Movement, and viewing Catholic Relief as a plot to strengthen the despotic state, he raised upwards of forty thousand supporters from the streets of London to march on Parliament with a petition for the reinstatement of the penal laws. Gordon's movement played on conspiratorial fears similar to those raised by the American conflict: rumours after the passage of the 1778 Act had talked of twenty thousand Jesuit priests poised to flood London by blowing up secret tunnels, and Benedictine monks poisoning flour supplies. One satirical print depicted the king in a monk's tonsure and some confidently asserted that he heard Mass in secret.[33]

The events of June 1780 proved that the apparently unopposed passage of the 1778 Act concealed deep and violent prejudices. The march to Parliament on the 2nd turned into a riot, unleashing what the contemporary writer Edward Gibbon called 'a dark and diabolical fanaticism'.[34] From then to 7th June London slipped from the grasp of its constituted authorities. Rioters attacked first the house of Chief Justice Lord Mansfield, the figure most closely associated with the reform, before going on to assault Catholic churches, private residences and symbols of state power. The prisons were opened, and at one point even the Bank of England came under siege. The local authorities had no civil police force to use against the rioters, and some shared their prejudices: one official refused to act to 'protect any popish rascals'. For the first few days of the troubles prominent figures remained reluctant to call on military forces, often for fear that the rioters would turn on their own properties in revenge. Officers leading the troops that were called in took the view, legally debatable law, that they could fire at rioters only after a specific order from a civil magistrate, and none could be found willing to give such an order. Only the personal initiative of the king himself, extracting a proclamation from his Privy Council that force required no such specific authorisation, allowed a counter-offensive against the disorders to begin.

Peace did not return to the streets of the capital until 9 June, by which time some 850 people were dead, half of them shot by troops, others killed by rioters, trampled in crowds or trapped in burning

buildings. Twenty-one rioters would be convicted and hanged, though Gordon escaped execution on a charge of high treason by arguing that there was no evidence his own actions had treasonable intent.[35]

In the wake of such appalling violence, unleashed to all appearances from the heart of the common people, there was no prospect of anything but a closing of ranks around established authority by propertied society. The Association Movement, already on the wane, dissolved, and a temporary revival in military fortunes, followed by the disastrous and unexpected surrender at Yorktown in October 1781, rallied British opinion, first elated, then gloomy, behind the Crown.

Further afield, however, the echoes of events in both Britain and America struck home in a further diminution of monarchical power. Ireland had been held by the English Crown since the Middle Ages, in theory an independent kingdom, but in practice subordinated to the will of the Westminster Parliament. The Irish Lords and Commons in Dublin could vote only on matters allowed to them by the dominant body, the Irish did not enjoy the rights and privileges the British took for granted, especially against arbitrary rule, and the Irish economy was held back by harsh and prejudicial tariffs and prohibitions on external trade, in a blatant effort to keep it a captive market for those whose wealth and votes carried power at Westminster. The strains of war on this economy, allied to a growing political consciousness among the propertied and Protestant elite, led to a movement through the war years to break the British stranglehold.

Led by regiments of Irish Volunteers raised in theory to defend against invasion, but now seeming to threaten insurrection, a campaign for 'Free Trade – Or Else' succeeded in extracting from Prime Minister Lord North effective freedom of Irish manufacturers to trade across the British Empire.[36] Ill-advised hints that such concessions might only be temporary, however, helped sustain support for a more political campaign. Standing committees and petitioning drew in all the respectable forces of Irish society, Anglican landowners and Ulster Presbyterians joining forces with a rising Catholic middle class to demand freedom from the tyranny of the Westminster Parliament. When Lord North was driven from office in March 1782, ending twelve years of personal struggle with the colonies in abject defeat, his successors were reformist Whigs (including both Fox and Pitt in their ranks) who quickly yielded to Irish demands. What might have been seen, and protested at, as a dire defeat for the interests of Britain slipped by in the wider context of transatlantic disaster, and the Irish Parliament in Dublin gained the right to set its own agenda, vote on its own laws and exercise financial control over military spending. Ironically, in light of the Gordon Riots, the Crown even had to palliate Irish Catholics by easing restrictions on their ownership of land, though it still declined to grant them political participation, and even this limited measure was seen as ominous by some Protestants. Even as it wrestled with traumatic global defeat, yielding up the Thirteen Colonies' independence in 1783 (thus losing the equivalent of a third of the population of England, a frightful blow) and ceding territories in the Mediterranean, Caribbean and Africa to France and Spain, the British Crown lived in a world where narrow sectarian religion, looking back to previous centuries of anxiety and alarm, still cast a long shadow.

The British system of power, which horrified Americans with its tyranny, appalled the French with its political licentiousness. Diderot, from an Enlightened perspective, had remarked in the 1760s: 'Elsewhere, the court commands and is obeyed. There [in Britain], it corrupts and does as it pleases, and the corruption of the subjects is perhaps worse, in the long term, than tyranny.'[37] In its ability to turn naked self-interest into collective power, it had no equal in the world, and represented a constitutional balancing act that neither the United States nor France dared to emulate. Yet both were drawn to it, by its real power and influence in their affairs and by the way it seemed to allow the state to float effortlessly on a sea of debt that would have swamped a less sturdy craft. From Canada to Jamaica, Gibraltar to Calcutta and even as far afield as Australia, with the arrival of the First Fleet in New South Wales in January 1788, British power was global. The might of the Royal Navy safeguarded the sea lanes of the world for a massive merchant fleet, and London was the emporium of the globe, trans-shipping cargoes by the thousands of tons from the tropics to the four corners of Europe (and still to North America in quantities that would humble French aims to profit from their republican allies).

To pay for all this the British state employed two spectacularly successful strategies. For almost a century it had possessed a Bank of England able to sustain the borrowing power of the state, and indeed actively to encourage the wealthy to invest in the state through interest-bearing bonds. This fluid and seemingly inexhaustible supply of money was further sustained by an ever growing burden of taxation, much of it levied on the import and sale of goods by an excise service whose ruthlessness entered into British (and American) legend. Half a century earlier the kingdom's annual budget had been around £5 million, of which some £2 million went to service the National Debt: in other words, to pay the interest on investors' bonds. By the 1780s the budget had risen to £13 million, and £9 million of this went in interest payments. Four-fifths of this total was raised in excise taxes, on items from newspapers and playing cards to hair powder and carriages; there was even a charge for employing menservants. Items of common necessity, such as salt, soap and candles, were also taxed, as were all manner of alcoholic drinks and imported goods, from French brandy to China tea.[38]

The Excise Service, which functioned as a recognisably modern bureaucracy, was loathed for this efficiency, which extended to rights of search on private property and summary jurisdiction in special courts – so much so that in 1782 the service's officers were disenfranchised by Act of Parliament, in a move that pandered to popular prejudice about their unjustified powers and possible influence.[39] Such a measure (and the slashing of duty on tea in 1785, catering to popular taste and admitting a lost war against smuggling) reflects the other side of the Hanoverian 'military–fiscal state'. Wondrously efficient at raising revenue it might have been, but that did not make the grandeur of its ambitions necessarily popular. Britain was still a small country in the 1780s, run as much, if not more, by personal relations as by any sense of wider public duty or responsibility. The suspicion of those such as the Association Movement that the powers of the state were put at the service of private interest was all too often well founded, and with the vast burden of taxation occasioned by the American War straining even Britain's well-formed fiscal sinews, the clash between an alert public opinion and an aristocratic political caste became more vivid by the day.

Fewer than two hundred titled noblemen headed the great landed families of England, sitting in Parliament by right in the House of

Lords (with the separate Scots nobility electing a small group from amongst themselves to join them). There were perhaps a similar number of untitled families able to claim equal wealth, mostly from landholding or imperial trade and plunder. These great families controlled networks of patronage, through intermarriage, local association and penetration of the machinery of state and business, that ran deeply through the life of society. Beneath them on the social ladder were some fifteen thousand other landowning families of the gentry, whose elder sons might have a claim on an income from family lands, but whose daughters would require marrying off and whose younger sons needed to find respectable careers. Some fathers would be influential enough to secure them for themselves; others would need to call on the great to act on their behalf.[40] For those who could make a claim on the patronage of the elite, such assistance was the natural and inevitable resort and was channelled through the Lords, and even more noticeably through the elected Members of Parliament, who sat in the House of Commons, in the cramped and inconvenient chamber of St Stephen's Chapel in the Palace of Westminster.

Membership of Parliament was, in the eyes of almost everyone involved in the political process, at least as much about satisfying the demands of one's friends, clients and family as it was about governing the kingdom. George III's Parliaments may have passed over fifteen thousand Acts in his long reign, but the vast majority were 'private': not legislation for the country at large, but legal authorisation for individual matters from divorce to the enclosure of specific pieces of farmland, sought and obtained by individuals with the money and influence to get MPs to act on their behalf.[41] Some members were the chosen representatives of the landed gentry, the traditional 'Knights of the Shires' elected (usually without opposition) by wealthy rural freeholders, but these were outnumbered over four to one by those who sat for 'parliamentary boroughs', of which there were 203, almost all returning two members. The distribution of seats bore no relation to population. While the far western county of Cornwall included twenty-one boroughs, each returning two MPs, Lancashire, increasingly the centre of an urban and industrial economy, had only six.

The manipulation of borough electorates was notorious. While there were some seven thousand voters in the City of London, and over twelve thousand in Westminster, making for turbulent and very public campaigning, most boroughs numbered their electors in the dozens or low hundreds. Some boroughs restricted voting to members of a municipal corporation, others vested the right in owners of particular parcels of land. The most notorious of these was the Pitt family's Old Sarum in Wiltshire, where there were a mere ten electors, none of whom actually resided in the borough, in fact an abandoned village. Boroughs of this type might well be condemned as 'rotten', but many more were known as 'pocket boroughs' and fell more or less openly under the influence of powerful families. Where electorates were small and wealthy, they could be bought with the assurance of favours; where there were a few hundred poorer electors, the influence of landlords over tenants and employers over workers could achieve the same ends. Only where there were either very many voters, as at Westminster, or a relatively large group of wealthy 'freemen' electors, as at Bristol, Norwich and York, did identifiable issues of politics and policy ever play much part in elections.

This undemocratic system, riddled with corruption and elite patronage, was yet seen by contemporary observers both as the harbinger of anarchy (a view common among absolutist Europeans) and as the linchpin of British liberty, prosperity and power (very much the established view in Britain itself). Parliament very neatly institutionalised all the disputes that might otherwise tear a country apart, as France was being torn apart by the end of the 1780s. On the one hand, the Crown could, through its powers of patronage, claim to control the votes of up to 180 'placemen' of one kind or another in the Commons, thus keeping a check on its independence. On the other hand, through their families or individual patronage, the titled aristocrats of the House of Lords also controlled up to two hundred seats.[42] Powerful men had a perfectly overt mechanism at hand to promote their own interests. They need not skulk in corners of a palace, plotting to bring down a minister by secretly blackening his name: they could get their friends to stand up in the Commons and do it openly. If they could influence enough votes, they could change the government without the need to wheedle their way into the mind of the king. And at the same time the power of the king and his ministers to reward individuals financially was a powerful incentive to loyalty. Revenue officers may have been disenfranchised in 1782, but that did not stop MPs' brothers, sons and cousins from holding

such posts, and there were many other offices available, not to mention the simple expedient of direct payment. The celebrated Dr
Samuel Johnson, lexicographer and wit, denounced official pensions
as 'pay given to a state hireling for treason to his country' – a fine
example of the era's independence of thought and speech – and
then accepted one for himself.[43]

Money and patronage thus lubricated every joint of the body
politic. If funds were raised through a level of taxation remarkable for
the age, twice that borne by any other major power, parliamentary
control of taxation nonetheless helped the country feel secure
against the threat of continental despotism. This was especially the
case among a Protestant people with long memories, for whom the
Glorious Revolution of 1689 and the century-long struggle against
'popery' that had preceded it were still the active constituents of
their collective identity. But the very virtues of this system were
also, in a changing context, providing dire threats to its security. If
patronage oiled the wheels of politics, then, from outside, the relationships it created could look very much like corruption, and if the
parliamentary system shielded the state from the effects of secret
factionalism, the overt dissent it allowed could, in time of crisis,
seem very like anarchy.

In the context of traumatic defeat, such anarchy seemed to loom
when Charles James Fox had joined forces with the ousted Lord
North to form, against the king's wishes, a coalition government in
April 1783. It was a cynical grab for power, by Fox in particular, and
this seemed to be reinforced when the new government brought
forward a proposal to give control of the vast resources of the East
India Company to commissioners appointed by Parliament, and thus
to partisans of Fox's Whigs. Indian affairs in general were at a critical
point, with the vast individual fortunes made in British dealings with
the country contrasting sharply with the parlous finances of the
Company itself. Obliged to fund military expeditions to consolidate
its position on many fronts, while also paying inflated dividends to
keep powerful shareholders happy, this great milch-cow of wealth
seemed on its last legs. Moral difficulties compounded its financial
peril, as liberal opinion began to agitate against the corruptions and
brutalities that the rulers of British India had judged necessary to
preserve their imperial power over the previous decade. Most of
these problems would simmer uneasily for several more years, but

Fox's India Bill was the occasion of a genuine constitutional clash, bringing William Pitt to power seemingly by undermining the power of Parliament – and thus the constitution itself.

It was the king himself who played the decisive part. Advised by Fox's opponents that the Bill was 'a plan to take more than half of the Royal power', and willing to bend the unwritten rules of constitutionality almost to breaking point to be rid of Fox, George III leaned on the House of Lords.[44] Unable to prevent Fox's supporters passing the Bill in the Commons by a large majority, the king could influence the much smaller number of peers enough, by what amounted to direct threats of future enmity in some cases, delivered by trusted intermediaries, to defeat the Bill by mid-December. The Commons passed a motion that to use the views of the king to influence a vote was 'a high crime and misdemeanour', thus meriting impeachment, and Fox himself roared that the question at stake was 'whether we are to be henceforward free men or slaves; whether this House is the palladium of liberty or the engine of despotism', but the fate of his government was sealed.[45] The king could use a defeat on a major policy measure as an excuse to strip his ministers of office, which he did on the evening of the next day, sending messengers to collect their seals of office and denying them a formal audience.

William Pitt thus came to office at the king's pleasure, without a majority in the House of Commons, and with a Cabinet around him composed of assorted grandees, some political neutrals and a coterie of his own young friends, almost all noted for their lack of parliamentary talents, at a time when command of the Commons was essential to political initiative. Little wonder that when his appointment was announced in the House on 19 December the packed occupants of the opposition Whig benches roared with laughter. Pitt's administration was denounced as the 'Mince Pie' ministry, doomed to be eaten up by Christmas. But Pitt and the king immediately showed their steel. As Parliament broke up for the Christmas recess, the royal prerogative began to be used in earnest. Political patrons were offered peerages, for themselves or, if they already had one, for favoured relatives. Holders of government office who were also MPs were forced to change allegiance or be replaced. Some who could not be bribed were again leaned on by the king in person, and then, like the Duke of Newcastle, leaned on their 'pocket' MPs: in this case, causing half to change sides and the other three to abstain or resign. With the writer and MP Horace Walpole noting cynically that 'They are crying peerages about the streets in barrows', it seemed an object lesson in the complaint of both Diderot and the Americans about the corruption of British politics.[46]

But it did not work immediately. When Pitt faced the Commons in January 1784 he still lacked a majority. In vote after vote he lost by thirty or forty and was forced to a masterful, but bare-faced, series of public lies about his prior knowledge of the moves to unseat Fox's ministry. On 16 January the House passed a motion that the continued existence of Pitt's government was 'contrary to Constitutional principles', and the opposition-supporting *Morning Herald* offered on 19 January a sinister portrait of the epoch:

> The cloven foot of absolute monarchy begins to appear, as is evident when secret influence rises superior to the voice of the people in their representative body . . . We have lost America – we have lost the dominion of the sea – we have nearly lost Ireland – and what is worse than all, the Constitution is at the verge of death.[47]

Despite such partisan portents of doom (with their own very characteristic entwining of imperial power and popular freedom), what the country faced was not so much a *coup d'état* as a stalemate. Fox plotted to impeach those who scorned the will of the Commons, and warned of 'universal anarchy' if the government did not acknowledge its position and resign, but the king gathered his ministers and warned them not to contemplate putting him 'bound hand and foot' into Fox's power, for he would rather quit the country and rule his other dominion in the German principality of Hanover.[48] With this very personal expression of the stakes in the game to encourage them, Pitt and his colleagues held on, and as they did so the other side of the British constitution, the side that promoted liberty, or anarchy, according to the observer's taste, began to come into play.

Public opinion, that amorphous force that the French were struggling in vain to harness, found easier and more direct routes of expression in Britain. From the start of 1784 public meetings began to be organised, gathering hundreds, and in major towns thousands, of individuals to express their support for the king and his government. The resolutions of these meetings, with their lists of signatures, began to arrive at Westminster at the rate of several a day as winter wore into spring, and Pitt's government survived defeat in vote after vote. It was, in its way, a rebellion against the power of Parliament, and certainly against the power of Fox's opposition Whigs to pursue their own interests while claiming to be the party of liberty. Pitt drove home the message of his own virtue in the public eye by conspicuously turning down a lucrative sinecure, worth £3,000 a year, that fell vacant at this very moment. The turbulent mix of public sentiment, virtue, vice and lurking violence at play was shown dramatically on 28 February. Pitt had been granted the Freedom of the City of London, and a huge crowd enthusiastically drew his carriage through the capital's streets. This crowd then showed alarming signs of wanting to attack Fox's house, but were pre-empted by the occupants of Brook's, a radical Whig club, who launched a concerted assault on Pitt's carriage. As Pitt's brother wrote, most of the mob were 'Chairmen', toughs who carried sedan chairs for hire, but others were waiters in the club, 'and several of the Gentlemen among them'.[49] Pitt himself had to be shielded from the blows of this group as they wrenched the doors of the carriage open, and after the occupants beat a retreat it was completely demolished. The empire that girdled the world, still reeling from the loss of the Thirteen Colonies, could scarcely ensure the safety of the Prime Minister from his opponents. For Britain to escape the crisis of its crushing defeat would take a truly remarkable turnaround, which as yet showed few signs of arriving.

# 3

# 'Vibrating between a monarchy and a corrupt oppressive aristocracy'

*The woes of France and America, 1787–8*

M arie-Joseph-Paul-Yves-Roch-Gilbert du Motier, marquis de Lafayette, was remarkable for many things beyond his name. A scion of France's old military aristocracy, whose father had fallen in battle when he was only two, Lafayette seemed destined at first for a similarly traditional career. Educated at the most prestigious of schools, the Lycée Louis-le-Grand in Paris, he enrolled as a teenager in the Royal Guards, and was an eighteen-year-old captain of dragoons when the Declaration of Independence was signed. Nothing in his background immediately suggested that he would rally to the cause of liberty. Tall, blond, acutely conscious of his own good looks and social distinction, Lafayette was every inch the aristocrat. When he first left his family's Auvergne estates to go to school in Paris, he had reportedly been astonished to see that not every peasant his carriage passed doffed his cap, as they did unfailingly at home. It was perhaps the opportunity for distinction that the American enterprise offered that first attracted him to it. His candid friend Thomas Jefferson, serving in 1789 as the American ambassador to France, noted that the marquis had a 'canine appetite' for such glory, while being 'as amiable a man as his vanity will permit'.[1]

Whatever the underlying cause, Lafayette rapidly acquired an infatuation with the American rebels and defied royal orders, and ignored the advice of Benjamin Franklin, to decamp across the

Atlantic (just ahead of an arrest warrant) with a letter from a US agent promising him a major general's commission in Washington's newly formed army. His willingness to discard this promise and serve as an unpaid volunteer persuaded a sceptical Congress to grant the commission anyway, though they may have intended it as an honorary post. However, for the next nine months he proved himself an able commander alongside Washington, who became a lifelong friend and father-figure. Lafayette was even to name his son after him.

Travelling back to France to cement the new alliance in 1778, Lafayette was lionised and promoted to colonel. He returned to America to further military glory, culminating at Yorktown in 1781. Still aged only thirty in 1787, a *maréchal de camp* in the French army, he was highly enough regarded in a country with no shortage of distinguished noblemen to be called as one of the 144 members of the Assembly of Notables. He remained devoted to the ideals he had acquired in the American cause, and also to the conviction that he ought to have a central role in bringing political liberty to France. In the hallway of his Paris mansion there hung a framed copy of the American Declaration of Independence and next to it a conspicuously empty frame, destined, he said, for a French Declaration of Rights.[2]

The fractious debates that had characterised the Notables under Calonne continued after his fall. Though Loménie de Brienne worked hard to cement a new package of reform proposals, it became increasingly clear that the Notables were not in a mood to help the Crown by wholeheartedly ratifying such a proposal. Indeed as May 1787 wore on many became more concerned than before about the root causes of the problems and the need to erect some permanent form of control over the monarch's government. It was Lafayette who dared to make this public. Speaking on 21 May, he noted the many admirable reforms that Brienne envisaged carrying out over the following five years and then asked if that point, five years thence, was not one that 'we should beg His Majesty to fix . . . for accounting for all these operations and consolidating forever their happy results by the convocation of a truly national assembly'.[3] Confined within the decorous language was a vast challenge to royal power. The comte d'Artois, the king's brother, who was chairing the session, asked Lafayette for clarification: did he mean the summoning of an

Estates-General? Yes he did, said Lafayette. The Estates-General
had not met since 1614. Its non-existence was, in the minds of most
contemporaries, a hallmark of monarchical absolutism. To suppose
that one might call an Estates-General and thus allow representatives
of the country to deliberate on royal policy in a national body, perhaps
even to challenge that policy, was a radical step. No matter that the
*parlements* claimed that right, nor even that, as Lafayette noted in his
memoirs, Brienne had confided to him a wish to install someday a
'truly representative government'.[4]

While Lafayette's proposal met with no visible response, the private thoughts of many of the Notables and their ilk were veering in
dangerous directions for the sanctity of the Crown. A well-connected
secret news-sheet reported in unequivocal terms the desire of many
to rein in royal power: 'Sometimes the chiefs of nations must be
recalled to their first foundations and taught that they hold their
power from these peoples that they treat too often as slaves. The
Notables have shown that the Nation still exists.'[5] Faced with growing rancour, Brienne wound up the Notables on 25 May, promising to
undertake the necessary reforms by royal authority. However, as this
programme went forward, even some of its supporters feared the
loss of royal power. The economist Dupont de Nemours, a colleague
of Calonne, criticised the direction Brienne was taking in a letter that
summer. The decision to create elective provincial assemblies, at
the heart of proposals to render the tax burden more equitable and
politically acceptable, meant, Dupont said, that the king was no
longer a monarch, but rather the magistrate of a republic, 'perpetu-
ally obliged to assemble his people and to ask them to provide for his
needs . . . the King of France becomes a King of England'.[6]

The 'King of England', as the French styled the monarch who
called himself King of Great Britain, France (still, and until 1801) and
Ireland, might have agreed with the negative implications of this
view after his fights with Charles James Fox across the decade, but
the King of France, even before giving away any formal powers, was
still unable to make his will felt in legislation. For Brienne's proposals to become law, they had to pass through the *parlement* of Paris,
which would turn out to be a much more formidable opponent than
the Notables. Among the judges of the *parlement* were figures such as
Duval d'Éprémesnil, who despite his own only recent ennoblement
was profoundly attached to an aristocratic view of power: he wished,

one contemporary wrote, 'only to make the *parlement* reign'.[7] D'Éprémesnil was forty-one, but many of the older members shared his views, more or less trenchantly. The much younger Adrien Duport, a mere twenty-eight, represented a faction among the judges who opposed royal policy for quite other reasons. A friend of Lafayette and other liberal nobles, Duport expressed in clinical prose the desire for a national assembly to do the work Brienne proposed: only such a body could legitimately 'correct and rejuvenate' the laws and make 'ministers responsible for all the abuses of a power that they have received solely for the happiness of the people'.[8]

Around the *parlementaires*, that amorphous public opinion that had been fought over for the past decade was finding new form and institutions. Pamphleteers and journalists for a press becoming increasingly heated over reform met with lawyers, clerks and even aristocrats in newly fashionable 'clubs' modelled on the British example. Like those in London, such meeting places progressed rapidly from offering reading rooms and general sociability to political discussion and even agitation. Almost all publication on such issues was still covered by blanket censorship, but a rising tide of material circulated illegally, sometimes even in manuscript. A theme that echoed through many discussions was phrased by one future revolutionary, Jacques-Pierre Brissot, in the high summer of 1787: 'we must say and repeat everywhere that the base of the Constitution is the right not to pay taxes without consenting to them'.[9] This echo of the American struggle was to find even stronger resonances in the *parlement*'s own deliberations.

To pass Brienne's reforms into law, the *parlement* of Paris was called together in its highest form, as the Court of Peers, which added forty-one dukes and Princes of the Blood to its usual 144 members. Beginning on 22 June 1787, Brienne offered up to them several measures of known popularity, one creating the new provincial assemblies, another freeing the grain trade from police regulations and finally, on the 28th, a measure converting the *corvée*, forced labour for road-building expected from peasant communities, into a tax. All passed with little dissent. If this was a softening-up exercise, however, it was proved to have decisively failed when on 2 July Brienne tried to get the Court of Peers to register a new Stamp Tax, making it illegal to transact many forms of public business on paper not bearing an official, paid-for stamp. As

one contemporary later recalled: 'a tax of this type had been the pretext for the uprising of the British colonies against their metropolis.
The orators of the *parlement* of Paris were proud to be able to repeat
the arguments of the Americans.'[10] The Court of Peers first inso-
lently demanded from the king new accounts to prove his need of
more taxation, and when he refused made the same demand again a
week later. Their insinuations against the Crown infuriated the
comte d'Artois to the extent that his own fulminations drew a stern
rebuke from the chair: anyone else who had so 'wanted in respect for
this Assembly' would have been sent immediately to the cells of the
Conciergerie prison.[11]

The combustible mixture of aristocratic pride and liberal ambition
that drove the *parlementaires* brought to the surface the demand
issued two months earlier by Lafayette. An anonymous voice had
yelled a call for the Estates-General in 2 July's stormy debate, and a
week later a more formal call garnered twenty-five votes in its favour.
On the 16th the *parlement* voted to prepare a formal remonstrance
against the Stamp Tax, and when a final version of this was approved
ten days later, the summoning of the Estates-General was integral to
the claim: the *parlementaires* wished 'to see the Nation assembled
prior to any new tax. It alone, instructed of the true position of the
finances, can extirpate great abuses and offer great resources.'[12] By
the genteel standards of public language, this was almost a declaration of war, and the royal response was emphatic.

On 6 August, a baking-hot day, the judges of the *parlement* of Paris
obeyed a royal summons to the palace of Versailles. Arrayed in their
scarlet state robes, packed into an audience chamber, they were, as
one wrote the next day, 'all in a steam-bath'.[13] They were there for a
*lit de justice*, a demonstration of the king's final power over them. In
such a session the judges' rights of deliberation were formally over-
ruled by the monarch's presence and his decrees were made law by
fiat. Thus the hated Stamp Tax and other measures were registered
against their will, while the king, whose majestic presence made
this possible, dozed off in the stifling heat, his snores audible to all.
What might have been read as a gesture of contempt (and was more
likely a product of Louis' habitual overeating) seemed more like an
expression of the king's political isolation when the judges
responded from their own Palace of Justice the next day. The *parlementaires* defiantly decreed the registration of these laws 'null and

illegal', and for the following week, acclaimed by crowds that had begun to gather outside their sessions, carried their audacity further. On the 10th they issued a formal indictment of Calonne for 'depredations on the finances' and three days later d'Éprémesnil garnered a massive majority for a declaration that the laws registered on the 6th were 'incapable of depriving the Nation of its rights'.[14] The stairways and courtyard of the palace were packed with people and the judges had to force their way to their carriages through a cheering, applauding mass.

The Crown's ministers struck back the next day when, in a manoeuvre that had been used in previous decades, they sent the entire personnel of the *parlement* into exile in the provincial town of Troyes to let them stew in their own juice away from the adulation of crowds and *salons* alike, and thus, it was presumed, to come to their senses. To further the measure, all the various clubs that had formed in Paris were closed by royal order. While this made political discussion more difficult for the denizens of the capital, it was unable to suppress the wider crisis in the state. The situation deteriorated. Many of the subordinate courts refused or protested at orders to accept the new laws. On 17 August the comte d'Artois, rapidly emerging as an enemy of reform, was jeered by a Parisian crowd as he arrived at one such court to force registration. His military escort drew their swords, precipitating a panicked flight. Within days police posts had been attacked, and a prominent barrister noted in his diary that the word among the crowds was ominous: 'So we shall have a civil war. Well then! We shall fight!'[15]

Several weeks of political stalemate followed, but it was the government, driven by its profound and unyielding need for money, that gave way the most as a settlement emerged in late September. The *parlement* returned to Paris on the 28th effectively triumphant, having seen the Crown obliged to withdraw the offensive innovations in taxation in return for registration of two conventional, and strictly temporary, tax increases. Political calm descended, but the advantage still lay with the advocates of an Estates-General. The Crown was still heading for bankruptcy and Brienne's administration was forced to go back to the *parlement* in November 1787 to register huge new loans.

To sweeten the deal a meeting of the Estates-General was conceded, to take place no more than five years thence, as in Lafayette's original request, when Brienne's other reforms had bedded in. The session on 19 November was held in the presence of the king, but it was not intended as a *lit de justice*, for the judges were permitted to debate the proposals, in the hope that a new consensus would be forthcoming. The king, however, after listening to repeated pleas for an Estates-General within the next year, brought the session to a close with the simple words 'I have promised the Estates-General before 1792; my word must suffice for you. I order the registration of my edict.' When his cousin the duc d'Orléans stammered a protest, appearing to make the audacious claim that the king's action itself was illegal, Louis blurted out a signal of his disregard for the *parlement*'s constitutional claims: 'It's legal because I want it.'[16] The king's will prevailed and *parlementaire* protests were struck from the record two days later, after Orléans and two judicial supporters had been sent into exile.

With the new loans in place and rapidly taken up by investors, the Crown could endure the protests that followed and over the winter of 1787–8 calm again descended. But nothing of principle had been resolved and in the spring the confrontation between ministers and *parlementaires* was widely sensed to be approaching crisis. Rumours that a new administrative *coup d'état* was being prepared surfaced first in the autumn, and with greater vigour in February 1788, and were entirely accurate. The king's ministers had given up trying to conciliate their recalcitrant magistrates and intended to abolish the political role of the *parlements*, replacing their role in the registration of laws with a single, compliant national Plenary Court. New lower appeal courts would also take much judicial business away from the *parlements*, thus breaking their influence over the legal system more directly.

With these moves imminent, the defiance of the Paris judges reached new heights. On 29 April they refused to license new arrangements for collecting the taxes they had agreed to authorise the previous September, and on 3 May they issued a decree in which they claimed to iterate the 'Fundamental Laws' of the kingdom: these, they said, included 'the right of the Nation freely to accord subsidies [i.e., taxes] through the organ of the Estates-General regularly convoked and composed', as well as 'the life-tenure of magistrates', and the right of the courts to register only those laws compatible with 'the fundamental laws of the State'.[17] In a pledge of defiance the judges also bound one another to 'take no place in any company, that should not be this Court itself, composed of the same personages and with the same rights'.

Two days after taking this stand the Paris *parlement* reinforced it when royal troops arrived to arrest the two judges who had drafted the text. A summons to yield up the men was greeted with defiant shouts from the assembled magistrates, forcing the troops to withdraw rather than assault the massed ranks of berobed noblemen. Though the two surrendered voluntarily the next day, this open confrontation sent the desired message to the provinces about the arbitrary treatment of the magistracy.[18] On 8 May the royal hammer fell as expected. Brienne's *coup d'état* became public and the *parlements* were summoned to submit to their subordination or face the dire consequences. The response was little less than a nationwide 'noble revolt'. Acting in the name of the Nation, and with widespread popular support, not least from townsfolk threatened with the loss of custom from exiled judges, *parlementaires* across the country expressed their principled objection to the changes. In Rennes, in Brittany, popular fervour was stoked so high that the chief royal administrator had to flee the city for his life. On 7 June in Grenoble, in the south-east, townsfolk attacked troops sent to close the *parlement* by hurling tiles from their rooftops. The nobility of several provinces gathered in unofficial assemblies to protest at the assault on ancient rights and freedoms, and the Catholic clergy, meeting as a national corporate body, refused a royal demand to double its usual contribution to state coffers, virtually halving it instead.

It rapidly became clear to the Crown that these protests could not simply be faced down. Though they were usually in the name of the Nation, they also had a clear aristocratic tint, and one of the first strategies tried by Brienne and his colleagues was to turn to popular support. Indeed the rhetoric of ministers became apocalyptic. Justice Minister Lamoignon was heard to say that because the *parlements*, clergy and nobility 'have dared resist the King, before two years are out, there shall be no more *parlements*, nobility, or clergy'. Brienne himself denounced the privileged for having 'abandoned the King', and now the latter 'must throw them into the arms of the Commons to have them crushed'.[19] These remarks would turn out to be prophetic, but in the short term the attempt to seduce non-noble opinion with printed propaganda and concessions about local representation failed to ease the crisis.

On the very day, 16 July 1787, that the august *parlementaires* had voted to defy the king's wishes, thus prolonging the paralysis of French affairs, the logjam of hostility that had held up progress in far-off Philadelphia finally broke. What became known as the 'Great Compromise' allowed the less populous states equal representation in the new Senate with the larger, while keeping population as the basis of seats in the lower House of Representatives. This seemed to ease the rancorous tensions between the different sectional interests at play, and in particular relieved the representatives of the majority of smaller states of the fear of a dangerous combination between the largest, Virginia, Pennsylvania and Massachusetts. At the same time, however, the anxieties about the new federal executive persisted. When the delegates from New Hampshire arrived in late July, having waited nine weeks before their state governor agreed to pay their expenses, they found the monarchical question still alive. One wrote home that 'feeble minds are for feeble measures', while 'vigorous minds . . . advocate a high-toned monarchy'.[20]

Such minds included Alexander Hamilton, who had made it quite plain that he envisaged America prospering under a strong king. Others in the old revolutionary tradition were suspicious that the 'vigorous minds' sought their own advancement, and perhaps consolidation into an aristocracy, under such a ruler. Hugh Williamson of North Carolina felt 'pretty certain that we should at some time or other have a king', but was no less opposed to it for all his certainty, arguing strongly against creating a presidential office that would allow a man to 'feel the spirit' of a king and progress towards installing himself as one.[21] Nonetheless, a single executive presidency seems to have been settled on by the great majority without significant dispute, probably largely because they knew that the spotless patriot Washington was bound to be its first holder. Abiding concerns about the nature of his eventual successor – 'General Slushington' as this spectre was dubbed – meant that it took sixty votes, however, to determine how he should be elected – by Congress, by state legislators, by the people at large – and a further sixty to settle on how long he should serve, and whether he might be re-elected or impeached.

Such was the hesitancy and the perplexity that reigned in the country at large, where scarcely a whisper of the Convention's work leaked out, that it is little surprise that wild rumours circulated. One swept the country in July, claiming that the Bishop of Osnaburgh was to be invited to become King of America. The absurd name, one of the courtesy titles of the Duke of York, second son of George III, hinted at the satirical origins of the claim in a disgruntled Connecticut Loyalist's pamphlet. But as reports came back to the Convention that the bishop was being toasted at society dinners, they felt obliged to act. Breaking their secrecy, if only in the negative, they allowed the *Pennsylvania Journal* to report authoritatively that 'tho' we cannot tell you affirmatively what we are doing . . . we never once thought of a king' – not strictly true, but enough to scotch the rumours.[22]

On 26 July the Convention created a 'Committee of Detail' to redraft their current set of decisions and questions into a workable order, and took ten days' leave to enable them to work in peace. The delegates kept remarkably well to their pact of secrecy, in some cases perhaps because it still remained entirely unclear to them what had so far been agreed. When the Convention reformed in the week after 6 August – slowly, as the individuals drifted back from leave – few of their basic fears were truly assuaged by the workmanlike draft text the Committee put in their hands. Another five weeks of heated talk lay ahead of them. Despite protests, concerns, arguments and alarms, there were forces that continued to compel the delegates towards agreement. In a very real sense the states and people of America had already begun to set the outlines of a country larger, yet more diverse, and in more need of careful central government, than even the old Thirteen Colonies.

In the South, Georgia had been scarcely more than a coastal strip under British rule, but now its claims rolled across half a continent to the mighty Mississippi river. Only this same year South Carolina gave up pretensions to a frontier on the same river, ceding to the realities of encirclement by its neighbours. North Carolina, meanwhile, maintained a nominal hold over its territory stretching to the Mississippi, already known loosely as Tennessee. Northward still further, Virginia's empire reached through the Appalachian chain to the confluence of the Ohio and Mississippi rivers, across the future state of Kentucky. Only three short years earlier Virginia's sovereignty had been asserted, according to a generous interpretation of its founding charter, to run the full northward length of the Mississippi, thus embracing a territory almost equal to the whole of the seaboard states. Somewhat problematically, this claim was cut across by similar provisions, made in an earlier age of almost complete igno-rance of the continent's internal geography, that gave New York, Massachusetts and even Connecticut title over vast vague swaths of land around and below the Great Lakes. In all the region bounded by the Lakes and the Mississippi and Ohio rivers, the last five years had seen at least some progress to resolution of this conundrum. First New York in 1782, then Virginia in 1784, then quickly the other claimant states had yielded their rights up to the common good and left to Congress the business of settling the disposition of this vast territory.

The legal quagmire of land-speculation claims had been one reason for the states to back away from their initial eager assertions. Another was the prospect of war with Indian nations confronted with, or cheated by, such avid speculators. Still a third was that the western lands were already taking on a new character. Down the Ohio river in one season in 1787 alone came over nine hundred ramshackle flatboats, bearing over eighteen thousand settlers, their livestock, wagons and provisions for a new life in the west.[23] The land over the mountains held the dream of freedom and independ-ence for the rootless among the coastal population, and for the many who still flowed in from the Old Country of the British Isles and further afield. The mêlée of organised land-grabs and individual hopes spawned a tumultuous process of asserted identities. Before the War of Independence Benjamin Franklin himself had been an investor in the proposed colony of Vandalia, to be carved out of the north-western lands of Virginia below the Ohio, and now, in 1787, inhabitants of north-western North Carolina honoured him with their claim to be the State of Franklin. Other names – Transylvania, Westsylvania – rose and fell with the fortunes of groups and schemes.

All this was not merely a question of internal disorder. Global pol-itics were in play. Spain held Florida and the west bank of the Mississippi and its outlet at New Orleans. A year earlier it had been proposed in Congress that the Spanish Crown be ceded the monop-oly of traffic along the great river in return for favourable terms on trade with its other colonies. The proposal fell, dismissed as a selfish move of the coastal mercantile elite, a scandalous neglect of the West's interests. That neglect, however, was so pervasive that some in Kentucky and Tennessee, where the only outlet for trade was down the Mississippi, thought the territories might prosper more if they switched allegiance to Spain wholesale. Moreover, there was no natural reason why the more north-western territories might not profit by directing their trade through the Great Lakes and the St Lawrence river, and the United States might see the old threat of France upon the Ohio replaced with a British West.[24]

Some in the Convention saw scarcely anything but evil about the process of expansion. Elbridge Gerry of Massachusetts, attuned to the interests of the mercantile elite of the coast whence he came, feared bluntly that population would flow to where land seemed almost free for the taking and that a tumultuous process would 'drain our wealth into the Western country'. His motion to prohibit forever the formation of western states outnumbering those of the seaboard fell, but only by five states' votes to four, and for some only on the premise that it was a fear too remote to be addressed. Others feared not the presence of wealth in the West, but its absence, with the result that the electorate of new states might be formed of an ignorant mass, their 'political talents' undeveloped in 'the remote wilderness', and prey to demagoguery. Therefore the suave New York landowner Gouverneur Morris moved that only property should determine the franchise in all areas.[25] This fell, as did his campaign against the admission of new states on equal terms with the old. He was bluntly reminded that it was the 'jealousy' of the British Crown, its 'fatal maxims . . . that the colonies were growing too fast' that had led to 'first enmity on our part, then actual separation'.[26]

Events had, in fact, rendered some of these concerns moot. On 13 July 1787 the old Congress produced the text known as the Northwest Ordinance, in which it placed all the territory north of the Ohio and east of the Mississippi under United States jurisdiction, with a governor, secretary and judges, and provision for an elected legislature once the settled population rose to reasonable levels. The ordinance's fifth article stated baldly that 'There shall be formed in the said territory, not less than three nor more than five States', and went on, 'whenever any of the said States shall have sixty thousand free inhabitants therein, such State shall be admitted, by its delegates, into the Congress of the United States, on an equal footing with the original States in all respects whatever.'[27] Regardless, therefore, of the fashion in which the delegates to the Convention viewed the threats and promises of the future, it was already clear that they were forming a nation that would have to step outside the bounds set by individual states' interests and alarms.

Other questions that continued to trouble the Convention were partly settled, but not laid to rest, by article six of the Northwest Ordinance:

> There shall be neither slavery nor involuntary servitude in the said territory, otherwise than in the punishment of crimes whereof the party shall have been duly convicted: Provided, always, that any person escaping into the same, from whom labour or service is lawfully claimed in any one of the original States, such fugitive may be lawfully reclaimed and conveyed to the person claiming his or her labour or service as aforesaid.

Slavery rose to the surface of the Convention's concerns in bitter debates in the searing heat of late August. George Mason, who was that most intriguing of Virginians, a slave-owning abolitionist (his plantation was not far from Washington's own Mount Vernon), raged against the slave trade, 'this infernal traffic', which he claimed with remarkable disingenuousness was perpetuated by British authority across the century, despite 'the attempts of Virginia to put a stop to it'. He spoke of slavery's 'pernicious effect . . . Every master of slaves is born a petty tyrant . . . the poor despise labour when they see it performed by slaves.' Already, supposedly, the settlers in the West were 'calling out for slaves for their new lands, and will fill that country with slaves' if given the chance. It was 'essential in every point of view' that 'power to prevent the increase of slavery' was placed in the hands of government.[28] Gouverneur Morris, who so disliked the poor, also had little sympathy for slavery, attributing to it 'the misery and poverty which overspreads the barren wastes' of the slave South.[29] But beyond these high flights of rhetoric the matter was mostly considered in the cold light of political and economic interest and practicality. Slavery was a settled social practice and if the slave-holders were prepared to concede, at least, that the transatlantic trade would eventually have to stop, they wrung a twenty-year moratorium on such a ban from the Convention, in mealy-mouthed language that hints at the conscious subversion of morality involved:

> The Migration or Importation of such Persons as any of the States now existing shall think proper to admit, shall not be prohibited by Congress prior to the Year one thousand eight hundred and eight, but a Tax or duty may be imposed on such Importation, not exceeding ten dollars for each person.[30]

Another clause later in the Constitution echoed the Northwest Ordinance, and would give bitter fruit through much of the century to come:

> No Person held to Service or Labour in one State, under the Laws thereof, escaping into another, shall, in consequence of any Law or Regulation therein, be discharged from such Service or Labour, but shall be delivered up on Claim of the Party to whom such Service or Labour may be due.[31]

Yet more fundamentally, when the time came to apportion representation in the new Congress, part of the 'Great Compromise' of the summer, slavery hung its shadow over the House of Representatives, where seats were to be granted to states according to 'the whole Number of free Persons . . . and excluding Indians not taxed, three fifths of all other Persons'.[32] Having thus dispatched, with little ado beyond flights of rhetoric, the problem of the unfree population, the Convention also backed gingerly away from the other great cultural dilemma of the age: religion. While Britain was caught between tolerating Catholics and privileging Anglicans, and even France, in a few short months, would grant limited civil rights to Protestants, America could scarcely do less than be tolerant. But it was a small and negative tolerance: a simple prohibition of religious tests for United States office-holders. Thus the question of the religious domination of Anglicans in Virginia, or Protestant sectaries in much of New England, was made into a non-issue.

As debate meandered on through August and early September there remained little overt consensus in the Convention. Every day some delegate or other voiced fundamental objections, often a matter had to be shelved after contentious argument, and frequently

slipped back in without discussion later. For the underlying agreement of most delegates, nurtured by continual reflection on the
parlous state of affairs under the Confederation, was in fact strong, if
largely unspoken. A new Constitution was needed, and the outlines
of the one they had been working on were clear. Moreover, and this
point was essential, the Constitution was not about setting the fun-
damentals of a society. The individual states retained a great deal of
power over their internal affairs, and they remained the basic building blocks of the sovereign system that was being erected. Edmund
Randolph, the young Governor of Virginia, had put the matter
bluntly in August: 'we are not working on the natural rights of men
not yet gathered into society, but upon those rights, modified by
society and interwoven with what we call the rights of states'.[33]
This was the reason why the Convention took perhaps its most
alarming decision, to outside observers, when on 12 September it
voted virtually unanimously not to include a Bill of Rights in the
Constitution. Put simply, the delegates thought it unnecessary.
Given the energetic debates and the endless fears expressed over
how far the powers of the new United States might spread, this was
extraordinarily complacent. It would prove a near-fatal flaw in the
plan as it proceeded forward outside the walls of the Pennsylvania
statehouse.

   The delegates came to sign the final draft of what they had so long
debated on 17 September 1787, a draft whose resonant phrases had
flowed largely from the elegant pen of Gouverneur Morris at the
head of a Committee of Style and Arrangement in the preceding
weeks. On this solemn day Benjamin Franklin himself, the cunning,
some might say dissembling, sage, made an opening speech that
wriggled around the notions of individual opinion and fallibility,
before bidding all present to sign the text, 'to make manifest our
unanimity', when it was quite evident that no such spirit existed.[34]
Edmund Randolph refused to sign, fearing 'anarchy and civil convulsions' when the people confronted the stark choice it offered
them. So too did Elbridge Gerry, fearing that the uncompromising
document would bring civil war between democrats (a party he
denounced as 'the worst of all political evils') and those 'as violent in
the opposite extreme'.[35] George Mason, the principled Virginian,
refused: he wrote that he foresaw the new government 'vibrating
between a monarchy and a corrupt oppressive aristocracy'.[36] In the

end only thirty-nine of the fifty-five men called to the Convention were both present and willing to sign.

The very next day, as the signers and non-signers dispersed to their widespread homes, the first conflict over the Constitution loomed in the very same room. The Pennsylvania Assembly, the state's single-chamber legislature, came into session, with a reading of the new text, including its injunction to form state conventions to ratify it. This mechanism had been explicitly written in by advocates of the new system, to avoid leaving the decision in the hands of existing political structures. Many in the Assembly, especially those from back-country districts who could see little gain for them in the elaborate new structures, did indeed object, and when ten days later the motion was put to convene a convention, they tried to block it by absenting themselves to their lodgings, denying the meeting a quorum. The issue was resolved the next day by a minor riot, in which populist advocates of the Constitution, known from now on as Federalists, had some of their Antifederalist opponents dragged from their lodgings by a mob and seated forcibly in the statehouse, making a quorum by their silent and enraged presence.

Thus, two months later, Pennsylvania was the first of the large states to hold its ratification convention, which saw five weeks of debate, as rancorous as the original Convention, before the Antifederalists lost the final vote two to one.[37] The matter was settled not by the debate, but effectively by ethnic and religious partisanship: James Madison acknowledged the presence of 'two fixed and violent parties' in Pennsylvania politics, and the Scots-Irish Presbyterians of the west lost out to the more numerous Quakers, Anglicans and Mennonites of the east, 'their old warfare carried on with new weapons'.[38] By then Delaware had already ratified after a much shorter meeting, and over the next month other small states, New Jersey, Georgia and Connecticut, did likewise. Public opinion here was far less divided, since the real threat they had always feared was the power of larger neighbours, not of a federal government.

One such large neighbour, the Commonwealth of Massachusetts, summoned its convention for 9 January 1788. With 355 delegates, it was a veritable parliament, and showed strong divisions. The coastal counties, with their attachment to maritime trade, sent strong Federalist majorities, while inland areas whose small farmers feared the power of distant states were solidly Anti.[39] Every time a 'well born' gentleman spoke up in favour of the Constitution, such men bristled, fearing 'the hideous daemon of aristocracy'.[40] The claim of the Federalists that the Constitution was a necessary remedy to the nation's ills made little sense to those whose prime enemies were the weather and the avarice of the merchants who bought their crops and mortgaged their lands. An old farmer, Amos Singletry, expressed their fears eloquently:

> Does not this Constitution . . . take away all we have – all our property? Does it not lay all taxes, duties, imposts and excises? And what more have we to give? . . . These lawyers and men of learning, and moneyed men that talk so finely, and gloss over matters so smoothly, to make us poor illiterate people swallow down the pill, expect to get into Congress themselves . . . and then they will swallow up us little fellows . . . just as the whale swallowed up Jonah.[41]

Others, including fellow 'plough joggers', as one memorably called himself, made calming arguments about the value of union, and countered that the 'lawyers, these moneyed men, these men of learning' were all in the same boat with the humble yeoman; but it was clear as the month progressed that the Massachusetts convention was not yet minded to ratify.[42]

Federalist strategy had to shift, and it did so by conceding ground to its opponents. If the Antifederalists feared so much in the new Constitution, then let it be amended. The local Federalist leadership used the mouthpiece provided by John Hancock, first signatory to the Declaration of Independence and Governor of Massachusetts (and promised a presidential nomination if Washington's Virginia failed to ratify). On 30 January he presented to the convention a 'Conciliatory Proposition' including nine specific changes limiting federal powers over taxation, elections and commerce.[43] For a week debate over this went back and forth, then the Antifederalist front finally cracked, for it was difficult to sustain a wholly negative objection to the project when so many specific issues were being addressed. On 5 February, after much havering, a final vote secured ratification, with the recommendation of amendments, by 187 to 168.

The process now slowed down again as no more states met in the winter. In April Maryland ratified, again with a list of desired amendments, and also with a formal protest from the minority appended, considering 'the proposed form of government very defective', requiring to be 'greatly altered' if the 'liberty and happiness of the people' were to be safeguarded. In May South Carolina ratified, though showing solid majorities opposed in its inland areas. New Hampshire agreed in June, another close vote, 57 to 46. As they did so, the convention of Virginia, the Old Dominion, was in session.[44] With a fifth of the Union's population, this meeting was crucial to the success of the enterprise. Although it was a much smaller gathering than Massachusetts's, with a mere 170 present, among them were towering figures in the history of the Revolution, and who in the debate now stood on one side or the other. Virginian society, of all the states, most resembled the ideal version of England to which the Whig rhetoric of liberty appealed – if one turned a blind eye to the tens of thousands of slaves. The Commonwealth of Virginia was ruled by a gentry elite of landowners and lawyers, proud of their ancestry and of their commitment to freedom, as they understood it.

Patrick Henry, who claimed credit for leading Virginia into the War of Independence with his parliamentary oratory, summoned this identity as he stood to condemn the Constitution: 'We drew the spirit of liberty from our British ancestors. But now, sir, the American spirit, assisted by the ropes and chains of consolidation, is about to convert this country into a powerful and mighty empire.' This was not a recommendation: 'There will be no checks, no real balances, in this government. What can avail your specious, imaginary balances, your rope-dancing, chain-rattling, ridiculous ideal checks and contrivances?'[45] Henry's turn to the stout defence of states' rights was in stark contrast to his protestations at the first Continental Congress of 1774, where he had boldly asserted: 'I am not a Virginian, but an American. All distinctions are thrown down. All America is thrown into one mass.'[46] But since then he had come to realise that his only real powerbase was with the Virginians, who feared subjection to New England mercantile pretensions.

Others mocked more openly the Federalist protestations of danger in disunity: 'the Carolinians from the south, mounted on alligators I presume, are to come and destroy our cornfields and eat up our little children!'[47] The tone of rancour was set on the first day of debate, 4 June, when Edmund Randolph, Governor of Virginia, performed a dramatic about-face. Having refused to sign the Constitution, he now advocated it, for Massachusetts's suggested amendments had changed his mind. With eight states already in favour, and the realistic prospect of remedying the document's defects, approval with Virginia's own suggested changes would be the best, indeed the only, course. In yet another of the Constitutional Convention's acts of bravado, the text itself decreed that it should come into effect when nine states had ratified. Virginia's moment to affect the outcome was now, and this was the only way forward 'without inevitable ruin to the Union'.[48] This performance was so astonishing that Henry stood next to assert boldly that 'something extraordinary' must have happened to change Randolph's mind – a quite clear allegation that he had been bribed or otherwise worked upon. After further furious exchanges the inevitable sequel in this gentlemanly world occurred and Henry's second saw Randolph that evening with a view to arranging a duel. Fortunately sense prevailed and thereafter debate was a little more tempered, but only a little. Still, the combination of the positive alternative offered by the Constitution and a formidable list of proposed amendments finally pushed a majority of ten to vote in favour three weeks later. They attached twenty desired amendments to the structure of the Constitution, and a further twenty-article Declaration of Rights.

The deed was now done. Technically New Hampshire's vote had secured the future of the Constitution, but Virginians had not known of it when they disputed. Ten states were now in, and New York followed a month later, though giving a majority of only three out of the fifty-seven delegates present, and after a particularly extensive and detailed public debate. This produced the pieces later to become known as the *Federalist Papers*, writings by the original leading advocates of the Constitution, notably Madison and Hamilton, in its favour. Though these would stand the test of time as an expression of the document's virtues, in 1788 they swayed few. The New York convention, to achieve its slender majority, had had to attach no fewer than thirty-two desired amendments, and a lengthy Bill of Rights.[49] The non-existence of such a document preyed on Americans' minds as they went forward with electing men to serve the new federal institutions as 1789 dawned. Antifederalist rhetoric had succeeded in raising dread spectres: Elbridge Gerry from

Massachusetts had denounced the Constitution as 'a consolidated fabrick of aristocratick tyranny' and a 'republican *form* of government' but 'founded on the principles of monarchy'. Federalist supporters tried to rebuff such points, yet seemed in some cases almost eager to embrace their implications. One noted publicist, Tench Coxe, wrote that the British balanced monarchy was indeed still an example to emulate, embracing again Hamilton's view of its model qualities: 'we did not dissolve our connection with that country so much on account of its constitution, as the perversion and mal-administration of it'.[50] Had Americans re-subjected themselves after only a decade of freedom? For many only time, and arduous debate, would tell. Almost the only thing genuinely settled was the identity of the first President. George Washington, saviour of independence, would be chosen in the first weeks of the new year to perform that function again for the new Republic.

France in the late summer of 1788 was looking desperately for a saviour, and for a short time thought that it had found one in the shape of a returning hero, Jacques Necker. Revered as the man who had piloted French finances through the American War, with many still believing his claim to have left office in 1781 with the accounts in surplus, Necker possessed a financial wizardry that seemed to offer the only way out of a spiralling crisis. In early July the government was at breaking point. With the catastrophic opposition to the *coup* against the *parlements* crippling political initiative, the Crown's precarious short-term credit collapsed as public confidence nosedived. Brienne had to concede an early but unspecified date for the Estates-General, and also liberated a flood of political commentary by explicitly revoking censorship on writing about the form that such an assembly should take. This in itself was also partly a manoeuvre to outflank the *parlementaires* and their allies, who clung to a rigidly traditional, noble-dominated version of the Estates. Here it would be eminently successful, but too late to save the government.

In the first half of August state credit reached an irremediable low. Two hundred and forty million *livres* in short-term borrowing was needed to cover the accounts, and no one wanted to lend. Brienne was forced on 8 August to suspend the Plenary Court and summon the Estates-General officially for May 1789. It was still not enough, and a week later, with just 400,000 *livres* in the coffers, less than a day's expenditure, the kingdom was effectively bankrupt. Interest payments were suspended, and some creditors paid off with long-term bonds, effectively extracting a forced loan from them. A short-term panic, briefly threatening a decisive run on the banks, gave those closest to the king, especially the queen and the comte d'Artois, all the ammunition they needed to destroy their former favourite. In a classic Court intrigue, like those that had brought down so many ministers in the past decades, Brienne learned on 25 August from Mercy-Argenteau, Austrian diplomat and Marie-Antoinette's political mentor, that he had lost her confidence. He tendered his resignation to the king at once. Waiting in the wings to take over was Necker.

Despite his Swiss birth (and family origins in Küstrin, Prussia), French affairs had taken up Necker's whole career. Apprenticed to a Paris banking house at fifteen in 1747, he had risen by the age of thirty to a partnership in the business, and only a few years later founded his own bank, which prospered largely on administering loans to the French state. In 1764 he married Suzanne Curchod, a Swiss pastor's daughter formerly betrothed to the English historian Edward Gibbon, and as a family man began to seek more of a public role. Over the next decade he served as a director of the French East India Company, defending its interests in polemics against government interference, and also wrote prize-winning essays in defence of state regulation of the grain trade and the centralist economic policies of Louis XIV's great minister Jean-Baptiste Colbert, in both cases going against the line of ministers in office.

Such activities positioned Necker ideally to be raised to ministerial power after the free-trader Turgot's fall in 1776. Promising to avoid both bankruptcy and new taxes, he had played the financial markets brilliantly at first, while also striking chords with 'Enlightened' public opinion: his wife's glittering *salon* was part of his political armoury for maintaining confidence, as were conspicuously forward-thinking (if almost cost-free) policy moves, including reforms to hospitals, the ending of certain forms of judicial torture in 1780 and, the previous year, a grand gesture in which the king abolished the last vestiges of serfdom on the royal domain.[51] Less visibly, but more controversially, Necker also fought hard to cut back on expenditure on venal offices, and to centralise the notoriously diffuse and shadowy networks of state financial management. It was political clashes over such issues and consequent loss of favour with the king that cost Necker his position in 1781. The king got through two more finance ministers in the next two years, before turning to Calonne and beginning the cycle of renewed efforts at reform that ended with Necker's triumphant return.

Necker in exile had retained his connections and his supporters, and also his interest in his family's advancement. When William Pitt made a visit to France with friends in the late summer of 1783, on the brink of his ascent to the premiership, Necker sought him out through mutual acquaintances and offered him the hand in marriage of his seventeen-year-old daughter Germaine. Pitt wanted nothing of it, but Necker had evidently seen a chance for establishing his only child in a position of influence: one she would gain in other ways in another decade, as Madame de Staël.[52] Given the depth of the French crisis in 1788, however, Necker had been reluctant to step back into the limelight. He had agreed to come back only if Brienne went, and had taken a week of persuading. His daughter wrote that he lamented the work he could have done if he had held office instead of Brienne since 1787: 'Right now, it's too late!'[53] Judging that the state's finances were indeed in an irreparable state, and the country on the verge of 'a general insurrection', he restored the *parlements* to their full powers and thus was able to stave off political discontent sufficiently to borrow the vast sums needed to get the French state to the end of the year intact.[54] Under Necker the government effectively sat back and did nothing for the rest of the year, while a new and not entirely unexpected conflict began to rage.

The *parlement* of Paris and its supporters on the streets of the city were exultantly triumphant, especially when, on 14 September, Justice Minister Lamoignon was forced to resign by the judges' absolute refusal to work with him. Two days later a mob attempting to assault his house, and that of Brienne, had to be driven off with bayonet charges. While the *parlement* condemned rioting as it re-entered its full functions on 24 September, it also opened an investigation into the actions of the police against crowds through the previous month, and one into Brienne and Lamoignon themselves. The Crown was powerless to intervene, its authority crippled by its recent prevarications – the inevitable effect, a commentator noted, of a state that revoked its own recently made laws 'as if they had been the work of madness and tyranny'.[55] But when the *parlement* sought to bolster its authority on 25 September by decreeing that the forthcoming Estates-General should unquestionably follow historic forms all its glory fell away. Such a form, last used in 1614, would condemn the vast majority of the population to be lumped into an unprivileged 'Third Estate', and thus to minority status, with the nobility and the clergy taking up two of three separate chambers and commanding a permanent majority in deliberations. Since July, however, in the press, and since Necker's return, in the political clubs allowed to reopen at his instructions, the Third Estate was finding an explicitly political voice. A host of pamphleteers had begun to offer their advice on the forms of the Estates-General and, necessarily therefore, on the political principles that should underlay such forms. Partisans of liberal reform joined circles of sociability that swelled almost at once into something approaching a liberal party. The wide spectrum of figures drawn into such discussions, and their prior entanglements in the complex politics of publicity under an absolute monarchy, can be exemplified in the pre-revolutionary careers of two very different outsiders: Jacques-Pierre Brissot de Warville and Honoré Gabriel Riqueti, comte de Mirabeau.

Mirabeau was the eldest in the fourth generation of a noble family that had been elevated from the merchant class of Marseille a century earlier. His father, Victor, marquis de Mirabeau, was a noted writer on economic affairs, sticking up for the cultivators of land against idle and parasitic landlords, and nicknamed, after the most famous of his works, *L'Ami des hommes*, or 'Friend of Men'. His relations with his son were not friendly, however. The boy was disfigured by smallpox at three and the father seems to have held out little hope for his future, packing him off to military school as soon as possible. Honoré Mirabeau grew up to be a large, ugly man gifted with a silver tongue, a surprisingly successful way with women and a talent for getting into trouble that made his early life read like a picaresque novel. In the late 1760s, while a young cavalry officer, he seduced his colonel's mistress, causing such a scandal that his father had him briefly locked away, using one of the infamous royal *lettres de cachet*, orders for arbitrary imprisonment often granted to save families from embarrassing offspring. In 1772, in an effort to gain respectability (and cash), Mirabeau sought to marry a rich heiress, but to do so he had to break her engagement to another man. Thus he bribed a maid to let him into her apartments and then claimed to her father that they had made love, forcing a rapid marriage. Already chronically in debt, he fell further in 1774 when a violent quarrel led to a second spell of detention, this time in the notorious château d'If. The following year, allowed out on parole from another fortress, he met and fell in love with a woman he nicknamed 'Sophie', to whom he wrote explicit love letters that later found notorious publication. Eloping to Switzerland and then Holland, Mirabeau survived by cultivating a developing talent for journalism (and pornography).

His escape with Sophie, however, had led to his being sentenced to death *in absentia*, and he was captured by French agents in 1777, thereafter spending five years in the château of Vincennes. Escaping the death sentence, and even having costs awarded against Sophie's father, by the force of his legal writings, he found on his release that she had killed herself. Further familial and erotic complications followed, including another exile in Holland, where he met a new lover; he spent some time in England with her. What is perhaps most remarkable is that throughout all this Mirabeau's reputation as a writer was growing. His attack on the system of *lettres de cachet* was much admired among the sympathetic Whig circles in which he moved in England, as was a pamphlet he wrote against the Order of the Cincinnati in America, picking up on current attacks on its hereditary status (and based on information forwarded by Benjamin Franklin).

Returning to France in the mid-1780s, Mirabeau tried to get subsidies from the Foreign Ministry to write propaganda, but ruined his chances by simultaneously producing polemics in a series of court cases and financial speculations. Despite this, he was sent on a covert mission to the Prussian Court in Berlin in late 1786, where Frederick the Great's death made his position crucial. Failing, however, to make a successful diplomatic impact, he returned, publishing a popular history of Frederick's reign while also failing to be appointed as secretary to the Assembly of Notables, largely because of yet another polemical publication. The rising crisis of 1787–8 saw him politicking furiously in liberal circles, founding a newspaper that disguised commentary on France amid its overt intent to digest the reports of English newspapers on their own politics, and renewing contacts with the circles of bankers and speculators he had engaged with before his Berlin trip.

Close to the centre of that circle was Étienne Clavière, a Genevan banker who also had close links with a much younger man, the son of a Chartres innkeeper who had fought his way to notice, and something approaching notoriety, through a series of journalistic schemes and international connections. Jacques-Pierre Brissot, who liked to add the aristocratic 'de Warville' to his name while it remained fashionable, had a past almost as chequered, if less picaresque, as Mirabeau's, and was about to enjoy almost as spectacular a rise. Born in 1754 and trained in the law, Brissot turned to writing in his late twenties. Within a few years he had embarked on ambitious plans for an international association of Enlightened men, centred on a newspaper published in London and Paris, and a public assembly maintained by subscription in the British capital. This *Licée de Londres* collapsed in a flurry of unpaid debts after Brissot had worked on it for almost a year. Dunned for money owed to his printer in London, Brissot had to be bailed out of prison by his business partner, with whom he then had a furious falling-out over the collapse. Returning to Paris in mid-1784, still embroiled in this row, Brissot was arrested by police agents and locked up in the notorious prison of the Bastille, on suspicion of writing and publishing some of the obscene and defamatory pamphlets about high political figures that continued to dog French affairs.[56]

The truth of the matter, which emerges only hesitantly from a fog of scurrilous accusations and hazy later recollections, is that Brissot had known and worked with some of the men responsible for writing such works in London, and may even have occasionally helped to ship a few copies to continental distributors. But he seems to have had no real part in the truly criminal end of the enterprise, which was the blackmailing of powerful individuals, and the French Crown itself, for large sums over the threat of publication of such texts. Nor did he, as enemies later charged, capitulate to police pressure and become a paid spy after his release in September 1784. Since his main initial accuser, Charles Théveneau de Morande, was all the things he accused Brissot of being – pornographer, blackmailer and paid police agent – this ought perhaps to be unsurprising. However, it seems Brissot may have nonetheless been part of the astonishingly close ties between opposition and police in 1780s Paris. The memoirs of Lenoir, the city's chief policeman until 1785, include cryptic notes suggesting that both Brissot and Mirabeau, linked together by their association with Clavière, supported the police by distributing 'packets of pamphlets . . . news bulletins reporting well or ill-attested facts', and that Mirabeau in particular was unscrupulously prepared to write against positions he had already taken, if paid enough. When Brissot's own memoirs note that he worked to support Calonne's plans, and was once paid by him to allow Mirabeau's more famous name to go on a work of his and Clavière's, a very complex picture emerges.[57]

Brissot was unquestionably an idealist, a *philosophe*, a thinker in his own right on, for example, penal policy and global trade. He also needed to live, and to support a family. He seems to have sought income wherever it would not directly contradict his core beliefs, but also to have put himself out in the cause of liberty and international co-operation. In 1787, again under pressure over polemical publications, he spent a second period in London, where he built a network of contacts among an emerging anti-slavery lobby. For the whole second half of 1788, when he might have been seeking new political sponsors in the hectic climate of Paris, instead he committed himself to a tour of the United States, in pursuit of connections for a new 'Gallo-American Society' that he and Clavière had pledged to fruitful exchanges between the two countries. Thomas Jefferson, ambassador in Paris, was familiar enough with him to note a few months later that 'Warville is returned charmed with our country. He is going to carry his wife and children to settle there.'[58] Alas for Brissot, such an emigration never happened. The rising ferment of revolution sucked him back into schemes for progress through political journalism that would make him a household name, along with Mirabeau and many others, across Europe, and then steer him to seemingly ineluctable doom.

With Brissot temporarily out of the picture in America, the new movement to promote the representation of the Third Estate had many other champions, and seemed at first to require little more than reiterated publicity to bring about the desired change. In this context the hostility of the *parlement* to the Third Estate was both a challenge and a gift. Educated public opinion was enflamed, writers expatiated on the futile prejudice shown by the judges and, as the *parlement* attempted to censor writings it deemed insufficiently respectful of its prerogatives, the storm merely grew. The barrister Target, one of the most respected trial lawyers in France, was among many who condemned absolutely the recourse to tradition in the *parlement*'s views: 'We must distrust the mania for proving what must be done by what has been done; for it is precisely what has been done that we complain of.'[59] Mirabeau had gone even further in a letter in August, declaring 'war on the privileged and on privileges', and Target backed him up in another text, calling on all those with privileges to use them to oppose the king, but to 'lay them down before France assembled'.[60]

Among all this controversy Necker tried to play the honest broker. The Assembly of Notables was reconvened in November 1788 specifically to advise on the form the Estates-General should take, but the wider rancour soon caught them up. Advocates of the Third Estate wanted at least that it should have the same number of representatives as the other two orders combined, 'doubling the Third' as it was called, and that voting should be by head to make the increase meaningful. Though the *parlement* of Paris in a belated bid to regain popularity came out for doubling on 5 December, a week later many of the king's own relatives in the Notables signed a declaration that there should be no concession on this point, or on voting by head. They had begun to read the writing on the wall and realised that it was not merely their exemption from taxation that might be threatened by the Third, but their whole existence as a privileged body. But the monarchy was now invested in letting the Estates-General go ahead, and indeed in the person of Necker believed it provided the only hope of a durable solution. With no agreement from the Notables, and scorning the voices of reaction, Necker passed through the king's council on 27 December 1788 a series of orders for the Estates-General: it would double the Third, but the more contentious issues of whether it would deliberate and vote as one body or three were left for the delegates themselves to decide. Likewise issues such as who qualified to represent the nobility in different regions were pushed out to those localities to decide, and no blockage was put on nobles or clergy representing the Third Estate if elected, in the hope of avoiding too direct a social confrontation. As the year ended it seemed quite clear to supporters and opponents alike that the majestic authority of the French Crown had been almost entirely sacrificed to the Nation.

That Nation was not, however, confined to actual members of the Third Estate. If Mirabeau was one somewhat disreputable example of a noble throwing his lot in with reform, there were many others pushing in the same direction who had a far greater claim to represent a real elite. Among them was the marquis de Lafayette, alongside a group of magistrates in the *parlement* of Paris already nicknamed the 'Americans' because of their zeal for a new constitution.[61] Lafayette, in correspondence with George Washington, had declared in December 1787 that an 'alliance' of these figures, desirous of a constitution and a declaration of rights, had been formed, and in November 1788 a new chapter in this progress opened. Profiting from Necker's relaxation of the previous ban on political clubs, the young *parlementaire* leader Duport began hosting a gathering known loosely as the 'Society of Thirty', described by the boisterously radical Mirabeau as 'a conspiracy of well-intentioned men'.

What was most notable about this group, in light of what was to come, was their remarkably high social status. There were, in fact, over fifty members of the 'Thirty'. Following the lead of Lafayette, the largest single group were from the established nobility. This category did include Mirabeau, but his disreputable presence was balanced by the prestige of the marquis de Condorcet, mathematician and philosopher, and considerably outweighed by almost twenty men with high military ranks, vast feudal estates or both. Alongside these were ten of Duport's own 'Americans' from the *parlement*, who in the early months of the Thirty's existence shared an uneasy alliance with half a dozen from the other, far more conservatively anti-absolutist faction of judges led by Duval d'Éprémesnil. Around these solid blocs were drawn in a small number of other men known for their political ideas and writings, including the *abbé* Sieyès, another like Brissot of humble origins, risen on talent and about to become enduringly famous.

Given Mirabeau's own career, one can readily detect irony in his anointment of any group including himself as *honnêtes hommes*, and it is undoubtedly true that interested motives could be attributed to many of these reformers. D'Éprémesnil's conservative *parlementaires* wanted real constitutional power for themselves, and in essence the position of Duport, for all its gloss of constitutional liberalism, was similar. Lafayette, alongside his lifelong commitment to the American example, was also an associate of the aristocratic house of Noailles, a grouping locked in bitter feud with the Polignac family,

favourites of Marie-Antoinette who had dominated Court patronage
for a decade. Many others among the military nobles in the Thirty
had been associated with a virtual mutiny of senior officers only
months earlier, protesting against reforms that would weaken the
hold of Court families over military appointments.[62] Most of the
other noble figures can be connected in one way or another to grievances at the treatment of themselves, relations or clients at the hands
of Louis XVI's administration. With singular ineptitude the king had
pursued a policy of neglecting the grandees of France in favour of
promoting provincial talent, seeking to cushion the monarchy against
Court intrigue, while propelling the country towards a crisis that had
united almost every strand of such opposition against him. And in
the powerhouse of political action formed by the Thirty, a far more
thoroughgoing challenge than any mere factional intrigue was given
shape.

By the end of 1788 the pamphleteering and behind-the-scenes
lobbying of the Thirty had already secured first the *parlement*'s and
then the government's consent to the doubling of Third Estate representation in the upcoming Estates-General. But it had also
nurtured a nationwide flood tide of activity. Pamphlets that made
their way from the pens of the Thirty and others to the towns
and cities of the provinces carried uncompromising messages, in
language that was new to public discussion and often highly
inflammatory. Late 1788 and early 1789 saw waves of writing that
denounced the nobility and clergy as parasitic, asserting that they
monopolised legal privilege for their own benefit, which was quite
untrue in a country where the privileges of lordship were for sale to
the highest bidder, and provinces, towns and even villages enjoyed
their own historic exemptions and rights.[63] Claims such as these,
and far more hysterical direct attacks and accusations of conspiracy,
created a running battle with the *parlement* of Paris, guardian of
public morality, which condemned numerous publications to be
banned and burned in these hectic months – stern actions that
simply produced more cries against censorship and warnings of
oppression.

The rallying cries of the Thirty and their imitators had their effect
in the concrete political realm. The middling classes of the country,
previously mere spectators at a distance to the turmoil of the elite,
now began to meet and deliberate. Once again, ironically, the

government itself had promoted their activity. Since late 1787 much of the country had seen the institution of provincial assemblies as part of the reforms of Brienne, and in other regions traditional provincial meetings of 'Estates' had been reinvigorated, both by and against ministers' wishes, in various cases.[64] Politics in provincial France had begun to have a real material basis for the first time in anyone's memory. While government reforms provided an example, the far wider networks of reading clubs and literary societies, an essential point of provincial educated sociability, were a nexus for the distribution of the printed matter suddenly flooding into small-town life. Taking the language of citizenship seriously, the lawyers, notaries, professionals and tradesmen of the provinces responded in kind. Over eight hundred collective petitions were sent to Versailles in the closing months of 1788 from town meetings convened by such local worthies to press the king for fair treatment of their kind.[65]

On 27 December, the formal declaration that the Third would be doubled, and that the press would remain free to discuss the Estates-General, seemed a victory for this pressure, which thereafter only redoubled.

---

# 4

# 'The seeds of decay and corruption'

*Britain, empire and the king's*
*madness, 1784–8*

Warren Hastings was a symbol of the possibilities of British imperial might. Born in 1732 to a family of former gentry who had lost their lands in the Civil War, he was sponsored in his education by a more prosperous uncle, until the latter's death when Hastings was fifteen left him in dire need of employment. A distant relative secured him a post as a clerk in the Honourable East India Company, and after studying bookkeeping he sailed for Calcutta in 1750, to spend almost all of the next thirty-five years in India. Swiftly educating himself in the languages of Bengal, Hastings rose with the Company as it entered its years of greatness. Still essentially a trading concern when he arrived, under the legendary Robert Clive it acquired armies, allies and military victories, and though Hastings remained always a civilian administrator he was steadily embroiled at ever more senior levels in an enterprise becoming a political force in its own right.

The East India Company, through the aggressive pursuit of its own interests, and not infrequently the private interests of its officials, secured by the mid-1760s a position for British power in India that was quite remarkable. Founded, and occasionally floundering, as a monopoly importer of Indian goods to Britain, it had long been entangled in political struggles to maintain a foothold in the regions where the most lucrative trade was to be had. The Company was harried by demands from home to pursue conflicting priorities, contesting through the middle decades of the century with equally enterprising and aggressive French imperialists and dealing with the near-frenzied, murderous, treacherous politics of a vast Mughal empire on the brink of dissolution, its princes and potentates possessed of huge wealth and unashamed luxury with which to bribe and suborn the Company's administrators and officers to their own interests. But the superior guile, cunning and outright single-minded greed of the Britons thousands of miles from home saw them raised to the status of effectively sovereign princes of Bengal, rulers of thirty million subjects, by order of the Mughal emperor, given at Benares on the Ganges on 12 August 1765. Through this rise Warren Hastings, a slim, studious, courteous figure at stark odds with buccaneers like Clive, had earned his administrative spurs in a series of trading and bureaucratic positions, and then spent the later 1760s back in England, a victim of the poisonous office politics that the Company raised to extraordinary heights. But he returned, first to a senior position in Madras in the south in 1769, and then to the governorship of Bengal two years later.

Hastings found a situation there in near chaos. Neither the men on the spot nor the Company's directors in London had accepted the implications of the 1765 grant of *diwan*, or tax-gathering powers. The local nominal ruler, the Nawab of Bengal, abandoned all effort to provide an administration of justice, seeing it as part of the *diwan*, while the Company preferred to treat the *diwan* as a simple revenue-raising structure, and to squeeze it ever tighter to defray the expense of the large tribute it had formally agreed to pay the emperor in return for it.[1] Alongside this collective disorder the Company's individual servants continued in Clive's piratical ways, accepting bribes from all and sundry in the complex games of local politics and pursuing the accretion of individual fortunes through abusive monopolies of local trade and other manipulations of tariffs, duties and customs. Clive himself, on a second tour of duty that ended in 1767, as poacher turned gamekeeper, bewailed the 'Corruption, Licentiousness and want of Principle' that seemed 'to have possessed the minds of all the Civil Servants', and failed in an effort to ban the private trading of such men, despite its being expressly forbidden by (and the men's supposed losses compensated by payments from) the Company itself.[2]

To complicate matters further, Bengal was beset by famine, aggravated by the tyranny of the Company's servants. Contemporaries
thought that a third of the population had perished, lands lay waste
and beggars and bandits thronged the roads. Beyond the human
misery all this provoked, it also left the Company in crisis, spending
far more than it took in and obliged to borrow £1 million from the
Westminster government in 1772 to tide it over.[3] In a whirlwind of
activity in his first two years in office, Hastings used military force to
suppress banditry and secure the frontiers against encroaching neighbours, restored regularity to internal administration, cut down on
ruinous bribes and subsidies to local nobles and princes, reformed
the decayed structures of customs and credit, created almost from
scratch functional local systems of justice and did much to restrain
the rapacity of individual Britons against Indians. Perhaps as a result,
when in 1773 the Westminster Parliament passed the Regulating
Act, rescuing the Company's finances in return for greater official
control over its activities, Hastings was raised to the rank of British
India's first Governor General, overseeing not just Bengal, but also
the Company's other 'Presidencies' of Madras and Bombay, and all
intervening activities. The significance of this office was embodied
in the salary and allowances attached to it: over £30,000, a veritably
princely sum, far more than that of a government minister. A further
decade of arduous endeavours followed, during which Hastings bat-
tled his own colleagues as much as the turbulent politics of India,
and found himself, sometimes to repair the errors of such colleagues,
extending the influence and outright power of the Company ever
further.

Such successes made Hastings and his supporters back home
active players in the intrigues against Charles James Fox's bid to
put the patronage of the Company under parliamentary control, and
thus, inevitably, involved them in the process that brought William
Pitt to office. Pitt was said to see Hastings as 'a very great and indeed
a wonderful man', while his colleague the Lord Chancellor passed on
the judgement that Hastings 'put an end to the late ministry as completely as if he had taken a pistol and shot them through the head
one after another' – flattery indeed, seen in a certain political light.
Hastings had his doubts, however, and as Pitt politicked furiously in
1784 to make the country ready for a general election, he wrote to his
wife that he firmly believed no administration would keep him on

'but as a cypher to keep the office open for the gift of their own patronage. I am not pleased to be made so pitiful an instrument.'[4]

High politics and low cunning were indeed being combined in Britain as Hastings wrote. News of the violent attack on Pitt's coach by Fox's supporters spread around the country, accompanied by Fox's own discreditable alibi – he was in bed with his mistress at the time – and the political fortunes of the opposition sank lower. Without modern party discipline the majority Fox commanded was steadily eroded by defections, and by mid-March the government was ready to call an election on its terms, which included the king personally borrowing £24,000 from a banker for the costs to be incurred. Like any other eighteenth-century election, that of 1784 brought out the worst of British politics in the eyes of observers. The majority of seats were decided, as always, by the wishes of powerful patrons, many of whom continued to be leaned upon heavily by the king and his gifts of honours. Sir James Lowther, who had given Pitt his first Commons seat, and continued to control a number of boroughs, was among those raised to the peerage. In the most open constituencies, where the votes of relatively poor individuals were up for grabs, expenditure on bribery, usually in the customary form of 'treating' electors to vast meals and unlimited supplies of alcohol, reached desperate levels.

The Foxites fought like demons to secure victory in the constituency of Westminster itself, with its thousands of voters. Fox stood for one of the two seats on offer, though he also had himself elected for Kirkwall, in the far north of Scotland, as an insurance policy. Beyond cash and drink, they resorted to blackening the names of their opponents in printed broadsides, to which the government supporters responded in kind. When the daring and beautiful Georgiana, Duchess of Devonshire, appeared in the streets on behalf of her Foxite friends, freely dispensing kisses to voters in return for their pledges, she was the target of ridicule and slanders, the worst of which compared her unfavourably to the 'sounder flesh on Portsmouth Common', home of the 'Brutes', hardened whores who serviced the fleet.[5]

Viciously satirical prints, rising in popularity with urban audiences, added their effects. The amateur artist James Sayers, who later received from Pitt the sinecure of Marshal of the Court of Exchequer, had already produced in December 1783 a defining new image of Charles James Fox as 'Carlo Khan', arriving on an elephant (with the face of Lord North) to seize control of the power and wealth of the East India Company. During the election campaign itself, Sayers showed Fox looking into *The Mirror of Patriotism*, and seeing there the armoured, scowling figure of Cromwell – emblem of dictatorship. The professional artist James Gillray had already been venting spleen on the Fox–North coalition before its fall: one image of April 1783, *The Junction of Parties*, showed the two men defecating into a pot stirred by the devil himself, the results signposted as 'the universal SALVE_ation of this Kingdom'.[6]

Despite these more ribald aspects, the most notable feature of the 1784 election was the support for Pitt among respectable propertied public opinion. Freeholding county electorates in particular rallied to the government, and in some cases, such as in Norfolk, opposition supporters with generations of local representation and patronage behind them could not even get a hearing at public meetings. The *Kentish Gazette* passed emphatic commentary on the result:

> A most complete revolution has taken place in the state of rep-resentation. Neither high rank, the most powerful influence, or acknowledged private integrity (the latter but a rare occurrence) have been able to serve the unpopular members. They are routed in all their strongholds, and it is beyond a doubt, that the Minister will come into Parliament with a very great majority.[7]

The election was a triumph for Pitt, who was indeed able to muster three-figure majorities on key votes. But the country overall was still in an atmosphere of crisis. On the level of pure politics Pitt poisoned the air further by instigating a formal scrutiny of all the votes cast in the Westminster contest. It was an attempt, perhaps, to deal a death blow to the reputation of Fox, who had sought to destroy Pitt so ardently, but one that would trail off into indecision after months of bitter wrangling. Nonetheless, Pitt now had what the French and Americans were so desperately to crave from their constitutional systems: legitimacy, and the power to do something about the crippling costs of the American War. Interest on the National Debt was consuming almost two-thirds of the whole government budget and had increased by a quarter in the war years.[8] Pitt turned his genius for detail, and his probity, to the problem immediately.

Reversing years of backstairs financial dealings, he ensured that a loan of £6 million was subscribed through sealed bids, opened before witnesses, rather than channelled at discount rates to political connections. He also succeeded in driving through Parliament a swath of new taxes on items of consumption, following the pattern of previous governments but with new intensity. Further dramatic changes followed, including massive cuts in the duty on tea, which combated smuggling and further boosted his popularity.

The problem of India was speedily resolved, to first impressions, with a new Act in July 1784, creating a royally appointed Board of Control to oversee the strategy of the East India Company, while leaving the appointment of Company officials to its directors. While all seemed smoothly done from Westminster, this was the last straw for Hastings in Calcutta. When he read Pitt's speech introducing the Bill, in which, to justify the need for reform, much was made of the problems and abuses of power in India, Hastings bridled, concluding: 'it is impossible that . . . he should desire me to remain, afford me his confidence or add to my powers'. He resigned his position and sailed for home in the first week of February 1785. On the voyage he recorded his firm and very telling belief that 'I have saved India, in spite of them all, from foreign conquest', but that politics had seen his hopes of raising an empire to prosperity 'vanish in an instant, like the illusions of a dream'.[9] He would return to something much closer to a nightmare.

While Hastings sailed for home, Pitt's hopes for further reform were dashed. For a year the Prime Minister laboured to reconcile further the politics and economies of Britain and Ireland, seeking to implement a radically liberated mode of trade between the two kingdoms, and to allow Irish commerce the freedom of the seas beyond the empire, while also bringing forth a modest contribution to national defence from the Irish taxpayers. Launched into a quagmire of competing interests, the scheme slowly and ignominiously sank, giving off eruptions of political vitriol as it did so. In the midst of this protracted failure Pitt also attempted in April 1785 to get the Commons to consider its own reform. He had been the first Prime Minister in British history to stand for election explicitly promising such reform – and he was to be the last for almost half a century.[10] Obliged to tiptoe round the king, who objected to anything that smacked of democratic change, but whose known opposition lurked in the minds of many MPs, Pitt put his reputation on the line. In so doing he was being entirely consistent with his former support for the Association Movement, and with his self-identification as an Independent Whig. He warned the House, in words that echoed Montesquieu's prophecy, that 'the best institutions, like human bodies, carried in themselves the seeds of decay and corruption', and stated that his proposals were remedies to this process, 'which the frame of the Constitution must necessarily experience in the lapse of years'.[11]

His plan would disenfranchise thirty-six rotten boroughs and give the seventy-two seats to areas of greater population, while also slightly extending the franchise overall. It was a modest proposal, and Pitt had earlier called it 'safe and temperate', but it fell on stony ground. Though Pitt had worked with Christopher Wyvill, leader of the 1780 movement, to whip up public support, strikingly few public addresses had been forthcoming, and the former Prime Minister Lord North, speaking against the Bill, captured the sentiment in quoting a popular play: 'What horrid sound of silence doth assail mine ear!'[12] Wyvill himself commented that the Prime Minister had been 'shamefully deserted'.[13] Even some of Pitt's close allies defected, and the opposition – under Fox, nominally committed to reform – voted tactically to inflict a resounding defeat by some seventy-four votes. Under the shadow of this defeat, and with the Irish plan still wending its way to its doom, Pitt faced challenges to several measures of his budget that spring. A tax on shop rents provoked riots, in which he was burned in effigy outside 10 Downing Street itself, and the strength of the rising constituency of industrialists forced the repeal of a tax imposed on cloth.

The power of this group, who under the banner of a newly formed General Chamber of Manufacturers were also working hard to block Irish access to their markets, marked the beginning of possibly the most decisive shift of all that was taking place in this epoch. Where the previous century had been ruled by traders, buying low and selling high in a vast global market place, the age of the industrialist, who could produce new goods ever more cheaply, was dawning. This was an era of buccaneering individualists who were also ruthless manipulators, self-made men who were conscious of their revolutionary impact on the country, but also often concerned to engross the profits of new techniques to themselves alone.

Richard Arkwright, a one-time barber and wig-maker, accumulated vast wealth in the 1770s by licensing a water-powered machine
for spinning thread. He was stripped of his patent by a court in 1781,
it being judged too vague and general to be upheld as a unique innovation. In 1783 he won the patent back, only to lose it in a titanic
court battle in 1785. Lancashire cotton-spinners who had some thirty
thousand employees and a vast amount of capital invested in
'pirated' machinery won the case, and the courts blocked any renewal of the dispute.[14] James Watt, the supposed 'inventor' of the
steam engine, owed his fame and fortune more to a ruthless exploitation of patents on the engines he built for Cornish and other mine
owners, and in 1784 took out an 'umbrella patent' that among other
things blocked anyone else from developing steam-powered road
vehicles. While this innovation might have seemed a distant
prospect, Watt knew that rivals had developed just such ideas, even
if only as scale models.[15] Others took a more expansive view. Josiah
Wedgwood, master-potter of Stoke-on-Trent, who used the most
advanced techniques of industrial management to produce the finest
ceramics of the age (and the most sophisticated marketing campaigns of the era to make them into desirable mass commodities),
was a leading light in the General Chamber. He shuttled between
the Midlands and London to bring it into operation, and wrung his
hands in frustration at the blinkered attitudes of those who preferred
the individual favour of the powerful to a collective case for their
economic well-being: 'the button maker makes buttons for his
majesty, and so he is tied fast to his majesty's minister's button hole'.
Through systematic connections of this kind, he complained, 'few of
the principal manufacturers are left at liberty to serve their country'.[16] Such service in this instance included helping to bring down
the Irish measures, but only a year later Wedgwood was engaged
with the government in negotiations for a much less prejudiced
enterprise, a commercial treaty with France.

The deal agreed, named the Eden Treaty after its chief British
negotiator, was a landmark move towards free trade between the
two powers. Envisaged in the peace treaty of 1783, the outcome was
far more favourable to the defeated British than they might have
hoped for at the time. French eagerness to open British markets to
their luxury goods blinded them – they were perhaps dazzled by
Calonne's fiscal juggling act – to the underlying strength of the

British exporting economy, and within a year the treaty was being blamed for a catastrophic slowdown in France's own mills and factories. Ironically for a deal that was soon to seem so transparently beneficial, it exposed the lingering weakness of British manufacturers' political position. Less dynamic trades quailed at any relaxation of state protection, and circulated dark rumours that Wedgwood, after defending them against Ireland, must have been bribed to capitulate to France. His General Chamber of Manufacturers was unable to stand the pressure and broke apart. Even William Eden, the politician who had worked closely with the General Chamber on the deal, subsequently dismissed such men as 'wavering and fickle . . . shy and sly, and snug and silent' when they gain, 'sullen and suspicious' otherwise, and 'confoundedly noisy, and absurd and mischievous' when they fear a loss.

Such language is a reminder that, beneath all the rhetoric of constitutional liberties, British politics remained intensely aristocratic. Little wonder that James Watt looked beyond his own empire-building to claim that 'our landed gentlemen' thought no more of 'mechanics' such as himself than of 'the slaves who cultivate their vineyards'.[17] In the political realm Pitt himself succeeded in passing the Eden Treaty through the Commons with a comfortable 134-vote majority, but not before Fox had opportunistically impugned his patriotism, claiming that 'the natural political enemy' of the nation wished to 'tie our hands' and prevent other, more advantageous alliances. Pitt retorted that such unalterable enmity was 'monstrous and impossible', a 'weak and childish' supposition.[18]

It was this level of political anger and dispute that Warren Hastings stepped into in the summer of 1785. Though initially he was greeted cordially by London society, the diarist Fanny Burney depicting him as 'one of the greatest men now living' and by virtue of his 'gentleness, candour, soft manners, and openness of disposition . . . one of the most pleasing', he was about to be painted as a villain and a tyrant of unparalleled infamy.[19] Arriving home with a modest fortune of £74,000 – a pittance compared with those made by other high officials and traders – Hastings was forced to commit almost all his funds to defend himself against charges that threatened him with utter ruin.[20] In so doing, those charges both challenged, and ultimately reinforced, the imperial commitment of British power in India, and by extension, across the world.

The Whigs around Charles James Fox, although no strangers to corruption themselves, had fastened onto the truly epic scale on which it was practised in India as a stick with which to beat government. This general concern, which spawned a series of scandals as Parliament wrestled to pass the Acts in the 1770s and 1780s that placed the East India Company under greater control, produced the particular interest in the problem taken by Edmund Burke. Born in 1729 of just-respectable Irish provincial stock, with a taint of Roman Catholicism that enemies whispered about throughout his career, Burke had begun a career in the law before becoming a factotum to Whig politicians in the early 1760s and entering the Commons in 1766. Paralleling some of the multiple talents of Benjamin Franklin, he had founded in 1758 a political journal, the *Annual Register*, which he continued to produce for over thirty years, and also acted after 1770 as London agent for the colony of New York, at £500 a year.[21] He developed into one of the great orators of his age, an advocate of the American cause and an enemy of corruption and the abuse of power. When his cousin William took up a position in Madras in 1777, Burke's interest was drawn to the monumental feats of corruption and greed that Company servants had undertaken in this Presidency in southern India. Here the local prince, the Nawab of Arcot, had been tied into a mesh of obligations to Britons that enriched the latter extravagantly while destabilising the politics of the entire region.

Company men had so contrived it that, in return for propping up the Nawab's affairs with loans at ruinous interest rates, they had acquired control of revenue-collecting rights, monopolised trade and received vast 'presents' from him. As the vicious cycle of debt and renewed lending accelerated, such men had even led the Nawab into wars with his neighbours, in pursuit of outright loot and new continuing revenues to service the expanding debts. Unlike Hastings, these were men with no great vision of governance, their concern being to make a fortune fast and go home to spend it. So egregiously rapacious were they that they had gone to the lengths of seizing and imprisoning the Governor, George Pigot, sent in 1775 to restrain them: kidnapped off the streets of Madras in August 1776, he had died in custody by the time furious orders arrived the following year for his reinstatement. The Nawab, to whom the vast expense of unearned money made no difference, and had allowed him to palm off the arduous work of revenue collection to eager Britons, rewarded those who had saved the system with further largesse, raising his debts to almost £2 million. The council members guilty of effectively murdering their chief were recalled to Britain, but let off with small fines.[22] The next Governor of Madras, who spent only two years there, was already a creditor of the Nawab when he arrived, and went home in 1780 with £750,000, including £180,000 in outright bribes. This 'Arcot interest' of moneyed men with much to hide had penetrated politics quite thoroughly when Burke began to campaign against it.

Another of these 'nabobs', Paul Benfield, who had bought a seat in the Commons with Arcot money in 1780, and funded up to eight others, attracted Burke's fulminations. He was a director of the East India Company and an alderman of the City of London, but in Burke's rhetoric he became 'a criminal, who long ago ought to have fattened the kites with his offal'. His entry into Parliament 'was managed upon Indian principles, and for an Indian interest. This was the golden cup of abominations; this the chalice of the fornications of rapine, usury and oppression, which was held out by the gorgeous eastern harlot; which so many of the people, so many of the nobles of this land, had drained to the very dregs.'[23] As such phrases make clear, at the heart of Burke's concern was the impact of these 'Indian' ways upon Britain, in an age when the Americans had revolted for 'English liberty' against despotic oppression and the Association Movement had raised the same fears at home.

Burke's attention was now drawn to Warren Hastings by Philip Francis. This ambitious Whig politician had sat on Hastings's council in Bengal from 1774 to 1780, where he had opposed almost every turn of the Governor General's active policies. Hoping originally to replace Hastings, he had seen himself increasingly marginalised in furious power struggles and not aided by the humiliating consequences of once being caught climbing down a ladder from a married woman's bedroom. Being publicly shamed by a rebuke from Hastings, who had one or two affairs to his own account, drove on a personal animosity that came to a head in a duel on 17 August 1780. Hastings shot him in the shoulder and, defeated on all fronts, Francis sailed for home a few months later.[24] There he began systematically to furnish documentation and background information to Burke that painted Hastings as every inch the 'Asiatic despot', an embodiment of the spectre that the Arcot affair had raised. Through the parliamentary combats over the various East India Bills Burke's growing conviction of the menace from the Orient grew, and Hastings's return and apparently favourable reception pushed him into action. He presented twenty-two counts of 'high crimes and misdemeanours' in the Commons in April 1786.

Hastings was charged with colluding in aggressive wars of annexation, unjustly driving a prince to revolt for the purposes of crushing him, confiscating a vast treasure from another prince's female relatives, taking bribes, awarding corrupt contracts, mishandling wars and in general with wicked and criminal conduct. Burke admitted to Francis that an actual conviction was 'a thing we all know to be impracticable', but thought of himself as acting for the honour of civilisation, to 'justify myself to those few persons and to those distant times, which may take a concern in these affairs and the actors in them'.[25] His language focused on moral reprobation rather than legal definitions, raising Hastings's conduct up as a great question of the age. When his target responded with a two-day presentation of legalistic screed, however, trying the patience of the fickle MPs, a glimmer of hope emerged that things would actually go further. Though one charge was voted down, on the second, the 'Benares charge' of oppressing the raja Chait Singh, notably with a fine of £500,000, there was a dramatic reversal.

Prime Minister Pitt stepped personally into the debate, transforming it from a party struggle between Whig opposition and royal favour towards Hastings into the general moral crusade Burke wanted. It has never been clear why Pitt agreed that the fine was an 'act of oppression . . . a very high crime . . . grinding . . . overbearing'.[26] Hastings thought he had been worked on that very day by Henry Dundas, a close political ally with his own East India Company axes to grind; biographers have assumed either that it was a political manoeuvre to distract the Foxites and absolve the government from responsibility, or indeed a sudden onset of refined morality. The truth is unknowable. In any case Pitt's example turned the government benches against Hastings, and a two-thirds majority against impeachment became an almost equally large majority for it on this charge, along with six others among the most serious articles. It took a year for the charges to be formally arrayed, but in May 1787 Hastings was condemned for trial before the House of Lords.[27] Long months would pass before he was actually brought to trial, and in that interval other problems continued to smoulder.

As events in America and France took a turn towards constitutional change in 1787, so the religious dimension to British politics revived divisions and revealed complex linkages between different nations and social realms. Rather than Catholics, this time it was the Dissenters, those who belonged to non-Anglican Protestant sects, who brought forward a claim for greater rights. The prosperous provincial base of their congregations, which supported flourishing 'dissenting academies' for educating future clergy and others, and underlay the rising industrial progress of the Midlands and North, was increasingly resentful of the elaborate regime of toleration under which they were allowed to exist. The Test and Corporation Acts, over a century old, barred them from civic and state office unless they compromised their faith by taking communion in the Anglican rite. Many in recent decades had chosen to ignore this requirement, taking local office 'with the hazard' by neglecting the communion and risking prosecution by local zealots. The wealthy could afford the risk to sit on a municipal council, as their only penalty would be to lose office, but it was not a chance worth taking for national office under the Test Act, which prescribed large fines and crippling civil disabilities for convicted violators (including, for example, the inability to receive inheritances). While some Dissenters bore up to the need for 'occasional conformity', and a few even managed to serve as MPs, they remained barred in practice from other important avenues of social and economic influence. The great chartered companies that controlled trade with India, Russia and the Pacific shut out Dissenters from their boards, and locally the boards of hospitals and other charitable institutions were equally closed, while less prestigious and more burdensome offices such as those of petty constable and poor-law overseer were open. Dissenters were welcome where they were needed, but not where they wanted to be.[28]

In early 1787 an eminent committee of Dissenters, including three MPs, piloted an initial petition for relief from these disabilities into the House of Commons. There had been no public meetings or outdoor agitation, merely discreet consultations with Prime Minister Pitt and other leading political and religious figures. The Whigs around Charles James Fox could be counted on for support, not least because the king was known to loathe the prospect of weakening the link between Church and state, but also out of good 'Revolution' principle. Pitt might have been expected to support the move, given his history of support for reform. However, he was dependent on the king's favour, and also strongly influenced by the Anglican clergymen who had tutored him at Cambridge University, and who remained among his close advisers. Fearing that no good could come of stirring up Establishment opposition, especially in the House of Lords, where the Anglican bishops sat and were opposed *en masse* to such concessions, Pitt spoke out against the Dissenters' motion: 'Were we to yield on this occasion, the fears of the members of the Church of England would be roused, and their apprehensions are not to be treated lightly.' As he went on, however, he rapidly passed from what seemed to be a religious argument to what sounded like an overtly political one: 'No means can be devised of admitting the moderate part of the dissenters and excluding the violent: the bulwark must be kept up against all.'[29] The motion fell by 176 votes to 98.

To understand how Pitt could associate the Dissenters with the prospect of a 'violent' intrusion into politics, we must look back to time immemorial, for that is where a certain breed among Whigs located their opposition to the conventional politics of the era. Beneath the surface of the venal and boisterous political life of the eighteenth-century political class, there had always been a strand of belief in the more essential virtues of English history (Englishness being, for such men, a far more meaningful label than newfangled 'Britishness'), and of an ancient constitution that lay sleeping, like King Arthur of legend, awaiting the call of a new generation. In part this tradition was stimulated by the history of the English Civil War, recalling the cry of the Levellers that 'the poorest he that is in England' had as much right to a political voice as any other. Believers took inspiration from the Glorious Revolution of 1688–9, producing in the years that followed a nostalgic vision of what the Revolution, by then sunk into factional business-as-usual politics, might have achieved. Despite attachment to a recent republican tradition, these men and their successors soon focused on looking further back, replacing the problematic heritage of Cromwell's brutal puritan republic, and the troubling democratic implications of the Levellers, with a more idealised vision of the historical sanctity of English liberty.[30] Throughout the first three-quarters of the eighteenth century successive coteries of men, often including peers of the realm, clergy and other elites, held themselves up as 'real Whigs' or 'Commonwealthmen', the true inheritors of England's revolutionary tradition. Though in political practice this drifted slowly away from radical idealism to being simply a more extreme form of opposition to encroachments of state power and religious orthodoxy (and a heightened sense of the fear of Jacobitical Catholicism), on the fringes of this grouping devoted idealists remained.

What was becoming a fully fledged political mythology was cast in print by a Yorkshire doctor, Obadiah Hulme, in 1771 in his *Historical Essay on the English Constitution*. This proclaimed that English politics under the Saxons had taken on a democratic cast as early as the fifth century and had been perfected under the kingship of Alfred the Great, the first true King of England, in the ninth century. Elective rather than purely hereditary monarchy, consultation of the Crown with an assembly of the nation, local popular assemblies, the safeguard of liberty by jury trial and of national defence by a local popular militia were all proclaimed to be part of this essentially democratic and libertarian heritage. Hulme drew parallels between the long-ago submergence of this system beneath the feudal yoke of the Norman Conquest and the restriction of the impact of the Glorious Revolution by decades of oligarchical legislation in the 1690s and 1700s. The fight for 'English' liberty was thus given both an ancient and a modern cast, and the text concluded with claims that were to dominate radical thinking for the next century – annual parliaments, reform of representation, a wider franchise and secret ballots.[31]

Works such as Hulme's, which called for 'associations' to pursue reform, were seconded by that of the teacher and writer James Burgh, emerging as the country slid towards war with the Thirteen Colonies. Burgh's *Political Disquisitions* of 1774–5 echoed Hulme's historical thesis and called for a 'Grand National Association for Restoring the Constitution' based on the formation of local groups across Britain, Ireland and America. The religious strain in such thought was also evident: Burgh beseeched God's aid to 'save the Protestant religion' from 'the infernal cloud of popish delusion', even inviting the deity to 'Arise, and come forth from thy sacred seat, clothed in all thy terrors.'[32] Ideas such as this were clearly in the air a few years later, in the dramatic juxtaposition of 'associational' campaigns for reform and violent anti-Catholic rioting that marked 1780. They also emerged from a context of London radical and religious opposition that was to carry them forward beyond the 1780s. James Burgh was a member of a society that met fortnightly at a London coffee-house. Since 1764 it had brought together scientific writers and experimenters with men from the religious fringes of 'Rational Dissent' and other 'friends of liberty'.[33]

The scientific, religious and political themes often met in the same bodies, like that of Joseph Priestley, an experimental chemist and Dissenter who in 1768 had published an *Essay on the First Principles of Government* that defended tyrannicide and asserted a right of revolution against oppression. Also regularly present was Dr Richard Price, a Welsh Dissenting minister whose papers on population statistics had been read before the Royal Society and who in 1776 wrote one of the most vigorous British defences of the American rebels, *Observations on the Nature of Civil Liberty.* In this he asserted that it was 'obvious, that all civil government, as far as it can be denominated free, is the creature of the people'.[34] Benjamin Franklin had been a regular of the group during his London years, calling it his 'Club of Honest Whigs', and he may have carried some of the group's published principles back across the Atlantic, for their ideas meshed seamlessly with much of the rhetoric of the Declaration of Independence and its attendant debates. He certainly conveyed its sentiments across the Channel, presenting a copy of Price's work to the statesman Turgot. The latter wrote to Price in 1778, hoping that the British 'will perhaps gain as much as America by this revolution' if the conflict led to a further constitutional upheaval, 'restoring annual elections' and other elements of the Commonwealthman mythology.[35]

As their relations with men such as Turgot and Franklin attest, these 'Honest Whigs' were not isolated figures. Price was the author of works on the dissolution of the National Debt that inspired Pitt's own policies in the mid-1780s. Priestley was an internationally renowned scientist, presently to be found contesting fame with Antoine Lavoisier of France for understanding the nature of oxygen. After their 1787 setback, the Dissenting leadership intensified their campaign of dignified lobbying through the following year, making more systematic contact with MPs, and especially closer ties with Fox's

Whigs. With a political system seemingly assailed on all sides, their
confidence grew.

The impeachment of Warren Hastings opened in the vast medieval
cavern of Westminster Hall on 13 February 1788. It was, quite literally, the trial of the century. Gentlemen and society ladies alike had
reportedly slept in nearby coffee-houses to secure themselves a seat.
The rush as the doors opened was likened to that for 'the pit of the
playhouse when Garrick plays King Lear'. Two hundred MPs turned
out, along with the 170 Lords who would be the judges of the affair.
The queen was in attendance, as were at least three royal dukes and
the Prince of Wales. Tickets sold for up to fifty guineas and the
double tiers of spectator seating remained packed, even as it took
two days to read out the dry particulars of the charges.[36] Amid the
glittering throng Burke rose on the third day to declare that brought
before their Lordships was 'the first man in rank, authority and station . . . the head, the chief, the captain-general in iniquity; one in
whom all the frauds, all the peculations, all the violence, all the
tyranny in India are embodied, disciplined and arrayed'.[37]

Burke spoke across four days, a performance of sustained rhetorical power that drew on all his strength. 'The credit and honour of
the British nation' was at stake. To condemn Hastings would 'reflect
a permanent lustre on the honour, justice and humanity of this
Kingdom'. It was crimes against 'eternal laws of justice' that they had
gathered to judge; at stake was 'our connivance and participation in
guilt, and our common share in the plunder of the East'.[38] At the core
of his indictment was the concept of 'geographical morality' that
he drew out, and condemned, on the second day of his speech.
Hastings's behaviour, Burke claimed, relied on the iniquitous idea
that what was proper and moral in Britain need not apply in India,
and thus that which was improper and immoral in one place might be
accepted and justified if done elsewhere.

To illustrate the lengths to which this might lead, Burke
addressed on the third day of his speech the tyrannical conduct of
Indian tax gatherers, supposedly under Hastings's ultimate authority.
Beginning with accounts of public floggings of recalcitrant farmers
and moving on to the whipping of men's children before them,
Burke ascended to descriptions of 'virgins whose fathers kept them
from the sight of the sun . . . dragged into the public Court . . . cruelly

violated by the basest and wickedest of mankind'. Married women suffered their violations 'in the bottom of the most cruel dungeons' before being 'dragged out, naked ... and scourged before all the people ... they put the nipples of the women into the sharp edges of split bamboos and tore them from their bodies'.[39] At this at least one female spectator fainted amid shrieks and general agitation, and Burke himself, overwrought, succumbed shortly afterwards to stomach cramps and had to resume the next day.

While that day brought less electrifying charges, the momentum of iniquity was kept up. Charles James Fox himself took the floor afterwards to launch the 'Benares charge' in a five-hour speech, modest by comparison with Burke, but packed with accusing detail. The playwright, MP and master of actorly rhetoric Richard Brinsley Sheridan, another chief spokesman of the opposition, repeated the charges he had lodged once already before the Commons about Hastings's seizure of the treasure of the 'Begums of Oudh', where the violation of these Muslim ladies' *purdah* gave the opportunity for further disquisitions on the sexual impropriety of imperial despotism. Sheridan also shamelessly played to the gallery, collapsing into Burke's arms as he completed his impassioned peroration.[40]

After the magnificent spectacle of the opening days of the trial, events would fade into anticlimax – it would take years to squeeze in enough sessions around all the other business of politics to hear all the evidence, and Burke's initial assessment that a conviction was 'impracticable' would be borne out. By the summer of 1788 both Fox and Sheridan thought proceedings should be abandoned, especially after the Commons had failed that May to impeach Elijah Impey, Hastings's alleged co-conspirator in the rigged trial and judicial murder of a Bengali opponent.[41] Burke single-handedly drove them to carry on, and if his dedication came to seem extreme it had been responsible for challenging the whole foundation of British imperialism in the East, at a moment when it was equally being called into question in the West. The impeachment of Hastings turned his 'salvation' of India into a component of a truly global crisis of British identity and destiny, one that would be resolved only through the lens of the epoch's other great crisis, in France.

At the end of 1788 resistance to 'despotism', defence of liberty and hope for radical outcomes from the French crisis all came together, uniting with the wider radical tradition of Whig politics, as the London Revolution Society prepared to celebrate the centenary of the Glorious Revolution with a dinner on 4 November 1788. The date was the birthday of the Protestant saviour William of Orange, chosen for its auspicious proximity to the date on which he had landed in England, 5 November 1688, which itself could not be celebrated without clashing with the even older anti-Catholic rites of Bonfire Night. Some three hundred Dissenters and radicals, including the Whig leader the Duke of Portland, the Lord Mayor of London and several other peers and MPs, met at the London Tavern in Bishopsgate, emblazoned for the occasion with the slogan 'A Tyrant Deposed and Liberty Restored, 1688'.[42] The London Revolution Society itself, which boasted a long history as one among a number of elite clubs set up earlier in the century to celebrate this heritage, had in recent decades faded into a more discreet social gathering. But the centenary and the atmosphere of the time had stirred it into new life, attracting 'many persons of rank and consequence from different parts of the kingdom', by its own published account of proceedings.[43]

After a hearty dinner during which forty-one toasts were drunk, some of them calling for such radical libertarian measures as the abolition of the slave trade, reform of penal law and the end of the naval press-gang, a motion was passed reaffirming the principles of the society and of the Glorious Revolution itself. They were carried unanimously in three articles:

1. That all civil and political authority is derived from the people.
2. That the abuse of power justifies resistance.
3. That the right of private judgement, liberty of conscience, trial by jury, the freedom of the press and the freedom of election ought ever to be held sacred and inviolable.

A Unitarian minister then gave an oration reaffirming the significance of these principles. Richard Price had been invited to do so, but was unwell. In his place his friend and colleague Joseph Towers beseeched, among other things, that

England and France may no longer continue their ancient hostility against each other; but that France may regain possession of her liberties; and that two nations, so eminently distinguished . . . may unite together in communicating the advantages of freedom, science and the arts to the most remote regions of the earth.[44]

It was a bold vision, and testament to the lively concern that the British radicals had for the state of the old enemy, even now moving towards revolutionary rupture. With further irony, on the night after this celebration of constitutional liberties, that constitution was thrown into turmoil by the king himself. In his fiftieth year George III had become noticeably more eccentric. From the summer of 1788 onwards, after he had recovered from stomach pains by taking the waters at Cheltenham Spa, his somewhat bustling manner degenerated towards mania. Long notorious for buttonholing people with eager questions capped with an enthusiastic 'What? What?', he now began to fuss and fume in equal measure, and by the autumn his physical symptoms returned and diversified. Agonising bowel pains were allied to leg cramps, rashes and delirium, and by late October he had appeared in public in such a state of disorder that near panic on the financial markets ensued.

He was given to impatient ravings, with a tinge of paranoia, announcing to the Lord Chancellor that 'You, too, forsake me', and returning to his most grievous complaint: 'I, that am born a gentleman, shall never lay my head on my last pillow in peace and quiet so long as I remember the loss of the American colonies.'[45] In his more lucid moments he suffered the most dreadful of fears, that of a man conscious that he is losing his reason. He wept on the shoulder of his second son, the Duke of York, as he told him: 'I wish to God I may die, for I am going to be mad.' His illness caused a temporary reconciliation with the Prince of Wales, but at dinner on 5 November some ill-advised remarks on the subject of murder, perhaps occasioned by the date, sent the king into a raging fury. He seized his son by the collar, dragged him from his chair and hurled him bodily against a wall, no mean feat considering that the prince was as grossly fat as his friend Fox. When examined by a doctor, the king's bloodshot eyes seemed like 'black currant jelly', and as he raved on to the point of exhaustion 'the foam ran out of his mouth'.[46] What Pitt called 'the most difficult and delicate crisis imaginable' was upon the government, and the nation.[47] In the words of the Prince of Wales to a younger brother, their father was now 'a compleat lunatick'. The British Constitution hung by a thread.[48]

There was now no meaningful improvement, merely more or less lucid episodes, and the king's madness was generally known to the world. A gaggle of doctors repeatedly examined him and he was subjected to all the absurd brutalities of an undeveloped science. If tying him to his bed was a measure for his own safety, keeping his rooms freezing cold as winter drew in was pointless cruelty. When the Privy Council, the king's highest advisers, examined these doctors under oath on 3 December, they acknowledged his current complete incapacity, but most nonetheless contended that the king would recover. Their pusillanimity led *The Times* to denounce the 'truly ridiculous' inconsistencies in their published bulletins.[49] Meanwhile the political consequences of the royal madness were unfolding in almost equal confusion and distress.

The news had brought Charles James Fox tearing back from Italy, where he had been holidaying with his mistress, certain that his hour had come. Crucial problems remained, however. Over the previous eighteen months his relations with the Prince of Wales, who in the early 1780s had been virtually dependent on him for political advice, had soured. In 1785, ignoring Fox's explicit advice, the prince had secretly, and illegally, married the Catholic widow Mrs Maria Fitzherbert. Two years later, as his debts piled up (which they did periodically throughout his adult life), a move to relieve them by parliamentary vote foundered on speculation about this marriage, but not before Fox had been brought to a formal public denial of its existence. That denial, in terms disagreeable to Mrs Fitzherbert, was then contradicted in several particulars by a new statement made (at the prince's behest) by Richard Brinsley Sheridan, whom both Fox and Burke came to see as seeking to replace the former as the prince's key political agent. So abject did the scandal become that George III decided to meet the debts in question out of his own pocket, to remove the matter from the public gaze. The prince, who could now reasonably expect to be advanced to a regency, had thus by his own conduct created divisions and abiding suspicions in the very party leadership that now had to negotiate his route to power.[50]

The previous session of Parliament had been prorogued in the normal constitutional fashion by the king's signature back in September, until 20 November.[51] As its suspension expired, its members gathered, though without formal authority, since the king's writ was required for their session to be opened. They bypassed this legal detail and agreed to summon themselves into session by circular letter after a further two weeks. Meeting on 4 December, although it was agreed that no legislation could be passed, the two chambers of the Lords and Commons agreed to form committees to examine the doctors further. Once again the testimony of the king's current condition was conclusive, and on 10 December the explosive matter of how to rule a kingdom with an insane king burst upon the floor of the Commons.

In the meantime new cracks had been driven into the shaky foundations of Whig party unity. Sheridan, acting in Fox's absence and with his own advancement in mind, had begun as early as 8 November to negotiate with Pitt's Lord Chancellor, Lord Thurlow, who was no great lover of his Prime Minister. With assurances of Thurlow's personal survival in office, Sheridan articulated a plan that would allow the Whigs to slip into power, albeit perhaps with some limitations on the regent, supported from within the government itself. Pitt's supporters, quailing as the king raved, latched eagerly onto news of divisions as offering hope for delay and defeat.[52] Fox's return from Italy launched him into a whirl of politicking, including a first tense face-to-face meeting with the prince since their falling-out over Mrs Fitzherbert. Fox was faced with a choice of going along with the plans launched by Sheridan, and thus acquiescing in the loss of his personal leadership, or working with those in the party who favoured a more overt claim on the power of a regency, and risking a break with those closest to the prince. Fox took the latter course, an acquaintance remarking, 'I want to know, how he has relished Sheridan's beginning a negotiation without him', and imagining him commenting, in a quote from Shakespeare, 'Saucey and bold, how did you dare to trade and traffic . . . and I . . . was never called.'[53] The words were those of Hecate, queen of the witches, to her consorts in *Macbeth*. The speech continues even more pointedly, in words the writer left out 'for fear of offending': 'all you have done | Hath been but for a wayward son, | Spiteful and wrathful, who, as others do, | Loves for his own ends, not for you.' Such devilish associations found an odd echo in reports from as far away as north Wales, where 'the Common people have an idea that Mr Fox administered Poison to the King and went abroad to await the effects of it'.[54]

Fox was encouraged to sidestep Sheridan's deal not just by personal ambition, but by the conviction among the opposition Whigs that the king's insanity was incurable and permanent. The government felt at liberty, on the evidence, to take the alternative view. Pitt himself wrote on 4 December that 'the Opinion of the Physicians is very favourable as to the Prospect of Recovery'.[55] Fox's own illness, brought on by his frantic nine-day journey from Italy, had caused him to miss the face-to-face scrutiny of medical evidence in early December, and he assumed that the dismissal of more pessimistic reports was mere politics. This, and possibly misleading reports from Thurlow, caused him to write off the government's view and look to a permanent and decisive settlement. Ever since his 'unconstitutional' expulsion from office and the bitter defeat of the 1784 election, Fox had been seeking to consolidate a party against the manoeuvres of those in power. Sheridan's deal with Thurlow had made Fox, in his own words, more 'uneasy' than 'any political thing I ever did in my life', and pursuing it was 'contrary to every principle of conduct I ever laid down for myself'. To suggest, as Sheridan did, proceeding by 'disclaiming all Party views' would cast aside all Fox's efforts of the last half-decade.[56] Thus it was that on 10 December Fox, still unwell and looking remarkably thin, opened with the claim of his patron, the Prince of Wales, to 'as express a right to assume the reins of government and exercise the power of sovereignty' as regent, as if his father had 'undergone a natural and perfect demise'.[57] At this Pitt is said to have slapped his thigh triumphantly and declared, 'I'll un-Whig him for the rest of his life.'[58] To the delight of his opponent, the advocate of parliamentary liberty and critic of the overweening power of the executive, who had cried up the 'unconstitutional' rise of Pitt with talk of impeachment, had just made a blatant claim on the divine right of kings.

He had done so, to make the irony even more delicious, on yet another cardinal date in the centenary of the Glorious Revolution that had decisively struck down such a claim as odious to the whole political nation. It had been on 10 December 1688 that the forces of the Protestant William of Orange, invited from the Netherlands by the leaders of Parliament to assume power in place of the Catholic James II, had defeated royal forces in the battle of Reading, and the next day that James had fled his capital, casting the Great Seal of the kingdom into the Thames. The rights and liberties of the 'freeborn

Englishman', and the limitations that these placed on the holders of royal office, were henceforth the lodestones of political culture, even if, as Fox's own miscalculation demonstrated, they were never without challenge. However, it was one thing to ironise about Fox's choice to promote the Prince of Wales's personal right to a regency, it was quite another to prevent it coming to pass.

Pitt immediately went for the constitutional jugular: 'To assert such a right in the Prince of Wales, or any one else, independent of the decision of the two houses of Parliament, was little less than treason to the constitution of the country.' Pitt went on to evoke 'a new question . . . of greater magnitude even than the question which was originally before them . . . the question of their own rights' as Parliament.[59] In attempting to avoid the political contamination of collaboration with a ministry he viewed as despotic, Fox had opened himself to charges of monarchical absolutism that delighted his opponents and baffled many supporters in the country. Two days later, in a further debate on the historical precedents available to be followed, Sheridan gave Pitt further ammunition, warning of 'the danger of provoking that claim to be asserted which had not yet been preferred' – in other words, that the Prince of Wales might literally seize the throne. Pitt could stand up for English liberty in replying that the Commons should 'do their duty in spite of any threat, however high the authority from which it might proceed'.[60] He managed to defer a decision still further by calling for a new debate on 16 December over the 'right and duty' of Parliament to determine the correct course of action.

Both Pitt and Fox had practically to drag themselves to the Commons for this crucial debate. The Prime Minister had a severe cold, while the rigours of Fox's return from the continent had driven him into a state of near collapse, suffering with something very like dysentery and believing death to be at hand. Nonetheless, both rose to the occasion with magnificent flights of rhetoric. Fox denounced the pursuit of precedents from the 'dark and barbarous' era of the fifteenth century, and mocked the notion that 'when the King of England is in good health the monarchy is hereditary' but that it should suddenly discover an elective character 'when he is ill'. Pitt countered cuttingly that, since Fox had publicly declared his intention of taking power in the prince's name, it was all the more important for Parliament to consider the character and powers of a regency carefully lest problems interfere with 'His Majesty's being able to resume the exercise of his own authority'; an authority that would see Fox cast from office, and that might therefore be impeded in mysterious ways, he carefully implied.[61] Pitt's time-wasting measures were approved by a majority of over sixty, and the rest of the year would be spent on technical debates. Each day won was a victory for the Prime Minister, but while the king showed no sign of recovery the ultimate triumph of Fox seemed assured.

Pitt's new strategy was to limit the nature of the regency itself, and he wrote privately to the Prince of Wales on 30 December indicating that the government, with its Commons majority seemingly solid, would propose a Regency Bill including what the prince denounced as 'such restrictions as no Dictator could possibly . . . ever have been barefaced enough to have brought forward'.[62] Among other limitations, the prince would be prevented from creating new peerages or making almost any other permanent appointments or pension awards. Meanwhile the royal household would be placed in the queen's care and the king's property would be safeguarded from disposal. Fox's Whig leadership helped the prince draft his reply, in which he denounced the plan as 'a project for dividing the Royal Family from each other – for separating the court from the state'.[63] Indeed it was, and Pitt insisted on the essentials of the plan, even as he worked to create further delay. The death of the Speaker, who presided over the Commons, allowed further time to be spent on an election to replace him with a pliant government man who could be relied upon to take Pitt's side if procedural issues were raised. Likewise Pitt seized on new opposition demands for a further commission to report on the king's health. Hoping for confirmation of insanity, the Foxites were disappointed by news of the doctors' greater optimism for recovery. It was now a race against time on both sides. The British Empire would enter the fatal year of 1789 headless, and with no sign of a clear resolution of that state.

# 5

# 'The base laws of servitude'

*Empire, slavery and race in the 1780s*

As the Westminster Parliament wrestled with the threat of despotic power, on the far side of the world an act of desperate coercion was under way. On 30 December 1788 a small boatload of British sailors from the settlement at Port Jackson, New South Wales, drew up in a cove and gestured towards two nearby Aboriginal Australians. Holding out small items of food and clothing to suggest they were offering gifts, the sailors lured the two men closer, seized them and succeeded in wrestling one into the boat, where he was tied up. He was returned to the ramshackle collection of huts and tents that made up the British imperial presence in the Antipodes. Here a handful of officers and some two hundred marines were trying to coax a productive workforce out of seven hundred convicts, almost a third of them women. As the British had been poorly supplied by an incompetent bureaucracy on departure, after almost a year ashore there was little progress in farming the arid soils. Relations with the locals, initially on a basis of mutual amused strangeness, were breaking down into violence as hungry convicts roamed the bush for food. The Governor of the tiny settlement, Arthur Philip, had determined that it was both right and necessary to carry out this kidnapping, in order to teach the captive sufficient English to act as an interpreter. Stranded among a population and geography that day by day revealed itself as more and more hostile, Philip was convinced that only this course of action could finally alert the 'Indians' of the land to the essential benevolence of the British. The captive, named Arabanoo, died of smallpox in May 1789, having yielded only a few clues as to the customs and ways of his people.[1]

As Arabanoo lay dying, attention in Britain was directed to the wider role of grim coercion in the maintenance of imperial power and wealth. On 12 May 1789 William Wilberforce stood in the House of Commons to make what is still regarded as one of the greatest ever parliamentary speeches. The MP for Hull had been a friend and confidant of William Pitt since his days as a rather dissolute Cambridge University student. After entering Parliament, however, Wilberforce experienced a religious conversion of particular intensity. Dedicating his life to reform of manners, he prevailed upon George III to issue a widely ridiculed Royal Proclamation against Vice and Immorality in June 1787, and also took up the abolition of the slave trade as his particular cause.[2] In his 1789 speech he presented the shocking facts of the trade, and left his listeners with a stark alternative:

> Sir, the nature and all the circumstances of this Trade are now laid open to us . . . it is brought now so directly before our eyes that this House must decide, and must justify to all the world, and to their own consciences, the rectitudes of their grounds and of the principles of their decision.[3]

That it would take almost another twenty years for Wilberforce to succeed in abolishing the transportation of Africans across the Atlantic in chains, and further generations to root out slavery itself from the territories of the British, French and Americans, testifies to the complexity with which Western consciences viewed the circumstances of slavery, and of all their other fraught and intimate connections with the new worlds of the eighteenth century.

Slavery itself was the great economic success story of the age. Six million Africans – equivalent to the entire population of mid-century Britain – were taken across the Atlantic during the eighteenth century, over three times more than in the previous century. The generation before 1789 saw shipments reach an all-time high.[4] Fully a third of all the commerce of Europe was bound up with slave-grown commodities: sugar, coffee, cocoa, cotton, tobacco, rice, indigo, from colonies founded by the British, French, Spanish, Portuguese and Dutch.[5] Half a century earlier the powers had united to stamp out the piracy that had been the scourge of the Caribbean, and since then even the vicissitudes of frequent wars had been tempered in the slave regions by the great common desire not to cut off the fountain of wealth that flowed forth from forced labour.

Vast sums of capital were invested in slavery. Merely to purchase a slave from his or her African captors at one of the established markets on the coast of West Africa cost anywhere between £15 and £29 in the 1780s, sums equal to the annual wage of a craftsman or even a clerk. The trade goods that made up much of this price themselves stimulated a rise in industry. Producing the masses of low-grade items for export kept thousands in work in the forges and workshops of Britain and France. One lot of 180 slaves, bought at the start of the great boom in the 1740s, cost their purchasers over four and a half tons of pig-iron, a ton of salt, half a ton of gunpowder, over half a ton of assorted textiles (including Indian cottons), three-quarters of a ton of assorted metal kitchenware and barrel-loads of beads, shells and crystals with their own local value as currency, as well as 92 cutlasses, 71 pairs of pistols and 164 muskets.[6] It cost around £8000 just to outfit a slaving vessel, which had to carry a crew almost equivalent to a small warship to manage several hundred desperate captives.

One ironic side to this investment was the nature of the effort put into keeping slaves alive on the terrifying 'Middle Passage' across the Atlantic. Though offering more space and air to the captives would have been effective, this would have meant reducing their numbers, and cutting profits to unacceptable levels. So instead slavers paid close attention to new developments in the science of diet and hygiene, increasingly offering a variety of foodstuffs, forcing slaves to 'dance' on deck under the guns of the crew and even sending doctors to give smallpox inoculations on the dockside in Africa. When the Pacific explorer Captain James Cook and his French counterpart Louis Antoine de Bougainville both made important contributions to naval hygiene practices, their innovations were adopted by slavers as well, as within a few years would be the issue of fruit juice against scurvy.[7] On the other hand, instances like that of the British slaver *Zong*, where in 1781 133 slaves were thrown overboard in mid-Atlantic after bad weather had left the ship short of rations, were viewed by all but a minority as cases for insurance against loss of cargo, not for criminal prosecution.[8]

Even with hygienic innovations, up to a tenth of the 'cargo' might die en route, and life expectancy for a slave who reached the Americas was no more than seven to ten years. Without constant replenishment the slave population would have declined annually by anything up to 4 per cent.[9] That, despite the costs of purchase and shipment, this labour-force rose so dramatically and continued rising, from around two and a half million at mid-century towards three million at the end, is stark testament to the rewards to be gained from investment in the slave system. The human costs are almost unimaginable. Some twenty-one million individuals were taken in raids by slave-hunting societies that ravaged the African coasts and far inland, wiping out the natural increase in the population over two centuries. Seven million remained enslaved in Africa and five million perished on or soon after the Middle Passage.[10]

What drove slavery was sugar: the first, and throughout this period still the greatest, slave-grown commodity. The back-breaking work of cultivating sugar cane had proved most effective when coupled with African slaves, partly because of the real unsuitability of Europeans for such extensive labour in the tropics, but mostly because of the cultural and political impossibility of holding them to such work. Hundreds of thousands of young men and women had crossed from Europe in the preceding two centuries as indentured servants, paying the passage with an agreement to be bound to serve for a period of years, seven or ten being common.[11] Yet rarely after the mid-seventeenth century had anyone tried to work plantations with such labour. The work was too hard, the people too prone to complain, to appeal for their rights, to escape – and too easily lost among the 'free' European population when they did. Indentured servants remained an important part of the general labour force in the United States in the 1780s (and had been supplemented until the 1770s by the even more unwilling 'servants' transported for crimes, who were sold off to individuals on arrival), but slaves, driven to work by the whip, dominated the economy of the Caribbean to an unprecedented extent.

The case of French Saint-Domingue (now Haiti) illustrates the centrality of slavery to the modern commercial economy of the 1780s. In the twenty years from 1770 the slave population of the island virtually doubled; as elsewhere, this was entirely due to swelling imports of new slaves, there being no 'natural increase'. By

1787 slave numbers had reached 465,000, at a time when there were 480,000 slaves in the whole of the British Caribbean. On Saint-Domingue thirty thousand Europeans and almost as many 'free people of colour', descendants of freed slaves or of interracial liaisons of all sorts, dominated this vast population by force. All free men over sixteen routinely went armed, and were organised into militia regiments supplementing a military garrison of several thousand.[12] Almost eight hundred slave-run sugar mills refined the plantations' products, sending eighty-seven thousand tons of sugar to Europe in 1787, twice the output of the largest British island, Jamaica, and supplying virtually all French demand. Meanwhile, thanks to extensive investment in irrigation works and agricultural experimentation, Saint-Domingue was also able to ship seventy-two million pounds of coffee in 1788–9, along with sizeable exports of indigo dyestuff and of cotton that serviced both French and British mills.[13]

The economics of slavery were complex. Estimates show that for both British and French islands gross output on the order of £100 per slave per year could be achieved, but 70–80 per cent of this was absorbed in running costs and more went in repayments to the merchants and bankers who extended credit for the purchase of supplies, new slaves and field improvements. Though a profit of up to 30 per cent on the plantation seems generous, French planters were said to owe ninety-nine million *livres* (equivalent to some £4 million) to Bordeaux and Nantes merchants in 1788, and a noticeable trend was estates falling into the hands of such absentees through foreclosure or sale. Those, like many of the French aristocracy, including the king's liberal cousin the duc d'Orléans, who invested in the general enterprise of slavery at a distance made more money than those who sweated over the slaves on site.[14]

The need to extract revenues from slaves to repay mountains of debt, or to remit funds to demanding absentee owners, helped to aggravate the culture of slavery, which itself was founded on acts of absolute brutality. Slaves were stripped of their culture along with their freedom: it was normal practice to break up family and social groups to hinder communication between slaves in their native tongues. This was just one of the layers of fear and suspicion that ringed slave existence, but it was never entirely successful. Slaves ran away when they could. In the inland areas of the larger islands, and in remote or mountainous tracts of the mainland colonies, 'maroons', bands of escaped slaves, lived a life that hovered between banditry and a real free society, posing a constant threat to plantation life both directly and by example. On Saint-Domingue new slave cultures emerged, with African and Catholic religious practices blending to produce voodoo, and even trusted slaves, who served as field overseers, coachmen or domestics, practising *petit marronage*: going absent without leave to attend ceremonies and to plot rebellion.[15] Slaves rose up periodically, when material conditions, political upheavals or some other opportunity persuaded them they might achieve something thereby – and sometimes just out of sheer desperation. As Benjamin Franklin quipped in the Constitutional Convention, well might southerners be more defensive about their rights than northern farmers, for 'sheep will never make an insurrection'.[16] Surrounded by slaves on the smaller sugar islands, some planter communities descended to virtual circles of Hell: fuelled by the rum that flowed from the sugar cane itself and driven by the knowledge that all that held down the slaves was force and fear, sadism and debauchery alike achieved free rein. Punishments for insubordination, even in the better-run colonies, were ferocious, and for rebellion of any kind, slaves could expect to be tortured to death for the edification of their fellows – burned or dismembered alive, nailed to trees, attacked by dogs; the variants were endless.

Thomas Thistlewood, who rose from an undistinguished farmer's son to be one of Jamaica's wealthiest planters, and a magistrate to boot, left records of his own increasingly sadistic encounters with this culture. Within weeks of his arrival in 1750 he had seen a planter whip a runaway slave and rub the wounds with salt, pepper and lime juice, then, when the man died, cut off his head and mount it on a pole. A slave who drew a knife was 'hang'd upon ye 1st tree immediately, his hand cut off, Body left unbury'd'. Thistlewood soon devised his own tortures to add to routine beatings and mutilations: for minor offences slaves were made to urinate and defecate into each other's mouths, and in the latter case gagged afterwards to prolong the agony. His was a reign of unremitting terror. He used the rape of slave women as an instrument of this terror, performing it publicly to degrade the watching male slaves. He also enjoyed his unlimited access to such women for his own pleasure, documenting 3852 sexual exploits with over 130 women, almost all slaves, until his death in 1786. And yet the only person for whom he expressed affection in his diaries was Phibbah, his slave housekeeper, with whom he lived and slept for thirty-three years, fathering a son, and freeing her on his death. It is perhaps only in the particularly well-documented ferocity of his activities that Thistlewood is unusual. In both his brutality and his curiously trusting affections he was a product of his time.[17]

In this gruesome context it is no wonder that the British move to offer freedom to runaway slaves had such a striking impact during the American War of Independence. Though the worst excesses of the sugar islands made the life of Virginia or New York farm slaves seem mild by comparison, their servitude was still no easy burden. The perils of it were clearly felt by Thomas Jefferson, who in his first draft of the Declaration of Independence assailed George III for 'exciting those very people to rise in arms against us, and to purchase that liberty of which *he* has deprived them, by murdering the people upon whom *he* has obtruded them'.[18] Such disingenuous rhetoric aside, the appeal of the British to the slaves led perhaps as many as a hundred thousand to flee their masters in the course of the conflict, a fifth of the states' slave population. Only fifteen thousand made it out with the British when they evacuated in 1781. A few lucky ones took service with French officers, but thousands of others were hunted down. Slave owners and their bounty hunters roamed the streets of New York as the British embarked, grabbing men and women back into bondage from the streets, or even from their beds. In a similar British evacuation at Charleston the ships were packed to capacity and troops patrolled the wharves to beat back the unlucky remainder. A few who managed to swim out and cling to longboats carrying the last Britons had to be hacked away with cutlasses, such was their desperation to remain free.[19] That so many thought freedom was to be found in the act of touching British soil is just one of the further complications of the era's treatment of servitude.

Both the British and French had long upheld within their legal tradition the notion that slavery was alien to their societies. In France the *parlement* of Paris had refused across the eighteenth century to register edicts dealing with the movement of slaves within the country, simply because the texts contained the word *esclave*, which they declared to have no meaning: 'No one is a slave in France,' was the common understanding of the maxim.[20] As a result, individual slaves, who were brought to France in their hundreds, usually as personal servants, were up to the 1770s able to petition successfully for their freedom, if they could get a lawyer and have their day in court.

In Britain the situation was less clear. Common-law tradition was silent on slavery, and Parliament had never pronounced on the subject. Yet there were probably thousands of slaves in Britain in the 1770s and 1780s, and in the port cities of the west particularly, with their thriving commercial links to the Americas, having slave servants was more normal than not for the mercantile classes. When such slaves and their supporters sought redress from the courts, results were ambiguous. In 1765 the slave Jonathan Strong, who had run away and been recaptured and beaten before escaping again, remained free only because his master did not pursue his case to its conclusion. The legal ruling in the matter retained a studied neutrality on the legality of slavery, though the Lord Chancellor himself came out strongly in favour of masters' rights. In the early 1770s the landmark 'Somerset Case', concerning James Somerset, the slave of a Boston customs official who sought to return him to the (then) colonies, produced a clearer outcome. Much against his political judgement (and his own material interests, as an investor in Virginia), Chief Justice Mansfield had to rule that, in the absence of a specific statute in English law, there was no right of a slave owner to remove a slave from the country: 'the state of slavery is of such a nature, that it is incapable of being now introduced by justice upon mere reasoning'.[21] Despite this passage, the judgement did not free the slaves who remained in England, though a Scottish court ruling of 1778 did deny masters in that country coercive control over slaves.

While British political opinion would be content to filibuster the matter for another generation, the French had taken a simpler route to dealing with the slave problem in the 1770s. The Minister of the Navy and Colonies, Antoine de Sartine – formerly, as the *Lieutenant-général de Police*, the country's highest public-order official – produced a new edict for the king's signature in August 1777. Noting that Africans in France were seeking freedoms that associated them to 'the superior beings they were destined to serve', he set out the necessity for controlling their presence more rigorously:

> Their marriages to Europeans are encouraged; the public houses are infected; the colours mingle together; the blood degenerates. A prodigious number of slaves removed from cultivation

in our colonies are brought to France only to flatter the vanity of their masters and of these same slaves. If they return to America, they carry with them the spirit of liberty, of independence and of equality that they communicate to the others; destroy the bonds of discipline and subordination and thereby prepare a revolution.[22]

The answer to this, and to the *parlements'* squeamish insistence that they did not recognise slavery, was quite simply to make it a matter of race. Since 1670 the *Code noir* or 'Black Code' had ruled French Caribbean colonies, defining such *noirs* as clearly inferior (although entitled, under the Catholic paternalism and royal absolutism of the time, to a certain standard of care and religious instruction). The new 'Declaration for the Police of Blacks' brought skin colour home to France as the marker of concern. 'Blacks' arriving from the colonies were supposed to be held in secure 'depots' at the ports while their masters conducted business, and then returned to the Americas with them. The law was in fact weakly enforced, not least because local authorities quibbled over the costs of maintaining these depots, and masters and ships' captains colluded to avoid the law by letting 'Blacks' off their vessels before summoning Admiralty inspectors. Registration of 'Blacks' in the capital actually increased to over seven hundred between 1777 and 1789: a small population compared with London's thousands, but evidence of the failure of this early attempt at racial exclusion.[23]

Over a hundred years before the upheavals we are examining, the poet John Dryden had captured in a phrase one of the essential myths that animated later generations' views of the New World. One of his characters, an Islamic 'Moor' as it happened, exclaimed, 'I am as free as Nature first made man, | Ere the base laws of servitude began, | When wild in woods the noble savage ran.'[24] Even earlier, in 1580, Michel de Montaigne had written in an essay ironically titled *On Cannibals* of the natives of the Amazon region (on the word of a single, and highly unreliable, informant): 'Among them you hear no words for treachery, lying, cheating, avarice, envy, backbiting or forgiveness . . . They are still in that blessed state of desiring nothing beyond what is ordained by their natural necessities.'[25] At the end of the seventeenth century John Locke could still anoint one of his *Two*

*Treatises on Government* with the bold assertion that 'In the beginning all the World was *America*', meaning thereby a state of nature, uncorrupted by power.[26] In the course of the eighteenth century these American idylls were supplemented by the newly discovered territories of the Pacific – the 'South Seas' that European imaginations rapidly populated with island utopias full of carefree, noble and sexually promiscuous natives. James Cook and the comte de Bougainville brought back to their respective capitals young Polynesian noblemen who charmed polite society with their 'natural' grace and manners. Court circles where all of life was a ritual of display proved highly susceptible to artificial demonstrations of 'native' accomplishments that were entirely in tune with their audience's preconceptions.

Writers such as Diderot and the *abbé* Raynal, collaborating on an epic history of the European intercourse with both East and West 'Indies' under Raynal's name, wrote unquestioningly of peoples such as the Tahitians and American Indians as being closer to nature, and therefore more pure and moral, than Europeans. Yet they also spoke of the European adventure of colonialism as a positive benefit, of trade and civilisation going hand in hand for mutual profit, both material and spiritual. Raynal in particular highlighted the ambiguity of the process:

> The produce of equatorial regions was consumed in polar climes. The industrial products of the north were transported to the south; the textiles of the Orient became the luxuries of Westerners, and everywhere men mutually exchanged their opinions, their laws, their customs, their illnesses, and their medicines, their virtues and their vices.[27]

Captain Cook, whose own complex encounter with the customary attitude of Hawaiian islanders to divinity and sacrifice ended with the roasting of his dismembered corpse in 1779, left a passage in his own *Journals* that highlights the questioning approach of even this dedicated explorer to the processes under way:

> What is still more to our shame as civilised Christians, we debauch their morals already too prone to vice, and we introduce among them wants and perhaps disease which they never before knew, and which serve only to disturb that happy tranquillity

which they and their forefathers enjoyed. If anyone denies the truth of this assertion let him tell me what the natives of the whole extent of America have gained by the commerce they have had with Europeans.[28]

This itself, while eloquent testimony to one man's disillusionment with a process he was instrumental in expanding, is at the same time still a reflection of fundamental European attitudes that were themselves based on fantasies. Time would show that idyllic Tahitian lifestyles incorporated patriarchal violence and brutal human sacrifice, while the happy tranquillity of the American 'noble savage' was a deeper and even more conflicted myth. Had the first European contacts with the New World not coincided with the outbreak of terrible disease, North America in the seventeenth century might have presented the spectacle of a settled agricultural civilisation.[29] The famed 'Pilgrim Fathers', cast up utterly unequipped on the shores of New England, had survived by taking up residence in an abandoned Indian village and learning local agricultural techniques. Even after the passage of epidemics that penetrated far ahead of European contact, devastating the larger centres of Indian settlement, groups such as the Iroquois Confederacy demonstrated the ability to maintain large-scale political organisation for both warfare and diplomacy with the ever encroaching power of the British and French.

The attitudes of Europeans who actually came into contact with American Indians veered sharply between the romanticised and the ruthless. Both French and British cultivated contacts with the nations in the borderlands between their colonial possessions in mid-century, and both used them as auxiliaries in warfare – thus the Seven Years War in Europe is the 'French and Indian War' in America (1756–63). The French held George Washington, then a young militia officer, personally responsible for the death of Jumonville, a French officer killed by Indians under his command in that war, while the Americans' own Declaration of Independence in 1776 denounced George III for having 'endeavoured to bring on the inhabitants of our frontiers, the merciless Indian Savages, whose known rule of warfare, is an undistinguished destruction of all ages, sexes and conditions'. The situation on 'the Frontier' by the 1780s was one of unremitting warfare between settlers and natives, but this was largely occasioned by the fact that the land being settled belonged to the Indians. British colonial authority's infuriating decision to hold settlement at the line of the Appalachians, which the new Americans had so joyfully over-thrown, had aimed at shielding the native population from outright spoliation. American independence cast the fate of the Indians to the four winds.

The Oneida people, members of the wide-ranging Iroquois Confederacy of the 'Six Nations', but numbering only six hundred individuals, had been allies of the victorious Americans. At the start of the war they had been promised 'every Blessing we enjoy, and united with a free people, your Liberty and property will be safe'. In 1783 Congress itself promised them the 'sole use and benefit' of their six million acres of designated territory, in what is now upstate New York.[30] Wary of such easy promises, the Oneida carefully worked in the next few years to consolidate their position. Not only did they invite Christianised Indians from more developed regions to settle and farm on lands leased from them; they even offered leases to prominent Americans whom they knew to be sympathetic, and drew in smaller-scale tenants from established border towns, working to establish a cultivated buffer zone under their control between their core territories and the rapacious movement of settlers and speculators. Holding the full panoply of legal titles and written leases, the Oneida were becoming capitalist landlords.

The State of New York, engaged in a furious political battle to secure its hinterland against competing claims from Massachusetts, scorned and mocked this process, labelling the Oneida as dupes of 'the private artifice of designing Persons' seeking to evade the state's self-granted monopoly on acquiring Indian lands.[31] By 1785 New York surveyors were already encroaching on Oneida lands and par-celling them up for sale. Nominal support for the Oneida from the federal government, in its near-helpless pre-Constitution condition, proved useless. The Governor of New York, George Clinton, warned the Oneida bluntly that six hundred Indians could not stand in the way of tens of thousands of settlers, and that New York would pro-tect them only if given rights over their lands: 'if this is not now done, it is your Fault and not ours'.[32] The Oneida signed away immediately some 460,000 acres, for $11,500. By 1787 the State of New York had sold around two-thirds of these lands for $125,955. By the end of the next year almost all of the territory of the Oneida and their neighbouring tribes, some eighteen million acres in all, had been signed away to aggressive speculators on a 999-year lease that would prove valueless.

The following months saw bitter legal fighting between the state authorities and the private individuals whom they saw as trying to steal the lands from beneath their, the politicians', noses. But the end result was the same – trickery allied to threats of overwhelming force removed the Indians' rights, left them on 'reservations' amounting to some 4 per cent of their original holdings and paved the way for a cascade of settlement in formerly virgin lands.[33] Within a few years the woods and streams of the region would be carved up into rigidly geometrical grids for sale, marked on a 1792 map with names redolent of the higher imperial culture the Americans thought they were bringing: Hector, Ulysses, Scipio, Brutus, Junius, Cato, Cicero, Homer, Solon, Virgil. At one edge of the territory came Dryden, Milton and Locke, as if thrown in as an afterthought, a recollection that this was not, in fact, imperial Rome.[34]

Changes in the way Europeans saw the world in the late eighteenth century boded ill not just for North American Indians, but for their counterparts across the globe. For long centuries Europeans had been powerful players in global networks of commerce and rivalry. Ocean-spanning maritime technology and increasingly powerful weaponry had given them ever more influence, but before this point they had remained in some senses comparable, even in their own eyes, to the other cultures with which they engaged. It had only really been at the end of the seventeenth century that 'the Turk', in the form of the Ottoman Empire, had ceased to be an active threat to Christian power, turned back from the gates of Vienna after a two-month siege in September 1683 (leaving behind, so legend has it, a stock of coffee that spawned a new fashion). It was out of the long European relationship with the different cultures of the Mediterranean that slavery itself, more or less extinct further north by the Middle Ages, had survived to be reinvigorated by the demands of the Atlantic trade. And slavery here was a fate that threatened not only black Africans. As North Carolinians argued over constitutional ratification in February 1788, one raised a dread spectre of national powerlessness: 'What is there to prevent an Algerine Pirate from landing on your coast, and carrying your citizens into slavery? You have not a single sloop of war.' At first glance absurd, such a fear was only too real.[35]

The Islamic 'Barbary Pirates' who operated out of a variety of empires and kingdoms from Morocco to Tripoli were, even at the end of the eighteenth century, a scourge of the seas. Their operations had taken over a million Christians into slavery since the sixteenth century, and their raiders were known to prey as far north as the shores of western England, and in one reported case, even Iceland.[36] To be taken by a 'Sallee Rover' was an accepted hazard of a sailor's life, and the wealthy and charitably inclined contributed to purchase such men's freedom with the same regularity as they funded missions to the heathen or supported widows and orphans. The United States, whose traders depended on access to the Mediterranean, paid out sums approaching 20 per cent of government revenues from the late 1780s to these states to ensure safe passage for its ships. Britain, France and other powers used both force and payment to achieve similar guarantees, which were only ever partially successful. Thomas Jefferson reported home from Paris in July 1789 that 'The capture of three French merchant ships by the Algerines under different pretexts, has produced great sensation in the sea-ports of this country, and some in it's government. They have ordered some frigates to be armed at Toulon to punish them.' Though this suggests a robust sense of superiority, two months later Jefferson reported that he was making arrangements 'for the redemption of our captives', undoubtedly from the Algerines. He had authorised the 'General of the Order of the Holy Trinity' to go 'as far as 3000 [*livres*] a head'.[37]

Many individuals captured by such pirates endured bitter years of imprisonment in the *bagnios* of Algiers and other cities, held as a public labour force, poorly fed and rented out in chain gangs to private individuals in need of hands. Conversion to Islam, for the enslavement of fellow believers was forbidden, was one route out, sometimes taken eagerly. Such 'renegadoes' were scorned by many who had not faced the threat of captivity, but often succeeded in becoming military or civil officials, and even slave owners themselves. Thomas Pellow, captured aboard ship in the Bay of Biscay, aged eleven in 1715, spent over twenty years in Morocco, becoming an officer in the sultan's army and accruing booty, and a wife from the imperial harem. Fathering two children and working with other

Europeans and the black Africans who made up the ranks of his slave unit, he had no thought of escape until his royal patron died and he was threatened by political upheavals. On his return to England in 1740 he wrote for his new audience a *History of the Long Captivity and Adventures of Thomas Pellow*, in which he tried to deny his all too visible assimilation into this multiracial Islamic society, but he was neither the first nor the last to 'turn Turk' so successfully.[38]

Though this was a zone of conflict, therefore, it was not one of evident superiority for either side, notwithstanding a constant rhetoric of religious intolerance, and even the apparently massive cultural boundaries between Christendom and Islam proved porous in practice. Further east the continued expansion of the Honourable East India Company had led to an embrace of Indian culture by British officials that was both more potent, and even more ambiguous, than that of the Barbary renegades. Many aspects of the Company's actions in India lacked any indication of cultural finesse. Crushing military victories in the 1750s had consolidated the role of what was once a trading concern as a fully fledged power on the subcontinent, and the exploitation of the inhabitants for personal enrichment had already made the home-from-India 'nabob' laden down with sudden wealth a figure of caricature (and envious disdain) in Britain. But much of this power came from the maintenance of complex political relationships with Indian princes and potentates. However corrupt their practices, it could not be denied that it was the participation of the Company's men within Mughal imperial politics, rather than any more domineering 'imperialism', that was the basis of much of this enrichment.[39]

Life for Company officials, either among growing British settlements in Calcutta, Madras and Bombay, or posted to more isolated positions in numerous princely courts, was marked at this moment by several levels of cultural interaction and sometimes contradictory blendings of influences. In the larger centres life could be conducted to some degree as in Britain. New buildings were erected in the finest traditions of Georgian neoclassicism and young men flush with cash could spend it gambling, drinking and horse-racing much as at home. The fact that many of the 'writers' sent out to do the Company's work were in their late teens when they began, and that the mortality rate from tropical diseases was ferocious, simply made this high life all the more rakishly present-minded.[40] At the same time the desires of such men for female company drove them towards relationships with *bibis*, young women, sometimes from quite respectable backgrounds among the Mughal gentry, who became companions, concubines and in some cases wives. Fully a third of those who died in Company service in Bengal in the early 1780s left formal bequests to such women and their children. These might include thousands of rupees in cash and even whole houses, servants and all. Clearly this was not merely prostitution or passing fancies, but a full-blown lifestyle, which brought with it for the women's families potentially valuable links of patronage and political support.[41] A hundred years earlier the East India Company had even made it an official policy to encourage liaisons for its ordinary soldiers: 'induce by all means you can invent our soldiers to marry with the Native women, because it will be impossible to get ordinary young women as we before directed to pay their own passages.' While the motive here is rather crudely financial, as the practices evolved, even senior officers were known to marry into high-ranking Muslim families, although some who did so already had wives and children back in Britain.[42]

Outside the confines of the British cantonments, Company officers' assimilation to local cultures might go still further. In an age when external dress was still a vital marker of social and cultural positioning, the fact that many shunned the stiffness of European garb in private and wore traditional light cottons as an informal 'undress' was notable in itself, but some went further and caparisoned themselves as Mughal noblemen. Sir David Ochterlony, scion of Highland Scots, born in Boston but driven out of Massachusetts by the American Revolution, joined the Company's army in 1777 and in later years, as Resident in Delhi, chose to carry on an almost entirely Eastern lifestyle of robes, palanquins and concubines.[43] While Ochterlony emulated the Islamic princely image, Charles Stuart, an enigmatic Irishman who appeared in India in his teens in the 1780s, took up Hinduism with evangelical fervour. Rising to the rank of major general in the Company's army, he also became legendary for his proselytisation in favour of Hindu ways of life, though here there was deep irony, for actual Hindus agreed that one had to be born into their caste system and that conversion was not possible.[44]

While the general's eccentricities led to his being mocked by his compatriots as 'General Pundit' and 'Hindoo Stuart', a wider current of concern at the 'Indianisation' of Company officials took hold from this very period. Ironically, comment on the influence of Indian ways on the British grew far more critical just as the serious philosophical roots of Hindu culture were being explored by Europeans for the first time. Since the first translations of Hindu law codes in the 1770s, the British elite had been fascinated with the revelation of what appeared to be ancient wisdom. Charles James Fox reported hearing Edmund Burke speak of the texts 'with an awe bordering on devotion'. One reviewer noted, with telling ambiguity: 'The most amiable part of modern philosophy is hardly upon a level with the extensive charity, the comprehensive benevolence, of a few rude, untutored Hindoo Brahmins.'[45] In Calcutta in 1784 the newly arrived Justice of the Supreme Court, Sir William Jones, founded a 'Society for enquiring into the History, Civil and Natural, the Antiquities, Arts, Sciences and Literature of Asia'. Governor General Hastings himself was its patron, and sought to 'diffuse a generosity of sentiment' through its works, remembering that the classics they studied 'will survive when British dominion in India shall have long ceased to exist'.[46]

While Jones ensconced himself among the Brahmins of the Ganges and studied Sanskrit – 'more perfect than Greek, more copious than Latin, and more exquisitely refined than either' – others were preparing an onslaught.[47] Alongside the refined acknowledgement of Sanskrit and Islamic cultures ran other, more disparaging trends. Whatever their past achievements, the present inhabitants of India were generally acknowledged to be sunk in political decrepitude. Hastings at his trial declaimed against the situation: an 'unavoidable anarchy and confusion of different laws, religions and prejudices, moral, civil, and political, all jumbled together in one unnatural and discordant mass'.[48] Moreover, as others noted, a 'spirit of extravagance' fostered by the 'malignant climate . . . and the uncertainty of life' threatened every European. Burke denounced the 'black banya', or factotum: 'persons without whom a European can do nothing' who came from the lowest class of 'natives, who by being habituated to misery and subjection can submit to any orders', but who became tyrants over their masters.[49] Travellers recalled how such men, or their sub-agents, battened on Britons fresh off the boat, and how they enriched themselves at their masters' expense.

Complete dependence on local servants seemed to be the fate of Europeans: the Calcutta diarist William Hickey in 1783 had sixty-three servants, including eight 'carrying sticks' and twenty to carry his palanquin. Female servants multiplied also, though some warned of the uselessness of maids recruited from 'idle and dissipated native women'.[50]

Charles Grant, one of the all-powerful directors of the East India Company, and an evangelical of ferocious conviction, launched in 1787 from London a campaign to install Christian missionaries in the Company's possessions. He viewed the Hindus as 'completely enchained . . . by their superstitions . . . universally and wholly corrupt . . . depraved as they are blind, and wretched as they are depraved'.[51] A half-century-long war was launched on the 'Brahminised' practices of the Company's own employees both in their public lives – payment of fees to temples for prayers, dedications and offerings of thanks for harvests, participation in local festivals, all of which were part of official policies of acceptance among the native population – and in their private affairs.

While Grant and his acolytes began to target the Company's religious toleration, another wave of feeling broke against its officers' cultural and sexual transgressions. Within the decade commentaries on India denounced the effect of 'the witcheries of the unhappy daughters of heathens and infidels' practised upon 'once blooming boys'. By 1805 widows had to have sworn affidavits that they were not of 'native blood' to receive official support.[52] Orders forbade the adoption of 'native' dress and practices (though some, like Stuart and Ochterlony, continued to ignore them), and more serious prohibitions were imposed on the offspring of Anglo-Indian relationships. A generation of children of mixed descent had already been sent 'home' to Britain for education, but this route to advancement was partly closed in 1786, when orphans of this ilk were barred from travel, and firmly shut off in 1791, when employment as an officer in the Company's service, civil or military, was closed to those not fully European. Funds to support orphan children were limited ever more firmly to Europeans, with some mixed-race children ending up being shipped into service in the Dutch East Indies.[53]

In the closing years of the eighteenth century a racial classification of Indians, in relation to one another and to the opposed poles of white Europeans and black Africans, the latter increasingly marked as absolute inferiors, took hold. While the refinements of Islamic civilisation were acknowledged, its martial and aristocratic virtues were associated with cruelty and despotism, the historical conquest of India set out as an episode, and heritage, of 'the most ferocious bigotry and rapine'. Hindu Indians, or 'Gentoos', were depicted by contrast as 'meek, superstitious, charitable', lacking 'that vigour of mind . . . virtues grafted on those passions' that made the British formidable.[54] Islam as a ruling religion was depicted as 'peculiarly calculated for despotism'. Giving untrammelled power to fathers and heads of households, it thus 'habituated mankind to slavery', while the Gentoos, for whom 'Happiness consists in a mere absence of misery', were doomed to suffer.[55] All this played on a rhetoric of 'Englishness' that for decades and indeed centuries had associated freedom with ferocity, and rights with conquest. As a pamphlet had put it in the 1720s, 'What has made us an Ingenious, Active and Warlike Nation . . . What has rendered us a Great, Wealthy, and Happy People . . . and what is it has made us Terrible to the whole World, but our English Liberty?'[56] A rising tide of racial prejudice meant that within less than a generation cultural assimilation through social and sexual liaisons went from a virtual norm to a career-ending transgression.

There was a cold logic to this, and one closely tied to the revolutionary liberty of the Americans. When Governor General Warren Hastings left India, his replacement, who agreed to go only after being specifically granted the supreme powers Hastings had failed to get, was Lord Cornwallis, commander of the army that surrendered to the Americans at Yorktown. His policy for India was quite explicitly to prevent the emergence of a 'native' class with European accomplishments, who might pose an insurrectionary threat. Company employees in India, kept from both landowning and intermarriage, were to remain outsiders, their affections held back to the 'mother country', dominating society from above – for its own good, of course. The process of cultural interweaving known across the Americas as creolisation was to be barred from India forever.

Cornwallis, accustomed to command, a player in British politics, but also a sober, plain-spoken man of restrained tastes, brought a radical shift to British India in far more areas than just sexual morality. Even before he arrived in September 1786 he set a new tone. Pressed by Pitt to take charge, he assented, 'Much against my will, and with grief of heart.' Unlike so many who had viewed India as a money-making opportunity, he foresaw 'all the plagues and miseries of command and public station'. He gained for himself powers to override the local administrators on the Company Council, and also insisted on being appointed military commander-in-chief for the theatre; but he refused the additional salary that came with that role.[57] In Calcutta he ostentatiously scorned the lavish drinking parties that were a prime entertainment for Company men, and publicly blenched when confronted with shameless tales of the corruption necessary to buy lucrative postings for offspring and relatives.

Warren Hastings, for all his efforts to reform the East India Company, had been the Company's man, rising through its ranks, negotiating and allying with Indian princes and potentates, speaking their languages and balancing their interests with those of his trading associates. Cornwallis was alien to all that, a genuine English aristocrat, who for both practical and deep cultural reasons could not imagine sinking into the various forms of 'going native' that had so visibly afflicted, to contemporary eyes, the previous generations of officials. Charged explicitly with reversing decades of corruption, Cornwallis fought hard against officials, including his own interim predecessor, who used every trick to block his threats to their peculations. In mid-1789 Cornwallis responded furiously to a slanderous bid to have him recalled, including the notion that, at forty-nine, he had become besotted with a sixteen-year-old girl. He wrote back to London that if his interim predecessor, Sir John Macpherson, was restored, 'the national character for sincerity and honour with native powers' that Cornwallis had been endeavouring to rebuild would collapse again through 'his duplicity and low intrigues' and 'system of mean jobbing and peculation'.[58]

Cornwallis saw the interests of all Indians being best served by a more bracingly British style of rule. In 1789 he authorised translations of compendiums of Hindu and Islamic laws, so that British judges could rule on native disputes without relying on potentially corrupt translators. He also drew on an expansive interpretation of the Company's *diwani* powers to give local agents criminal, as well as civil, jurisdiction in minor cases, making them more like British magistrates. In a striking gesture of overt racial supremacy he ordered that all cases with European defendants should be tried only by the British judges of the Calcutta supreme court. He wrote to London in

1789 that criminal-justice reforms would be 'useless and nugatory, whilst the execution of them depends upon any native whatever', and ordered Company men to oversee all trials of Indians by native judges 'and be particularly careful that the sentences should be executed on those who are found guilty and that the innocent should be released'.[59] Although a few years later he would go even further by removing the powers of Company collectors to judge their own conflicts with their populations, his complete faith in British conceptions of justice, without regard whatsoever for local traditions, was part of a step change in the history of India.

Rejecting so firmly the 'geographical morality' that Burke had lamented in Hastings's rule, Cornwallis was nonetheless equally firmly of the view that Indians 'must be ruled by an absolute power', as he put it in 1786, and in a letter of late 1789 he tellingly invoked a contrast with his earlier experiences and underlying sympathies:

> Let not my Americans, therefore, be like the deluded, besotted Indians, among whom I live, who would receive Liberty as a curse instead of a blessing, if it were possible to give it to them, and would reject it as a vase of poison, that, which, if they could taste and digest it, would be the water of life.[60]

This paternalistic approach bore fruit in ways that were of unarguable benefit: regulations to protect native weavers against unscrupulous merchants, a recoinage to relieve the 'vexation and extortion' practised by money-changers on the peasantry and, on 27 July 1789, a proclamation promising the 'utmost rigour' of punishments against the 'inhuman and detestable traffic' of Indian orphans into slavery overseas.[61] But it also brought about jarring alien interventions into the complex customs of Bengali society, none greater than the famous 'Permanent Settlement' that Cornwallis drew up in the same summer months of 1789.

Ever since the Company had acquired its tax-gathering powers in 1765 it had been vexed by its inability to extract a steady revenue stream from this supposed sovereign right. Taxation demands under the Mughal system passed down from local rulers to the rural labouring population of *ryots* via the *zemindars*, a class of local gentry whose social status and wealth derived essentially from the right to gather taxes, and cream off surpluses, on behalf of higher authority. The system was a sort of fiscal feudalism, the *zemindars* a largely but not entirely hereditary class ranging from village bigwigs or minor nobles up to substantial local lords. The raja Devi Singh, whose tax gatherers had run rampant in 1783, furnishing Burke with his most colourful passages, was acting as a *zemindar*.[62] The crises of the previous decade, including devastating famines, had produced a situation that, to British eyes, was one of near-total collapse, with what should be an orderly transmission of sovereign requirements turned into a battleground and a desert of evasions and oppression.

Cornwallis's solution was to impose a permanent valuation of lands and taxes owed upon them, and to consolidate the rights of individual *zemindars* to their title over particular territories. In his words, 'In a country where the landlord has a permanent property in the soil it will be worth his while to encourage his tenants who hold his farm in lease to improve that property', whereas a temporary lease merely encouraged exploitation: 'Will it not be his interest . . . to exhibit his lands at the end of it in a state of ruin', to discourage others from outbidding him, and to minimise his expense if he does lose the lease.[63] As is evident here, the Indian situation encouraged a confusion between the European concepts of 'tax' and 'rent', and the rights of the *zemindars* to demand payment, which came essentially as grants from higher authority, were here transformed into a personal possession, property in land in a British sense. Cornwallis held no particular brief for the *zemindars* as a group: 'It is immaterial to government what individual possessed the land, provided he cultivates it, protects the ryots, and pays the public revenue.'[64] But this conception was precisely the problem, for the *zemindars* did not 'possess' or 'cultivate' the land, and they certainly had no interest in 'protecting' the *ryots*. But similarly the *ryots* themselves did not match up to the picture of a settled tenantry that Cornwallis so complacently evoked.

Extracting revenue from the Bengali agricultural classes involved a much more complex collision of rights and assumptions than the British rulers were capable of digesting. Devi Singh's tactics, for example, were an extreme version of a violence common to revenue-collecting activities, but a violence that the *ryots* understood and were even able to use. In defying violence, labouring groups consolidated a position that was ultimately resistant to the notion of settled authority. As one *ryot* remarked to a British collector in the 1790s, 'though I presented the *zemindar* my back [for a beating], I never gave him my money; and how do you expect I will give it to you now?'[65] The constant negotiations and fluidity of tenancies, and fluctuating levels of payment, that had infuriated the British for decades, were key to the *ryots*' efforts to extract the maximum from those who held wealth and apparent power. Complex webs of short-term credit, rent reductions, concessions and negotiations were necessary to hold *ryots* to the land. Bengal was an underpopulated country, with much land left waste, and one of the *zemindars*' hardest tasks was getting *ryots* to farm their fields. Better offers from other *zemindars* might tempt them away, or equally they might leave on their own account if conditions were unsatisfactory. Part of the violence of Devi Singh's actions, which produced a widespread rebellion, or *dhing*, in 1783, was his effort to short-circuit such negotiations under the incessant pressure of British revenue demands that ignored all this complexity. Seizing cattle and oxen, for example, stripping *ryots* of mobility, was one such device, and was more important in bringing about the massed protests of the *dhing* than simple physical attacks.

The *dhing*, around Rangpur in 1782–3, and in several other districts between 1787 and 1789, was revolt, but deeply structured revolt. *Ryots* formed protest camps outside local revenue collectors' offices, appointed their own 'Nabob and Dewan and all the necessary officers of regular government' as one Company official reported, exchanged tokens of loyalty and raised funds to support their expenses.[66] Revenue offices were burned, but overt violence first came from the *zemindars*' guards: only after one crowd was fired on with deadly results did a local collector suffer decapitation and dismemberment as condign punishment. After an initial agreement to reduce collections was broken by the local agents, violence became more widespread and the Company's officials called in their army. One overt engagement killed or captured most of the rebel leadership, and the Company's forces approached a further contingent by disguising themselves as locals, before throwing off their concealment and opening fire indiscriminately. The survivors had no choice but to straggle home in defeat.

This crushing of a revolt that had begun as little more than a rent strike reflected the vast gulf between the *ryots*' and the Company's perception of their relative situation. Petitions had been as much a part of the initial protest as actions. One such expressed the *ryots*' view of the matter to the British authorities succinctly: 'You are head of one country, we have a thousand countries to go to, You are Chief, we are Ryotts, you will therefore order us Justice.'[67] The Permanent Settlement was an effort to do just that, in the eyes of Cornwallis and his administrators, with fixed rents and formal written notices to the *ryots* of their tenure. But this was the justice of an agricultural improver, who saw benefit coming from stability and imagined that the *zemindars* could be persuaded to act as paternalistic landlords. Other protesters in the first years of the Settlement's operation had a more realistic view. Refusing to accept the *patta*, or written notice of tenure, they declared that the landlords 'are wealthy and we are poor, so they should be bound and we free'.[68] The imposition of the Settlement deprived the *ryots* of their 'thousand countries' and would cause them to sink into abject, grievously exploited poverty in the decades to come. The best intentions of modernising reform came to nothing, blinded by a failure to attend to the cultural differences that had been a firm part of Warren Hastings's perception of India.

As the British position in India mounted further towards supremacy, so the fortunes of French India had irretrievably declined. At one point, under the buccaneering Governor General Joseph François Dupleix in the early 1750s, French influence had extended over three-quarters of India's southern peninsula and her possessions encompassed much of the country's south-eastern coastline. In the era of the Seven Years' War this territory was reduced to a rump of trading posts, but the ambition to check British power and maintain valuable alliances persisted. French agents, in some cases merchants and in others military officers on more or less unofficial reconnaissance missions, visited the princely courts of southern India in the later 1760s and early 1770s, reporting back on British ambitions and the potential for their defeat. One such officer, Louis Marc-Antoine de Valory, spent three years exploring the political and military situation of Hyderabad, Madras and other centres, issuing a warning in 1777 that the British would seek to conquer all of India if they lost the American colonies. Such was the confusion of French efforts, however, that officers such as de Valory were often regarded as dangerous adventurers by the commercially minded administrators of the French possessions. When he returned home he met further confusion, being refused reintegration to his regiment by a commander who saw his absence as a fortune-hunting jaunt.[69]

French 'volunteer' officers also served as commanders and trainers to the armies of various allies, most notably and effectively that of Haidar Ali, Sultan of Mysore, in the 1760s and 1770s. This state was central to the politics of southern India. Lodged between the large, British-influenced but hopelessly decadent territories of Hyderabad to the north and the smaller, spice-producing states of the tip of the peninsula, Mysore ranged alongside the British possessions around Madras, a permanent threat to control of the whole region, or rather, a state with its own ambitions for such control. The Muslim general Haidar Ali had seized control of Mysore from its weak Hindu prince, who subsequently faded from a figurehead to a nonentity. Prosperous, vigorous and militarily well organised, Mysore had obtained concessions from the British at Madras by aggression in a war of 1767, including a promise of support in case of outside attack. When a few years later the Hindu Mahratta Confederacy launched an attack from the north against Mysore, the refusal of the Madras establishment to assist Mysore fomented a severe grievance. Successfully fending off Mahratta aggression, and indeed expanding his own territories at their and Hyderabad's expense, Haidar Ali's Mysore was a prime candidate for an alliance with the French, which was secured as France entered the American War in 1778.[70]

A massive invasion of the British territories around Madras in 1780, supported by French troops and naval forces, caused Warren Hastings some of the most unsettling months of his career. Haidar Ali's 100,000 troops routed the first British units sent against them, killing or capturing the whole force of over 700 European and 3500 Indian soldiers. Only the frantic rallying of British forces from across the subcontinent, along with a successful naval campaign to prevent the landing of French reinforcements, prevented a total defeat. War raged on in the south, and the baton of opposition to the British passed in December 1782 from Haidar Ali to his son, Tipu. The succession was attended by the French, whose officers surrounded the dying Haidar and kept news of his demise secret until Tipu could be summoned back from his command to take up the reins of office and continue the war. The entanglement of Mysore with the French was not entirely profitable, however. With the support of French guns and engineers, Tipu was making solid progress on a siege of the key British fortress of Mangalore in mid-1783 when news of the Anglo-French ceasefire arrived, forcing him to break off the attack and sign a treaty restoring the *status quo ante* the following year.[71]

Tipu Sultan, as he was known, grew in the following years in the eyes of the British to be a monster of legendary proportions. More devoutly Muslim than his father, he displayed a religious devotion, including eventually the notion that war against the British was *jihad*, that caused him to be condemned by Cornwallis in 1789 as having a 'general character of bigotry . . . jealousy and hatred of Europeans'. Reports of brutality and summary executions, hardly uncommon in the jurisdiction of Indian rulers, were written up by British agents as 'barbarity unknown in any civilised nation'.[72] What troubled the British perhaps above all was the energy and technical advancement of Tipu's army and economy and its continued connections with the French. Though the French refused to station troops officially in Mysore after 1783, they could not stop Tipu recruiting French soldiers, engineers and gunners to work for him, even from the convalescent hospitals. Such men kept his army well drilled in European techniques, while the explorations of Tipu's own craftsmen and ironsmiths produced modern artillery, including fearsome rockets later adopted by the British as one of their own 'secret weapons'. Such were the military fruits of a much wider modernising drive. Like Cornwallis himself, Tipu minted new coins to regulate the economy and glorify his rule; he also encouraged overseas trade and thought about agricultural improvement.

Ironically, and epochally, the French were breaking with their previous policy of seeking to expand in south India just as Tipu was gearing up for another engagement with British power. The headquarters of their eastern possessions was moved offshore, to Île de France (Mauritius) in 1785. Two years later the trading posts in India were put under royal administration as their parent East India Company, which had lost its monopoly in France in 1769, descended towards bankruptcy. In 1789 the French Asiatic establishment was placed under a fixed budget of 700,000 *livres*, making military action effectively impossible.[73] Rebuffed by Tipu after seeking a local trade treaty in 1788 – the sultan had already sent ambassadors directly to France, seeking a wider alliance – the cautious and parochial-minded French administrators at their post of Pondicherry wrote of him as 'cruel, avaricious, vain and very ill-humoured ... hates all Christians'. They had 'lost all confidence' and regarded him as corrupt, added another in 1789.[74]

At the same time that the French in India were saying this, Governor General Cornwallis was receiving intelligence reports claiming that Tipu had an army of up to 153,000 men, including 1500 European cavalry and no fewer than 2000 pieces of artillery, and that at least one American ship had loaded munitions from Europe to supply him. Many such accounts he dismissed as 'foolish and incredible', but it was clear that for the first time in India British power faced a modern army, independent of restraint by European allies, but with the best of European technology at its disposal.[75] For the first time also, British power was overtly defined as the dominant force in the subcontinent, and here is the significance of the events that followed. When Hastings faced the armies of Haidar Ali in 1780, he did so to defend British trading power, as a Company servant. When Cornwallis learned of Tipu Sultan's attack on his southern neighbour of Travancore in December 1789, he had already issued orders that this was to be considered an act of war against the Company for strategic reasons. Having provoked Tipu by arrogantly taking control of a neighbouring territory, the Guntoor Circar, in 1788, and lending troops to his enemy in Hyderabad, Cornwallis now took the opportunity for a trial of strength, to assert the official, military and imperial supremacy of British power across all India.

There can be no doubt that Tipu was an aggressive ruler, with every intention of adding his neighbours to his domains if he could. The campaigns that Cornwallis led over the next two years, deploying tens of thousands of British and Indian troops, hundreds of guns (including a siege train drawn, unprecedentedly, by elephants) and hundreds of thousands of civilian followers, happened in the name of moderation and restraint, of keeping the peace of India. They ended with Tipu agreeing to Cornwallis's terms under threat of final and humiliating siege, surrendering his two young sons as hostages for two years into Cornwallis's care, and seeing his domain shrunk by almost half, augmenting his enemies' strength against him. The war that began in 1789 opened a decade in which British military domination of India would become unchallengeable, and de Valory's prophecy of 1777, that India would replace America under the

British thumb, came to pass, defining the politics of imperialism around the globe for the next century.

While America's lesson of independence was not lost on the imperial projectors of Britain, it is clear that in the complex stew of colonial relations, this period was a turning point inspired at least partly by the other lesson of the Atlantic economy – stigmatisation and exploitation by race. To return to where we began, the British convict settlement clinging to the shores of what would become Sydney Harbour, the story of its relations with the Australians is one of swift movement from Enlightenment optimism to racial denigration. Governor Philip, in a letter written some time in mid-1788, wrote of the natives with thoughtful observation:

> I have reason to think that the Men do not want [i.e., lack] personal Courage, they readily place a confidence and appear to be a friendly and inoffensive people unless made Angry and which the most trifling circumstance does at times. Three convicts have been killed by them in the woods . . .
>    They . . . are fond of any very Soft Musick, and will attend to singing any of the words which they very readily repeat. But I know very little at present of the people.[76]

Thus, despite attacks on his charges (for which he blames aggressive convicts), Philip gives the benefit of anthropological doubt to the Australians, and seeks only to know more about them. He believed profoundly, however, that they could be taught to act and think like Europeans, to abandon a way of life based on hunting and foraging, and thus be redeemed for civilisation, and for their own good:

> It is undeniably certain that to teach the shivering savage how to clothe his body, and to shelter himself completely from the cold and wet, and to put into the hands of men, ready to perish one half of the year with hunger, the means of procuring constant and abundant provision, must confer upon them benefits of the highest value and importance.[77]

That this should take place while a swelling convict and settler population was taking land that the Aboriginals had roamed for centuries, driving them from their best hunting grounds and watering places with alien concepts of private property, seems not to have entered Philip's mind as a problem. He left for home at the end of 1792, replaced by a military governor at the head of the New South Wales Corps, a band of soldier-entrepreneurs who would make an economically thriving colony through the ruthless abuse of convict labour, and complete scorn for the Australians. Where Philip had encouraged sobriety and equality of provisions, the new administration cut convict rations and bought 7500 gallons of spirits from a passing American ship, which at once became a new currency. Drunkenness among the Australians, black and white, would become endemic within months.[78]

David Collins, who had sailed out with Philip and the First Fleet, and served as both Judge-Advocate and Governor's Secretary, had at first seemed more offended by the behaviour of the convicts than by that of the Australians. The former he denounced repeatedly in his writings: 'There was such a tenderness in these people to each other's guilt, such an acquaintance with vice and the different degrees of it, that unless they were detected in the fact, it was generally next to impossible to bring an offence home to them.'[79] The Aboriginals he viewed initially as 'children of ignorance', best left alone 'under a dispensation to keep them happy in their liberties', though this also meant keeping them away from the expanding settlement.[80] As British power grew over the following years he became a more sensitive observer of Australian ways, noting how jealously those tribes in greater contact with the British guarded the material privileges that resulted. This merely resulted for him in a yet more negative assessment of their ultimate character: 'Although they lived among the inhabitants of the different settlements, were kindly treated, fed and often clothed, yet they were never found to possess the smallest degree of gratitude for such favours.' Even children who had spent their formative years among the whites and who 'might be supposed to ill relish the lives of their parents' more often than not fled back to the 'same mode of savage living'.[81]

As the watershed year of 1789 passed, a vast simplification of European relations with the darker-skinned ranks of humanity was in full flood. It is going too far to say that the model created by African slavery became dominant, because even that model was in the process of change. Older arguments about biblical precedent were giving way to a discourse of natural inferiority. There is a true irony in the image produced by Josiah Wedgwood for the anti-slavery campaign at just this time – an African man, kneeling in chains, with the legend 'Am I not a Man and a Brother?' The prevailing winds of Western thought, which had backed and filled around this question for the last century, were now setting in to answer with a decisive negative. Slavery might be entering a long decline, but the very length of it would show the force behind the new racial contempt and fear that the West had begun to brandish on all sides.

# 6

# 'That offspring of tyranny, baseness and pride'

*Abolitionism, political economy*
*and the people's rights*

Villiam Wilberforce's great speech of May 1789, calling on
Britons to look slavery in the face and examine their consciences, was only one facet of a genuinely international movement
that attracted support at the very highest levels. When Olaudah
Equiano, formerly known by his 'slave name' of Gustavus Vassa,
published his ground-breaking first-person account of life as a slave
in that same month, the work was prefaced by an impressive list of
subscribers. Personally supporting the publication of *The Interesting
Narrative of the Life of Olaudah Equiano, or Gustavus Vassa, the African.
Written by Himself* were the Prince of Wales and his brother the Duke
of York, five other dukes (and several duchesses), another seventeen titled noblemen, four bishops, two generals, an admiral, three
naval captains and eleven MPs, alongside dozens of clergymen and
other gentlefolk, including Josiah Wedgwood and John Wesley,
founder of Methodism. Granville Sharp and Thomas Clarkson, leaders of the movement Wilberforce had recently joined, had put
themselves down for two copies each.[1]

While fashionable Whig sympathies had clearly been raised by
Equiano in 1789, in general those unequivocal in their condemnation
of slavery were those who worked with a religious conviction. Some,
such as Sharp, were relatively isolated voices within mainstream

denominations. His reading of scripture had led him to pronounce in 1776 that all 'Tyrants, Slave-holders, and Oppressors' would be subjected to 'God's Temporal Vengeance' and that 'under the glorious Dispensation of the Gospel, we are absolutely bound to consider ourselves as *Citizens of the World*; that every Man whatever, without any *partial distinction* of Nation, Distance, or Complexion, must necessarily be esteemed our *neighbour*, and *our Brother*'.[2] Such sentiments were also embedded within Dissenting sects, and of these, none were more active than the Quakers.

In America, Quaker groups had abhorred slavery since an historic meeting in 1688, and moral pressure had obliged many Quakers, and others susceptible to religious logic, to free their slaves over the succeeding generations. A handful of activists took a further step by forming a society to promote a general abolition at the Sun Tavern in Philadelphia in 1775. Lost in the travails of revolutionary politics, this group was refounded with greater vigour in 1784, as the new Republic contemplated its future nature. Many individuals, influenced by the rhetoric of revolutionary and republican liberty, would free their own slaves in the decade to come, but this was not enough to turn the tide, and abolitionists strove to organise for more structural change. The same year saw the gathering of the New York Manumission Society, which admitted Alexander Hamilton as a member, along with another Founding Father, John Jay. At least three other states formed similar groupings shortly thereafter. The Pennsylvania Abolition Society, which persuaded the ever active Benjamin Franklin to become its president in 1787, would prove the most vigorous.[3] It pursued an elitist, legalistic policy, seeking out men of influence to attract to its cause, and its finances, and working primarily through court cases where existing laws could be used to defend individual slaves or freedmen and establish principles of liberty and equity.

It remained always an uphill struggle. Pennsylvania passed a law in 1780 freeing native-born slaves when they reached the age of twenty-eight (the original proposal had been eighteen years for women and twenty-one for men, but that had not survived debate). Future decades saw many such individuals simply sold down the river into the South just before their date of liberation arrived. There were still some seven thousand slaves in the state in the 1790s. New York, which held over twenty thousand slaves, did not even pass such a gradualist law until 1799, while Massachusetts, which had declared slavery illegal by a court decision in 1780, saw many influential figures argue that this had been a mistake, creating a class of free black paupers who were a threat to the social order.[4] Men as eminent as John Adams, James Madison and George Washington himself all feared that a challenge to slavery could be a challenge to the existence of the United States, as well as a check on its prosperity, while Thomas Jefferson, whose enlightened sensibilities had tempted him into blaming Britain for the very existence of slavery, kept his own slaves, and wrote in a 1787 work that manumission was the prerogative of individual slaveholders, not government.[5]

In truth, the notion of ending slavery filled even those who supported it with fear and trembling, especially on the western side of the Atlantic. It was no accident that the most vigorous campaigners – such as Wilberforce and the two great idealists who had brought him into their pre-existing campaign, Clarkson and Sharp – focused on ending the transatlantic slave trade, rather than slavery itself. The former was an activity, with all its bestialities, that could simply be stopped, without raising the far more serious dilemma of what to do with those who would become ex-slaves. Benjamin Franklin, in an address for the Pennsylvania society in November 1789, noted:

> Slavery is such an atrocious debasement of human nature that its very extirpation, if not performed with solicitous care, may sometimes open a source of serious evils. The unhappy man, who has long been treated as a brute animal, too frequently sinks beneath the common standard of the human species.

Thus Franklin proposed for the society committees of Inspection, Guardians, Education and Employ, who would see to fostering, schooling and apprenticeship for free blacks, but also 'superintend the morals, general conduct, and ordinary situation of the free Negroes'.[6]

The dread prospect of 'free Negroes' running wild had been raised to new heights in the consciousness of Europeans by the very men who called for an end to slavery. In the middle years of the century the philosophical tide had set against the institution, with figures as diverse as Montesquieu, Rousseau, Voltaire and Samuel

Johnson denouncing it in literary forms. When these essentially abstract condemnations had little effect, a new generation from the 1760s had begun to use a more apocalyptic register. Louis-Sébastien Mercier wrote a ground-breaking vision of the far future in 1770, *The Year 2440*, in which he imagined, among many other things, a statue raised in Paris to the 'Avenger of the New World', the black Spartacus who had begun the general uprising that had freed the bondsmen of the Americas. It was a process Mercier depicted as one of universal massacre, as the oppressed took their revenge on the whole society that had kept them down, and 'the soil of America drank with avidity the blood that it had awaited for so long'.[7] The epic and influential work of the *abbé* Raynal on the history of European colonisation in the 'Two Indies' – ghostwritten in parts by the committed libertarian Diderot – made similar play of the fate that awaited settler societies if they did not reform, but such appeals tended more to harden hearts against the slaves than to invite liberation at risk of future massacre.

Nor was it clear, in the work of many abolitionists, whether such liberation would actually mean the emergence of equality between former masters and slaves. The rhetoric of human spiritual equality was in full flow. Wedgwood's 'Am I not a Man and a Brother?' joined the language in which Franklin petitioned Congress in February 1790: 'Mankind are all formed by the same Almighty Being . . . and equally designed for the enjoyment of happiness.'[8] But actual schemes for liberation often turned out to have motives that were somewhat more material. The abstract definitions of Enlightenment thinking in the middle decades of the century had taken other turns besides that of apocalyptic prophecy. Political economy was a leading language of the day by 1789, and it prompted incisive thought into the 'problem' of slavery from quite other angles.

William Pitt himself was not immune to the arguments of emotion and enlightened sentiment. When the Commons debated (unsuccessfully) the repeal of the religious Test Act in May 1789, he noted how the spirit of enlightenment 'was . . . pretty generally felt on the Continent . . . owing to the universal intelligence that had spread itself through all ranks of people, which had contributed to enlighten their minds, soften their hearts, and enlarge their understandings'. Two years later, in a further abortive attempt to move against the slave trade, he was memorably direct, saying bluntly that 'the truth was, that we stopped the natural progress of civilisation; we cut off Africa from improvement; we kept down that Continent in a state of darkness, bondage, ignorance and blood'.[9] There can be no doubt of Pitt's earnest conviction of the evils of slavery and the trade, and under the influence of the Anti-Slavery Society and Wilberforce, he had enthusiastically pushed for diplomatic agreement in 1787–8 on a general abolition. Granting Wilberforce access to the papers of the customs service to pursue his research into the scope of the trade, Pitt also directed his envoy Eden to raise the prospect of a joint treaty with France to abolish transatlantic trafficking. By January 1788 Pitt was highly optimistic, writing to Eden that he believed 'you will find the French government in a disposition to concur with the measure in its fullest extent', and thus also able to influence the Spanish and Dutch governments to join an abolition.[10] A Bill to end the trade was forced off the Commons agenda in 1788, ironically by the 'humanitarian' impeachment of Warren Hastings, though a minor measure to improve conditions of carriage in slave ships was passed. Responses from Spain and the Dutch were not encouraging, but Pitt saw great prospects from the arrival in power of Jacques Necker. Out of office in 1784, Necker had shown interest in a 'general European concert' to end the slave trade, and Pitt was hopeful that his return would now 'enable us to settle something'.[11] This drive at the highest level was matched by the internationalism of the most committed activists.

February 1788 brought the formation in Paris of the Société des Amis des Noirs, or Society of Friends of the Blacks. Unlike the British and American groupings, this was not principally motivated by religion, but by a more secular spirit of Enlightenment and progress. Its two leading lights were men with great, if turbulent, revolutionary futures ahead of them. Étienne Clavière was fifty-three years old, a financier and political economist of note and a man who had already had to flee the failure of one revolution, in his native Geneva in 1782. He spent two years in Ireland and England before settling in Paris, where he revolutionised the insurance industry, setting up France's first modern life-assurance company in 1787. Continuing a collaboration with Jacques-Pierre Brissot that had begun with pamphleteering and grown into the 'Gallo-American Society', Clavière's foundation of the Friends of the Blacks tapped into a wider circle of idealism.

Its foundation was announced in the new newspaper run by Mirabeau, disingenuously named the *Analysis of English Papers*, but increasingly offering a commentary on French affairs. On 31 January 1788 the paper published a letter from Brissot and Clavière in which they declared they had been 'named as agents and correspondents' by the London abolitionist society.[12] Brissot had been in London in late 1787, still embroiled in the fallout of his earlier failed schemes, but this move launched him into far greater respectability. The Friends of the Blacks attracted what might be called a 'reform aristocracy'. The marquis de Condorcet, perpetual secretary of the French Académie des Sciences, joined, as did the *abbé* Sieyès from the future Society of Thirty. Lafayette became a member at once and wrote that he was sorry that 'the National Assembly was still too far off to be able to share in the glory which the English Parliament is about to gain' – a very telling phrase in his thinking, since the Estates-General would not take on the title 'National Assembly' for over a year, and it would be a revolutionary innovation when it did.[13]

When the Estates-General did loom, Condorcet wrote in impassioned terms to Lafayette about the issue of slavery:

> It is in the Estates-General that the cause of the Negroes should be pleaded, and it is to you, the hero of American liberty, the wise and zealous advocate of the noble resolution on behalf of Negroes, the generous man who has devoted part of his fortune and some of his brilliant youth to the search for ways to break the chain that his eyes ought ever to see – it is to you that belongs the defence there of Liberty and the Rights of Man, which are the same for all, no matter what their colour or their country may be.[14]

We should note, however, that Lafayette provides a telling example of the intricate connection of slavery to society. Much as his fellow liberal the duc d'Orléans profited from investments in Saint-Domingue, Lafayette owned plantations in French Guiana, on the coast of South America. Here, though the well-meaning marquis instructed his managers to carry out experiments in agricultural improvement, to pay slaves at least a token salary for their labour and to refrain from corporal punishment, there is little evidence that such noble intentions were followed through on the ground. Lafayette, like hundreds of such wealthy investors, continued nonetheless to take the remittances from slavery as part of his considerable income.[15]

While Condorcet's rhetoric might be emotive, the goals of the Friends of the Blacks were more coolly programmatic. First, international agreement was to be sought to end the slave trade. As Sharp, Clarkson and Wilberforce organised public opinion in Britain's parliamentary state, so the society would lobby the Ministry of the Navy (which also controlled colonial affairs) in France's absolutist monarchy to the same ends. Following the achievement of this goal, a multi-generational gradual abolition of slavery itself was envisaged, linked to a radical shift in the basis of engagement with Africa and the Caribbean.[16] Here the thinking of Clavière and his associates linked up with the views of Pitt, and indeed Adam Smith, whom Pitt viewed as a mentor.[17] Trade and industrial progress were the keys to advancing 'civilisation'. The Friends of the Blacks wrote of mechanisation of sugar-cane processing revolutionising an industry held back by the irrational demands of slavery. They also envisaged Africa opening up to the commercial penetration of European trade, and indeed saw that as coming about through renewed, albeit more temperate, forms of colonisation. While there could be no swift liberation of the slaves, for their 'moral faculties' were insufficiently developed, there could be a process of making them and the Africans 'susceptible to numerous needs to which their civilisation gives birth', and thus yoking them to dependence on manufactures while drawing from their societies the produce of agriculture and mineral extraction.[18]

Pitt struck a similar note in yet another abortive debate in 1792. He likened the condemnatory position of some about Africans to a 'Roman Senator' who could have said of the benighted Britons, '*there* is a people that will never rise to civilisation – *there* is a people destined never to be free', and he went on to perorate epically about the prospects for a free Africa:

We may live to behold the natives of Africa engaged in the calm occupations of industry, in the pursuits of a just and legitimate commerce. We may behold the beams of science and philosophy breaking in upon their land, which, at some happy period in still

later times, may blaze with full lustre; and joining their influence
to that of pure religion, may illuminate and invigorate the most
distant extremities of that immense continent.[19]

As the Roman language makes clear, it was empire that would bring
these benefits, and that would thus enrich the European metropolis
even more than the regions on which he proposed to shine 'the
beams of science and philosophy'. It was a long stretch from being
humanitarian to being egalitarian, and what was accommodated
easily in the idealistic rhetoric of abolition was to fit far less comfortably within the structures, and strictures, of societies built on
property and colonies. Revulsion at slavery might have penetrated
the highest echelons of politics and begun its slow crescendo among
the educated public, but this development coincided with an accelerating denial of traditional freedoms to the working population of
these same societies. The political economy that taught forward-
thinking statesmen the folly of enslavement to the whip would lead
them to see no evil in enslavement to the machine, and produce a
generation of strife.

The ties that bound together the working people of Britain, France
and the Americas were intricate and subtle. At one level they were
composed of the parallel evolution of quite different societies from
agriculture and handicraft towards industrial production, and the
attendant pressures and conflicts of that process. At another level
they reflected the similar tensions that even these very different
societies experienced between the wealthy and powerful, and those
who were neither. At a third level, individuals could, by force or
choice, weave their ways through two or three of the different set-
tings of this fluid, Atlantic world. One such was William Brown, a
sailor who had the bad luck to be captured after demanding a shilling
from a householder during the Gordon Riots of June 1780, 'or by
God I have a party that can destroy your house presently'. Tried, convicted and hanged only five days later, he had pleaded with the court
to spare his life, offering to re-enlist in the navy. It was there his troubles had probably started, for he had been in the crew of HMS
*Serapis*, which nine months before his death had fought an epic duel
off the Yorkshire coast with the American John Paul Jones's
*Bonhomme Richard*, itself named in token of another connection, for

this was the title under which Benjamin Franklin's famous almanac had found renown in France. It was to France that Jones sailed with Brown and five hundred other prisoners after *Serapis* succumbed, and from there that Brown must have made his way home, under the perilous and shadowy circumstances of a Channel crossing in wartime, to the penniless condition that would earn him death for the price of a day's work.[20]

While Lord George Gordon's rabid anti-Catholicism might have raised the mobs that terrified propertied London that June, there was far more to their actions than religious prejudice. Their most spectacular deeds, the opening of the prisons of the capital amid scenes of arson that observers likened to 'the final consummation of all things', showed a contempt for the law and its instruments that reflected a dramatic tension over just what it meant to be a member of society. 'A vast concourse of people' were gathered, and the keys of Newgate prison were brandished like magical talismans, their very sight causing the main gates to be opened by a terrified turnkey.[21] One leader of the crowds, whose friends later pleaded insanity on his behalf, offered a strikingly lucid account of his motivations when put on trial: it had all been for 'the Cause', he said, and only when asked did he elaborate, as if it were self-evident, that 'there should not be a prison standing on the morrow in London'.[22] Those who worked for their living had long had to fight for the respect of those above them, and to secure what they felt were their rights. In the years approaching 1789 the workings of the economy and the majesty of the laws were combining to threaten the skills, the rights and the very freedoms of those who worked with their hands.

The sorts of freedom enjoyed by the eighteenth-century common people were rough and ready by modern standards. Insecurity was their usual lot. In Britain in particular, the common people had long moved away from living from the land and were dependent in one form or another on payment for labour, some in agriculture but more in the new staple industries that had swelled across the century. Country districts across northern England in particular were occupied more by spinners and weavers of cloth, makers of stockings and shoes and by many kinds of other household-based proto-industries, than by farming alone. Similar scenes abounded in France, though here such industrious districts co-existed with a far wider peasant class: Normandy and the lower Loire Valley were filled with cotton- and linen-weavers' cottages, in Flanders the wool trade flourished, while to the south, around Lyon and Nîmes, it was silk that was spun and woven on thousands of frames and looms. In towns, goods were being produced increasingly on what we would now call an industrial scale, including shoes and clothes to be sold cheaply to other workers or shipped as bulk cargo to American and other markets. The cutlers of Sheffield, the iron workers of Saint-Étienne or the trinket-makers of Birmingham, where the smoke of a thousand forges marked the surrounding area as the Black Country, all showed how dramatically industry could concentrate even when its individual units remained small and hand-driven.

Both Paris and London were centres of fine and luxury production: tailoring for royal courts, goldsmithing, carriage-making, fine lacquer-work and a hundred other intricate and skilled occupations supported burgeoning populations. Alongside the genuine luxury trades, there was a growing market for the appearance of luxury at a better price. Social aspiration and material transformation – for example, coloured cottons replaced silk brocades – combined to see both the rising middle classes and spendthrift young workers decking themselves out in previously unattainable finery. Innovations in technology led ceramics to replace pewter and silverware for crockery, bringing easily replaceable splashes of colour to tens of thousands of homes. As techniques of engraving and printing improved, so coloured prints (from the religious to the scatologically political) also came to be seen even in workers' homes, along with increasing numbers of books, for literacy among the urban workers, educated in parish and charitable schools, was a majority achievement from mid-century on.

None of this, however, provided stability or security for these populations. Much work was seasonal, most obviously that linked to agriculture, but also, for example, tailoring, which fell into depression every summer as aristocrats fled the cities for their country estates. Aristocrats were also notorious for not paying their bills, and while tradesmen might hanker after a noble clientele for the tone it lent their business, they might also find themselves laden with years of ignored invoices. As ever more of the population grew dependent on what we now think of as waged work, it is instructive to note just how problematic that 'wage' could be. Money itself was often a commodity in short supply. Britain's Royal Mint had issued new copper coins only once in thirty years by the 1780s, and that had been a small batch of halfpennies. By some estimates as much as two-thirds of all the small change in circulation was faked.[23] Wages just could not be paid on time, so that even in the Royal Dockyards, where a contented workforce might be thought a matter of national security, workers were often owed a year or more's money and then paid in paper drafts that had to be discounted by brokers to produce hard cash.[24] In such an atmosphere money wages could be only part of a worker's remuneration, so the custom of many trades was to supplement them with perquisites.

What were customary rights for one party were for the other, their employers, outright theft. In the dockyards the right to take waste wood was known as 'chips', while in tailoring scrap cloth was 'cabbage' and hatters called the practice 'bugging'. Customary practices and dishonesty shaded into one another: watchmakers might feel entitled to keep gold filings, but a shoemaker who pawned fine leather and replaced it with cheaper stuff presumably knew he was committing a theft. Dock workers who sewed pockets inside their coats for smuggling out sugar, or weavers who impregnated cloth with kettle steam to raise its weight and price, had likewise crossed a clear line.[25] Or had they? Workers spoke out about the 'oppressions' they suffered from employers: lies about market conditions to force down agreed payments, dishonesty in weighing or measuring finished goods, false deductions from payments, and payment in 'truck': goods or other items at inflated values instead of an honest rate of exchange. In 1787 one Sheffield cutler even tried to insist that his workers provide thirteen knives in every dozen he paid for, occasioning a vitriolic poetic response:

> That offspring of tyranny, baseness and pride
> Our rights hath invaded and almost destroyed
> . . .
> And may the odd knife his great carcass dissect;
> Lay open his vitals for all to inspect
> A heart full as black as the infernal gulf
> In that greedy, blood-sucking, bone-scraping wolf.[26]

As this language of rights makes clear, what was taking place in the decades up to 1789 was a struggle as political as any revolution, and one that workers were slowly and steadily losing. Specific legislation against 'embezzlement' in shoemaking and other trades had been passed in the 1720s and 1730s. Acts against hatters in 1749, watch-makers in 1754 and worsted-weavers in 1777 criminalised what workers regarded as customary practice and went against natural jus-tice by presuming guilt. The Worsted Acts allowed conviction on the unsupported oath of the employer, and other Acts made failure to return surplus items theft by default.[27]

The conflict was political, social, technological, logistical. In the eighteenth century employment was not recognised as a contract between equals. Where workers agreed with a supplier to turn raw materials into finished goods, those workers saw themselves not as 'employed' at all, but as free contractors, especially as they usually worked without supervision and in many cases in their own homes. Even in organised workplaces, such as docks and dockyards, workers strove to retain that idea that they were independent and had their customary rights, because the alternative was servitude. Not for nothing were employers in the eighteenth century usually termed 'masters'. Domestic servants came by law, in all these countries, under the paternal authority of their master; they were not 'free' as an independent worker was. Many in the 1780s still shipped out to the Americas under indentures, bound to servitude for a term of years. And to see the end point of the process, one had only to look to the slaves of the sugar plantations. European workers knew a great deal about slavery. In London alone there were thousands of ex-slaves, and similar numbers in the Atlantic seaports of both Britain and France, and the experiences they had escaped from were part of the common currency of resistance. Forms little better than slavery also prevailed even in the heart of the manufacturing dis-tricts. Orphan boys and girls were regularly sold in job lots to masters for work in mills and factories, where they lived as prisoners of poverty and in many cases perished of neglect or accident.

Exemplary employers such as Josiah Wedgwood and his Birmingham friend Matthew Boulton, who both opened pioneering new works at the end of the 1780s, were exceptions to some of these practices. At Wedgwood's Stoke potteries, culminating with the 1789 opening of the Etruria works, and at Boulton's complex at Soho in Birmingham, crowned in 1788 with a steam-powered coining mill, regular wages and humanitarian treatment were the norm. But this went along with a control over the work process that was alien to skilled workers, and with an intensifying regime of fines and other punishments to hold them to that control. Such men would brook no challenge to their place as master in their own house, and as such practices revealed their productive superiority and began to spread steadily across the land, this represented an epochal shift in the nature of work. It was a view that also carried across the Atlantic, so that American workers, who might have seemed more fortunate than most, faced prejudice and scorn. The lands of the United States certainly bore none of the marks of the feudal past that disfigured Europe, an absence that continued to baffle travellers from the old continent. The French consul general in America in the 1780s, the marquis de Barbé-Marbois, related an anecdote about stopping some Massachusetts harvesters in their fields and interrogating them about their burdens – who was the local lord, what duties did he impose, how high was the tithe, what taxes were levied on alcohol or tobacco? The man addressed 'started to laugh' and told the marquis that justice in America was 'neither high nor low' (common forms to describe lords' rights), 'but perfectly fair and equal for everyone, and we could not make him understand at all what sorts of beings lords of the village were'.[28]

Undoubtedly such men's burdens were lighter than those of the French, with none of the ties of lordship to bind them; and unlike in Britain, there was to all appearances an abundance of land for families to set up independently, and workers were free from the constraints of a market economy and 'masters' of all kinds. Certainly their revolutionary experience in the 1770s had stood many in good stead when it came to asserting their rights as citizens. In Philadelphia artisans and craftsmen, or 'mechanics' as the age called them, were active in local bodies, following the traditions of self-help that Franklin had helped to start decades earlier. Here and in Boston committees of mechanics were prominent in promoting, and subsequently celebrating, the ratification of the new Constitution. But that assertion itself was sometimes borne of tension. In New York, where mechanics held seats on the state legislature, they were often rebuffed for their presumption. The Federalist champion Alexander Hamilton warned them in 1785 that 'there is a certain proportion or level in all the departments of industry. It is folly to think to raise any of them.'[29] A General Society of Mechanics sought incorporation from the legislature that year, creating an organisation to oversee workers' rights, which was granted but later vetoed by a higher state court. It reasoned that 'a community of free citizens pursuing the public interest' should be protected from the formation of 'corporations, influenced by partial views'.[30] The existence of a Chamber of Commerce, representing the 'partial views' of the wealthier merchant community, was ignored.

This kind of self-serving protection of local elites was one reason why the mechanics of the seaboard cities came out strongly in favour of the new Constitution, since it offered at least the promise of a larger, countervailing power to such interests. The stout Massachusetts yeomen who had shrugged off Barbé-Marbois' ill-informed questions were of course the same class that had risen a few years later in Shays's Rebellion, as merchants and politicians conspired to grind them under a burden of unfair tax and debt. While Washington had despaired of such events as a 'triumph for the advocates of despotism', Jefferson had been more sanguine, offering from his ambassador's post in Paris one of his most famous aphorisms: 'The tree of liberty must be refreshed from time to time with the blood of patriots and tyrants.'[31] This view, which essentially shrugged off the matter, was easy to take from a Parisian *salon* in 1786. It would be less so by the end of 1789.

In France the war over work was fought on different ground, with even higher political stakes, but with remarkably similar outcomes. While in Britain trades tended to be organised as loose associations of individuals, and the medieval structure of craft guilds was reserved for prosperous remnants of an older order, such as those who governed the City of London, the guilds in France were an active part of the absolutist political system. Guild authorities, made up of those who had paid substantial fees for a 'mastership' in a particular trade and town, had formal police authority over wide-ranging aspects of working life. They controlled access to trades through apprenticeship standards, they oversaw the employment of qualified workers or 'journeymen' by masters, they set prices and standards of materials and workmanship and they defended the local monopoly of their trade against both unlicensed outsiders and encroachment from other guilds with neighbouring specialisms. By their very existence the guilds sucked workers into conflicts in several ways. Their insistence on their rights of police over the workplace challenged journeymen who negotiated as individuals with specific masters, especially when those individual masters were themselves often in conflict with the guilds. For the guild hierarchy was not a disinterested authority – guilds had their cliques and their cabals, their favourites and outsiders, and the regulations they enforced could be treated laxly or punitively at the whim of the officers involved. Moreover, when guilds clashed among themselves, most often over who had the right to undertake a certain work process or sell a certain kind of product, journeymen and other workers were embroiled in legal argument and sometimes physical confrontation.[32]

Such tensions were part of the atmosphere of guild life, but other conflicts reflected more directly on the nature of the workers themselves and their claims of right. While British workers were all too often limited to fruitless petitions and poetic laments, French journeymen had legal recourse for their grievances. As the central role of the *parlements* demonstrates, France was a highly legalistic society, and the rights and wrongs of working practices and disputes frequently ended up in the courts. Journeymen, organised in their own associations, hired lawyers and defended their rights against masters on the basis both of abstract legal principle and the specific rights they said derived from guild statutes. Like British workers who defended their customary rights, French journeymen set out a vision of themselves as autonomous and dignified individuals, unfairly abused by masters who assailed the spirit of free labour in search of unjust profits. The world of work, in this interpretation, was under constant attack by those who would reduce its inhabitants to slavery.[33]

This view found ironic, but short-lived, support from the French state itself. Under the idealistic Finance Minister Turgot in the mid-1770s there was a brief attempt to abolish the entire structure of the guilds and introduce a genuine free market in craft production. Anyone who paid an annual levy was to be allowed to register as a trader, employ journeymen and sell items without geographical or other restriction. While 'liberated' journeymen reportedly rioted in joy, and also overwhelmed officials with their demands for registration, the guilds and their friends in the legal hierarchy (who found adjudicating on their disputes to be a very profitable core business) helped force the collapse of the measure as part of Turgot's overall fall from grace. Noteworthy also in this episode was the attitude of the royal police who were given the task of registering 'free' workers. Hard-pressed, they began to find spurious reasons for refusing registrations – spurious in terms of the legislation, but meaningful in their own minds. Workers unable to display sufficient moral credentials, and those lacking in solid community foundations or known to the police for other reasons, were refused the right to trade.[34] The notion that the guilds existed specifically to police their workers, always built into the structure of their practices, grew more intense after Turgot's experiment. When the guilds were 'restored' the state seized the opportunity to modernise their structures. This meant amalgamating many guilds into larger, more coherent bodies, but it also meant writing out of their new statutes any defence of workers' rights.

In the last decade before 1789 French workers saw their influence over their work decisively challenged. Not only did their recourse to the law dramatically shrink, but in the workplace itself they had to face new threats. In the restored guilds money became the only criterion for mastership, and in addition to this dilution of influence, workers also faced up to the legal right of such masters to employ unqualified people as *alloués*, or 'hired men', alongside and in place of those who had passed an apprenticeship.[35] To French administrators who had absorbed the free-market lessons of the Enlightenment, and who looked to the growing power of a British manufacturing sector freed from antiquated restrictions, this policy seemed the only way forward for greater national prosperity. Combined with other features of life in the 1780s, however, it was a recipe for growing social tension.

Populations in both Britain and France were rising rapidly, and on an accelerating curve. From some five or six million in the early decades of the century, the British population was on course to double within another two decades. In France, which began the century in several episodes of famine with a population of around twenty-one million, a third again had been added by 1789, half of them within the last generation. The explanation for this is complex. In Britain a wave of agricultural innovation had certainly increased productivity, with new systems of crop rotation, more scientific programmes of breeding and the introduction of a variety of machines to reduce wastage in sowing and harvesting. This was facilitated, and made concrete in the countryside, by a significant wave of 'enclosures', the consolidation, usually by Act of Parliament, of lands formerly farmed under medieval arrangements of open 'strips' into fenced and hedged plots where individual landowners could innovate free from customary restrictions. But in France there was little of this, and indeed observers spoke with despair of the poverty of the countryside and its resistance to change. With three times the surface area, France achieved some of the support for its extra population simply by taking more wasteland into cultivation, but both the French and British also relied more and more on foods, grain especially, brought from international markets. Between increased productivity in some regions, and greater reliance on long-distance and international movements of food, the majority of the population that lived partly at least from forms of waged work was increasingly dependent on buying rather than growing its food.

Just as the burgeoning force of the free market in employment was straining social relations, so too the impact of such markets on consumption created anxiety, outrage and sometimes violent protest. In the traditional mentality of this and earlier centuries it was immoral and unjust to seek profit at the expense of those who needed to eat. Markets in food were a service for the common good, not an opportunity for enrichment. Legislation in Britain dating back to the sixteenth century forbade practices such as 'forestalling' and 'engrossing': keeping food back from markets or buying it before it reached them, to drive up prices. In France the royal police supervised food markets, particularly for grains and flour, determining prices and finely monitoring quality and quantities of deliveries. In both countries laws and regulations kept the first hours of market days for local people to make purchases, keeping out wholesale merchants until others' needs were satisfied, and hedged all aspects of the trade around with cautions and prohibitions.[36] All this was true, and yet at the same time highly inconvenient to governments who saw free circulation, created by profit-seeking merchants, as the real answer to supply problems. Such problems were real: the advances in agriculture had still not ruled out the possibility of shortage in years of bad weather and goods could still be moved no faster than a wagon or a barge could carry them.

But for the ordinary consumers of British and French towns and cities – and increasingly in the villages, where land was parcelled among a growing population, and waged work was coming to dominate family budgets – the free market for grain was a threat to existence to be met with legitimate resistance. In the half-century before 1789 there were five major waves of food-rioting, 'insurrections' or 'risings of the poor' in Britain against high prices, and countless smaller protests.[37] In France the situation was aggravated as official and well-publicised moves to withdraw controls from markets seemed to accompany shortages, and thus these were often viewed as deliberate conspiracies to starve the poor. After several episodes in the 1760s of abortive reforms, Turgot's short-lived administration tried once again, in parallel with his attack on the guilds, to strip the police from the market place. The result was the 'Flour War' of 1775.

The spark for a dramatic explosion of social grievances came at the market town of Beaumont-sur-Oise, near Paris, on Thursday 27 April 1775. On the 22nd a price of twenty-six *livres* for a sack of mixed wheat and rye had provoked murmuring, and when the next market, five days later, appeared well stocked, customers expected to see a fall in price, and were reported later to have clearly threatened violence, saying that 'starving or being killed amounted to the same thing'.[38] When one trader demanded thirty-two *livres* per sack he was seized and dunked in the local fountain, then dragged to the office of the municipal authorities, where demands were made for an order to lower prices. Adhering to the free-market regime, the authorities, in the shape of the local senior notary, refused, but then had to watch as the crowd seized full control of the market place, drove out the merchants and sold off the grain for twelve *livres* a sack. This action went by the name of *taxation populaire* and was acclaimed by the common people as a time-honoured right in periods of crisis. Only three men of the state's mounted police were in the town, and one of those was a fifty-five-year-old invalid. Neither the initial riot nor its contagious spread could be checked.

The next day the neighbouring town was the site of pillage as soon as its market opened, word having been carried by individuals from Beaumont of the previous day's events. On that same day a grain barge moored at a mill on the Oise was stripped of a shipment worth over nineteen thousand *livres* by individuals from at least seventeen villages. Although they reportedly set a price of eighteen to twenty *livres* per sack, the owner of the grain said only some three hundred *livres* had actually changed hands. Over the following days the disorders spread rapidly, reaching the market of Versailles on 2 May and ripping through Paris on 3 May, when only police action to close the gates of the central markets protected them from pillage. Reports said that over a thousand individual bakers' premises were stripped. Once again money was sometimes paid at the popularly determined 'just price', sometimes not.

Incidents fanned out across the Paris Basin, amounting eventually to some three hundred separate disorders over twenty-two days. On twelve occasions barges or carts were intercepted en route to urban markets, and there were over eighty riots that began in markets, of which almost half spread to take in systematic searches for grain stored in urban property for wholesale distribution. This was a developing economic trend in grain-exporting areas, and one which, in the people's mind, stank of secret conspiracy to keep grain away from open sale. Doors were battered down, proprietors threatened with murder or arson and huge stocks of grain disappeared, again usually with only token payment at best. It was also in the grain-exporting areas that the most widespread form of disorder occurred, where over two hundred communities experienced expeditions of peasants to the premises of prosperous farmers, which they stripped of grain stored on site for later sale. As in the urban disturbances, rioters brooked no interference and did not hesitate to break into barns and storerooms, or to issue threats to those who tried to stop them. Nevertheless, in all these episodes, which frequently involved the actions of hundreds of people at a time, no one was killed or even seriously injured. To restore order on the state's terms nonetheless took twenty-five thousand troops and three months of effective martial law across the region.

In Britain similar fears of the export of grain – a practice supported, much to the anguish of the population, by official state bounties intended to promote trade – led to smaller-scale but no less determined opposition. At Padstow in Cornwall in 1773 a contemporary recorded that in 'the devil and all of a riot'

> Seven or eight hundred tinners [tin-miners] went thither, who first offered the corn-factors seventeen shillings for 24 gallons of wheat; but being told they should have none, they immediately broke open the cellar doors, and took away all in the place without money or price.[39]

The sense of right involved in such assaults was captured vividly in a notice nailed to the market cross in Carlisle, on the English–Scottish border, one day in 1783. Naming two local merchants, it went on:

> This is to give you warning that you must Quit your unlawfull Dealing or Die and be Damned your buying the Corn to starve the Poor Inhabitants of the City . . . to send to France and get the Bounty . . . but by the Lord God Almighty we will give you Bounty at the Expence of your Lives you Damed Roagues.[40]

Riotous protest was nothing unusual. When Benjamin Franklin first came to London in 1764 he was able to write home that he had witnessed in a single year 'riots in the country about corn; riots about elections; riots about work-houses; riots of colliers; riots of weavers; riots of coal-heavers; riots of sawyers; riots of chairmen; riots of smugglers in which custom-house officers and excisemen have been murdered and the king's armed vessels and troops fired at'.[41] More than once in the middle decades of the century the king's own carriage had been chased and stoned in the streets of London, though never, as Pitt's had been in 1784, physically smashed. Such had been the fervour of supporters of John Wilkes, a disreputable radical MP in the late 1760s, that the cry 'Wilkes and No King!' had resounded through the streets of London, while ministers and peers had their windows smashed, and troops had to put down one riot with gunfire.[42] It is a telling marker of the acceptance of such disorder in the political culture of the time to note that Wilkes, rehabilitated, was Lord Mayor of London by 1780 and proved himself one of the stouter supporters of order during the Gordon Riots of that year.

A remarkably casual approach to violent protest, provided it stopped short of actual bloodshed and widespread destruction, was taken to be an essential component of 'English liberty' as contemporaries defined it. While in many aspects of social life, as we have seen, French practices converged with those of the Anglo-Saxons even when approaching from a very different direction, this was one point on which there was a basic philosophical divergence. French practices of law and order were governed by a notion of *la police*, a term far more capacious than is commonly registered by the humble

English usage of the same word. For the servants of the French state, the population was something to be controlled. It was this belief that placed such value on the role of the guilds in licensing and chastising unruly workers, and which had led state officials to undermine Turgot's free-market experiments with their own moralising concerns. While London, a city of a million people by the 1780s, lacked any police beyond ineffectual parish constables and the handful of famous 'Bow Street Runners', the 650,000 Parisians were watched over by hundreds of uniformed officers of the *garde* and *guet*, and by a permanent military garrison. Moreover, Paris was also surveyed by a more secretive police force. From the *lieutenant-général de police*, down via a network of *inspecteurs* to a force of *observateurs*, *exempts* and more or less criminal informers and agents, the monarchical state penetrated what it saw as a dangerous underworld. Such officers were willing to intervene to break up criminal gangs and networks of prostitution, though just as likely to 'turn' such people for their own ends, and occasionally to live off their earnings. The police also investigated and monitored groups from homosexuals to poets, anyone who might produce by word or deed destabilising consequences for a royal, Catholic moral order.[43]

Those who did contravene often faced a spell in a royal prison as a result: in Paris this might well be the feared Bastille, though the nearby château of Vincennes was also frequently used. Those whose words were taken to be genuinely seditious – the equivalent perhaps of one caught in London saying, 'Wilkes and No King' – might be locked away for years, interrogated repeatedly about associates and co-conspirators, in the conviction that dissent from the lower orders was always a symptom of disturbance begun higher up. Thus, while in Britain it was a matter of accepted fact that politicians stirred up mobs for their own purposes, whether at notably riotous Westminster elections or elsewhere, in France even the very shadow of such activity was pursued with a rigour that frequently surpassed reason.[44]

Contradictions continued to abound on both sides of the Channel, however. The 1775 Flour War showed that French communities in and around Paris were not to be cowed by *la police* when their material interests were stricken, and the evolution of the British 'Bloody Code' across the century challenges a libertarian view of Anglo-Saxon justice. There were some two hundred offences on the English statute book at the end of the 1780s for which the penalty was death. Almost all were for crimes against property, and over a hundred had been added in the course of the past three-quarters of a century. Across the century as a whole, capital convictions in London, the only area for which reliable statistics exist, fluctuated, from over a thousand in the 1710s to a low of some 411 in the 1750s, rising again to 1162 in the 1780s. Many sentences were commuted, on a rising trend through the latter half of the century, but the total of actual executions still rose from 281 in the 1750s to 517 in the 1780s – almost an average of one execution a week.[45] Until 1783 hangings were carried out at the notorious 'Tyburn Tree', near today's Marble Arch, where scenes of disorder were common. Public execution was a spectacle intended to exert an exemplary influence on the lower orders, and the extent to which they turned it into a sort of customary fair became increasingly troubling. For that reason, hangings were moved to the rebuilt Newgate prison in the City, remaining public but within a more controllable environment.[46]

It is notable that executions did not run in parallel with the rising definitions of capital crime. The law was understood at least as much as a threat as a system of punishment. For most crimes in Britain the victim had to initiate prosecution and potentially bear its costs, so grandiose statutes were reduced in practice to the willingness of a property owner to pay out to see a malefactor punished; or not, if the evidence was lacking. Where offences were against the state, pursuit was more uniform, but this too could expose contradictions and dilemmas in the use of capital punishment for social control. The shortage of coinage in Britain, as noted earlier, produced an epidemic of forgery or 'coining' in the 1780s in particular. When this involved gold or silver coins it was a crime of high treason. The traditional penalty for this crime, for a man, was to be hanged, drawn and quartered, a fate so medieval in its barbarism that it had been all but abolished and replaced by simple hanging. For women, however, the penalty for high treason was to be burned at the stake. Twice within a year, in June 1788 and March 1789, that sentence was carried out in front of Newgate, as it had been in 1786. While some newspapers denounced the 1788 execution as 'torturing barbarity on the body of [an] unhappy female', other publications simply used the executions as an occasion to trot out hackneyed verses on the suffering and repentance of the victims, of the kind long sold to accompany both Newgate executions and their more raucous Tyburn predecessors.[47] Though the March 1789 execution was to be the last of its kind, the practice being abolished soon after, it was noticeable that a decisive force in the debate was the personal revulsion of the sheriffs, the men obliged to oversee the actual burning, rather than a wider public concern.

Britain faced a genuine crisis in its systems of social and criminal control in the 1780s. Since 1718 the preferred solution for dealing with most criminals – those who had been sentenced to hang and then reprieved, and those convicted of many lesser crimes – was transportation. Until 1776 a rising tide of individuals had been shipped across the Atlantic to the Americas: some fifty thousand in all, including ten thousand women, mostly young, and mostly guilty of little more than petty theft. Transportation filled a gap between corporal and capital punishment so effectively that while whippings were carried out by the hundred each year in London alone, the whole country had a mere 653 prison inmates in 1776, over four hundred of whom were debtors, not criminals.[48] Transported by private contractors, and frequently sold into service on arrival, the flood of undesirables into the Thirteen Colonies was one of the many grievances held against the Crown by the Americans that prompted the Declaration of Independence. With this avenue thus blocked up, convicts began to pile up in Britain. Through the war years the situation was difficult enough. The infamous 'hulks', old wooden warships moored in rivers and harbours, were stuffed with inmates, while thousands of other prisoners languished in the local jails normally reserved for those awaiting trial at the seasonal Assizes. Peace in 1783 brought a massive demobilisation of soldiers and sailors, flooding the labour market and driving many, especially young men, into the sort of crimes of desperation that pushed up both the number of capital convictions and the numbers of convicts sentenced to transportation. The result was to be a stark, epochal shift in dealing with the problem of crime, and the related concept of social control – *la police*, in the French sense – that underpinned the definition of that problem itself.

British, and more particularly English, justice in the eighteenth century rested on two fundamental premises. One was that determined criminality was something that should be expelled from the body politic, either through the finality of execution or the notionally temporary forms of transportation to distant realms. This would not change in the years after 1789. But a second premise, that punishments should be exemplary, and accompanied by a tempering degree of mercy, amnesty and reprieve, fell away sharply. Harsh corporal and capital sentences, passed in large numbers, then whittled away at in customary displays of clemency by judges themselves, and further on appeal for royal pardons, seemed to do nothing to stem a rising tide of crime in the 1780s. The avenue of transportation was reopened, and tied ever more closely to imperial expansion, with the departure of the First Fleet for New South Wales in 1787. Over the next eighty years Australia would absorb some 158,000 convicts. But far more would pass through radically new systems of imprisonment being developed within Britain itself. For some, such as the former High Sheriff of Bedfordshire, John Howard, who between 1777 and his death in 1790 campaigned tirelessly to expose and improve the shockingly unsanitary and immoral condition of prisons, the issue was largely one of humanitarian concern. But even within this the notion that a remoralisation of prison conditions could make them into places of essentially coercive reformation ran close to the surface.

Under Howard's influence regional reformers in Britain through the 1780s sponsored the construction of jails on new lines – cells, not communal rooms, and segregation by sex and category of prisoner – all designed to prevent them being places of moral contamination. Regimes of management and treatment of inmates were introduced, with the idea of correction and discipline, rather than merely punishment. If the hardened criminal was still essentially given up as lost, and destined for Botany Bay, others might still have a chance. As the sonorously named Sir George Onesiphorous Paul put it about his reforms in Gloucestershire, 'Few men have been hanged for a felony, who might not have been saved to the community for the correction of a former misdemeanour.'[49] From these notions of disciplined correction, which ran in parallel with those of Enlightenment thinkers elsewhere, emerged new conceptions of the right and duty of society (which meant the powerful) actively to shape the behaviour of its members (which meant those with less power). As an idea this would culminate with the elaboration by the polymath philosopher Jeremy Bentham of his *Panopticon*. This scheme, drafted in 1787 and published in 1791, envisaged a building wherein surveillance of all activities all the time was possible. Prisoners, but equally easily factory workers or even schoolchildren, were here imagined as subjects of an overseer's continuous, hidden gaze, which would work on their minds to drive them to behave correctly. From a British thinker emerged the notion that *la police* could be cast in stone, and a model, albeit never fully implemented, for institutions across the world for the century to come.[50]

France, meanwhile, was facing up to the limitations of *la police* in holding back discontent and its associated disorder. Despite the alarming experience of the Flour War, there had been a good deal of smug commentary on the subject of the Gordon Riots, and the impossibility of Paris ever falling out of the control of the authorities. Yet at the same time anxieties grew through the 1780s. The writer Louis-Sébastien Mercier, who produced an encyclopedic survey of Parisian life, felt that insubordination had been 'visible in the common people for several years, and above all among the trades', with a 'neglect of all discipline' that could bring 'the worst effects'.[51] Surveys of the artisan population carried out after stern police regulations were passed in 1781 revealed that many, if not most, were colluding with masters to avoid the official forms of registration required, and going on to form independent workers' groups to assert their autonomy from these new burdens.[52] Throughout the conflicts of the state with the *parlements* that marked 1787 and 1788, the police had repeatedly lost control of protests and demonstrations, and at the moments of the judges' greatest triumphs seemed on the point of yielding the streets entirely to their enflamed supporters.

Out in the French countryside a more sombre conflict, bringing together deep-seated grievances and new conditions of emergency, was bearing down on the common people as 1789 approached. One of its seeds lay in a strange occurrence noted by Benjamin Franklin:

> During several of the summer months of the year 1783, when the effect of the sun's rays to heat the earth in these northern regions should have been greater, there existed a constant fog over all Europe, and a great part of North America. This fog was of a permanent nature; it was dry, and the rays of the sun seemed to have little effect towards dissipating it.[53]

A plume of smoke and gas from the volcanic Laki Fissure in Iceland produced a pronounced deterioration in the weather through this year, the next and into 1785. How far this caused the string of poor harvests that followed is ultimately unfathomable, but what is clear is that French agriculture suffered a slow-burning disaster – in 1785 a failure of forage crops caused by extended drought, in 1786 a poor harvest in the west of the country and a forage-crop failure so severe that many were forced to sell off their livestock.[54] In 1787 a uniformly poor harvest attended the first signs of major political breakdown, stirring tension, and this was turned to real fear by the weather in 1788, when a wet spring retarded the growing season and across a swath of central France crops were devastated by a freak hailstorm on 13 July. As winter drew in, with snowfall and frosts from November of a severity not seen in living memory, it seemed that nature herself was conspiring to add an apocalyptic tinge to a rural landscape already racked with troubles.

Although in some respects rural life in France was being driven by forces of innovation – for example, in the spread of manufacturing work – in other ways the peasantry were burdened by a long history of subjection. While fewer than in Britain had seen their traditional rights to pasture animals, gather firewood and otherwise make use of common land restricted by enclosures, and more had access to their own productive fields, almost all laboured under a regime of feudal exactions that had faded away across the Channel over a century before. Land in France was subject to a series of charges, and the owners and tenants of land to a series of onerous obligations, that descended directly from the rights of the medieval nobility. Hundreds of years earlier the martial nobles of France, like other countries, had defended the communities under their authority as 'seigneurs' – most often from the depredations of other nobles – and had offered them justice in their courts, and charity in times of hardship, in return for a series of payments in money, labour and produce. This was an advance, for the peasants, on an even earlier situation in which their services had been extracted as part of the real unfreedom of serfdom. The extraction of dues from the peasantry became increasingly a financial relationship, and by the eighteenth century had developed for many a clear disconnection with the older notion of a community where patronage reciprocated respect. The feudal or seigneurial rights to payments, which might include charging for local monopolies on milling and bake ovens, and sometimes tolls on bridges and markets, along with rights over harvests, were bought and sold as commodities themselves. Seigneurial status was a desirable possession for the upwardly mobile, and a valuable and secure source of income. By the 1770s and 1780s it was common for successful businessmen to sell up their enterprises and buy a package of feudal rights: a step on the route to future social advancement for their children, alongside the purchase of offices in state administration, for both individual nobles and the monarchy sold off their prerogatives for cash.

Peasant communities thus found themselves legally bound to make payments to individuals who had no connection with their community, who offered none of the old compensations of patronage in return, and who increasingly viewed their seigneurial rights as a resource to be enhanced in any way possible. Indeed both new and older seigneurs in the last third of the century put increased effort into researching, and in some cases inventing, entitlements to payments. In Burgundy seigneurs claimed rights for payment to maintain their châteaux, on the grounds that these 'fortifications' defended the community, and renewed ancient rights to demand 'gifts' on the marriage of their daughters. In the south-west one community was hounded through the courts by a feudal agent claiming dues on a new crop, the potato. As this case implies, peasants were not at all eager to pay up, and we know of these cases precisely because they came to court, sometimes with the seigneur as the plaintiff, but often with the community lodging protests against innovations or extensions of asserted rights.[55] In a countryside increasingly pressured by population growth, and with the middle years of the decade dominated by poor harvests, the rising tide of aggression and counter-aggression over seigneurial rights entrenched a bitterness that was shortly to find explosive outlets.

Rumours of a general uprising, in support of the *parlements* and against the despotic royal state, had begun in the summer of 1788. By September of that year the effects of the poor harvest were already being felt in Normandy, where angry crowds prevented the transport of supplies out of their localities. Many also began to default on the shares of the harvest they were due to pay their seigneurs, and to the Church as its tithe. Meanwhile poor weather and the trade treaty with Britain conspired to drive up unemployment in the textile towns and the surrounding countryside. Larger cities began to fill up, or so was the perception, with the desperate poor in search of charity (or loot, it was feared, as such wanderers were tagged as 'brigands' almost at once). Conversely, the rumour began to circulate that all the various shortages that the country was experiencing came from a plot by those in power, both to make money from inflated prices and to drive the population into the subjection that royal plans were alleged to foreshadow. As rivers froze and olive groves shattered in the cold, the French were caught between the unprecedented excitement of expressing themselves through an Estates-General, and the dread that all their hopes might be snuffed out.

# 7

# 'Constant effort and continuous emulation'

## *The revolutions of cotton and steam*

On the thoroughly auspicious anniversary, 5 November 1788, even as George III was hurling his son across the room in maddened fury, Major John Cartwright held a topping-out ceremony to celebrate completion of his new weaving mill at Retford, Nottinghamshire. Major Cartwright, a gentleman's son, had served as a naval lieutenant during and after the victories of the Seven Years War. For five years he had acted as a magistrate while posted to the Newfoundland station, and acquired a warm sympathy for colonial liberty. Returning home in ill health in 1771 (and acquiring his new rank in the local militia), he became a disciple of the 'Commonwealthman' tradition of political radicalism, and on the outbreak of the American Revolution wrote two noted pamphlets. The first, *American Independence the Interest and Glory of Great Britain*, argued like several others for radical reform at home, to come as the fruit of acknowledging the Americans' rights. God-given rights, in the idiom of the age: 'a title to the liberty of mankind . . . is the immediate, the universal gift of God'; as rights 'not derived from any one, but original in every one . . . the rights of sovereignty reside in the people themselves'.[1] The second, *Take Your Choice*, produced in the independence year 1776, was a landmark publication, for it set an agenda for radical ambitions not to be bettered in generations – a clean sweep of all the corrupt ways of Parliament, a universal manhood franchise, annual elections, equal constituencies and salaried MPs. The 'choice' it offered was spelled out on its first page: 'Representation and Respect – Annual Parliaments and Liberty', or 'Imposition and Contempt – Long Parliaments and Slavery'.[2]

Four years later, as the Association Movement reached its peak, Cartwright had founded the Society for Constitutional Information (SCI), aiming 'to revive in the minds of their fellow-citizens, THE COMMONALTY AT LARGE, a knowledge of their lost rights', and thus to 'restore Freedom and Independence to that branch of the legislature which originates from, represents, and is answerable to THEMSELVES'.[3] Among its dozen other founding members were two clergymen, two doctors, various gentlemen and scholars, and Richard Brinsley Sheridan. Though the era of the Gordon Riots and defeat in America closed down the possibility of immediate success, the SCI set to work propagandising steadily through the next decade. It had links with the Dissenters, who pursued their own enfranchisement down to 1789, and with the London Revolution Society, whose great centenary feast Cartwright perforce missed to attend the completion of his own project 150 miles north.

In honour of the date, and the major's beliefs, it was named Revolution Mill, and 'an hundred of King William's shillings were given to the workmen to regale themselves'.[4] For a man of revolutionary sentiments the enterprise was of a suitably innovative character. When it began operations a few months later it contained over a hundred looms, powered by the largest steam engine that Boulton and Watt had yet built, and thus, quite simply, the largest steam engine in the world – thirty horsepower, twice the size of anything else in existence. Unfortunately, like so many other pioneering enterprises of this time, Revolution Mill, funded by Cartwright and a group of local friends, collapsed into bankruptcy within a year. It was, however, the first attempt to put full-sized power-looms into operation, and to run them by steam. If its failure left the major deeply troubled – he wrote that 'the apprehension of the loss to my friends . . . must sit heavy on my mind' – he might have been even more troubled if he had known how little liberty his own 'Revolution' would foreshadow.[5]

Industrial progress is always full of paradoxes. In creating the wealth on which modern society's freedoms are based, it has often also created subjection and misery. The unhesitating integration of mass slavery into the development of the sugar trade, one of the first recognisably 'modern' commercial networks, is a case in point, and so too is the massively complex process that would build an industrial revolution on slave-grown cotton. The story began in India, from where for over a century the East India Company had done a brisk trade importing fine-quality Indian muslins, calicoes and other plain and patterned fabrics for the European luxury market. The exceptional quality of these materials, and the potential sales value of increased and more local production, drove British traders to investigate their origins closely. Cotton itself was no mystery; it had been grown across the tropical and subtropical latitudes since pre-history, and indeed particularly fine 'Sea Island' cotton came from a variety first discovered under cultivation in South America by the Dutch, and subsequently brought to various Caribbean colonies. The Indians, however, were seen to have particular advantages in the manufacture of cloth, summarised by Richard Orme after his mission to investigate the Bengal trade in the 1770s: 'As much as an Indian is born deficient in mechanical strength, so much is his whole frame endowed with an exceeding degree of sensibility and pliant-ness.' Thus, as the catalogue to an exhibition of images of Indian cotton manufactures put it a few years later, 'the delicate touch, and fine finger of the effeminate Hindoo, gives a degree of softness and flexibility to the thread, which no machine the art of man has yet formed, can at all equal'.[6]

Against this alleged racial distinctiveness was pitted in the 1780s the technological ingenuity of the European, and in the eyes of the East India Company there soon appeared the spectre of defeat. In March 1787 they wrote to their factors in Bengal sharply reducing their orders for 'low priced Doreas' cloth, and bidding their agents encourage the production of the 'finer assortment of mulmalls': the highest-quality cloths. In August 1788 they wrote in even greater anxiety, for there now existed the political threat of a ban on imports, so successfully could British manufacturers argue they had substi-tuted for them with domestic products, and the Company urged that 'The utmost attention must be paid to the manufacture of all our piece goods in general, but more particularly the muslins of the finest Dacca assortments' – because they not only 'yield the greatest profits', but, tellingly, 'interfere the least with the home manu-facturers' whose power was rising so steeply. By 1792 such was the competition that the chairman of the Company himself recorded the 'very trifling quantity of India goods at present worn in Great Britain', and foresaw these sales 'very speedily reduced to nothing in consequence of the low price and great perfection' of British goods in all but the most luxurious categories.[7]

This competition was achieved, of course, with machinery. But such machinery built on a long history of hand production, the original meaning of 'manufacture'. As early as the 1720s Britain was taking in 1.5 million pounds of raw cotton for spinning and subsequent weaving into cheap fabrics: normally mixed with a warp of linen on the loom, for greater strength and ease of handling (and because manufacture of pure cotton cloth was banned by law, to protect the East India Company's monopoly). From the 1750s the Company itself preferred to concentrate on more luxurious goods, opening a gap in the market for home production. By the 1770s this sector was using five million pounds of imported raw cotton annually and had already begun the first moves towards mechanisation.[8] Both spinning and weaving had been subject to continual experimentation and improvement for centuries. For example, the large spinning wheel so familiar from fairy tales and antique shops was a fourteenth-century improvement on the hand-held distaff and other smaller devices, and Adam Smith himself reckoned it increased an individual spinner's output 100 per cent.[9] 'Engines' for carding cotton, the preliminary process of straightening the fibres to make them spinnable, were developed in the mid-1700s, and in 1770 James Hargreaves patented the machine later known as the 'Spinning Jenny', a hand-driven device that took the power of one spinning wheel to multiple bobbins: sixteen in the first designs and later many more.

The Jenny, invented in Lancashire, proved a godsend to the local handloom weavers who were the heart of the British cotton trade. As one account put it, the weavers 'saw with surprise children from nine to twelve years of age manage them with dexterity, whereby plenty was brought into families formerly overburdened with children'. Released from reliance on spinners who had begun to demand high prices for their thread, the handloom weavers flourished on their children's labour, previously useless as weaving was a highly skilled business reserved to adults. But pressures of competition soon drove engineers and entrepreneurs to produce bigger Jennies,

Thomas Paine: propagandist, revolutionary and bridge-builder. *(Bridgeman Art Library)*

Benjamin Franklin, in the fur hat that won the hearts of the French. *(Bridgeman Art Library)*

George III, seen in 1794, recovered from 1789's madness and before his long final decline.

*(Bridgeman Art Library)*

Louis XVI, portrayed in his coronation robes, the awkward face of the man perched atop the splendour of the image.

*(Getty Images)*

Jacques Necker, spikily self-conscious of his virtue; his quest to save the crown through the Estates-General would provoke an attempted *coup*, and a revolution. *(Bridgeman Art Library)*

Charles Alexandre de Calonne, in the full glory of his personal elegance, helped stoke the problems even Necker could not solve. *(Bridgeman Art Library)*

The French Assembly of Notables, here arrayed in the elegant chamber that caused caustic comment even before they met. *(Bridgeman Art Library)*

James Madison, the Virginian intellectual, his frailty amply on display in this portrait from the year of American triumph, 1783. *(Getty Images)*

Alexander Hamilton, the Caribbean-born adventurer – a typically vigorous image from the early months of his tenure as President Washington's Treasury Secretary. *(Getty Images)*

George Washington as President of the United States, in the sombre and restrained dress he wore to his weekly levees. *(Getty Images)*

Charles James Fox as a youthful, though already rotund, statesman in the closing years of the American War. *(Bridgeman Art Library)*

Fox in caricature as a rabble-rousing radical. *(Getty Images)*

William Pitt the Younger, here as statesman and also pensive youth, aged twenty-eight, with five years of the premiership behind him and his greatest trials still ahead.

*(Bridgeman Art Library)*

Pitt in caricature, here quite literally 'bottomless' as he expounds on the happy fiscal conditions of 1792.

*(akg-images)*

The BOTTOMLESS-PITT.

The Comte de Mirabeau, the picaresque and pockmarked rogue who became a parliamentary titan. *(Bridgeman Art Library)*

The Marquis de Lafayette, handsome, vain and arrogantly committed to his own version of the liberty and equality that would be good for France.
*(Bridgeman Art Library)*

that only adults could work, and that required space in workshops and larger buildings: eighty and even 130 spindles were known by the later 1770s, and in 1779 angry workers in the Blackburn area attacked such larger machines, breaking many up as a threat to livelihoods. Nonetheless, numbers continued to grow and some twenty thousand machines were said to be running in 1788.[10]

The Jenny still required immediate attention from an operative, to move the action back and forth to wind on the threads, but meanwhile in 1769 Richard Arkwright had patented a machine for spinning that could be driven continuously by a water-wheel, drawing on earlier ideas coming from the silk trade, where machinery to spin without stressing the delicate threads had been patented, but not widely used, decades earlier. This 'water-frame' was installed by licence in a series of mills and came into even wider use after 1785, when Arkwright lost a momentous court case in defence of his patents. But both Jennies and Arkwright water-frames produced a yarn that was relatively coarse compared with Indian handmades. Samuel Crompton of Bolton, a weaver who as a boy of sixteen in 1769 had worked a Spinning Jenny, laboured a decade later in the attic of his home to bring the Jenny and the water-frame together. His hand-built water-driven machine soon thus became known as the 'mule'. With a delicate balance of twisting and stretching, the mule proved capable of spinning yarns twice as fine as a water-frame.[11] Crompton failed to patent his machine, and as Arkwright's patents, which governed various aspects of spinning with machinery, lapsed, the market was opened up to entrepreneurs who exploded into imitation and improvement.

Since its first importation to Europe, cotton had always been part of a global economy. Raw cotton from the eastern Mediterranean, or Levant, was shipped to Europe in bulk quantities by the later eighteenth century, and cotton manufacturers in Britain had petitioned in 1786 for advantageous terms in the Eden Treaty with France, since the latter's industry had both easier access to the Levant, and a more developed Caribbean cotton cultivation on Saint-Domingue. In March 1788 British muslin manufacturers petitioned Prime Minister Pitt on the scale and prospects of the trade in raw cotton: 'Independent of about five million pounds of cotton wool which is raised in the British West India Islands, the nation pays annually to foreigners for this article about £1,000,000 sterling.' This sum 'could with great propriety and justice be transferred to the East India Company', if it agreed to import raw cotton, rather than finished goods.[12] The Board of Trade, the British government's high-level economic policy body, proposed that the Company should import at least half a million pounds of finest raw cotton, which it agreed to, disappointing the manufacturers who had hoped for no less than six million pounds annually. The Company was pressed by the demand for fine cotton from Indian spinners, and was also reluctant to give up a lucrative export trade to China, where demand was high, and the voyage shorter and cheaper. When 300,000 pounds did turn up in London in 1790, it was of poor quality, enhancing the urgent race already under way for new supplies.[13]

British merchants, and their government, scoured the world for cotton. Portuguese Brazil, supplying under 500,000 pounds each year in the early 1780s, spurted to a trade of 2.5 million pounds in 1787 and 4.8 million in 1789.[14] From 1786, under official encouragement, the governors of various British Caribbean possessions offered bounties or other incentives for cotton cultivation. In India a Polish-born botanist by the name of Anton Pantaleon Hove, commissioned by the Board of Trade itself, spent 1788 and 1789 taking samples of seeds from various cotton-growing areas. These were diligently passed on to the Caribbean, where the results of cultivation were reported back and acted on to improve the quality of the product. Enquiries passed by way of Moscow and the Levant for seeds of Persian cotton, a sample of which had grown well in the colonies.[15] At the end of 1787 the Board of Trade heard the results of experiments in spinning cotton from Senegal, West Africa, which yielded a superfine thread. In the same year the anti-slavery activist Thomas Clarkson founded the Sierra Leone Company. This followed on from an earlier Committee for the Relief of the Black Poor and proposed settling ex-slave refugees from the former North American colonies in West Africa, with cotton-growing as one of their prime employments. Richard Arkwright was another investor, but the project crashed tragically within a few years: native cottons proved of poor quality, imported seeds did not flourish and pests and diseases ate at plants and men alike.[16]

Meanwhile another exodus provoked by the American War, of Loyalist merchants and farmers from the southern states to the British Caribbean, became a reverse flow in the mid-1780s, taking with it the seeds of new varieties of cotton. As experiments began with growing new 'upland' varieties, away from the narrow coastal zone where delicate 'Sea Island' plants already flourished, cotton became part of a debate on America's future. While some such as Thomas Jefferson saw America as a land waiting to be filled by independent yeomen, shunning the corruptions both of urban life and slave-driven agriculture, others foresaw a great future coming from the combination of those very things. Tench Coxe, an economic thinker who had recovered his place in American life after an early flirtation with Loyalism in the 1770s, was by the mid-1780s a great promoter of industrial development and an agricultural base that would support it. Ever since inter-state trade had given the pretext for the meeting of the Annapolis Convention in 1786, leading forward to the new Constitution, on to his appointment as Assistant Secretary of the Treasury under Hamilton in September 1789, Coxe agitated for the newly opened expanses of the South to be filled with cotton. Founding a group called the Friends of American Manufactures, he wrote in 1787 that, compared with 'before the revolution', 'The perfection of the manufactories in Europe has raised it to such a pitch, that . . . the price has risen 50%.' Tobacco, on which Carolina and Georgia planters had hoped to build their post-war fortunes, had already proved a disaster: the *Pennsylvania Gazette* reviewed the future of southern plantations in 1788, noting that tobacco exhausted the soil, required extensive labour and in any case produced a poorer crop in the new lands than in its existing Virginia range. Prices were also falling, as were those of wheat and Carolina rice, with markets ever harder to find.[17] The *Gazette* pressed the case for cotton vigorously: one slave could tend seven acres, and with almost unlimited land for planting, the value of such slaves, currently languishing, could only rise. The argument was clinched for the newspaper by word from across the Atlantic: 'It is well known,' it wrote on 23 April 1788, 'that the cotton manufactories in Great Britain will take any quantity' coming from America, where the cotton crop was 'deemed by good judges to be now only in infancy'.[18]

The prospects for growing southern cotton had been clear to the British merchants eager to supplement their supplies, and some had reportedly visited the area in the mid-1780s to press the case for more development. A mere 1500 pounds of cotton passed through Charleston, South Carolina, for Britain in 1785, but 32,400 in 1787 and 84,600 in 1788. Adding that and other ports together, the trade exploded to over 500,000 pounds in 1789.[19] Ironically, this very success would hinder the aims of Coxe and his fellow friends of manufactures. Far from expanding, America's cotton manufacture contracted in the years around 1789, because its cotton mills simply could not compete with the efficiencies of the British industry. The British consul in Philadelphia reported in 1789 that, even after raw cotton had crossed the Atlantic, and recrossed it as cloth, 'The Manchester goods are sold for 25% less' than local produce. As he went on to note, redoubling the ironies, Manchester merchants had recently been able to slash their prices further, giving a 'sensible check' to American manufactures, thanks to the additional profits made after the Eden Treaty with France.[20]

Some in America, however, remained optimistic. Among their number was George Washington, who wrote to Thomas Jefferson in February 1789 about the exciting prospects he saw for 'manufactures and inland navigation'. Information to hand made him think that Georgia and South Carolina could yield cotton 'of a most excellent quality, and in such abundant quantities as to prove a more profitable species of agriculture, than any other Crop'. With this, and 'the introduction of the late-improved Machines to abridge labour', he foresaw 'almost infinite consequence to America'. He particularly tied it to the development of canals and waterways, writing of connections to be made from Lake Erie to the Ohio river, and from the Ohio to the Potomac river, a survey of which lay in his hands at that moment. The 'abundance of water' allowed for extensive navigation, albeit with 'canals and locks' to skirt the worst patches of geography: 'I need not describe what and how extensive the rivers are which will be thus in a wonderful manner connected,' the statesman almost gushed. He had personally journeyed once again along the Potomac towards its upland sources, scouting locations for 'Mill-seats' that could be secured against the particular dangers of a rigorous climate: spring 'freshes' or floods, 'or the breaking up of Ice'.[21]

The enthusiasm of the president-elect (the Electoral College had met to confirm the expected result the previous month) had been prompted by a house guest, a 'Mr Milne, an English Gentleman', who by Washington's account 'has been for many years introducing those [cotton] manufactures into France, and whose father is now carrying them on (under the protection of government) at the Royal

Chateau of Muette in Passy'.[22] In this innocent phrase is concealed a whole history of international espionage, chicanery and greed that wove the economies of France and Britain tightly together in desperate competition. While Washington's mind was still clearly running to water power, the sharp edge of innovation across the Atlantic had already turned to steam.

Steam engines used as giant pumps, principally for raising water to keep coal mines dry, were an established feature of the eighteenth century. A handful of early 'Newcomen' designs had left British shores for France as early as the 1720s, but there was little demand for these relatively inefficient models, as France, unlike Britain, had barely started on the road to a fossil-fuel economy. The English firm of Boulton and Watt, driven by the former's entrepreneurship and the latter's engineering talent, and cemented by a completely ruthless approach to patent protection for their innovations, emerged in the 1770s as the sole supplier of improved, far more efficient and reliable engine designs. Quite extraordinarily, the first of these new machines to cross the Channel did so in 1779 – in wartime, to an enemy nation. Boulton and Watt secured a special export licence from the Privy Council by arguing that their sale would actually inhibit French development: if they did not supply the engines, 'the French will be obliged to establish manufactories capable of furnishing them not only with Fire Engines but also with many other kinds of Cast Iron goods of a larger size than can now be made in France', harming 'a beneficial branch of commerce' in Britain.[23] The licence they granted to their French partner, Périer, allowed him to produce two further engines from their design. Rather predictably, this deal was reneged on, and evidence suggests it was always Périer's intention to set up independently: by 1789 the Chaillot works established by this trade had produced perhaps as many as forty engines, though few seem to have made a successful impact.

Boulton and Watt faced many kinds of piracy. Their various works were tourist attractions in the later 1780s, and as they developed intricate new means to smooth out the reciprocating action of a steam piston, eventually perfecting a rotating action capable of driving machinery, such tourists were often spies. Their famous Albion Mill at Blackfriars, London, where two engines drove twenty huge millstones to produce 150 bushels of flour per hour, was visited in June 1787 by a French marquis and two members of the Académie des Sciences. The nobleman and one of the scientists were discovered sketching the mechanism secretly, and Boulton angrily banned them from the equally revolutionary Soho metal-working mill in Birmingham, where they were heading next: 'They might have obtained more Knowledge if they had behaved like philosophers and gentlemen, but they are thieves and should be treated as such.'[24] The practice continued nevertheless: one Spaniard openly reported the findings of a 1788 visit to the Académie at the end of 1789, and did not blush about the underhand way his information was acquired.

Steam was just one aspect of a concerted drive by foreign governments, particularly the French, to get their hands on British manufacturing technology. British customs officers even blocked the attempted smuggling of machinery to America in the 1780s.[25] Traditional mercantilist economics had made retention of skills and trade secrets a matter of state policy for centuries. A long procession of Acts of Parliament even made it illegal for skilled workers to leave the country, something extended to the cotton trade by an Act of 1774. Another in 1781 prohibited exports not just of machines, but of any parts, tools, plans or drawings that might assist in building them.[26] Needless to say, this did not stop anyone. At least twenty different individuals and families of British textile workers and machine-makers were being supported in France by the royal administration in the 1780s.

One of these was the family of James Milne, who as early as 1779 had offered various designs of simple machines for cleaning and spinning cotton to the French Crown for around 200,000 *livres*. The family settled in France, and were soon petitioning for another payment of 500,000 *livres* for what were essentially copies of Arkwright's water-frame, though they would assert vigorously that Arkwright had copied them, and tried to lodge legal protection for their own 'inventions' with Paris magistrates.[27] The Milnes became part of Finance Minister Calonne's plans for economic expansion in 1785, and it was at this point that they were given the buildings at La Muette, not far from Paris, where they were to build machines for carding and spinning cotton. Others worked equally hard to turn clandestinely gained knowledge to profit: a group of industrialists in the town of Louviers paid spies, and brought over two Englishmen, to make Arkwright's water-frame work on the more arduous task of spinning wool, rather than cotton: and here the French were almost equal with the British, as only two firms had made this leap in Britain by 1787.[28] Indeed the pace of innovation in Britain in the 1780s seemed to be matched by an accelerating speed of French piracy, aided by the entrepreneurial spirit of internationally minded Britons (or traitorous thieves, according to taste). Crompton's mule, busily pirated in its own country, was brought to France in 1788 by Philemon Pickford, a machine-maker of Ashton, Cheshire, who assembled a hundred-spindle machine at Brive and went on to build another at Melun the same year. The merchants of Amiens, at the heart of the region hit hardest by the Eden Treaty, paid two English workers already in France to go home and obtain spinning machines in 1788. They returned with a water-frame and a 160-spindle mule, which were set to work as a public exhibition to encourage emulation.[29]

All this was fully supported by the French Crown. The government's 'inspectors of manufactures' regularly toured innovative plants, sending reports and recommendations to the centre, and that centre dealt directly with individuals bringing in technology. William Douglas, a mill owner with several Arkwright-driven spinning mills around Manchester, even offered to move his business lock, stock and barrel to France at the end of 1788, apparently because of a sudden sharp dip in local prospects: Necker's government, harassed by preparations for the Estates-General, did not take up his offer, and twenty years later he was still employing over thirteen hundred workers in England and north Wales. The French also had actual secret agents attempting to smuggle machinery and designs out of Britain in the 1780s. One, Bonaventure Joseph Le Turc, was a military engineer who spent over a decade as a roving spy. He succeeded in getting stocking-looms out of the country in 1785, for which he was paid 10,000 *livres*, and a further assortment of machines for preparing raw cotton and wool for spinning the next year. In 1787 he tried unsuccessfully to persuade one of the men who built Boulton and Watt's engines to leave the country, but returned to France with secret technology to mechanise the production of pulley blocks for the navy. A plant to produce these critical items was set up under his management at Lorient, and shown off to the ambassadors of Tipu Sultan, Britain's great rival in southern India, and thus eagerly courted by the French, when they visited in 1788. Too few workers were yet trained, however, for the French to acquiesce in their guests' suggestion that a companion plant be built in Tipu's domain to help challenge British supremacy.[30]

French manufactures found themselves in a critical dilemma, expressed quite clearly by expert commentators after the signing of the Eden Treaty. There were 'over fifty years of constant effort and continuous emulation' behind the British technological lead, and the French hardly knew where to start. Should they, for example, mechanise some processes, and draw in hand-workers for complementary tasks, or focus on all-through mechanisation, at huge cost, but possible strategic advantage? In 1788 the French equivalent of the British Board of Trade noted that the British 'have marched from invention to invention at a pace so rapid, that French industry, plunged into despair and nearly destroyed', had been almost unable to follow.[31] One consequence of this concern, ironically self-defeating, was to latch onto any prospect for simplifying the mechanical production process. With their inspectors trained in science, rather than trade, scorning the notion of complicated 'secrets' to processes that the Enlightenment should make clear to all (and with a concern for the ability of relatively unskilled French workers to grasp such processes), the French government frequently fell prey to those who claimed to have taken out 'unnecessary' complications. One such was George Garnett, who arrived in 1787 proclaiming that he had successfully 'simplified' Arkwright's water-frame and carding machines. He had actually removed the mechanism's most delicate parts, which ensured that the thread emerging was of fine enough quality to weave with, but this did not stop him being paid for his 'inventions', and to set up a plant for making carding machines in Rouen early in 1789.[32] It is noticeable that the French government was willing to pay upfront for claims of excellence and innovation, while the British tended to work through 'bounties' on actual production and exports. Paying by results seemed, in this case at least, distinctly superior.

Nonetheless, the pioneers of mechanisation in France did produce results. Milne's machine-makers produced two sets of machinery in 1786, four the next year, six the next and ten in 1789.[33] One of their main customers was the duc d'Orléans, the king's liberal cousin, who had invested along with a series of elite backers in a large plant in Orléans itself. By the end of 1788 eight sets of machinery were being run by hand, by forty skilled male workers, paid in total some 9600 *livres* per year. It was determined that a steam plant could be put in, to run many more machines, at only twice the annual cost of these men's wages. When this plant was finished it employed almost exclusively children and women, mostly 'widows, infirm, unable to earn their living elsewhere', and thus extremely cheap. However, the start-up costs had been huge. Building the factory, 133 feet long and on seven floors, cost five times the original estimate of 120,000 *livres*, and the engine and its gearing added another 136,000. The building costs alone absorbed all the start-up capital of the company the duke had put together, but he had signed a commitment in August 1788 'to furnish the funds necessary for the construction of the building', and so had to pay the rest. As a multimillionaire he could afford it, and the plant worked on solidly throughout the revolutionary years.[34]

Such costs, the price of moving ahead into uncharted technological waters with such large-scale schemes, crippled other plans launched with royal protection at the same time. One factory at L'Épine, opened under the personal patronage of Calonne, ran into a huge deficit of 144,000 *livres* by the spring of 1789. The plant manager, himself an investor, recorded a catalogue of woes: he was

at the point of ceasing work at the establishment, for lack of funds, those given have in large part been absorbed by losses caused, either by epidemic maladies ... which have killed or driven away many workers, or by the state of trade which has caused a fall in the price of cotton, or finally by a lack of sales.[35]

As if illness and economic troubles were not enough, the threat posed by mechanisation to livelihoods was realised early by French workers, and felt particularly harshly as the economic crisis bit deep. In November 1788 the female spinners of Falaise, Normandy, petitioned royal officials against spinning machines and went on to burn down one prominent plant. In response the local royal agent proposed that 'to prevent popular uprisings in future' action should be taken 'to prohibit the use of machines for spinning cotton'. The populace certainly seems to have shared this view, in the short term. An 'English manufactory' in Rouen was burned on the emblematic date of 14 July 1789, as was the establishment of the 'inventor'

George Garnett, and several others in the coming weeks and months.[36] A major mechanised plant at Louviers, judged by Arthur Young in October 1788 as 'the most important that one can find in France', was shut down in July 1789 to avoid the threat of attacks, though its own workers, now feeling the pain of unemployment, successfully petitioned for it to be reopened in November.[37]

Development of the cotton industry in France produced a number of lasting edifices in the years up to 1789 – for example, the monumental Orléans spinning plant was matched in grandeur by the cotton-printing works set up by Oberkampf at Jouy, giving the world the pastoral images of *toiles de Jouy* to this day.[38] But overall an industry heavily reliant on operating with individual investors and protectors from the highest social echelons, frequently sheltered inside semi-monopolistic royal *privilèges* or functioning only through state encouragements of other kinds, could not hope truly to compete, outside their domestic market, with the raw power of the emerging industry of Great Britain. Nonetheless, the dilemma of the French, racing to catch up, was matched in some respects by that of the British manufacturers, racing to stay ahead. The new machines needed power, for which one obvious option was water-wheels. Here Lancashire had a great advantage, in its steep valleys running from the Pennines to the River Mersey and the Irish Sea, fed with abundant rainfall, and close to the commercial hubs of Manchester and Liverpool, the latter already grown fat on the slave trade and always eager for new cargoes. From the first waves of mechanisation right through to the mid-nineteenth century, ever larger and more efficient wheels would take power to mills that almost literally choked some valleys. More sophisticated designs incorporated dams to hold back flow during the dead hours of the night, releasing it to power larger wheels in the daytime, but such dams could occasion bitter dispute, for upstream there was always another mill, threatened with a loss of the vital 'fall', the difference in water levels, that made it possible to run a wheel at all.

Water-mills would continue to grow in size and power, where fortunate situations allowed, but they could not be the true engine of a revolution. There were never enough sites for water-wheels to meet all the demand for power, and besides, the careful positioning of such mills, and the extensive hydrological works required, put them beyond the reach of many starting entrepreneurs. Some early experiments with spinning machines had used donkeys to turn a large axle to make power, just as areas without water or wind had used animals to grind grain for centuries. 'Horse-wheels' played a crucial role in the 1780s as the cotton trade mushroomed. In the Lancashire town of Oldham, for example, six spinning mills were built in the late 1770s, three water-powered and three horse-driven. By 1788 there were twenty-five mills in Oldham, the majority worked by horses. The inventor of the water-frame himself, Richard Arkwright, ran one of his mills in Nottingham at this point with a horse-wheel twenty-seven feet across and nine feet high. When Boulton and Watt consulted to replace it with a steam engine in 1790, they noted that the nine horses harnessed to it 'seemed to be very much loaded, so much so that they were obliged to be changed frequently', and could still only drive the shaft at fewer than ten revolutions per minute. To reach the desired fourteen revolutions, the engineers decided that an engine rated by their own system at twelve horsepower was required.[39]

Arkwright had already used a steam engine as early as 1780 in another mill, but this was a pumping engine designed, as many were in these years, to recover water passed through a water-wheel and return it to an upper reservoir. As water was a precious resource, and steam power did not yet give an action smooth enough to drive delicate machinery, this was an efficient use of resources in a tight situation.[40] He did the same in 1783, this time for a cotton-spinning mill in Manchester, where the combination worked three thousand spindles. One of Boulton and Watt's few competitors, using an extremely simple if inefficient pumping design not covered by their patents, was also combining these 'Savery engines' with water-wheels in Manchester in the mid-1780s. But in 1784 Watt patented the complex 'parallel motion' necessary to turn the rise and fall of a piston arm into smooth rotation, and installed it successfully at Albion Mill in 1786.[41] One of the main gains that Watt and his customers saw from this advance was simple economy: he wrote in 1791 that 'an Engine to drive ... directly will not cost much more than half the money of one to raise the water to do the same work and will not consume 2/3 of the fuel in the same time'.[42] The firm installed one engine in 1785 – which proved a failure as the machinery had been built, inexplicably, out of square with the buildings – and one, more successfully, in 1786, and orders then began to rise from a trickle to a stream. Before 1789 virtually all their orders came either to replace existing horse-wheels or offer a supplement to water power in times of drought; but after then, the trade expanded dramatically into new construction. They would build 110 steam plants by 1800, 92 of them for cotton mills, and no fewer than 50 of those in Lancashire.[43]

Very nearly all of this mechanised growth was in spinning, and the preliminary processes of carding and roving. But 1789 remains significant also in the weaving of cotton, even if only as a marker for the future. The 'Revolution Mill' that Major Cartwright set up and tried to run throughout that year employed a new form of power-loom invented by his younger brother, the Reverend Dr Edmund Cartwright. He had worked on a power-loom ever since being told, in Manchester in 1784, that such a thing was impossible owing to the deep complexity of the motions involved. Within a year, with no experience of working looms, he had designed a mechanical prototype that took 'two powerful men to work the machine at a slow rate, and only for a short time' before their strength gave out. But after he had patented this, 'I condescended to see how other people wove', and was astonished at their 'easy modes of operation'. Starting again from a more practical basis, he patented a new machine in 1787, which he believed would be 'exceedingly simple and cheap'.[44] He decided to build a plant on some land at Doncaster that had come from his recently deceased wife's estate. The power for this plant came from a horse-wheel, but the following year he opened another factory near by, this one run by an old-fashioned Newcomen steam engine. Both plants struggled to run successfully, as the power-looms still faced numerous problems of refinement, but the example was enough to encourage his brother John into his scheme at Retford. No fewer than 108 looms were installed in the Revolution Mill, on three floors of a building 123 feet long and 29 feet wide.[45]

The difficulty with commercial power-loom operation was that there were very many handloom weavers around to compete with it. As late as 1800 weaving was taught as a skill to the inmates of poorhouses and prisons around Manchester, and many impoverished Irish came across via Liverpool and picked up the trade too. Unlike spinning machines, which had actually provided work for idle hands in their early stages, power-looms were an obvious and immediate threat. The only commercial enterprise to take up Cartwright's machines and install them in a large factory was the Grimshaw Brothers of Manchester. They saw their premises, where five hundred looms had been planned, burned to the ground in 1791 after only a month's trial operation. It was exactly the fate that anonymous letters had threatened even before it opened.[46] Until further refinements made power-mills truly economical, and the continued burgeoning of the trade outstripped even the capacities of the handloom weavers, weaving by steam remained just a sign of things to come.

Early cotton mills were often very small – one built 'on Henry Ashcroft's farm in Eccleston' in 1784 to use the new-fangled water-frames was 52 feet long and 31 feet wide, and was fitted out at a modest cost of £493.[47] One pamphleteer in 1787 claimed that by that year £715,000 had been invested in building 'water-frame factories', but this was probably a gross exaggeration. Many mill owners got their start by buying up disused buildings, including corn mills, barns and, as was common in Oldham, for example, in these years, even private houses, with 'the rooms laid together' to make space for the machinery. One steam-powered cotton mill sold as a going concern in 1794 was in buildings 'heretofore used as sugar houses, warehouses and stables', but had subsequently accommodated ten thousand spindles, with room and power, the advertisement claimed, for five thousand more.[48] Many factories were built speculatively and then changed hands at a loss through bankruptcy or less spectacular failure. There was already a keen trade in advantageous premises. A sudden downturn in 1788, probably occasioned by over-enthusiastic expansion after the Eden Treaty, put a new wave of properties on the market. Robert Owen, later one of the great cotton-spinning magnates, and a keen social reformer, got his start in 1789, by his own account, from leasing a factory and subletting all but one room, where he directly employed a mere three men.[49] Both the costs and the size of buildings would creep up steadily, and competition for ever larger machines added its own burdens. As we have already seen, many of the machines that drove this first phase of mechanisation were designed, and in some cases hand-built, by individual entrepreneurs. But from the late 1780s designs began to become standardised – by 1795 machine-makers were offering 180-spindle Crompton mules for £38, plus extra for 'gearing' to attach to a power source. Firms were also already going bust, putting their machinery onto a lively second-hand market, where a full set of machines for handling calico printing was had in 1788 for £269, and three years later a small, steam-powered cotton mill for a mere £420.[50]

The real costs in the cotton trade were raw materials – which in the case of weaving meant the finished products of the spinning trade. It was in such materials that tens of thousands of pounds were invested, and fortunes could be made or lost on the back of fickle markets. While the price of cotton cloth was highly variable, dependent on quality and the demands of fashion and incorporated numerous costs of bleaching, spinning, carding, weaving and printing alongside the materials themselves, the price of cotton yarn is much easier to chart. For fine cotton yarn at one hundred hanks per pound weight, the price noted in Manchester in 1789 was thirty-four shillings a pound, little more than half the cost of equivalent materials from Crompton's own hand-worked mule in 1780. By 1792 that price had halved again, to only sixteen shillings a pound, where it remained stable for the rest of the decade before dipping under ten shillings in 1798. It would trickle lower, to between five and seven shillings in 1810–15, but the drastic changes had clearly taken place around 1789.[51] The explosive competition unleashed by mechanised production drove down costs, yet also raised the prospect of huge gains from supplying entire new social classes to whom these products now became available. It was a race to the bottom that would impoverish many, and ruin some, but which changed the face of the world.

Between 1780 and 1789 total British imports of raw cotton soared from 6.8 to 32.5 million pounds. In the following two decades they doubled and redoubled. In 1788 almost none of that cotton came from the United States; ten years later one-fifth did; by 1807 more than half; and as the total rose in later years America continued to supply a third to a half of this burgeoning trade.[52] Southern planters harvested some two million pounds of raw cotton in 1791, already quadrupled from a few years before, and a massive increase on the minuscule trade of a decade earlier. By 1801 that had risen to a huge forty million pounds, the figure doubling again in the next ten years and reaching 182 million pounds by 1821.[53] To even begin to reach this level of production, another revolution had to take place, again involving machines.

Cotton fibres are harvested attached to the seeds of the plant. In the case of Sea Island cotton, chance and cultivation combined to fuse the individual seeds into a clump, and make the long fibres fall off with a gentle tug. But the ecological pay-off was a delicate plant that would not grow outside coastal zones: hence the scouring of the world for viable 'upland' varieties. These produced seeds scattered through the fibrous boll and firmly attached to the shorter strands they gave.[54] Human ingenuity had long produced solutions to this problem, beginning with a simple arrangement of a slab and hand-held rod, which, used with care and dexterity, could pinch seeds free with a rolling motion. These were known in India as early as AD 500, and in the American South-West at the time of the Spanish incursion, and were in use across the Old World as late as the nineteenth century. But clearly they were slow and laborious. In the fourteenth century the Chinese produced a new system, later spreading with modifications to India, which worked something like a mangle: twin rollers, turned in opposite directions by hand or foot, formed a pinch-point into which the harvested bolls could be fed: seeds were pinched off and fell back, fibres passed through to the other side for collection. These kinds of machines, which doubled the output of the older devices, spread far and wide, and were known in the Mediterranean before Columbus set sail.[55]

With slave labour abundant, and crops still small, in early eighteenth-century cotton cultivation in the Caribbean the primitive slab-and-rod devices were still in general use, but double-roller machines came onto the scene from mid-century. These seem to have been reinventions, rather than adoptions of the Old World models: in 1733 a French inventor produced a large metal double-roller machine and was given a royal grant in reward, but local planters declared it a failure. Smaller machines began to flourish, however, and the *Encyclopédie* of the 1750s carried pictures of ones driven by foot-power with flywheels much like spinning-wheels. Such machines became well established in the coming decades.[56] This relatively stagnant technology produced a drastic bottleneck in production, as the mechanisation of textile production and the expansive dreams of planters and politicians began to build up a huge pressure for change. Early experiments with driving larger rollers by water or animal power were disastrous. Slave hands fed the cotton between the rollers, mere fractions of an inch from mutilation – fractions that too often proved too small for safety, ruining both the slaves and the cotton. The action of the machines overall, with the seeds falling back towards the operator, was not easy to mechanise as it stood. But ingenuity struggled on.

In 1788 Joseph Eve announced in the *Bahama Gazette* that he had invented a self-feeding machine, or 'gin' as they were known, capable of taking power from wind, water or animals. Only nineteen years old, Eve came from a Philadelphia family with noted scientific connections. His father had been an associate of Benjamin Franklin in his philosophical gatherings a generation earlier, but was expelled from the city, and the United States, after apparently doing a deal with wartime British occupation forces to keep his gunpowder mill in production. The young Eve struggled, as so many inventors did, to raise funds to take his design further, but after a few years was securing testimonials from satisfied planters. Their letters reveal that they had been employing teams of slaves on batteries of foot-driven gins, and still found it hard to make the work economical. Now the machine merely needed to be tended by a slave who filled a hopper with the cotton bolls and took away the raw cotton fibre on the other side. One planter said Eve's machine saved 'eighteen hundred days' of slave labour, enough in itself at a time of year when 'the slave's work is most valuable' to raise an extra two tons of cotton.[57] News of the potential of these innovations soon spread, and around 1789 numerous experiments across the American South were going on with forms of self-feeding machines. This was the context into which stepped a Massachusetts-born tutor, fresh from Yale University, in 1792, and in six months he had 'invented' a machine that solved the ginning bottleneck forever.

Eli Whitney's cotton gin has long passed into legend – a tendentious legend, borne of his own hard-fought legal battles to secure a patent – of how an ingenious Yankee overcame southern indolence and moved an industry from hand-work to mechanisation overnight.[58] As we have just noted, it was in fact more the capstone of a long process, much as Crompton's mule built on those who came before, and one in which many individual experimenters may have contributed to the one design Whitney claimed as his own. In some respects a remarkably well-designed machine, in others it was an ugly brute-force solution to the underlying problem. Whitney's gin did not trouble to gather all the fibres that could be plucked from the seeds. Rather, using a roller set with wire brushes, and later with toothed blades, it ripped enough fibre from the seeds to be viable, and did so at high speed. The resultant short-staple cotton was hideously crude in comparison with the products of more careful techniques, but it was good enough for the machines of Britain and the vast markets for cheap cloth across the world into which they were plunging headlong. With this final bottleneck bridged, King Cotton was ready to be born: and thus, for almost three-quarters of a century, millions more would be held in a slavery that had seemed to be fading into history at just this moment.

# 8

# 'This general agitation
of public insanity'

*France and Britain in the spring of 1789*

'What is the Third Estate? *Everything*. What has it been until
now in the political order? *Nothing*. What does it want to be?
*Something*.' The author of these words, Emmanuel-Joseph Sieyès,
was an unlikely revolutionary firebrand. Forty in 1788, he had risen
from undistinguished beginnings as the son of a tax inspector in the
southern port of Fréjus by lending his talents to the most conservative of France's institutions, the Catholic Church.[1] From his studies
at the elite Sorbonne in Paris, he progressed in the only way a
commoner could, by taking on the administrative burdens that
noble-born bishops scorned in favour of country leisure and Court
attendance. Thus by the 1780s he was comfortably established as
vicar-general and chancellor of the bishopric of Chartres. For a man
of his abilities the actual burdens of this role were light, and he was
able to cultivate his other talents as a student of the Enlightenment.
He read and wrote voluminously, an acute and acerbic observer of
the collapsing political world around him, though he kept much of
his production to himself, not risking publication of his more incendiary analyses.

Like Montesquieu and the American Founders before him,
Sieyès was grounded in John Locke's empiricism and liberalism,
though he went on to engage extensively with the writings of the
generation of *Encyclopédistes* who were then steadily dying out. With

his official duties at Chartres no more than a day or two's travel by coach from the *salons* of Versailles and Paris, Sieyès became a fixture in the discreet private debates of a forward-looking elite. As these burgeoned into the meetings of the Society of Thirty his ideas grew more forceful, and increasingly public as he joined the pamphlet debate. After an *Essay on Privileges* in late 1788, which condemned the nobility for monopolising social advancement, it was in the febrile atmosphere of January 1789 that Sieyès produced a two-hundred-page excoriation of privilege and assertion of political rights for all productive citizens, *What Is the Third Estate?*, which opened with the stark assertions above. As this and similar productions circulated, the other side of the political conflict now brewing was coming to life. When the agenda had shifted dramatically from royal despotism to unjust privilege, those whose lives and values were founded on that very thing began to react vigorously and uncompromisingly.

As the second Assembly of Notables failed to reach agreement at the end of November 1788, the prince de Conti noted in a meeting with the other noble leaders of that body that it was vital that 'all these new proposals be forever outlawed and that the Constitution and the ancient forms be maintained in all their integrity'.[2] Days later Conti and the other royal Princes of the Blood delivered a memorandum to the king himself, which contained an undisguised demand for continued subordination of the Third Estate: it should 'cease to attack the rights of the two leading Orders; rights which, no less ancient than the Monarchy, must be as inalterable as its Constitution; [the Third] should limit itself to soliciting the reduction of taxation, with which it may be overburdened'.[3] In provinces where Third Estate opinion was already showing itself particularly radical, such as Brittany, Provence and Franche-Comté, noble movements of intransigence rose up in response. In Brittany a petitioning movement of nobles against 'Patriot' claims gained the support of the *parlement* of Rennes, and provoked street fighting between gentlemen and student commoners. The Breton nobility ultimately boycotted the Estates-General *en masse*, laying the groundwork for a decade of conflict. In Provence likewise, any collaboration with Third Estate forces was shunned, and conservative nobles abandoned the regular electoral procedures to send a dissenting delegation to Versailles to protest at the entire concept of the remodelled Estates-General.[4]

In areas without the relatively close-knit networks of these dissenting provinces, many nobles felt at a loss to respond to continued waves of Patriot propaganda: 'These men are seducing others with their pens,' lamented one noble officer in early January 1789, 'and we write nothing at all.'[5] Those few nobles who did write, outside the charmed circle of the Society of Thirty, revealed an intense attachment to privilege as the lifeblood of their being. Even the intellectual marquis de Montesquiou-Fezensac, a prominent Freemason and member of the Académie française, who condemned those of his fellow nobles who 'superstitiously hold even the most absurd beliefs in high regard, as long as those beliefs are sufficiently ancient', was only prepared, in his pamphlet *To the Three Orders of the Nation*, to imagine voting by head for measures of taxation, advocating voting by order for all other matters.[6] A retired soldier, the baron de Luppé, called his pamphlet *Reflections of a Citizen on the Forthcoming Assembly of the Estates-General*, but there was little of a Patriot's understanding of citizenship in his denunciation of 'this general agitation of public insanity' for voting by head. This would lead to Third Estate demands for 'honours, positions and dignities' that were the nobility's alone by right. Such change was unconscionable, for 'the mingling of classes has always led to the fall of empires'.[7] Achard de Bonvouloir, a Norman gentleman, would not even grant, as Luppé did, concessions on taxation: 'The Third is after our swords even more than our purses,' he announced, 'their pretensions are boundless' and only a total determination to refuse change could fend off the destruction of the nobility: 'the whole universe seems in the throes of convulsions'.[8]

To read the closing paragraph of Sieyès' *What Is the Third Estate?*, after over twenty-five thousand words of argument for the parasitic nature of privilege and the nobility, is to see what such men feared: 'Do not ask what is the appropriate place for a privileged class in the social order. It is like deciding on the appropriate place in the body of a sick man for a malignant tumour . . . It must be *neutralised*.'[9] At almost the same time the words of the king himself circulated into the towns and villages of all France, with the publication of regulations for the elections to the Estates-General itself. Implicitly these abandoned any attempt that might have been made to 'manage' the electoral process actively. Beyond the barest details of geographical constituencies, and special treatment for a few sensitive areas, the clergy, nobility and commoners of France were left to select their own representatives as they saw fit. Beyond insistence that participants be adult male taxpayers, there was not even any attempt to limit the franchise to those who might favour order or defend property. Necker's, and the king's, trust in the virtues of public opinion was on open display, and the text included a particularly frank reference to the procedure for the statement of grievances that traditionally accompanied such an election: 'His Majesty wishes that everyone, from the extremities of His realm and from the most remote dwelling-places, may be assured that his desires and claims will reach Him.'[10] With these words everyone, from the highest seigneurs of the nobility to the lowliest peasant sharecroppers, was invited to denounce any aspect of the social and political order to which they objected. And so they did.

The vigour with which the French population expressed their grievances had much to do with their dire situation – in a winter of ghastly cold, after several years of poor harvests, with trade on the wane and uncertainty all around, they might well have felt apocalyptic. But what flowed from the recording pens of thousands of village and town meetings showed far more than mere helpless fear. Though they lived under an absolute monarchy, where their voices were in theory nothing in the public order, townsfolk and peasants had always had politics to deal with. Even the humblest country-dwellers lived in communities that held meetings and deputed officials, sometimes by election and sometimes by nomination of state administrators or the local lord, to conduct business, assess taxes, co-ordinate harvesting, find funds to repair churches, negotiate (or litigate) with neighbouring communities over common lands, rights of access, boundary stones and a thousand other things. Communities dealt with seigneurial agents for feudal dues, with contractors for the collection of the church tithe, and with the demands of an ever more intrusive administrative state for responses to surveys and censuses of crops, households, vagrants and all manner of other queries that a bureaucrat's fancy could create.

The men who passed on such demands, the unpaid sub-delegates of regional *intendants*, lived in the same small towns as many, and out into the villages themselves the middling class of those who lived from the law, from subcontracting the practice of seigneurial justice or from the collection of feudal and church incomes, spread itself thinly and ever presently. Such men brought connections and influence, and often bitter local feuds, with their own resonances of politics, into the orbit of all. In towns themselves the political web was woven even thicker. Municipal politics could bring prestige and privilege – and even, in larger centres, noble status – to councilmen, and the many reform schemes of the 1780s had revived a competitive interest in its pursuit. The craftsmen of the towns, with their guilds, drew their own diagrams of litigious political infighting, and the greater proximity of real centres of power, principally the many and overlapping law-courts, gave added focus to awareness of conflict and competition. It was in the towns too that the middling classes pursued their strategies of cultural and political advancement, and where the intellectual agendas of reading clubs and the politics of reform had already overlapped decisively in 1788.

Between those middling classes and the nobility, or at least those parts of it that read books, there had been a growing *rapprochement* in the decades of the Enlightenment. The liberal members of the high elite that joined the Society of Thirty were matched by those of lesser means who had flocked to buy the *Encyclopédie* in an earlier generation and who were stalwarts of provincial academic and cultural networks. As in Paris the ranks of noble judges, gentlemen, financiers and bishops mingled, so too it was in smaller cities, and from some perspectives the writings of those such as Sieyès looked to be fomenting conflict out of nothing. But the pamphlet war exposed real divisions, which were only solidified by the new electoral process. So much was new, in the calling of an Estates-General after 175 years, that those who looked for change could only anticipate it. But in reaching for the shadow of an all but medieval institution, the reformers gave equally strong weapons into the hands of those set against all their goals.

An Estates-General was a *consultative* assembly. It brought things to the attention of the king and requested action upon them. Nowhere in its history was there a sense of it having an independent initiative, and those who had argued for it had done so with the idea that it alone could legitimate royal reforms – but reforms proposed to it from the monarch's ministers. In these two senses of consultation and legitimation rested the idea that such a body was in effect a form of negotiation between sovereign and subjects: a view dangerous to absolutism, but also difficult to reconcile with the partisan divisions arising over privilege. In the electoral process that division was decisively hardened, even as the challenge to absolutism was reinforced.

Over 250 geographical areas sent final delegations to the Estates-General, from each of the three orders. In most cases those areas corresponded to *bailliages*, the jurisdictions of royal courts, but in some cases smaller *bailliages* were amalgamated and in some areas other divisions were used, for it was entirely typical of the monarchy's complex structure that uniformity should be impossible. Each order met separately. Nobles attended these meetings directly by right. The clergy elected representatives, producing bodies dominated by parish priests, a challenge to the established hierarchy of monasteries, cathedral chapters and bishops. The Third Estate representatives were gathered by election from every rural parish, and from preliminary meetings among the guilds and other formal organisations of urban life. These local meetings, over forty thousand of them, produced their own *cahiers de doléances*, registers of grievances, which were reviewed in the production of a *cahier* for the final *bailliage* meeting, to be taken forward, alongside *cahiers* from the nobility and clergy, to the gathering at Versailles.

Striking divisions emerged between nobility and Third Estate, and also between the local grievances of rural parishes and the final documents of their order. The nobility closed ranks, shunning in its electoral meetings the very many more recently ennobled figures, notably those who had risen through the ranks of royal courts and administration. Almost three-quarters of the 322 deputies chosen bore titles – counts, dukes, barons – a distinction that over 90 per cent of the nobility lacked. Many were eminent in Court politics and national life, and almost all possessed fortunes beyond the reach of their humbler peers and far above anything mustered by those of the Third Estate. Less than a quarter of those elected could be said to live in rural seclusion – Versailles, Paris and the great centres of regional political and military life predominated. Over 80 per cent of the delegates had served as military officers, including nineteen who had fought in the American War, and many others with a record of active service elsewhere. As a body primarily made up of military aristocrats, elected to represent a wider, but no less proud, class, the noble delegation set itself firmly against the values of both the reforming absolutist state and the aspiring commons.[11] Among the top twenty issues raised by noble *cahiers* were the evident problems of the kingdom: the need for new forms of taxation (with suggestions that purely fiscal privileges could be sacrificed for the common good), the demand for regular meetings of the Estates-General to oversee financial matters, some more liberal concerns with personal liberty and censorship; but also, very clearly, a concern to retain voting by order in the Estates-General, and an overall unwillingness to broach the issue of privilege in general.[12]

The some six hundred deputies sent by the Third Estate to Versailles were, above all, provincial lawyers: a third of the whole delegation sat as judges in royal or other courts (some undoubtedly helped to election by their role in chairing the local assemblies); another third were men of the law, from elite Parisian barristers to legal scholars and jurists, and from small-town notaries to those who had qualified in the law but now lived from landed income. Only a few came from the machinery of the state, though of these a handful were eminent, including several who had worked at high positions in the Finance Ministry. There were around fifty doctors, teachers and writers, sixty wholesale merchants and forty other traders, bankers and manufacturers. Some forty others were farmers, all of the more prosperous kind, and a final twenty lived as 'bourgeois' from rental incomes.[13] At least fifty-eight of the Third's deputies possessed personal nobility, largely gained through office-holding or purchase. Only seven had inherited their status, though among these was the firebrand Mirabeau, who had ostentatiously scorned the noble assembly in Provence, where only the most restrictive definition of nobility was accepted, to get himself elected by the local commons instead.[14] Perhaps a majority of the whole six hundred lived in ways that showed they aspired to nobility as part of the normal pattern of eighteenth-century social mobility: landowning was widespread, and judgeships and other offices were the natural route to privileged status for those educated in the law.

It is all the more remarkable then that when this group and their peers who elected them sat down to sift out composite *cahiers* from the grievances of the many communities that sent them, they directly attacked, after the travails of royal taxation, noble status itself. Voting by head in the Estates-General was the fourth most common demand, and in their top twenty the Third also complained of noble dominance of military careers, unfair taxation on non-noble land purchases and noble privileges within the legal system, amid positions shared with the nobility on personal freedoms, censorship and the need for the Estates-General to meet regularly and control taxation. In some regions the disagreement was relatively minor. In the *bailliage* of Vic, in the rolling countryside of north-central France, the phrasing of noble and Third Estate documents showed such similarities that they must at least have been compared by their authors in draft. The reforms of taxation and administration they demanded were virtually identical, as were their concerns for personal freedom (and an anti-Semitic suggestion that loans by Jews should require independent authentication). But differences lingered: the Third wanted all taxpayers included on a single roll, dispensing with a key sign of privilege; where the nobles wanted the sale of judicial office abolished, the Third wanted to end distinction of birth in all royal appointments; on measures of state economy and rigour the Third was generally harsher and more thoroughgoing; and on a key point the Third was for voting by head and the nobility by order.[15]

In other regions such relatively polite difference was already impossible. The *cahiers* of Mâcon in Burgundy show divisions exacerbated by growing social unrest. The nobility wanted voting and deliberation in separate chambers of each order; the Third insisted deliberation be in common, and voting by head with a doubled Third, and even suggested that the Third could form a genuinely national assembly alone if the other orders refused to join it. The nobles demanded the preservation of seigneurial rights in full; the Third would variously abolish, restrict and investigate reform of such rights. The nobles wanted better pay for soldiers and officers, stricter discipline in the army and more autonomy for military commanders. The Third demanded the opening of military appointments, alongside all others, to commoners, and an oath for all troops never to take arms against civilians (except when ordered by an Estates-General). While these demands show shared areas of concern, and in others there was closer agreement, the goals of the two bodies were sharply different, raising the potential for a serious clash.[16]

While the *cahiers* carried to Versailles in the spring of 1789 presaged conflicts over the national political direction, their composition had left behind in the countryside an extraordinary movement of protest and outright rejection of the old order. Urban notables had sifted out almost all the specific demands of individual parishes, treating them as unworthy of attention in the context of the larger constitutional crisis. What did it matter, for example, that the southern parish of Saint-Vincent-Rive d'Olt lamented that 'there is a hospital established in the town of Luzech; our community pays towards this hospital, and yet our poor do not receive any aid from it'? But closer inspection reveals that such issues were part of a far larger pattern, a concern with injustice, arbitrary impositions and privilege that ran through the tens of thousands of individual *cahiers* like a golden thread. The same community asked bluntly: 'The lands of nobles and the Church, should they not be submitted to taxation? Why protect them from it?'[17] Lignères-la-Doucelle, in Normandy, was systematic in its approach to the injustices of both taxation and privilege. Beginning with a direct request to replace all existing taxes with a single land tax and a business tax, they asked for the complete abolition of all the privileged corps of judges and officials who controlled the existing tax regime, the suppression of all taxes on consumption goods, the ending of all privileges regarding exemption from taxation, the redemption of seigneurial dues on land and the outright abolition of other seigneurial privileges, such as milling monopolies, forced labour and personal jurisdictions. Noble status, they declared, should be limited to a reward for honourable public functions: 'That no nobility be granted by payments nor otherwise than by arms or service rendered to the state.'[18]

While nine of the parishes' top ten grievances focused on state taxation, the top specific complaint being the hated and iniquitous tax on salt, next came the privileges of the clergy and nobility, and all the various elements listed by the denizens of Lignères came in the first fifty of a very extensive list of concerns.[19] Bitterness spilled out between the lines of documents that normally preserved a respectful tone, often drafted by local clergy or judicial officials. Saint-Vincent complained, 'Our community has so many charges to which it is subjected by a dozen seigneurs who have these rights recognised as easily as one changes a shirt.' Longnes, a village near Paris, lamented 'the abuses which occur in the opening of some useless road like that of some seigneur to communicate with his château'.[20] Vitry-sur-Seine, in the same region, had stated its wishes uncompromisingly as 'the total suppression of all privileges whatsoever' and listed some twenty other specific concerns.[21]

Taken as a whole, the parish *cahiers* portray a complex engagement with the ills of French society. A number concern themselves with, for example, the problems caused by the rootless poor, while urban communities draw attention to the difficulties of trade under a regime of local exceptions and private tolls on roads and rivers. Many of the comments are perceptive, few are totally unmeasured and there is no call for outright material expropriation, or denial of the need for state taxation. But there is an overpowering groundswell of evidence that a system that was fundamentally against the interests of the vast majority was now being critiqued clearly by that majority and that, as a consequence, sweeping change was expected.

What complicated this picture, and tipped it into open conflict even before the *cahiers* had been completed, was the dire material state of the country. In Normandy the previous autumn fears over grain shortages had already mobilised crowds and made wagon drivers too fearful to move supplies. As winter set in, attacks on shipments were rumoured across the country, as was the fear of a 'famine pact' – that shortage was a deliberate move by evil aristocrats to beat down the people. Even state officials contributed to such rumours. In Normandy the Mayor of Le Mans denounced the police for taking bribes to conceal illicit grain shipments. In Paris it was rumoured that the judges of the *parlement* had failed to act against the conspirators: 'the plan originated at too high a level', one diarist noted.[22] With urban unemployment soaring and much of the country snowbound, conditions went on worsening. By January 1789 reports were emerging of collective attacks by peasants on seigneurs in the east of France, demanding an end to their privilege, and the release of 'hoarded' food stocks. The convocation of the Estates-General added fuel to a gathering fire, and once the harshest of the weather began to lift, massive unrest developed.

March and April 1789 saw collective attacks on markets and grain stores across French Flanders, in the north, and stretching into the Orléanais and Normandy. In the far south-east rioting developed into something more systematic. On 14 March in Manosque, some thirty miles north of Marseille, the local bishop was stoned by a crowd who accused him of encouraging hoarding. As electoral assemblies began to meet in this region some ten days later, there were minor disorders in Marseille, but serious revolt in the neighbouring city of Toulon, where workers in the naval arsenal had gone unpaid for two months. Over the following week violence spread: to Aix on 24 March, and in an arc to the east, encompassing at least a dozen towns across an area forty to fifty miles wide.

This rioting was no mere wanton destruction. Posters put up in Marseille noted that workers had been excluded from the electoral assemblies, and called for protest: 'it is right and proper that our opinion be heard; if you have courage, show it now'.[23] In the towns of Barjols and Saint-Maximin protesters forced the submission or replacement of local officials. At Riez another bishop was attacked in his palace as a hoarder, and also forced to hand over the papers and titles of his feudal rights. Monasteries were treated similarly – one was sacked in Barjols – as were some châteaux. Seigneurial mills, with their irksome monopolies, were destroyed in the town of Pertuis, and across the region lawyers and agents for feudal lords had their archives confiscated and destroyed, and were forced to pay back recent fines they had enforced and to make formal renunciations of their masters' rights. In the town of La Seyne the protesters even extorted payment from their victims for the time they had had to spend away from work.

Once this week's work was done feudalism was dead in this region in the eyes of the general population, as were many local taxes and the tithes of the Church: they simply refused to pay. In the Alpine valleys of the Dauphiné similar events occurred in mid-April. Peasants from the village of Avançon had already warned their seigneur, a judge in the Aix *parlement*, that they saw the Estates-General as having freed them from all pre-existing dues. On Sunday 19 April they went further, driven by the prevailing shortages, and decided to demand back from him the grain they had paid him the previous year. An armed band set out from Avançon on the 20th, recruiting help from neighbouring communities, and invested, invaded and searched the seigneur's residence, neither stealing nor damaging anything. As the seigneur was away, his servants were forced to promise that he would formally renounce his rights by the 26th. When the mounted police were called in, the peasants remained defiant, threatening to drive their cattle into the seigneur's crops. When cavalry were summoned the villagers simply decamped to the forest until they left. Cooler heads prevailed when formal legal action was threatened, and the deadline for the peasants' demands passed without a formal victory, but the seigneur noted that it was now physically impossible to pursue the collection of his dues.[24]

Such physical action was counterpointed by a campaign of letter writing from villages across France that had seen their grievances excluded from the final Third Estate *cahiers*. Ministers were bombarded with reiterations of their complaints, but were powerless to respond, and the tidal wave of direct action continued to swell. Conflict reached Paris itself in the last week of April, as the reported remarks of two manufacturing employers were taken as signs of a plot to cut workers' wages. With food prices spiralling out of control, and amid severe agitation only days ahead of the meeting of the Estates-General, thousands marched behind effigies of the two men, carrying placards announcing that 'By order of the Third Estate' they were to be hanged and burned. Cries were heard of 'Death to the rich! Death to the aristocrats! Death to hoarders!', and on succeeding days first the house of one man, Henriot, was sacked, and then the larger residence-cum-factory of the other, Réveillon, was besieged, sacked and burned. Hundreds of troops failed to prevent the violence, which was carried out to cries of 'Long live the Third Estate! Long live the king!' with a semi-formal fury – the contents of both buildings were torched in huge bonfires, rather than looted. Restoring order after the destruction of Réveillon's premises, the enraged and humiliated troops killed dozens – some reports made it over three hundred – fomenting anger for the future.[25]

There was perhaps no more contradictory observer of the revolutionary scene in 1789 than Thomas Jefferson. As a youth he had every opportunity to sink into dissipation – at fourteen in 1757 he had inherited his five-thousand-acre estate and all its many slaves – but instead he had made himself a philosophical polymath by intense study, and proved an energetic legislator in the decades to come. If he was no hero – and his enemies made charges about his conduct as Governor of Virginia during the War of Independence that came very close to accusations of cowardice – he was an exceptional thinker. Before his unfortunate experiences as Governor, he had drafted over 120 Bills for the state legislature, including landmark texts on religious freedom, and political, judicial and educational reform. Jefferson produced in 1784 a report on the western territories that would evolve into the Northwest Ordinance of 1787, and specifically excluded slavery from the new lands. He went to Paris in 1785, replacing Benjamin Franklin as ambassador, with grand plans for the future good: in July 1785, for example, he wrote of a plan to abolish invidious distinctions between nationalities, to have all nations offer 'mutual adoption by each of the citizens or subjects of the other' when they came into contact.[26]

Tall, slender, upright and elegant of manner, blond and refined of appearance, Jefferson settled remarkably well into French society. Unlike his predecessor, he made no effort to cultivate intriguing rusticity or to charm by difference: rather it was as a smooth imitator of courtly manners that he insinuated himself into refined company. Not that French aristocrats eager to share the lustre of the man who wrote the Declaration of Independence needed much encouragement to seek him out, and the charming widower – he had lost his wife in 1782 – was never short of company of either sex. He rented an elegant home, the Hôtel de Langeac, adjacent to the parkland of the Champs-Élysées. Though not large, this bow-fronted pavilion offered the refinements of comfort Jefferson was used to, a substantial garden he laid out in an informal 'English' fashion and a base close to the fashionable districts of the capital in which to host dinner parties, receptions and the business of diplomatic agency.[27]

As French affairs of state deteriorated in 1787, Jefferson was a caustic observer of early efforts at reform. The failure of the Assembly of Notables that year made him furious: 'This occasion, more than anything I have seen, convinces me that this nation is incapable of any serious effort but under the word of command.' The reason for this anger, however, lay in an unexpected direction: the casual mockery with which the Assembly had been greeted. 'The people at large view every object only as it may furnish puns and bon mots: and I pronounce that a good punster would disarm the whole nation were they ever so seriously disposed to revolt.'[28] As elite and popular defiance of the Crown grew over the next year, however, he developed a more sanguine view, and wrote to the French ambassador in the USA in May 1788: 'Courtiers had rather give up power than pleasures: they will barter therefore the usurped prerogatives of the king for the money of the people. This is the agent by which modern nations will recover their rights.'[29] Jefferson struck a less cynical note in discussions he had through that summer with Lafayette and Thomas Paine, the latter in Paris promoting his bridge. Lafayette wrote to an American friend that the three were 'debating in a convention of our own as earnestly as if we were to decide upon it', though the matter in question was the American, rather than French, Constitution.[30]

By December 1788 Jefferson wrote in more idealistic terms to Washington about the French: 'The nation has been awakened by our revolution, they feel their strength, they are enlightened, their lights are spreading, and they will not retrograde', although at this point he foresaw the Estates-General gaining little more than the right to its continued existence. Writing in January 1789 to the Welsh radical cleric Richard Price, Jefferson thought that issues such as freedom of the press and a declaration of rights might be raised, 'But probably they may not obtain these in the first session'. He went on nevertheless that there had been 'an illumination of the public mind as to the rights of the nation' and 'natural progress' would now see 'the establishment of a constitution which shall assure to them a good degree of liberty'.[31] By early spring the processes of election to the Estates-General continued to cause him to revise his views of his hosts further, writing to a compatriot that 'The frivolities of conversation have given way entirely to politics.' He went on:

> The press groans with daily productions, which in point of bold-ness make an Englishman stare who hitherto has thought himself the boldest of men. A complete revolution in the government has, within the space of two years ... been effected merely by public opinion, aided indeed by want of money which the dissi-pation of the court had brought on.[32]

To Paine, Jefferson was even more optimistic: 'there seems to be but one opinion on the principal points', and that opinion favoured the Third Estate.[33]

As Jefferson watched the drama unfold he was joined in Paris by the draftsman of the American Constitution, Gouverneur Morris. In a striking indication of the small circles in which the leaders of America moved, Morris, who was later to succeed Jefferson as ambassador, had come to Paris on private business, provoked in part by one of Jefferson's own early successes. In 1786 he had per-suaded the French Crown to abrogate a deal between Robert

Morris, the American financier, and the French state tobacco monopoly, which had given him exclusive right to sell American tobacco into France. While Jefferson had opened up the French market to competing American suppliers, loss of this right had cost Robert Morris, whose financial affairs were of epic complexity, dear. Indeed, although currently serving as a US Senator, he was en route to a catastrophic bankruptcy. Gouverneur Morris, no relation, but a business associate, travelled to Paris in the hope of establishing some new advantageous deal to relieve this embarrassment.[34] Bearing letters of introduction from Washington and Franklin, he lost no time in plunging into a social whirl. Despite the impediment of a wooden leg, the product of a fall from a moving carriage in his youth, Morris deployed suave manners that made him very popular among the female inhabitants of aristocratic Paris. He was soon sharing the sexual favours of the comtesse de Flahaut with Charles-Maurice de Talleyrand, Bishop of Autun and future revolutionary diplomat.

Such happy debauchery probably displeased Jefferson less than Morris's tendency to get mixed up with groups whose views leaned towards the frankly reactionary, but Jefferson was in general no fan of Frenchwomen's taste for public association. In the same letter to Washington that had praised France's awakening to Enlightenment, he had observed that 'the influence of women in the government' threatened all reform, as well as accounting for 'the desperate state to which things are reduced in this country'. Such behaviour, he noted, 'fortunately for the happiness of the sex itself, does not endeavour to extend itself in our country beyond the domestic line'.[35] Whatever Jefferson thought of Morris and the company he kept, he could not refuse him hospitality (though only his social polish saved his habit of sniffing round for diplomatic and commercial news from becoming irksome) and the two watched the events of the spring and summer of 1789 unfold side by side.

Jefferson introduced Morris to Lafayette on 22 April, and both counselled the marquis on policy for the upcoming Estates-General, agreeing that he should speak out only on 'important Occasions'. Jefferson wrote unsympathetically of the suppression of the Réveillon riots in the city a few days later as a punishment 'universally approved'. He commented that such destructive actions were the work of 'the most abandoned banditti . . . unprovoked and unpitied'. Morris's social circle went further: his diary recorded a dinner party at which the 'Magnificence of the hanging Match' that followed the repression was applauded.[36]

Jefferson was also an observer, albeit at a distance, of the turmoil of British politics during the madness of George III. Thomas Paine wrote to him from London on 16 December 1788 with the 'old news' of the king's collapse, and summed up the political consequences: 'a change of Ministry is expected and, I believe, determined on'.[37] Jefferson began a reply on 23 December, but it was not dispatched, with various additions, until mid-January – as Jefferson wrote, 'such a correspondence between you and me cannot pass thro' the post, nor even by the couriers of ambassadors', and had to be sent with a private individual heading the right way. By the time Jefferson replied, telling Paine about experiments with steamboats, encouraging the work on his bridge and noting that temperatures had fallen to minus 9.5 Fahrenheit, he was also concerning himself more officially with the regency crisis.[38] On 11 January his letter home to Secretary of State John Jay included a profile of the Prince of Wales's character, an issue 'becoming interesting' in the circumstances. He had gleaned the information from someone who had dined with him, and who began to discuss the prince's acquisition of French from French servants as a child:

he led him from this to give an account of his education, the total of which was the learning of a little Latin. He has not a single element of Mathematics, of natural or moral philosophy, or of any other science on earth; nor has the society he has kept been such as to supply the void of education. It has been that of the lowest, the most illiterate and profligate persons of the kingdom, without choice of rank or merit, and with whom the subjects of conversation are only horses, drinking-matches, bawdy-houses, and in terms the most vulgar. The young nobility who begin by associating with him, soon leave him, disgusted with the insupportable profligacy of his society, and Mr Fox who has been supposed his favourite, and not over-nice in the choice of company, would never keep his company habitually. In fact he never associated with a man of sense. He has not a single idea of justice, morality, religion, or of the rights of men, nor any anxiety for the opinion of the world.[39]

Jefferson charitably noted that the prince's sexual morals had improved since taking up with his mistress (and now his secret wife), Mrs Fitzherbert, 'an honest and worthy woman'. His conclusion was nonetheless that 'For the peace of Europe it is best that the king should give such gleamings of recovery, as would prevent the regent or his ministry from thinking themselves firm, and yet that he should not recover.'[40] The arrival of a Foxite ministry under a regent still seemed certain when Paine wrote again from London a few days later: 'I am in some intimacy with Mr Burke and after the New Ministry are formed he has proposed to introduce me to them.'[41] As late as 9 February Jefferson was writing to a friend that 'The king continues as raving mad as ever. I never heard of so furious a Maniac.'[42] Such was certainly the view of Paine, Fox and their friends, but it was rapidly being overtaken by events, much to their discomfiture.

On 2 February 1789 Miss Fanny Burney, Assistant Keeper of the Wardrobe to the queen, was walking in the gardens of Kew Palace when an unexpected figure lumbered up to her, hoarsely crying her name. A short-sighted and timorous old maid of thirty-seven, Burney fled, but was brought up short when she heard other voices clamouring for her to stop. As she recorded in her voluminous journal, this meeting with a king who had shortly before been a raving madman was terrifying: 'I wonder I did not really sink, so exquisite was my affright when I saw him spread out his arms! Involuntarily, I concluded he was about to crush me.' Instead he kissed her tenderly on the cheek and made kindly remarks about her well-known travails with her grumpy superior, the redoubtable Mrs Schwellenberg. They spoke for some minutes before the king's increase in agitation persuaded his doctors to lead him away.[43]

This episode marked the confirmation that George III had begun to recover from his 'madness', now widely though not conclusively viewed as a delusional state brought on by the physical and possibly hereditary condition porphyria.[44] The leading light among the professional physicians who attended him, Dr Richard Warren, maintained as late as 5 February that the king was 'as deranged as ever', but then he was the Prince of Wales's personal doctor.[45] The king was actually in the charge of Francis Willis, a seventy-year-old clergyman become doctor who ran an asylum in Lincolnshire where genteel lunatics (who could afford to pay up to £1000 a year) were treated humanely but firmly. Together with his sons and a team of attendants, Willis had taken the king in hand in December 1788, believing most of his troubles to come from nervous stress and over-work. To deal with the madness itself, strict confinement was used, including tying the king into a chair and gagging him when he could not restrain his outbursts of sexual profanity. Though a gruesome series of medicines, including strong emetics, were given to work on the king's physical disorders, Willis also continually worked to recall him to self-mastery, reprimanding his outbursts sternly and con-frontationally. Improvements were rewarded, and by January the king was allowed to shave himself under supervision and take walks in the grounds, though his relapses into ranting fervour still nec-essitated occasional recourse to a straitjacket. As early as 7 January, answering questions before a parliamentary committee, Willis stated: 'His Majesty does everything in a more rational way than he did, and some things exceeding rational.' Dr Warren bluntly dis-agreed, telling the same committee two days later: 'I see no symp-toms of convalescence.'[46]

In other exchanges Warren had been blunter still, taking the line of his patron that Willis's optimistic prognostications were 'mere fab-rications' for a 'sinister purpose'.[47] For those who hoped to see the Prince of Wales take the throne as regent, the possibility of recovery could not be admitted. Prime Minister Pitt, however, relied on that prospect for his political life, and continued to weather the growing crisis of a paralysed constitution with the help of a swelling tide of public opinion. By early January concerned municipalities and meet-ings of citizens from Aberdeen in the north through Glasgow, Leicester and Cambridge to Southampton on the Channel had reg-istered their approval of Pitt's conduct.[48] The opposition Whig response, calling counter-meetings in several Yorkshire towns, for example, was less successful. At a meeting in the London Tavern on 7 January, opponents in the audience caused uproar when it was announced that a motion for an address of thanks to Pitt had been carried by a show of hands. As the chairman scuttled out down the back stairs, a Foxite replacement held another vote, which it was announced had defeated the motion by five to one. But the govern-ment continued to acclaim the original vote in the press, printing over four hundred signatures of 'the Merchants, Bankers and Traders of the City of London'. Pitt's stand for the rights of Parliament, made possible by the opposition's botched strategy, continued to pay off.[49]

One Foxite response, indicating quite clearly the elitist basis of their position, was to mock the petitioners. The inhabitants of Yorkshire, one correspondent reported, were 'horribly infatuated' with Pitt, while the *Morning Herald* sneered at one address from Gateshead in the far north as a place populated by 'shopkeepers of the *lowest* order'. Attempts by opposition pamphleteers to assail 'Prince Pitt' as one who had 'already destroyed the People's Rights' and sought to 'raise himself above the prerogative by *seizing on the Sovereignty of these Kingdoms*' had little effect.[50] Government supporters were not above deploying scorn and ridicule themselves, however. The London Tavern disruption was dismissed: the opposition could never show 'such a mass of riches' as had supported Pitt's stand, and their opponents did not dare publish their own names and whereabouts, for fear of 'some very disagreeable visits to garrets and cellars' by bailiffs in pursuit of debts. The same report, in *The Times*, mocked the leaders of the opposition more generally, noting how the restrictions on the powers of regency would prevent permanent pensions being given to the 'virtuous matrons of the immaculate party' and naming the mistresses of assorted Foxite leaders. Their party overall was damned as 'an assemblage of Dukes, Earls, Blackguards, Sharpers, Captains of the Road, and Parsons of the Fields – all seeking for power, places, and pensions, by any means, fair or unfair'.[51]

Though Pitt succeeded in producing a Regency Bill that would keep many of the king's powers away from his son, he could not ultimately prevent the regency from coming to pass. The extreme caution and division among the king's doctors worked against the Prime Minister, as even into February there was no agreement that George was definitively recovering. From the 5th a week of debates in the Commons moved the Bill forward. The Whig spokesman Edmund Burke voiced the view of the prince's party in no uncertain terms as debate opened. Though the Lord Chancellor himself was now of the opinion that 'it would be indecent' to proceed with such a Bill, given developing news from Kew, Burke was emphatic: 'The whole business is a scheme . . . to bring back an insane King.'[52] He was called to order that day for the extravagance of his claims, as he was to be on several more occasions through the week. Two days later government supporters laughed through his speech, and diarists and commentators thought he had fallen prey to mental disorder himself: 'violent almost to madness', said one; 'appeared to have lost his own reason', observed another. One mocked the contrast with the sad fate of the king: 'Burke walking at large and him in a strait waistcoat!'[53] Burke's vehemence was particularly striking as it came after his own claims back in December that 'if ever there was a question which peculiarly called for temper and moderation', it was that of the regency. But he excused himself on 6 February in the Commons by asserting that it was 'a deep consideration of the great importance of the subject, and not from any censurable imbecility of temper' that he grew heated.[54]

Burke's alarm was lodged deeply within his self-perception as a guardian of the unique historical liberties of the English Constitution. As he had fought against the tyrannical treatment of the American colonists, and as he was currently embroiled in making an example of the 'oriental despot' Warren Hastings, so on the matter of the regency he saw fundamental issues at stake. In the first place his view of the succession was that it had been settled by statute in the years after 1689: Pitt's pursuit of fifteenth-century precedents for the regency was not merely barbaric, as Fox had called it, but an attack on settled law and rights. Burke honoured what he saw as a complex balance between monarchy and liberty. On the one hand, trying to play the issue out before popular opinion was a breach of the rights of the monarch: 'The disposition of the Sovereign power is not in the will of the People,' as his notes put it. In the Commons in late December, he had declared it 'his sole pride and exclusive glory . . . to speak against the wishes of the people whenever they attempted to ruin themselves'. But as he also wrote, 'the settled, known, hereditary succession of the Crown is an invaluable part of our Constitution. That is as much our inheritance as the inheritance of the Royal Family.' Thus the powers of the Crown were prevented from becoming 'the object of private pursuit'.[55]

That pursuit concerned him greatly, and was wrapped up with the whole history of the past decade. In particular, the rise to power of Pitt, through dubious use of royal prerogatives and influence, set a fearful precedent for what Burke perceived as a grab for power under the guise of protection of the rights of Parliament. Pitt's moves to limit the powers of the regency amounted to an invasion of executive prerogative – in the worst case, a seizure of sovereign power for himself. Burke's notes again sketched this out, referring to the pattern of Pitt's career in office:

> It is curious to observe how the power of Mr Pitt . . . revolves unto itself and forms a compleat . . . unity. He first establishes in the Crown the sole power to nominate its minister. The chance of events then enables him through Parliament to name a King. It is established as a principle that the Crown is incontroulable [*sic*] in the appointment of its ministers; and it devolves upon the ministers to appoint those who have the power of appointing ministers without controul.[56]

By early February, though he continued to rage in the Commons, in private Burke saw the limited regency as a *fait accompli*, but he still thought that the Whig opposition ought to accept it only 'to prevent further outrages upon the constitution' and should then 'absent ourselves from Parliament until favourable circumstance should call us to it' in protest.[57] The provisions in the Regency Bill for announcing the king's return to health – without outside medical examination, by an announcement 'under the Queen's hand' – horrified him. In debate on 11 February he revealed he had made careful enquiries into the current state of understanding of lunacy, even visiting 'those dreadful mansions where these unfortunate beings are confined', and what he had learned alarmed him greatly: 'Some, *after a supposed recovery*, have committed parricide, butchered their sons, hanged, shot, drowned, thrown themselves from windows.' He was shouted down, but raged on: 'Such is the danger of an uncertain cure – such is the necessity to see that a sane sovereign is put in possession of the Government.'[58] A Pitt taking absolute power under a regency was displaced, in these fears, by a Pitt taking the same power under a king fraudulently attested as competent. Burke stood almost alone on these points, and the Bill moved forward regardless.

On 16 February the Bill moved to the House of Lords, and the next day Charles James Fox, convalescing from his own stress-induced illness at Bath, wrote to his supporters in the capital to scotch reports of a royal recovery and to ask them to 'let me know by return of the post on what day the Regency is like to commence'.[59]

He was buoyed by news that the Irish Parliament was exercising the independence it had won earlier in the decade, and was preparing to welcome the Prince of Wales as Regent of Ireland by a congratulatory address, and without limitations on his powers. During his stay Fox had continued to fire off letters making arrangements for coming into power. The matter of who was to have assorted Cabinet positions had been settled after arduous haggling in December.[60] Fox, though he had spent so much energy trying to give the Whigs a coherent political position in the past years, was also unquestionably a product and advocate of a system that gave the victor all the spoils of public life. With the major offices disbursed, he was now settling more minor matters: a chaplaincy for his brother-in-law, a position in Ireland for a cousin, various regimental commands for the military relatives of supporters. More vindictively, he insisted that an Irish official who had insulted the Whigs in 1785 be dismissed, threatening to be 'quite vexed if he is not'.[61]

Alas for Fox, it was not to be. On the very day he wrote of the regency's commencement, the king's doctors issued a public bulletin placing him in 'a state of convalescence', and within two days the regency had faded into history, the Bill was dropped and both Pitt and public were exultant. The political class, however, remained riven with bitterness, as one nobleman commented on 21 February: 'we have seen no times when it has been so necessary to separate parties in private company. The acrimony is beyond anything you can conceive. The ladies are as usual at the head of all animosity and are distinguished by caps, ribands and other such ensigns of party.'[62]

Many on the opposition side doubted the king's full recovery, and continued to fear what they had learned of Pitt's conduct, should a relapse occur. One noted: 'Pitt will without scruple hazard the public tranquillity . . . rather than be removed from power; and the popular cry which has been excited . . . by extraordinary management will enable him to cope (under the King's name) with all the influence of the Prince.'[63] Nonetheless, general rejoicing could not be gainsaid, and when Parliament opened for a new session on 11 March, London was illuminated in the king's honour, all the great houses showing lights in the shape of crowns, 'G.R.' ciphers, and the slogan 'Rejoice', while firecrackers flew around the streets. The following day Thomas Paine wrote bitterly to Jefferson:

With respect to Political matters here, the Truth is, the people
are fools. They have no discernment into principles and consequences. Had Mr Pitt proposed a National Convention at the
time of the king's insanity he had done right, but instead of this
he has absorbed the right of the Nation into a right of
Parliament . . . Therefore he has lessened instead of increased
the rights of the people, but as they have not sense enough to see
it they have been huzzaing him.[64]

His pique was compounded by a sense of missed personal and political opportunity, as he explained: 'Had the Regency gone on and the
new administration been formed I should have been able to communicate some Matters of business to you both with respect to
America and France.' Paine had clearly been working his Whig contacts, 'as an interview for that purpose was agreed upon and to take
place as soon as the persons who were to fill the offices should succeed'.[65] Failure led him to more splenetic observations: the British
'cannot be excited by any thing they hear or see to question the
remains of prejudice . . . but for national puffery none equals them.
The addresses which have been presented are stuffed with nonsense of this kind. One of them published in the London Gazette
and presented by a Sir William Appleby begins thus – "Britain, the
Queen of Isles – the pride of Nations – the Arbitress of Europe, perhaps, of the world."'[66]

As the king slowly returned to physical as well as mental health –
he had lost over forty pounds in weight since October – celebrations
grew, climaxing in a grand service of thanksgiving at St Paul's
Cathedral in London on St George's Day, 23 April 1789. Paine had
noted that 'Those about him have endeavoured to dissuade him
from this ostentatious pilgrimage, most probably from an apprehension of some effect it may have upon him.' But this proved to be no
more than a last flicker of hopeful ill will. The king's appearance, and
that of his Prime Minister, produced an authentic wave of public
jubilation. Cheering crowds took the horses from Pitt's carriage and
drew it in triumph through the streets of the capital.[67] It seemed that
the near-permanent crisis that had endured since Pitt first came to
office had at last passed. Looming across the Channel, however, was
a challenge that would transform British politics more completely
than could be imagined on a fine spring day in 1789.

———

# 9

# 'Highly fraught with disinterested benevolence'

*Empire, reason, race and profit in the Pacific*

While London celebrated the return of reason to its king, on the other side of the world a voyage conceived in service of the twin goals of reason and imperial majesty was about to fall into madness. Fletcher Christian, the earnest, able son of distressed gentlefolk, master's mate and acting lieutenant aboard His Majesty's Armed Vessel *Bounty*, had by late April 1789 been driven beyond the bounds of restraint. A shipmate later recalled Christian saying on the 21st, 'I have been in Hell for weeks', and seven days later he was to echo those words to his superior, William Bligh, as the latter pleaded with him to see reason and recall their friendship: 'That – captain Bligh – that is the thing – I am in Hell – I am in Hell.'[1] On the night of 28 April Christian and a little over half the *Bounty*'s crew took the ship, in the most storied mutiny of all time. What most of those stories, centred so often on Bligh's tyranny and the sexual allure of Polynesia, have overlooked is the remarkable interlocking of historical currents at work in the tale. From the dispatch of the ship on its mission to the wanderings of the forlorn mutineers, the whole episode is wrapped in the global shifts of this particular moment.

Bligh's voyage took place at the behest of the West Indian planter interest, and his mission was to feed the slaves of the British Caribbean. The breadfruit cuttings he was to bring back would grow into trees that could yield several hundred melon-sized, high-energy fruits without significant regular tending. Slaves could be fed, so the project went, from the resources of their own islands, without detracting from their productive labours, and also without reliance on imports from the newly independent United States or other foreign powers. To tie the project still further into the mesh of empire, the original plan had been for one of the ships that made up the First Fleet transporting convicts to Australia to carry on to the South Seas for this collection mission. The man whose plant-gathering exploits had led James Cook to christen the convicts' destination 'Botany Bay', Sir Joseph Banks, was the scientific and political linchpin of Bligh's quest.

The son of a wealthy gentleman MP, Banks had been educated at Harrow, Eton and Oxford, where his passion for natural history had blossomed. Inheriting his father's landed estate in 1761, aged eighteen, Banks had, like Jefferson, resisted the temptations of wealth and devoted himself to scientific study. Elected to the Royal Society, Britain's elite scientific institution, at twenty-three, and distinguishing himself shortly after with a botanising expedition to Newfoundland and Labrador, Banks was a natural choice for Captain Cook's first epic voyage in 1768–71. He made botanical discoveries in Brazil, Tahiti, New Zealand and Australia, and his accounts of this voyage secured his scientific fame. From 1778 he held the position of president of the Royal Society, where he would remain at the helm of British scientific endeavour for forty-one years.[2]

Banks's letters on the planning of Bligh's voyage show his overarching interest in uniting scientific investigation with the exploitation of such discoveries for imperial gain. They also reveal his mind for detail: one letter contained, among other instructions for the care and watering of the young plants, a scheme for driving rats out of the holds onto 'a boat with green boughs' laid alongside, by means of 'a Drum kept going below'. Such detail excluded much concern, however, for the men who would make the trip: 'as poison will constantly be used to destroy [the rats] and the cockroaches, the Crew must not complain if some of them who may die in the ceiling make an unpleasant smell'.[3] The same letter also included an early variant of the vessel's route, taking it first to New Zealand to gather examples of the native flax plant there, which Banks had seen on his own voyage, and thought might have valuable properties for making canvas and rope. A second draft of the plan dropped the flax, but instead sent the ship homewards via the Malay Peninsula, where

'Mangosteens, Jacks, Durians' and other tropical fruits could be procured in living examples for transplantation.[4]

In May 1787 Banks wrote a long letter to the government's Secretary for War. Setting out from the good news of the recent establishment of a Botanic Garden at Calcutta, and its plan of communicating with that of St Vincent's in the Caribbean, Banks launched into a long disquisition on the productive benefits of a world-circling quest for transplantable items. Noting that 'Our politic neighbours, the French, have preceded us several years in the execution of similar projects' and had introduced nutmeg and cloves from the East Indies to the West, Banks offered numerous suggestions from his own encyclopedic botanical knowledge of potential successes. The 'best kind' of mangoes might be reared, and many other fruits, including the 'lichee. A fruit which the late Governor General, Mr Hastings, is said to have imported from China.' Basmati rice, and 'Naugharbussee Bamboo', far superior to the bamboos imported to the Caribbean by the Spanish from the Philippines, could be brought, and the mysterious 'small black seed with which shauls are allways packed', and which drove off moths, would be worth exploring, as 'its value will be great in Russia' and other countries with a large fur trade. The 'Cheh root' used to make red dye, and the 'Cajir Gautch', a palm whose sap made an alcoholic drink, were also named. Banks then listed around a dozen products of the Western hemisphere that might equally well be tried in the East, and over a dozen varieties of roots, grains and fruits where different varieties from the two Indies could be crossed productively. He closed by noting: 'I shall ever think myself happy when I have the honour to be called upon to throw my small assistance towards perfecting a plan so highly fraught with disinterested benevolence as this.'[5]

Banks was an ardent promoter of the 'Republic of Letters', the international brotherhood of intellectuals that such disinterested benevolence pointed towards. Through the years of the war with America he had kept up correspondence with scientific authorities there and in France, such higher concerns seen as legitimately surpassing mere political enmity. With war officially over, in the mid-1780s Banks developed more formal links across the Channel, and in 1787 he was admitted as an honorary member of the French Academy of Sciences, where disinterested endeavours were given even higher priority than in Britain and the marquis de Condorcet led a scintillating elite from his post as perpetual secretary to the Academy. The following year this co-operation was cemented by joint participation in a complex effort of mathematical surveying, the 'triangulation project' designed to determine the relative positions of the two countries' royal observatories at Paris and Greenwich, and thus to help set the baselines for mapping the world more accurately.[6]

Mapping and direct exploration were at the heart of the scientific efforts Banks and his French counterparts promoted. The voyages of Captain Cook symbolised this, for, as their contemporary Edward Gibbon wrote, they were seen to be 'inspired by the pure and generous love of science and mankind'. Benjamin Franklin was instrumental in ensuring that American forces were ordered not to interfere with Cook's last voyage (though tragically, by the time the instructions were given, Cook had already been slaughtered) and Banks rewarded this effort with a Gold Medal from the Royal Society to honour Franklin's 'sentiments of general philanthropy'.[7] Cook's voyages had their counterpart in a circumnavigation of the world between 1766 and 1769 by a French expedition led by the nobleman, soldier, diplomat and mathematician Louis Antoine de Bougainville. Though, ironically, Bougainville discovered little of note – he was beaten to Tahiti, for example, by a rival British circumnavigation team – his fame rivalled Cook's because his account of Tahiti entered the language of the Enlightenment. Denis Diderot wrote a famous *supplement* to Bougainville's account, in which the 'noble savages' of the South Seas stood almost transparently for a critique of European corruption.

As Bligh's *Bounty* sailed towards the Pacific, another French expedition was circumnavigating that great ocean. Jean-François, comte de La Pérouse, had led two ships in an epic voyage for over three years, from Chile to Alaska, south to California, across the whole ocean to the Philippines and north to unknown regions of Korea, Siberia and northern Japan. On Siberia's Kamchatka Peninsula Russian official hospitality brought welcome contact with civilisation, including mail, and orders from France to investigate the new British colony at Botany Bay.[8] For the underlying truth of these great disinterested endeavours was that they fitted into both the pattern of Enlightenment scientific internationalism and the mould of imperial expansion and rivalry. Both Bougainville and the British captain who beat him to Tahiti claimed the land for their sovereigns, and the two

Crowns would continue to squabble over the territory for another half-century before France prevailed.

Closer to home, Joseph Banks would ardently promote the British annexation of Iceland (and its flourishing fisheries) after the turn of the century, even stretching logic to argue that 'Iceland is by nature a part of the group of islands called by the ancients "Britannia", and consequently that it ought to be a Part of the British Empire'. In 1788 Banks helped found the Association for Promoting the Discovery of the Interior Parts of Africa, concerning which he wrote to a French colleague: 'I certainly wish that my countrymen should make discoveries of all kinds in preference to the inhabitants of other kingdoms.'[9] Banks's fertile mind was ever at work to find ways of putting such discoveries to economic use, and he was a tireless proponent of agricultural experimentation in Britain's new Australian colony. The more aggressive side of his thoughts also came out in later correspondence. He was happy to allow for foreign settlements on the continent, 'under the moral certainty of its getting into our hands in time of war', but aggressively opposed allowing the Americans to interlope in trade with the motherland: Governors should be instructed to enforce a ban 'with severity'.[10]

It is intriguing to see in the correspondence of Thomas Jefferson how the national and international dimensions of Banks's interests were paralleled, and necessarily sometimes inverted, by the American's concern for science and country. Their circles of acquaintance firmly overlapped, whether from the angle of Thomas Paine and his bridge-building schemes, or in correspondence with Cassini at the French Royal Observatory, where Jefferson on 3 July 1789 wrote asking to set his watches by their measure, and promised to keep them going until he could 'start the tracing of a meridian line at home'.[11] In the same letter in which Paine reported to Jefferson that Banks had read a paper about his bridge to the Royal Society, he also noted his discovery of an inventor's 'geometrical wheelbarrow', a surveying machine for virgin lands, concerning which Jefferson was eager for more details.[12] La Pérouse's voyage interested Jefferson enough to mention it (along with Paine's bridge) in a letter to the provost of Harvard College, thanking him for an honorary degree; the return of the ships, he wrote, would 'add to our knowledge in geography botany and natural history'.[13] Through Paine, Jefferson learned from Banks of the death of an American explorer, John

Ledyard, in Egypt in January 1789. He was on the first stages of an expedition that had hoped to cross Africa from the Red Sea to the Atlantic, but died of illness while still making arrangements in Alexandria. Ledyard, only thirty-eight at his death, had already tried, at Jefferson's suggestion, to cross the Eurasian continent and reach America overland, but had been turned back by Catherine the Great's police in 1788, having reached Yakutsk in east-central Siberia. Both Banks and the marquis de Lafayette had bankrolled this epic journey.

Through another London correspondent, Benjamin Vaughan, Jefferson heard that Banks had experimented with different varieties of 'dry' rice seeds from the uplands of the East Indies, and Jefferson sought some of the same seeds to send home to the Carolinas for American experimentation. On 17 March 1789 Vaughan indicated how close the links were between such projects: 'We expect the bread-fruit vessel to leave us some of these seeds, when she arrives . . . and I will take measures for your supply as soon as possible from that quarter.'[14] Jefferson was also exploiting his friendship with the former French government minister Lamoignon de Malesherbes, a noted amateur botanist, to seek 'some seeds of the dry rice of Cochin-China'. He stressed, in language echoing Banks's formulations: 'Your zeal to promote the general good of mankind by an interchange of useful things, and particularly in the line of agriculture.'[15] Malesherbes responded with an invitation to dine with him and two men with experience of rice-growing in France's Indian Ocean possessions. Jefferson was also eager to introduce the olive tree to the southern US states, calling it 'one of the most precious productions of nature [that] contributes the most to the happiness of mankind'.[16]

But the language of Enlightenment rationality and co-operation was not the sole register in which Jefferson regarded agriculture and trade. The expansion of American commerce, if necessary at the expense of others, was an ever active concern, and he was eager for American suppliers to take up a French bounty for imports of grain, offered by Necker's government from November 1788, as 'The apprehension of a want of corn has induced them to turn their eyes to foreign supplies'.[17] Reports in April 1789 that such cargoes were clearing a 100 per cent net profit rewarded his efforts to oblige Necker to overrule the 'chicanery' of customs officials and actually pay the bounty as advertised.[18] Jefferson had a long correspondence with various Charleston merchants about the prospects for shipping Carolina rice to Constantinople – and the perils of Barbary piracy en route. If such a discussion brought home the grimmer realities of global trade in one fashion, Jefferson's own lobbying of the French government to encourage the production of cheap cloth for export to America, including the items known expressively as 'negro plains', was a reminder that this *philosophe* was also a slave owner and representative of a society dependent on servitude.[19]

Jefferson was also an avowed enemy of Britain. Though at least once in correspondence in the spring of 1789 he called himself an 'Englishman' – in connection with his amazement at the 'boldness' of the new French press – he was committed to doing down the commerce of the old overlord.[20] He welcomed even the far-fetched notions of St John de Crèvecoeur, the French-born New York farmer and writer, that 'within Two Years' American ships and goods might dominate trade with India, and much of his discussion with French and American merchants alike concerned fostering trade links to bypass old connections via Bristol, Liverpool and London.[21] In a letter to George Washington of December 1788 he allied the advantages of the new federal government and its powers of taxation to the need to combat continued British control of the seas: 'all the resources of taxation will be necessary for the safety of the state' at some point soon, for 'who can avoid seeing the source of war in the tyranny of those nations who deprive us of the natural right of trading with our neighbours?'[22]

His zeal to do down what he saw as domineering British activities led Jefferson at the end of 1788 into an extensive investigation of an industry poised, like so many others, for an epochal global advance: the hunting of the great whales. In the process of helping to overturn a French move to close their ports to all 'foreign' whale oils, he demonstrated that a Franco-American agreement would save the French almost five million *livres* that they would otherwise have to find, to subsidise a native fishery to compete against a British trade run rampant. British exclusion of Americans from their trade, he asserted, had seen their fleet double to over three hundred ships in the past three years alone, while the Americans out of Nantucket could barely support eighty, a fall of three-quarters since the early 1770s. While Jefferson's arguments for the interests of the French in allowing Americans to land their catch there succeeded in opening their ports, his letter to Washington also reported gleefully that the move would put one hundred British ships out of the trade, 'and 150 ere long'.[23]

Such optimism was to be blunted by a voyage already under way. The stout London whaling-ship *Emelia* rounded Cape Horn on 20 January 1789 on a mission to collect a significant government bounty for whaling voyages to the South Seas lasting at least eighteen months. So swiftly did she fill her holds that on the return voyage she had to lurk off Gravesend for several days, extending her absence to qualify for the bounty.[24] Scarcely fifteen years before, European and American whaling had been confined almost exclusively to the North Atlantic. The famed Nantucket whalers had reached the coasts of Brazil as the American War broke out, to see their trade devastated by sanctions and blockade. Now a race was on to open the seas of the whole world. The prize was the sperm whale, its rendered oil being worth three times the price of the 'common oil' gleaned from Greenland right whales, and the spermaceti, the waxy 'head-matter' drawn off from its bulbous 'case', selling for double again.[25] Sperm oil, and particularly spermaceti candles, burned longer, cleaner and brighter than other light sources, even the costly beeswax candles of the rich. With the swelling beginnings of an industrial revolution that could no longer work to the rhythms of the seasons, artificial light was an essential component of growth and progress. Whale oils also lubricated fine machinery without clouding, clogging or putrefying as other animal and vegetable fats did. The wheels of the nineteenth century would turn on the product of great cetaceans harpooned from matchwood boats, racing across the vast swells of the world-ocean.

British whalers and statesmen alike had seen this development coming, agreeing high bounties in the 1780s even before the deal that sent the *Emelia* south. Nantucket whalers were lured to settle in Nova Scotia after the American War with the prospect of entry into the British trade, and a few years later some would even be paid to settle in west Wales. The French had tried to compete. When another scheme to import a hundred Nantucket families to England had been rejected in 1785, the ministry thinking the cost too high, the French had offered a bounty to settle the men in Dunkirk. Only nine families came, however. Other French efforts to compete, drawing on technical excellence, as with their cotton mills, seemed to founder always in the face of British economic drive. For example, a state-of-the-art rendering plant at Rouen, built in the late 1780s to extract wax from sperm oil, could not halt the flow of men, ships and goods into Britain.[26] The British government's Act for the Encouragement of the Southern Whale Fishery in 1786 swept aside the monopoly of the defunct South Seas Company to open the prospect of voyages round Cape Horn. The more sternly defended monopoly of the East India Company, which prohibited ships from taking cargo east past the Cape of Good Hope, was circumvented with another kind of government help. The long voyage could not be made to pay without some outbound cargo, and a new kind became available in 1787. Two of the ships that carried convicts in the Australian First Fleet were whalers, though neither managed a successful hunt on arrival. By 1791 five whalers would sail with the Third Fleet, and go on to return via the whaling ground off Peru located by the *Emelia*, completing a circuit of the globe. There they found three former Nantucket ships out of Dunkirk, and five Americans. Eighteen British ships also made the voyage that year, rising to dozens in the years ahead.[27]

Whalers would slaughter both their prey and whole populations of other animals – seals notably – for food, in the remotest corners of the world in the decades to come. They would also impose themselves brutally on isolated populations, especially in a quest, on their years-long voyages, for the pleasures of female company. In this they joined more 'official' explorers in forcing their expectations upon such cultures, at gunpoint if necessary. The grimmer side of the Pacific exploration written up by the Enlightenment as the discovery of 'noble savages' was always there, when one looked. Captain Cook, before he had been cut down in Hawaii, had used force and fraud often enough against recalcitrant locals, to retaliate for attacks, or just to get what he wanted. The very first encounter of Europeans with Tahiti, when Captain Samuel Wallis of the Royal Navy anchored his ship offshore on 21 June 1767, was consummated by a wave of musketry and cannon fire, driving off a massed canoe attack with major casualties.[28] A month of feasting and fornication that followed, though it helped cement the image of the place as a paradise, did not take away the underlying danger or brutality. La Pérouse's expedition was assaulted at a landfall in Samoa in December 1787, losing a dozen dead, and others who succumbed to their injuries as they voyaged on.[29] The British First Fleet they met in Botany Bay on 23 January 1788, which abandoned that beguilingly named place for

the less barren and windswept inlet that would become Sydney
Harbour, found deadly conflict in every step of its relations with the
Australians. And the day before William Bligh faced the mutineers
on the *Bounty*, he had held three local Tongan chiefs hostage in his
rage against thefts. He had called Fletcher Christian a thief too, for
opening a coconut from the ship's store. In his anguish that night the
latter had gathered timbers and supplies, torn up his personal papers
and seemed to intend to raft ashore and desert. Instead he and his
fellows took the ship.[30]

The *Bounty*'s crew, like almost all their fellow long-distance travellers in this era, lived under conditions hard to imagine. They had
sailed over twenty thousand miles in a vessel eighty-five feet long
and twenty-four feet wide – forty-six men and a mass of stores enduring everything that the ocean could throw at them, including an
unsuccessful attempt to round Cape Horn, and a reversal of course,
to pass by South Africa, that added months to their journey. They
were crammed in even more than was usual, for the largest habitable
space in the ship, the captain's cabin, had been taken over with stag-
ing to house the plants they were to collect. Lieutenant Bligh, as
captain, dwelt instead in a windowless cabin eight feet long. The
other senior men – master, boatswain, surgeon, master's mates and
midshipmen – were in even more cramped quarters, and the seamen
slung their hammocks where they could.[31] To make things worse,
the ship carried a wearisome freight of anxieties and expectations,
nowhere more fraught, perhaps, than in the mind of William Bligh
himself.

Bligh was of an old naval family, and his father, who died in 1780,
had been Chief of Customs for the port of Plymouth. He had long
been set for a naval career and was entered on the ship's books of
HMS *Monmouth* aged only seven, a common ruse to accumulate sea-
time, and hence future seniority, for the sons of friends and relations.
He was actually at sea by his mid-teens, and must have proved himself a young man of superior ability, because at twenty-one no less a
navigator than Captain Cook requested his services as sailing master
for his third, and final, great voyage. Here, however, the tragic ambiguity that dogged Bligh's career raised its head. At this age he could
legitimately expect a lieutenant's commission, while becoming a
master – a mere warrant-officer – was a step outside the smooth hierarchy that led to future command.

Bligh took the position and distinguished himself with his diligent service, only to see it brought almost to naught by Cook's gruesome death. He did himself no favours by failing to conceal his view that the cowardice of others present had been an essential factor in the captain's loss, and he was marginalised from even the small share of glory that remained. The charts and soundings he had meticulously drawn up were published, mysteriously, under another's name.[32] His voyage with Cook, and its acrimonious aftermath, might have been an object lesson in the world of personal connections that ran the Royal Navy. Among his fellow officers, for example, was James Burney, brother of the Court diarist Fanny. (Also aboard ship, serving as a humble corporal of marines, was John Ledyard, the future ill-fated explorer.) Like almost every other significant figure involved, Burney produced an account of events, and became embroiled in bitter controversy. The result of this was that he, with his social-climbing connections, was one of only two officers from the voyage to be promoted to captain in the decade that followed.

Burney had already experienced the benefits of good social connections: he had had to wait only a year for a commission as lieutenant after passing the qualifying examination, while most of his fellows had waited between four and eight years in the lean pre-war navy to gain an appointment. The one among them who had waited the longest, John Rickman, had taken sixteen years to gain a lieutenant's berth. Of entirely undistinguished family, he was the only officer on the voyage never promoted again, and despite his being on the other side of the bay from Cook's death, accounts increasingly foisted blame onto him for stirring the Hawaiians to anger in a preceding incident.[33] One of the other officers, accused of actual cowardice in many accounts written by witnesses in the immediate aftermath, was whitewashed when official documents were compiled. This man, John Williamson, was the only one beside Burney to become a captain, and was tied through his Irish family into the circles of patronage that surrounded Charles James Fox's Whigs. This was not enough in the 1780s to guarantee his success in life, but certainly enough to save him from vilification in a highly politicised and socially conscious affair.[34]

Bligh doubtless watched all this manoeuvring with ill-concealed disgust. Though the expanded wartime navy of the early 1780s gave him his lieutenant's commission, he was thrown on the beach, with a new wife to support, at the close of hostilities in 1783, and for four years served as a merchant captain for his wife's uncle, shipping the products of slavery from the Caribbean. Lacking as he did Burney's or Williamson's social connections, appointment to the *Bounty*, even if still only as a humble lieutenant, was a return to the paths of future promotion for a man now worried about stagnation as his mid-thirties loomed. Bligh's history was thus emblematic of the fluidity of the naval world in its relation with the wider social reality of a largely aristocratic society. But it was also, during his fateful voyage, to be conditioned by another kind of fluidity, one that linked Bligh's quest to fulfil Joseph Banks's scientific and imperial goals to another question of the age, the relationship between reason and custom, progress and tradition, self-interest and the common good.

Below the surface of the rule of the famous Articles of War, which made a naval captain second only to God aboard ship and enjoined flogging or death for all forms of disobedience, was a reality of a professional community, especially in peacetime, that clung to traditional rights and cast a critical eye on pretensions to supremacy. Bligh would tangle repeatedly, for example, with John Fryer, the man who filled his old position of sailing master. Despite Bligh's eminent navigational skills, he was stuck with an associate who regarded directing the ship's course as, at least in part, his prerogative. And when Bligh clashed with other senior men, as he did repeatedly with the ship's carpenter, William Purcell, the limits of his authority were revealed. As possessors of Admiralty warrants, such men were punishable only by court-martial, and for the good of the ship Bligh was forced to accommodate himself to behaviour that was little short of mutinous, long before even reaching Tahiti.[35] Bligh's solution to Purcell's behaviour – to threaten him with withdrawal of rations unless he worked as ordered – was effective in his eyes, but merely highlighted one of the other abiding tensions among the crew.

Because the ship was so small, Bligh was forced to undertake the duties another officer normally carried, the purser, and there was no more detested figure aboard an eighteenth-century warship. Pursers dealt with rations and stores, for which they were responsible to the Navy Board, and had to provide sureties out of their own pockets. Notoriously, they covered this risk by scrimping on rations issued, over and above the fact that they were allowed to keep an eighth of everything issued to cover wastage: thus a 'pusser's pound' had only fourteen ounces, and their common nickname was 'Nipcheese'.[36]

Bligh, forced to carry the purser's sureties on a meagre lieutenant's salary, was meticulous in keeping his books, and in requiring the master, Fryer, to countersign them as rules obliged. Such was the tension raised between these two that in October 1788, on the voyage out, Fryer had tried to extort a sort of certificate of good conduct from Bligh, in return for his signature on the books. Bligh in return held an extraordinary ceremony in which the Articles of War were read, emphasising the master's duties, and Fryer publicly signed, intoning that he did it 'in obedience to your Orders, but this may be Cancelled hereafter'.[37] The heavy implication was that he suspected dishonest accounting, a slur that resonated with the crew. When Bligh, with his undoubted captain's authority, cut rations, or substituted one kind of food for another, as he had to on the long voyage and afterwards in Tahiti, he was also acting as purser. Thus, in the men's eyes, he was acting for his own profit and against their real sense of customary right and entitlement to certain rations. It was a classic, emblematic confrontation of the era, between a man with law and reason on his side and others with custom and interest on theirs.

To compound matters still further, Bligh found himself contending with that ultimate cliché of the sail navy, an incompetent drunken surgeon. As a devoted follower of Captain Cook's methods against scurvy, Bligh was horrified to discover, shortly after the Fryer incident, that some of his men were suffering the effects of poor nutrition, and dosed them furiously with essence of malt and sauerkraut. The surgeon's lethargic reckoning that every vague pain some men suffered thereafter was scurvy, combined with his reluctance to help enforce the diet and exercise regime Bligh insisted on, drove the captain into a fury. His own inspection of the men showed no sign of scorbutic symptoms, and the surgeon declared himself sick with a 'paralytic affection'. The man was blind drunk, and Bligh had to search his cabin, confiscating all his alcohol, to get him to sober up enough for one last crucial duty. As they arrived at Tahiti, the surgeon was needed 'to examine very particularly every Man and Officer' for signs of venereal disease. He did so, declaring, no doubt to general rejoicing, that all were 'totally free from the Venereal complaint'.[38] That situation would not last.

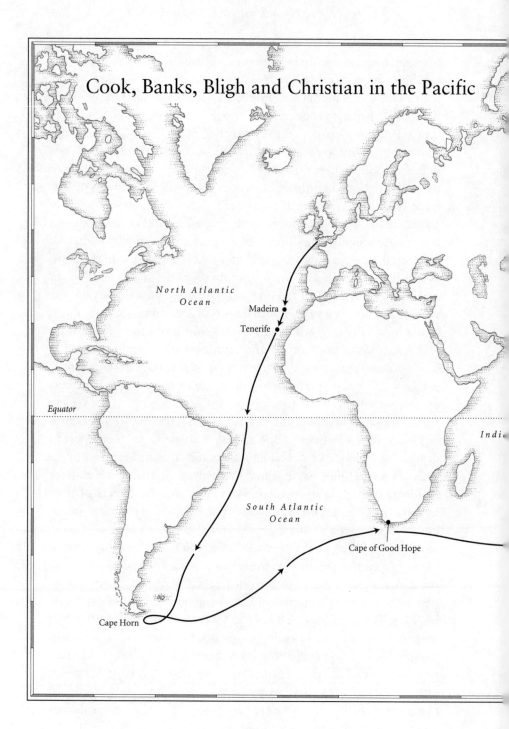

# Cook, Banks, Bligh and Christian in the Pacific

*North Atlantic
Ocean*

Madeira •

Tenerife •

*Equator*

*I n d i*

*South Atlantic
Ocean*

Cape of Good Hope

Cape Horn

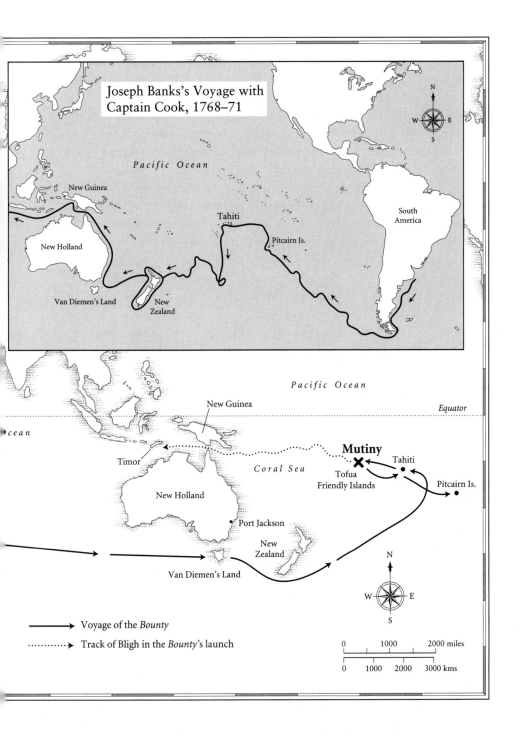

Joseph Banks's Voyage with
Captain Cook, 1768–71

*Pacific Ocean*

New Guinea

Tahiti

Pitcairn Is.

South
America

New Holland

Van Diemen's Land

New
Zealand

*Pacific Ocean*

Equator

New Guinea

Timor

**Mutiny**

Tahiti

*Coral Sea*

Tofua
Friendly Islands

Pitcairn Is.

New Holland

Port Jackson

New
Zealand

Van Diemen's Land

Voyage of the *Bounty*

Track of Bligh in the *Bounty*'s launch

| 0 | 1000 | 2000 miles |

| 0 | 1000 | 2000 | 3000 kms |

The *Bounty* stayed at Tahiti for five months, far longer than originally planned, as the delay of the failed rounding of the Horn meant
it now had to ride out the stormy season before departing. In those
five months the crew showed the same porous willingness to blend
with 'Indian' life as had the young men of the East India Company.
Much of that porosity was due, as elsewhere, to sexual liaisons. The
Tahitian women were everything that sailors' legend already said
them to be – golden-skinned, beautiful (especially to bandy-legged,
pock-marked Britons with nothing but themselves to stare at for
months) and both sexually available and experienced in ways little
short of a dream come true. As Bligh put it, 'Even the mouths of
Women are not exempt from the polution [sic], and many other as
uncommon ways have they of gratifying their beastly inclinations.'[39]
The delights of Tahitian culture sucked the men in, and most soon
found themselves welcomed by local chiefs and other heads of
households, who became their *taios*, hosts and guardians. The fact
that the British could supply them with items, especially metals, in
short supply in Polynesia was at the root of this exuberant welcome,
no doubt, but, as elsewhere, it drew them into local life. Many soon
exhibited tattoos, an art form of the region first brought to European
attention by Cook's voyages. Some stuck to mottos and heraldic
emblems, but others went further in accepting the Tahitians' notion
of proper tattooing. An eligible bachelor had to have his entire but-
tocks blackened with tattoo – a long and painful process. Among
several who endured this for the sake of their welcome was Fletcher
Christian.[40]

Christian's position on the voyage had always been an odd one, for
he was rather a liminal figure. His family was old and once well-to-
do, but had slipped into such impoverishment through living beyond
their means that relatives had had to club together to save his widowed mother from debts of over £6000 in 1779, and she had moved
to the Isle of Man, where outside courts' writs did not run, to be free
from further legal threats. Fletcher, a younger son, had to make his
own way, and after an uncertain start had entered the navy as a midshipman at the uncommonly advanced age of eighteen in 1783. He
spent over two years aboard the frigate HMS *Eurydice*, much of it on
a cruise to the East Indies. During this time he proved his worth, and
was raised to master's mate, the traditional holding position for a
young gentleman who had not yet gained a lieutenant's commission

but might be expected to do so. On his return from the voyage he, like Bligh, found himself unemployed, and family contacts advised him to seek out the latter, in his new role as a merchant captain. Christian must have impressed by his enthusiasm, as his offer to serve as a common seaman, given a lack of officer berths, was taken up for one voyage, and on a second Bligh rated him as a 'gunner' and treated him as one of his officers. Indeed he seemed to become a protégé, and Bligh's continuing influence brought him aboard the *Bounty*. Here again he was initially rated as 'able seaman', but was raised to master's mate and acting lieutenant three months into the voyage.[41]

Christian was young, eager, vigorous, popular with the men, thirsty for experience and adventure – and thus potentially a thorn in the side of Bligh, who was slight, pale, anxious about his own finances and the perilous success of the voyage, and prone thus, as fiction has painted him ever since, to gratuitous irascibility. Something very like penny-pinching seems to have come between him and Christian during their stop in Cape Town. Acting as a banker, as he had learned to do when a merchant captain, Bligh lent money to Christian and others in the expectation that they or their relations back home would redeem the debts at a profit. Ill will began to creep into Bligh and Christian's relationship – one that others had noted had something of infatuation in it initially for Bligh towards the younger man, so charming, so eager to please, so grateful for chances to learn.[42] Christian was just the sort of man to see no harm in the crew's rising contempt for Bligh and his ways, and to affect not to notice the underhand mockery so easily inflicted on a man who could not control his temper but insisted on controlling everything else. While much of the crew, and Christian and the other 'young gentlemen', spent their free time on Tahiti in frank debauchery, Bligh played diplomat to local kings and queens, took anthropological notes and agonised over the growth of the seedlings in a nursery he had set up inland. He tried to keep Tahitians from the ship (where they were all too likely to steal anything not bolted down, and sometimes even those that were, for profit or adventure), prohibited uncontrolled trade with them, sought to confiscate 90 per cent of the foodstuffs brought aboard for the ship's stores and generally opened himself to mockery and disregard.

Discipline began to fall apart. Three men deserted, and remained

at large on the island for three weeks before the local king was able
to find intelligence of them, and Bligh led a party to track them
down. But he was so short-handed he could not clap them in irons for
the voyage home and had to be content with a few dozen lashes,
which for hardened seamen was little more than could be expected
for a routine bout of drunkenness. Bligh was not a flogging captain,
but nor was he one who could command respect in other ways.
Master Fryer was wilfully negligent, it seemed, allowing a man who
had helped the deserters to escape from the ship, while covering
himself with a mealy-mouthed note sent to the captain. The
boatswain, in charge of sails and rigging, allowed the spare canvas to
rot in the hold: 'scarce any neglect of duty can equal the criminality
of this', Bligh raged in his log, but neither this man nor Fryer could
be removed, for he had no 'Officers to supersede' them, and even
'considering them as common Seamen', he was not 'capable of doing
without them'.[43]

By force of will and rage Bligh dragged the ship's company back
together for the voyage home. Young plants filled the cabin, and
assorted stores crammed the holds. The men, in the end, did not
come on board particularly unwillingly, and indeed by one account
'Everybody was in high spirits'. They looked forward to earning
good sums for the 'artificial curiosities' of the South Seas they had
stuffed into every available space, and some had already planned the
narratives they would write of their adventures for an eager and curious public. But Bligh's rages only grew. His contempt now extended
to all those put under him, after further negligent incidents: 'No
order[s] for hours together were obeyed by them and their conduct
in general is so bad that no confidence or trust can be reposed in
them.'[44] He had a long and arduous voyage to look forward to, in
which a thousand tender seedlings had to be protected from salt
water at all costs, and a second, more purely naval priority fulfilled.
The Admiralty wanted charts and soundings of the Endeavour
Straits, along the north coast of Australia, a difficult and precise job
for a captain and crew in harmony: it must have appeared an agonising prospect for Bligh. No wonder his accusations grew after they
weighed anchor on 4 April 1789, and he had the crew aloft near midnight on the 21st, when, Fryer later recalled, Christian spoke to him
bluntly, 'Sir your abuse is so bad that I cannot do my Duty with any
Pleasure. I have been in Hell for weeks with you.'[45]

Accounts of the mutiny itself, and of the various adventures that followed, would always be clouded with inconsistencies and contradictions. But a few points stand out, and all reinforce the power of imperial culture at this moment in world time. The fate of Bligh is one of them. Cast adrift in the South Pacific with the loyal half of his crew, nineteen men in an open launch twenty-three feet long and less than seven feet wide, with a haphazard assortment of rations that could not hope to last them over a week, and barely a hand's breadth of freeboard above the waves, Bligh sailed 3618 nautical miles to safety. It was an astonishing feat, done with a few basic navigational tables, an old quadrant and Bligh's memory. Attacked by locals at their first landfall not far from the site of the mutiny – one man had his brains beaten out on the beach – and thereafter wary of all contacts, they skirted Fiji and the New Hebrides before making landfall at last on the northern tip of Australia, resting and feeding on the beaches but ever alert for attack. Bligh doled out the rations with an iron will and did not lose his irascibility: on one occasion he had to be restrained from assaulting the useless carpenter Purcell with a cutlass, but it was the equally despised Fryer who saved him from committing murder. Their disputes continued when they reached safety at the Dutch port of Coupang, on Timor, for Bligh still could not keep discipline among such recalcitrants, and caused further discontent with his mercantile ways over the advance of funds. These were funds for which he had to pledge personal sureties to the cautious Dutch, however, and which enabled the whole crew, less a few who tragically succumbed to illness in the fever-infested port, to be repatriated within the year.

The global reach of Western trading power brought Bligh and his men home, just as the global ambition of the scientific navigator got them to safety. Bligh had written in his log that as soon as they set out in the boat 'I felt an inward happiness which prevented any depression of my spirits; conscious of my own integrity and anxious solicitude for the good of the service I was on – I found my mind most wonderfully supported.'[46] What is even more intriguing is the great support the mutineers found in the ways of imperialism, though these were to destroy almost all of them in the end. From the start they formed a volatile mix of equality and hierarchy. They made themselves uniform clothes from sailcloth – a curiously symbolic gesture against rank – but made Christian their captain and gave him back the great cabin. The breadfruit plants, Bligh's burning obsession, had been pitched overboard within hours of his departure. Then they sailed away, to an island on which no European had landed before but which Cook had charted, Tubuai, over three hundred miles south of Tahiti. Their first contact with the natives was marked, as it had been twenty years earlier at Tahiti, with spears and gunfire, followed by cautious politics. But there were not enough spare resources on the island to feed the mutineers, and provide them with women – a veritable obsession – so a return to Tahiti was required. There they extracted hundreds of hogs, fifty goats, assorted other livestock, nine women and twenty-five men from the locals with a story that Bligh had met Cook again (his death having been systematically concealed) and needed supplies for a new settlement.

The new settlement on Tubuai, as Christian planned it, was 'Fort George', complete with a hundred yards of earthen ramparts twenty-five feet high and twelve feet thick, an eighteen-foot-wide ditch, watch-towers, drawbridge and cannon at the corners. And the Union Jack flying over all.[47] It took six weeks to build, in July and August 1789 – the mutineers' Bastille, going up just as the Parisians would set to work tearing down theirs. By the time it was finished it was already evidently a folly. The outward signs of European power could not conceal from local chiefs that this was a small and fissiparous band, and armed expeditions to gain local co-operation grew more bloody, and also more pointless. On one such expedition, the mutineers later recalled, they gunned down perhaps 120 men and women, and achieved no peace from raids and thefts. To overcome the threat of their band dissolving into murderous quarrels, Christian had them all swear 'articles' of reconciliation, but also had to concede the abandonment of Tubuai. On 15 September 1789 they set sail again for Tahiti. There sixteen men were left, while eight sailed with Christian, along with twelve Tahitian women, one female infant, five Tahitian men and one Tubuaian. Almost all of the islanders appear to have been kidnapped, the ship departing for a turn round the island that became a long voyage.[48]

Christian's party sailed to Pitcairn Island, where they burned the *Bounty* and tried to establish a farming settlement. The tale of their fate is even more cloudy than most of this narrative, surviving only from recollections gathered decades later. But it seems that the men came increasingly to treat their Polynesian fellows as slaves, as well as working on resentments and sexual jealousies among themselves, and that, by ones and twos, they murdered each other, or were murdered by the Tahitians – such was Christian's fate, bashed on the head as he tended his garden – until only one remained. Able Seaman Alexander Smith, as entered on the *Bounty*'s books, had been taught to read by another mutineer, and under his original baptismal name John Adams found religion through the Bible and the *Book of Common Prayer*, and brought peace to the island through an idiosyncratic interpretation of those works, breeding new generations of men noted by visiting sailors for their extreme physical prowess, and women for their beauty.[49] If Pitcairn became a sort of fable, a Garden of Eden in reverse, paradise made out of evil, the deeds of the other mutineers left on Tahiti were more particularly resonant of this time.

Using the power of the still-magical memory of Cook, the men claimed a kinship with the Tahitians that ensured them a welcome. Many returned to the homes of the *taios* that had adopted them during their original stay. But this was not an easy homecoming. The guns and tools of the Westerners were devices to be used in the complicated politics of the island, and the hospitality of the Tahitians was expected to be repaid with loyalty. When James Morrison, boatswain's mate, revealed to some of his comrades his plan for building a seaworthy vessel and escaping, to the Dutch East Indies or even the Americas, they had to conceal this purpose from their hosts. They did so partly to ensure that they were willing to assist, but partly also from fear that such an escape, once discovered, would mean death for any who remained. Their vessel, a half-decked schooner of some thirty-one feet, had to be presented as an addition to local life; and would end up serving as a warship in the conquests of the Tahitian king. To build it required truly astonishing feats of improvisation. Morrison, along with two carpenters' mates, the cooper and the armourer, controlling the labour of several others, and roping in Tahitians when they could, cut each plank, thirty feet long, with a handsaw, taking a whole tree trunk for each one. When they heated them to bend onto frames, many split and had to be remade from scratch. They had no fine tools, and hardly any metal implements beyond a few saws and adzes. They had to experiment with tree sap and animal fats to make resins and pitch for caulking the seams, and build their own barrels to store water and provisions. To salt pork, they boiled seawater first, but it took a day to make a pound of salt, weeks to make enough to salt a single barrel of meat. Sailcloth was substituted with the local woven matting, and when the Tahitians realised its necessity, they made it, like anything else they could, a bargaining chip for aid in their own disputes.[50]

It was desperate, slow, back-breaking, soul-sapping work, for months on end, but it produced a vessel that the Tahitians themselves acknowledged put their canoes to shame. Could a handful of men of another culture, semi-literate by their own standards, thrown up on the far side of the world, in fear of their lives, have blended knowledge, ingenuity and local adaptation, the imposition of their will, diplomacy and fine craftsmanship in a similar way? The mutineers' real tragedy was that they made themselves and their vessel indispensable to the military ambitions of the Tahitian king Pomare. The finished schooner served as the centrepiece of several expeditions, and Morrison's crew were never left with the leisure to accumulate sufficient supplies for an escape. They were still on the island when the long arm of the British Empire and Royal Navy arrived to capture them a month shy of two years after the fateful mutiny. HMS *Pandora* took Morrison's schooner into service as a tender, while its makers lived chained in a box on the ship's deck. Given as a gift to the Dutch Governor of Timor, the vessel, named *Resolution* by Morrison but renamed *Matavy* by her captors, lived on as an ocean-spanning trader, a remarkable testament to her builders' skills. She was first used to trade for sea-otter furs across to the northwest coast of America, and spent a later period voyaging all across the Pacific as far as China, where she finally disappeared from history.[51]

James Morrison's own itinerary stands for some of the other ways in which the imperial culture could take hold of individuals. With his fellow mutineers he suffered through another epic voyage when the *Pandora* was lost on the Great Barrier Reef, en route to chart the same straits that Bligh had been bound for. Returning via an open-boat voyage to Timor, and to Portsmouth for court-martial, Morrison was convicted, but pardoned on account of good character and service, and re-entered the navy, though not before he had published an account of the mutiny that laid such blame on Bligh's bad character that the latter could only splutter about 'vile falsehoods' and 'malicious insinuations' in a letter to Joseph Banks.[52] Morrison served as a gunner on both West and East Indian stations, and was lost when HMS *Blenheim* foundered with all hands off Madagascar in 1807 – a ship taken to sea after suffering damage from running aground, on the orders of an officer more anxious to reach his new station at the Cape than to consider safety. If Rear Admiral Sir Thomas Troubridge had been as wily a professional sailor as James Morrison, the latter and all his crew might not have paid with their lives for his pride.[53]

As for Bligh, cleared of blame for losing his ship, he was to have a career dogged by mutiny and recrimination. When the sailors of the fleet rose against poor pay and conditions in 1797, Bligh was one of the captains at the site of the most serious troubles, the Nore, where the River Thames meets the North Sea. Though he was not singled out for the mutineers' attacks, and went on to a valiant career in naval actions over the next decade, on several occasions his legendary temper was brought up against him. In a litigious age naval officers brought each other to trial surprisingly often, and in 1805 Bligh was charged with acting in a 'tyrannical and oppressive and unofficerlike manner', shaking his fist in the face of one of his lieutenants.[54] Though the court-martial found the charge unfounded, and indeed 'frivolous', Bligh's reputation pursued him through another extraordinary episode in the South Seas. Ageing, and with little personal influence in the naval hierarchy, his health afflicted by long-term effects of his open-boat voyage, he was offered a new position by his indefatigable supporter, Banks.

The governorship of New South Wales offered Bligh a warm climate, a solid salary and a relief from the rigours of seaborne command, and he took it up in August 1806. In a little over a year he so antagonised the leaders of local society that they led a military *coup* against him and left him virtually a prisoner aboard a naval vessel until the business was recalled to Britain for court-martial two years later. Though this was dismissed by some writers as the 'Rum Rebellion', and confined to issues about the alleged illegal distillation of spirits – still in use, as they had been since the early 1790s, as a local currency – other accounts suggest more complex motives. Bligh's interventions (intemperate as usual) had threatened to disrupt the rise of a local propertied class of military officers and entrepreneurs, and he had also scorned them socially. At court-martial the defence even claimed, playing on Bligh's reputation, that he had used language 'too gross to be repeated' towards soldiers of the New South Wales Corps.[55] Putting aside the absurdity of licentious soldiery objecting to being sworn at, such a charge nonetheless brings us back to a core issue of social identity highlighted by the original mutiny of 1789.

As competing accounts of the mutiny circulated in the nineteenth century, new scraps of information came to light from many directions. One collector of folk tales recalled in the 1850s hearing over thirty years earlier from a survivor of Bligh's boat voyage that 'two scoundrels' had led the mutiny, being able to influence the rest of the crew 'because they were genteelly connected'.[56] Bligh's lack of breeding, and its outward display, may have haunted him not just before fellow officers, but among his rebellious crew itself. One of the two 'scoundrels' was, of course, Fletcher Christian. The other was a midshipman, Edward Young, whose identity makes the cultural twists of this moment even more ornate. Twenty-three by the time of the mutiny, he was recorded on the ship's books as coming from St Kitts, in the Caribbean; Bligh described him as dark-complexioned and other sources openly named him as a 'half-caste'. But he was also the nephew of Sir George Young, an influential naval officer with connections in the East India Company, and an advocate, alongside Banks, of the Botany Bay colony. Edward was most likely the illegitimate offspring of Sir George's brother Robert, an East India Company captain who had died at sea in 1781.[57] Such an individual's identity was extraordinarily multiple: a 'negro' by American standards; but 'genteel', and more influential on that score, by one account at least, than Bligh himself. He was a product of imperial diaspora, who followed his fellow 'scoundrel' Christian to Pitcairn Island, and kept, by other accounts, better relations with the Tahitian 'blacks' than the other mutineers could manage, dying not by their hands but of an asthma attack in 1800 (having taught John Adams to read and write).[58] By the time he died someone of his parentage could no longer hope for the opportunities he had enjoyed: dark-complexioned bastard offspring were unwelcome in the new empires of the nineteenth century, and certainly none could hope to lead men astray from their loyalties on the strength of being 'genteelly connected'.

# 'Deep rooted prejudices, and malignity of heart, and conduct'

*President Washington and the war in the West*

Chosen unanimously, as everyone had expected, by the US Electoral College as President in January 1789, George Washington stood as the human linchpin of the new republic's existence. How exactly he was to be more than just a living symbol was, nevertheless, a genuinely troubling question. His supporters deluged him with praise in the only language of the time that seemed to fit. 'You are now a king,' one had written on news of his election; and on 23 April – St George's Day, and the same day as the London triumph of the other King George – he was rowed ceremoniously across the Hudson river to New York, where the new government was to reside. A chorus on an accompanying boat sang new words to 'God Save the King':

> Thrice welcome to this shore,
> Our Leader now no more,
> But Ruler thou;
> Oh, truly good and great!
> Long live to glad our State,
> Where countless Honours wait
> To deck thy brow.[1]

Crowds along the route of his week-long trip from Mount Vernon had lauded him at every stop; triumphal arches and flower garlands, roaring cannon and tedious speeches had made popular and political adulation clear. Though this may have buoyed him on his way, no one who had sat through all the raging arguments about monarchy that occupied the Constitutional Convention, or who had read the reports of bitter ratification debates, could be entirely happy at this seeming confirmation of those fears.

Washington was an intriguing man, whose early career oscillated between a quest for military glory and a quiet assumption of civilian responsibilities. Born in 1732 into the solid landholding classes of Virginia, the proud and stately 'Old Dominion', by the age of twenty-three he had been propelled by his martial tastes to the rank of colonel of militia, holding down a thankless command in the western wilderness, 350 miles of open frontier along the Ohio valley threatened by French and Indian raids. Early daring exploits had brought this promotion, and put his name in the ear of King George II in London. They had also made him something of a bogeyman to French patriots of the time, who charged him, in prose and patriotic odes, with responsibility for the death of a French officer, killed treacherously, they claimed, by Washington's Indian troops. The dashing Washington, the finest horseman in Virginia, who stood a head taller than most contemporaries, seemed marked for distinction in British service. But his frontier command earned him little besides valuable lessons in the finicky and frustrating business of supply and logistics. He quit in 1758, with the frontier now secured by French abandonment of their key post, and Washington's own military future seemingly damned by an inability to obtain the regular king's commission he ardently craved. How different his destiny might have been had he possessed a few more influential Court connections.[2]

But Washington was not to be a king's officer any longer, returning to his estates (he inherited the celebrated Mount Vernon from his brother at this point), marrying the eligible widow Martha Custis and taking up an elected post in Virginia's own legislature, the House of Burgesses, all within a few months. From this point and through much of the next twenty years, he would cultivate the character of a gentleman – something that, in its time, meant a very specific and public kind of person. He held a quasi-public position, with authority and responsibility not merely over slaves and tenants, but also extending a more diffuse but very real penumbra over neighbouring farmers, labourers and craftspeople, the whole reality of a community that looked to him as a patron. The fundamental inequalities of this role, which jar on modern sensibilities, were merely natural, at least to Virginians of the time, even if the bustling streets of Philadelphia and Boston might be breeding a more egalitarian type of American. Washington was, with all the ironies it implied, living the life of almost the ideal type of English country squire (or indeed, in a slightly different register, the role of a conscientious French country nobleman). His continual service at a higher level of representation and responsibility, as a local justice, member of committees and burgess in the legislature, consolidated the reputation of a man who dealt fairly, spoke infrequently but wisely and could be counted on to follow the proprieties in any matter of import. Such matters came to include, by the end of the 1760s, resistance to the threat posed by British arrogance to the natural rights and liberties of Virginia.[3]

It was the fact that he fitted this character so well that helped lift him, with almost no dissent, to the chief command of the rebel armies, once the Continental Congress of 1775 had agreed on the dire necessity for such a post. A Virginian would unite the disparate geographical tendencies of the states, when the fighting to be done was in (and might seem to be for) New England, and Washington was the quintessential Virginian leader, who had come to the sessions in military uniform – an unspoken message of his willingness to serve. In his first months of action it seemed as if Washington, who had doubted his own abilities for the role, had regressed to his youthful enthusiasm for the dashing offensive. An early reckless quest for decisive battle soon gave way, however, to a Fabian strategy of the army as threat, by its very existence tying down and weakening over-confident British forces, as guerrilla war and the growing presence of European allies brought victory slowly closer.

Meanwhile Washington rediscovered the grim realities he had learned on the French frontier in the 1750s, that war for generals must be first about logistics, not tactics. Perhaps the true mark of his stoic greatness was his persistence in maintaining an army that all the forces of the time seemed to threaten with dissolution, from surly militiamen to ingrate politicians, greedy contractors and sullen suppliers. Without his constant labour his troops would have melted away in a fog of broken enlistments, unpaid bills and rotting, inadequate provisions. The measure of his commitment to the work is shown by the extraordinary way in which he took his leave of his staff in New York in late 1783, at what was planned as a banquet in his honour. Unable to do more than pick at his food, he asked each man present to come up and take his hand, but as they did, near-blinded by tears, he took each one in his arms and kissed him. None could speak, so emotive was the atmosphere, and Washington left for his home at once, pausing only at Annapolis to tender his formal resignation to Congress.[4]

In retirement Washington remained a figure of awe, so much so that home life at Mount Vernon was almost constantly interrupted by respectful visitors insisting on intruding – some distinguished, others merely nuisances, but all seeking to consult him on the direction of the Republic. As he tried to return to the gentleman's life he also maintained an interest that had been close to his heart ever since his youthful days on the frontier: the acquisition and consolidation of fertile land in the West. By the 1780s he was in possession of tens of thousands of acres of such land-grants, making him a significant, and not always scrupulously honest, player in one of the greatest speculative bubbles of the age – one that would ruin many a less prudent investor.[5] It was in this guise of private entrepreneur that Washington had been a key advocate of the improvement of navigation on the Potomac, so placing him at the heart of the dispute that led to the Annapolis Convention, and thus to Philadelphia in 1787.[6]

What is particularly intriguing to note is how much of Washington's assumption of the quiet dignity of a true-born gentleman was an act. His own family background was far more chequered than he cared to admit. In the late 1780s a friend essayed a biography while staying with the retired general, who himself annotated a draft. Washington added, for example, a comment that his ancestors who settled in Virginia in 1657, two brothers, brought with them 'a considerable inheritance'. As far as we can tell, however, these men were the sons of a clergyman dispossessed in the Cromwellian upheavals, and arrived with almost nothing.[7] Washington glossed over this and allowed the draft to add that 'almost every branch of their offspring still possesses a considerable portion of property and respectability'.[8] In truth, many branches had died out, Washington descended from a line of semi-impoverished younger sons and he himself was the late-born son of a second marriage. His father, Augustine, was not the leisured gentleman one might imagine, but spent most of his time managing an ironworks. He did send two of his older sons to England for a gentleman's education, but George was probably taught his letters at home by a 'convict servant', a transportee from Britain.[9] It was only the death of his half-brother Lawrence that made George a landed proprietor, and his marriage that made him prosperous.

Moreover, the 'property and respectability' that Washington yoked together were far from always running hand in hand. The same draft biography comments that the sons of the Virginia gentry were too inclined to become 'indolent and helpless' from the support given by their servants, 'if not imperious and dissipated from the habit of commanding slaves and living in a measure without control'.[10] Washington himself was zealously regular in his habits, as his triumph in the war demonstrated, but he had written, shortly after that victory, of his fears for the country that might 'like a young heir, come a little prematurely into a large inheritance . . . run riot until we have brought our reputation to the brink of ruin'.[11] As he prepared to step into the role of President he was surely conscious of just how much that position, like the position of gentleman, was indeed a role to be taken on, and played carefully.

Though the president-to-be (as everyone rightly assumed him) had been a leading player in co-ordinating the campaign for ratification of the Constitution, even lending Mount Vernon for use as a strategic headquarters, he had kept a very evident public silence. To be seen to be anxious for power was simply not done, and it was one of the traits that made a man like Charles James Fox so odious to many across the Atlantic. Washington carried this a stage further, and even in his private reflections rarely voiced anything but hesitation and lamentation about the burden shortly to descend on him. Alexander Hamilton went so far as to write to him demanding he stop such mutterings: he had 'pledged to take a part', and that was that. But even the day before his inauguration Washington told a friend that his assumption of office 'will be accompanied by feelings not unlike those of a culprit who is going to the place of his execution'.[12] At the same time as he denied all ambition he was consulting with political allies about priorities, for example writing to Lafayette, amid the turmoil of election for the Estates-General, about American plans for foreign policy.

*

Waiting for Washington in New York was a man his opposite in many ways. John Adams had been elected Vice-President of the United States as 'runner-up' in the Electoral College, where each voter cast two ballots. He garnered only half as many votes as Washington – thirty-four to his unanimous sixty-nine – and was later to discover that Alexander Hamilton had caballed to keep his total down, so as to avoid a tie, and the possibility of a vote in Congress to decide the presidency.[13] The low total, and the later discovery of its reason, stung him to the quick, for he was a man who often seemed to live on resentment and antagonism. Adams was born a few miles from Boston, Massachusetts, in 1735, the son of a farmer. A graduate of Harvard, he hesitated as a youth between careers as clergyman or lawyer, before settling on the latter, though always combining such a specialism with the virtues (particularly in his own mind) of being an independent farming man. Restlessly active and voraciously erudite, he plunged in his middle years into the cause of independence with a zeal that made him as many enemies as friends – and later rather more. At the Continental Congress he had been the proposer of General Washington for commander of the rebels' forces, and he made a habit of cutting debate and quick, decisive action ever after. From drafting political treatises to overseeing the manufacture of arms, and later as a diplomat arranging vital deals with French politicians and Dutch bankers, his role as a leading light of the American Revolution was indisputable. When he returned in 1788 from diplomatic service in Britain, he, like Washington, kept conspicuously quiet about further political ambitions. But his wife and helpmeet Abigail confided in a letter to their daughter that he thought anything other than the vice-presidency would be 'beneath him'.[14]

Such a private conviction marked a man who had raised resentment to the level of an obligation. It was a 'Passion, implanted by Nature for the Preservation of the Individual', as he had written while in the Continental Congress, 'he must and ought to feel it. Nay he ought to indulge it and cultivate it. It is a Duty.'[15] Adams's obsession with his own prickly virtue, the dual inheritance of his classical learning and New England Puritanism, wrestled constantly with his driving ambition and conviction of his superior worth: while he raged against slights real and imagined, he was brutally honest about his own flaws (and his triumph over them) and saw no reason not to be equally brutal in dissecting the faults of others. He seemed to relish the unpopularity this brought as further evidence of his distinction. It was a mark of the great extent of his real abilities that he retained any political friends at all, and was indeed the obvious choice for Vice-President. The role remained problematic, however, and perhaps particularly so for Adams. His restless energy and intellectual superiority would be confined to serving as a reserve, a spare in case Washington should suddenly expire, and meanwhile his main official occupation would be to preside over the Senate, where the Constitution specifically said he 'shall have no vote, unless they be equally divided'.[16]

For the residence of the new legislature, New York had committed funds to build a Federal Hall, mostly in the hope that a pleasing home would lure Congress into remaining there. The building was a solid rectangle in faintly classical style, with a thin, steeple-like tower at the centre, the frontage relieved by a slightly anaemic gesture towards a classical portico (in the 1830s it was taken down and replaced by an edifice with a much grander set of stone columns). But the decoration of the building, working variations on stars and laurels, and crowned by a huge eagle in the pediment, set the mark for a new 'federal style' and was widely applauded.[17] Here, on 21 April, John Adams had been welcomed with little ceremony as Vice-President, and taken his seat for the first formal session of the Senate. After an unusually modest opening speech – he had begged to be excused if 'from inexperience or inadvertency' he strayed beyond propriety – he set the tone for an uneasy month ahead by posing the question of protocol for the President's entry: should Adams leave the Chair, should the Senators greet the President seated or standing?[18] They made little progress on this issue, and for Washington's inauguration on the 30th it proved moot: all rose as one when the president-elect entered to meet both Houses of Congress gathered in the Senate Chamber along with diplomatic agents and officials. Both Adams and Washington seemed flustered at points in the ensuing scene, the former seeming to forget his few formal words of welcome, the latter mumbling a rather anodyne address after his oath-taking, his hands visibly trembling. The moment nonetheless moved some watchers to tears, and the shortcomings of its splendour were passed over by the majority of more impressionable witnesses: one elected Representative called it 'an allegory on which virtue was personified'.[19]

In trying to carry forward this notion Adams revived the debate that he had begun his office with – how should the President be addressed? The matter had already been raised by a handful of Senators, who bandied around the call for some sort of worthy title: 'Excellency', one suggested (a title Washington had often been addressed with as commanding general). A committee was formed and came back with the grandiose suggestion 'His Highness the President of the United States of America and Protector of the Rights of the Same'.[20] The project might have died there – the House of Representatives had passed a motion with almost no debate to restrict the title to 'President of the United States' – but Adams's punctiliousness and inability to let go of an argument kept it running in the Senate for over two weeks. As the presidential issue floated around, other matters of protocol as inane as whether congressional messengers should make 'obeisance' as they left the chamber bounced back and forth with increasing acrimony.[21] The Vice-President would later claim that he wanted only clarity and would have been content with a simple 'Sir' to address Washington, but the flurry of suggestions, including 'His Elective Majesty' and 'His Mightiness', all rebounded to give Adams the appearance of a closet monarchist.[22] A suggestion that he be dubbed 'His Rotundity' became a wildfire jest, and the whole episode brought little but mockery down upon a man for whom such treatment was pure torture. Moreover, it produced a palpable distance from Washington himself, who was advised that Adams was becoming 'odious' by it.[23] Thus the unfortunate Vice-President was driven even further from the circles of government.

Ironically, Washington himself was groping for a sense of how to play his role, and leaning towards what his ardent adviser Alexander Hamilton called 'a pretty high tone'.[24] Clearly he could no longer behave as a private gentleman, calling on others and hosting parties at his pleasure, otherwise claims of faction would inevitably follow. Moreover, his rank needed to be preserved. On a visit to Boston a few months after his inauguration, Washington wrote to advise the Governor, John Hancock, who was still nursing the failure of his own political ambitions, that he would be unable to pay him an official visit unless Hancock first attended the President. The Governor recovered remarkably quickly from the illness that had been keeping him at home, and was obliged to acknowledge the social supremacy of the higher office.[25] At an everyday level, complete presidential seclusion would be counter-productive, however: as Washington later wrote, not only would it close off his access to 'the many' who might bring him 'useful information', but it would be seen as 'an ostentatious show of mimicry of sovereignty'.[26] The compromise he settled on, though it shunned the grandeur of a Court, had little of easy democracy about it. Once a week Washington held 'levees' for an hour: a form of open house where the President, dressed formally in powdered hair, velvet suit and sword, greeted guests with a bow but never a handshake. Beyond a few words to each guest as he made a formal circuit of the room, he preserved such a notable taciturnity that the occasion when he bent to kiss a widow on the cheek went down in history.[27] In preserving a rigid public dullness, Washington hoped to set the presidency above the political fight, even while, in the privacy of government, he had his own very particular ideas about how to proceed.

Among the debates of Congress in its first months there were a number of lively exchanges over the very nature of government – for in truth the United States did not yet have one. Executive officers – ministers – were hanging on in caretaker positions from the old and almost powerless Confederation administration, and the legal basis for a new set of ministries was in the hands of Congress to establish. How those ministries should relate to the President raised the vexed question of monarchy yet again. The Constitution specified that he should nominate officials, with the 'advice and consent' of the Senate – but should he also have the right to remove them? One Virginia Representative, Theodorick Bland, argued that this would risk every new president 'turning out the great officers', and he might thus 'throw the affairs of the union into disorder'; moreover, 'would this not, in fact, make the President a monarch, and give him absolute power over all the great departments of Government?'[28] Another Virginian, John Page, denied absolutely that government required the unity or 'energy' afforded by strong leadership: this was 'the true doctrine of tyrants ... Energy of government may be the destruction of liberty.' Page carried his argument to grandiose lengths: for him, 'Indecision, delay, blunders, nay, villainous actions in the administration of Government, are trifles compared to legalizing the full exertion of a tyrannical despotism.'[29]

Evidently all the old arguments of the 1787 Convention were still alive for many. If there was to be a United States government, then the Antifederalists in Congress wanted one subordinate to the elected legislature, serving effectively at its pleasure, not the President's, and as far as possible divided in its aims. Federalists, however, had the strength to ride out these claims. James Madison, the ardent chronicler of those earlier debates, was now the director of Federalist strategy in the House of Representatives. As early as 19 May 1789, when the proposal to create a Department of Finance was raised, he diverted debate away from this most controversial of positions – for the power of taxation was the most detested potential of this new government – to the undisputed ground of foreign affairs. Here Madison carried a proposal for a new department, headed by a single minister, 'who shall be appointed by the President, by and with the advice and consent of the Senate; and to be removable by the President'.[30] Though the matter required lengthy deliberation in the House, it was eventually carried in this form, establishing a precedent. In the Senate, where that body's own prerogatives were at issue, the debate was more testy, and closer. Senator William Maclay, who had been Adams's bugbear in the wrangling over titles, saw Madison as one of a Federalist cabal trying to seize the whole executive power and 'exalt the President above the Constitution, and depress the Senate below it'.[31] On 16 July a tied vote on Madison's form of words was broken in its favour, no doubt to Maclay's utter vexation, by the casting vote of the Chair, John Adams.

There was less dispute over the creation of a Department of War: with fewer than a thousand men serving in the United States Army, it was not seen as a great instrument of despotism. Much of the rest of the summer, however, was taken up with argument about the creation of what was to become the United States Treasury. Revenue was, after all, at the heart of the creation of the Constitution itself, and a well-organised set of fiscal affairs was essential to remedying the parlous state of indebtedness that had driven down the Confederation. In a very real sense the Treasury was the government, insofar as it interacted with the people. The United States in 1789 ran the office of its President with a single secretary. The Secretary of War had three clerks and a messenger. Abroad were salaried a grand total of five diplomats (three in Paris, one of whom was a mere clerk), and the State Department at home had only four clerks, an interpreter and a doorkeeper. The Treasury, as established by Congress, had no fewer than twenty-seven staff at its headquarters, including five senior appointments below the titular Secretary. Moreover, in the country at large, the Treasury took under its wing the network of local postmasters, tax collectors, the Customs Service (including, in time, a maritime force of Revenue cutters) and eventually the staff of a national bank. It also co-ordinated government purchasing, including supplying the army.[32]

This powerful body should be controlled, Antifederalists argued, by more than one man. The finances of the Confederation had not prospered early in the 1780s when they were put in the hands of Robert Morris, the banker and speculator widely known as America's richest man. Though Morris had been credited with piloting the finances through the war years, and his political career continued – he was currently sitting in the Senate – his rule had been displaced in the executive by a Board of Treasury, removing the power of the position to a committee under closer scrutiny of the legislature. Madison again led a fight in the House to avoid such a solution, and once again to place the office in the hands of a man serving at the President's pleasure. The fight with the Senate was even harder, and the House had to throw back a Senate demand for the power of removal before the latter body could be brought, again, to a tied vote and Adams's decision.[33] The position of Secretary of the Treasury went, in September 1789, to Alexander Hamilton, who would use it to foster an ardently national vision of economic development, including a precocious drive for industrialisation, while constantly affirming the independence of the executive from close scrutiny. The victory of the Federalist position on these matters was confirmed a few days after Hamilton's appointment, when the House voted to abolish its own Ways and Means Committee, set up two months earlier with such oversight as its goal.[34]

Beneath the apparent benign inactivity of Washington, and perhaps only because of his reassuring presence, the Federalists succeeded in creating a government based on just the 'energetic' principles of unity and action that their opponents most feared. Moreover, Washington himself was far from the mere symbolic figurehead his public appearances might suggest. Though some might resent it, and particularly the vigorous Hamilton, who visualised himself as Prime Minister – as William Pitt was First Lord of the Treasury to another elderly George – the general had firm ideas about his position and relation to government. As he later wrote, the purpose of creating government officers was 'to assist the supreme Magistrate to discharging the duties of his trust'. He issued pithy instructions to his ministers, dwelling on the efficient conduct of administration: 'System to all things is the soul of business. To deliberate maturely, and execute promptly is the way to conduct it to advantage.' Mature deliberation required the gathering of 'well authenticated facts' that would allow judgement of '*right* or *wrong*, according to the actual state of things'; prompt execution would avoid 'one thing treading on the heals [*sic*] of another' – a state in which 'business will never be *well* done'.[35] Moreover, in the operations of government, as Thomas Jefferson, shortly to be his first Secretary of State, later recalled, Washington made himself the linchpin of decision-making: all correspondence flowed through his office, even if only to be sent back with tacit approval, but often 'with an informal note, suggesting an alteration or a query'. Thus Washington 'formed a central point for the different branches; preserved a unity of object and action among them; exercised that participation in the suggestion of affairs which his office made incumbent upon him; and met himself the due responsibility for whatever was done'.[36]

A last obstacle to the unfettered exercise of executive prerogative was removed in a celebrated episode of confusion and embarrassment in August 1789. Following the letter of the Constitution, and after two weeks of discussion to establish a procedure, Washington went, with his Secretary of War, Henry Knox, to seek the Senate's 'advice and consent' on a proposed treaty with Indian nations adjoining the southern states. The President arrived with the seeming intention of leading some sort of seminar – a prepared paper was read by Adams from the chair, concluding with a series of questions for discussion. But the event was a fiasco: irritating noise from the street outside contributed to making debate fractious, and matters of procedure and the need for more information came up again and again. Senator Maclay was a leader in posing difficulties, and confided to his journal that he thought the whole affair an attempt to 'tread on the necks of the Senate'.[37] Ironically, after an adjournment across the weekend, a second session resulted in unproblematic approval of the President's proposals – but he would never again seek congressional advice in person before embarking on a course of action, and even his replacement habit of written consultation on diplomatic initiatives died out within a few years.

In one respect at least, the Senate's rejection of Washington's overture closed out a radically different possibility for the evolution of American government. The position of the Vice-President in the Senate had troubled many Antifederalists – Elbridge Gerry, George Mason and Edmund Randolph had all queried it in the original Convention, and during the ratification debates it was called 'unnecessary and dangerous', a 'complication of powers and prerogatives' that was 'intolerable'. One acquaintance even wrote to Adams himself that the Vice-President's 'sole business seems to be to intrigue', and that the two elected figures, President and Vice-President, 'will easily govern the two Houses to their will'.[38] Such fears, however, glossed over other potentials for the legislature's influence on the executive. Placing the Vice-President in the Senate, and giving the latter its 'advice and consent' role, laid the road open to its cultivation as a presidential council – a group of senior advisers, especially on diplomatic affairs, that the British monarchy embodied in the Privy Council, and every other significant state had in some form or other. In such states senior aristocratic figures often belonged to such bodies by right, and a democratic replication, through the Senate, of such rightful consultation, with the limitations it implied on executive prerogative, is an intriguing alternative path for Washington's government to have followed. It was certainly one that Adams would have welcomed, as he had been deeply critical of the lack of such a council. However, through its own fears of subordination, the Senate blocked this avenue, and Washington's ministerial appointments, with their conditions set in the teeth of senatorial resistance, emerged as the first American Cabinet. The separation of powers, gestured towards but not actually enforced by the text of the Constitution, was borne of the jealousies between those powers even as they came into operation.[39]

The subject matter of Washington's abortive consultation that led to this situation revealed an even more profound and bitter irony. Washington and Knox had been working hard to evolve an ethical approach to Indian relations. In the run-up to this treaty, Knox, who had been at Washington's right hand through the Revolutionary War, shared with him a view that 'the independent tribes of Indians ought to be considered as foreign nations, not the subjects of any

particular state'. Only binding federal treaties should govern relations with them, and moreover, 'Indians being the prior occupants
possess the right of the Soil . . . To dispossess them . . . would be a
gross violation of the fundamental Laws of Nature and of that dis-
tributive justice which is the glory of a nation.'[40] For the next year
the two men worked to identify and foster leaders in the southern
nations with whom such agreements could be created, and were to
sign a landmark treaty in 1790 with the Creek Nation, defining
and protecting its boundaries, and going on to forbid private or
state encroachments by presidential proclamation. Unfortunately
the Treaty of New York was rendered worthless by the facts on the
ground. Just as the legislators of New York had dispossessed the
former Six Nations of the Iroquois Confederacy, so those of the State
of Georgia, egged on by bribes and promises of land-grants, signed
away the lands of the Creek – some fifteen million acres – to speculators of the 'Yazoo Companies', and white settlers carried on pouring
west.[41]

Westward movement was the great imperative of the American
society being born around its fledgling institutions. Whatever the
misgivings it had raised in the Philadelphia Convention, the process
could not be – and to the minds of most Americans, should not be –
stopped. The Ohio river, which flowed westwards for almost a thousand miles from Pennsylvania to the Mississippi, was the symbol, the
goal and the means of transport for much of this intensifying movement. Washington himself had stood on the banks of the Ohio in
1770 (as he had fought in the region as a young officer fifteen
years earlier). The 'River of Many White Caps', Ohiopeekhanne, as
the locals called it, flowed between banks wooded so richly with the
dark timbers of cherry, oak and walnut that they became known
as 'black forests'. Hickory, beech and poplar too beckoned the
pioneer's axe, their felling revealing a rich earth that promised an
easy life from the honest toil of farming. No wonder, as Washington
wrote on that 1770 trip, that 'the people of Virginia and elsewhere'
were 'exploring and marking all the lands that are valuable' – that,
after all, was exactly what he was doing himself, beginning a career
in land speculation that would continue for decades.[42]

South of the Ohio, the Kentucky territories of Virginia had
expanded at lightning pace, from first handfuls of settlers in 1775 to
a population of over seventy thousand by 1789. Tales of the rich

lands of the West, and their easy availability, circulated widely. In European accounts this was a landscape of pastoral imaginings, where people could live free from the constraints of society. A generation of romantic dreams found outlets in poetic and prose visions of a land without care, where honest work earned honest rewards, and each man was his own master. But the cheap land in Kentucky was almost all gone. The northern bank of the mighty river beckoned, apparently free for the taking.

One town established north of the Ohio was named Gallipolis, 'French City', symbolic of the international lure of the frontier. Within months Americans in Paris would be beguiling disillusioned aristocrats with tales of natural life in the West, touching off a brief 'mania' for their proposed settlement on the Scioto, one of the Ohio's northern tributaries. If few actually made the voyage from Paris, others made up for their reluctance. What had been a trickle of people down the river was now a flood: 18,370 people (and 7986 horses, 2372 cows and 1110 sheep) were counted on boats going down the Ohio in 1788.[43] North of the river, that flood collided with the backwash of another, hidden tide of population, as the Indians of the Algonquian peoples prepared to make their last stand. In so doing they would reveal the grim reality of backwoods life, the weakness of the federal government's hold over its people and the strength of the expansionist drive that forced Washington to start his new country's first war.

The world between the Ohio and the Great Lakes, a zone the French had called the *pays d'en haut*, the upper land, was one of constant interchange between Indians and Europeans. Henry Hay, son of a former British lieutenant governor, and nephew (on his mother's side) of long-established French traders, wintered in 1789 at Kekionga, a strategic junction for the fur trade north of the Ohio valley, and left a revealing journal of his visit. From childhood Hay had been an intimate of local Indian leaders: the chief Le Gris reintroduced him in 1789 to his now grown son, or 'brother and old play fellow as he called him'.[44] Ethnic groups intermingled freely: French and British kept up a round of civilised visits and recreations, including both Indians and the French-Indian *métis* in their social calendar. Henry Hay was capable of noting that one man's daughter was 'very brown', and another he dismissed (in French) as having 'a little of the peasant' about her. But such niceties did not stop him being polite to them, or meeting, after a carriage ride to a fellow English-man's house, the latter's brother, 'wife and two sisters-in-law (Indians)'. Local Indian chiefs regularly ate meals in the leading Europeans' houses, taking 'tea, also madeira', and parties of Indians returning from hunting camps were greeted with general, and some-times raucous, celebration. After a loud party had woken him, Hay found himself shaking hands with a strange Indian woman at his bedside at three o'clock on New Year's morning.

This life was not without its tensions. Hay recorded that almost every European traded with the Indians in some capacity, and much of it was an effort 'to get what he can by fowle play or otherwise . . . a Rascally Scrambling Trade'. Moreover, the uncrossable lines of social and ethnic disgrace still existed, and for Hay these had been breached by men such as one Montroille, 'who has abandoned him-self totally & lives among the Indians . . . such Rascalls ought to be . . . totally excommunicated from the Indian country'. We should note that a central grievance against Montroille and his ilk was that they 'fill the Indians Heads with very bad notions & think nothing of Robbin the Traders Property'.[45] This hints at one form of structural tension in this odd in-between life, but there were others, far more serious, and growing stronger. During Hay's visit word arrived that a trader had been taken captive by the Wea Indians for betraying one of their war parties to the Americans. Though this turned out to be a false alarm, the complexity of responses is telling – the chiefs at Kekionga offered to send envoys to obtain the man's release, and traders provided the goods for a ransom. But at Kekionga at the same time lived prisoners of these same chiefs held for ransom them-selves. Hay met an Irishman they had freed, who was awaiting the spring to go home across the Ohio. Yet more ominously, an Indian showed Hay the dried heart of an American, killed after being cap-tured as revenge for deaths caused to the Indian's own family.[46] A war was going on, one sincerely regretted by many on both sides, but also eagerly pursued by others, a war that echoed back to the very origins of the life of the *pays d'en haut* over a century before.

The Algonquian Indian nations of this land – the Weas and Wyandots, Shawnees and Ottawas, Sauks, Fox, Wabash and Potawat-omis, Miamis, Hurons, Kickapoos and Delawares, and many others – were all refugees. Their journey to the North-west had begun as a consequence of the relations of the Iroquois Confederacy with the first wave of European settlements in Canada and New England. Europeans brought iron weapons, and soon firearms, to Indian nations who had previously had only stone tools. They also brought both an insatiable demand for beaver and deer pelts and a conquerors' mentality to the acquisition of land. From the 1640s, for over a generation, this combination had driven the Iroquois to a series of devastating attacks against their neighbouring peoples westwards along the Ohio from their homelands east of the Great Lakes. Iroquois traditions of enslavement and sacrifice aggravated the toll on their enemies, as they pursued the people as much as they did the fur-rich lands. Along the way whole nations were wiped out – the Eries, and a group known to history only as the Neutrals, who themselves made war on the *pays d'en haut* in the 1640s before succumbing to the Iroquois onslaught. Driven away, the Algonquian peoples took refuge in the western half of what became the Northwest Territory. They could go no further north, because the winters there were too long and harsh, and to the west the Sioux peoples defended themselves vigorously against incursions. At the end of the seventeenth century this process left much of the Ohio valley virtually depopulated. The Iroquois withdrew to their ancestral lands as captives became harder to find, and they became locked in ever more complex struggles with the European powers.[47]

The world that was slowly constructed by the refugee populations was one in which European influence was ever present. French fur traders and missionaries were entering the region at the same time as the fleeing Indians, and though the influence of religion would be variable, the demand for furs would provide an anchor for a recovering society. The Algonquians had to survive not only the Iroquois, but also the plagues that European contact had brought: measles, and particularly smallpox, would continue to ravage their populations, but over time their way of life restabilised. Belying the image of the Indian as a nomadic warrior-hunter, much of Algonquian life revolved around agriculture (even though the actual raising of crops was seen as women's work). In the southern ranges of their lands buffalo still existed to be hunted, but even these were only a supplement to tended crops, as were the huge sturgeon taken from rivers and lakes. A French observer noted that the 'savages' preferred maize, kidney beans and squashes: 'If they are without these, they think they are fasting, no matter what abundance of meat and fish they have in their stores.'[48] Such agriculture, however, still had its perils. The growing season was short in the higher latitudes, and early or late frosts could imperil a whole year's supplies. Famine dogged the Algonquians' footsteps, and continued to do so right into the 1780s – 1782, 1784 and 1787 saw poor harvests and real hunger, and in 1788 the snows lay six feet deep from the Ohio to Lake Erie. In 1789, already on the brink of starvation, the Indians delayed their spring planting through fears of an American invasion, and then saw their crops assailed by pests and frost.[49]

At this very time, surprisingly, the Indian populations in the region were growing – a token of a long-term recovery from the plagues of the previous century, and possibly also of a further integration into the profitable channels of European trade.[50] Henry Hay and his ilk brought goods of all sorts to the nations of the Ohio, and undoubtedly contributed to their relative long-term prosperity. But, compared with the tens of thousands of settlers arriving every year, these peoples were still, in their villages and war bands numbering by the dozen or the hundred, helpless before a tidal wave. The engagement of the European empires with the Algonquians had also entrenched the preconditions for the epochal struggle now under way. The Ohio valley had been a source of conflict for much of the century. French influence extending down from Canada via the Great Lakes had made the Algonquians into effective allies, as well as trading partners, as struggles with the British developed in the middle decades of the century. That allegiance turned towards subordination in the later 1740s, and French arrogance produced a 'republican' rebellion among Ohio Indians against their own compromised chiefs. In 1747 Pennsylvania's leadership sent gifts to support this rebellion, and it became part of the endgame of 'King George's War', the North American component of a European conflagration known as the War of the Austrian Succession, 1740–8.[51]

Complex political and military manoeuvres brought most of the rebellious Indians back under French oversight, but a series of small 'republics' along the Ohio became prizes in a game of imperial influence in the early 1750s. Both British and French saw the valley and its peoples as the key to continental domination. William Johnson, leader of Indian policy in New York, wrote that 'if we lose them . . .

it must be our own faults & the consequences may be very bad'. The French Governor La Galissonière constructed a colonial domino theory that made the Ohio essential to retaining Canada, Louisiana and even the Caribbean colonies.[52] The French resorted increasingly to force to maintain their influence, but succeeded in stirring up more rebellion against themselves. Crushing this in 1752, the French-appointed leader Charles Langlade, a *métis*, led allied Ottawa and Chippewa Indians against rebels weakened by raging smallpox. After capturing their stockade, Langlade delivered up the rebel leader to his troops, who killed, cooked and ate him. They had already ripped the heart from a wounded British trader and eaten it before his horrified fellows.[53]

Murder, torture and cannibalism marked the turbulent world of the *pays d'en haut*. Indians were renowned for their casual willingness to butcher and consume captives when on the march, and there is something particularly chilling about accounts, from within Indian traditions themselves, of war parties steadily working their way through captive women and children as they traversed the great forests, sometimes tracked by grieving relatives who recognised the remains left behind and took their own bloody and ferocious revenge.[54] Originally Iroquois customs of the torture stake, the ceremonial dispatch of captured fighters, infiltrated the Algonquian realm. Tied over burning coals, or sometimes tethered among them and allowed to struggle, a warrior was supposed to show his strength by defying his captors, abusing them and calling down a death blow from an enraged opponent. This horrified and disgusted European observers accustomed to quite other ideas of chivalry – and those Europeans unfortunate enough to suffer this fate found it prolonged and intensified by their own misplaced pleas for mercy. But savagery was far from being all on the side of the Indians. Their ways with captives may have been grim, but Europeans had little to boast of in their own traditions of hanging, drawing and quartering or burning at the stake. From the very beginnings of the Iroquois raids along the Ohio, the intensification of violence in the Indians' realm could be attributed to the Europeans – if at first only indirectly, then by the middle decades of the century quite decidedly directly. The Algonquian nations, like their Iroquois cousins further east, were compelled to join in wars not of their making, and which ultimately threatened to make them the side-dish of an imperial feast.

British expulsion of the French from Canada during the Seven Years' War – known in North America as the French and Indian War – brought at first an easing of the strain on the *pays d'en haut*. However, the vision of control over the region that the British introduced was a more dangerous one for the Indians than the French had possessed. While the French governors had posed as 'Onontio', a father-figure, offering to mediate inter-tribal conflicts, the British saw more to gain from bilateral agreements with different groups, who could be played off against each other and supplied with arms in return for profitable trade goods. Although in practice they were often sucked into mediation, and fomenting war seemed less useful in reality than it had in theory, the British did not offer the same kind of overall stabilising association that the French had. Moreover, within a decade the perilous consequences of British hegemony for the very survival of the *pays d'en haut* were becoming apparent.

The eagerness of both French and British to enlist Indian allies in backwoods fighting had stirred yet further the lurking fear of the 'savage' among settler societies. By the 1770s many of those Europeans who defied British authority to settle over the Appalachians, in the western lands of Pennsylvania and especially the zone south of the Ohio that would become Kentucky, already saw themselves at war with 'the Indian'. When the Kentuckian George Rogers Clark launched a rebel invasion of the *pays d'en haut* in 1778, he told the captured British Governor of Detroit that 'for his part he would never spare Man woman or child of them on whom he could lay his hands'.[55] Indian resistance to encroachment had notoriously turned Kentucky into a 'bloody ground', and the buckskinned delegates from these regions who came to the Constitutional Convention in 1787 would still travel armed to the teeth against 'savage' raiders. The Indians named all such people 'Big Knives', a name Clark and others bore with pride and used to build alliances of convenience with some groups against the control of the 'English'. But the Big Knives brought repeated violence, unhesitating brutality and ultimately an exterminatory mentality to all their dealings. Clark's 1778 expedition failed, and over the following years the Americans' initial military advantage in the back country melted away – or rather was washed away in the continual round of near-random slaughter of Indians that rebellion against British paternalism seemed to have licensed.

The culmination of this attitude was the infamous massacre at Gnadenhutten on the Tuscarawas river, north of the Ohio, in 1782, when a whole community of converted Christian Delaware Indians was captured returning to their abandoned village to gather food.[56] Accused by inveterate Indian-hating militiamen of being thieves and raiders – because they possessed the impedimenta of a settled existence, from axes to tea kettles, that did not 'belong' to Indians – they were condemned to death and had their skulls crushed with a cooper's mallet in a local slaughterhouse. Over ninety died, mostly women and children.[57] When the Delawares in return pledged to spare no prisoners, and wiped out a Pennsylvania militia expedition, subjecting its leader, Colonel William Crawford, to a particularly pitiful ordeal at the torture stake, they were just, for the Indian-haters, reverting to type.[58]

The French, and their Spanish allies who held the Mississippi, tried to turn the back-country war against the British in a more structured fashion, but were unsuccessful in doing more than launching a few raids. The British themselves found it hard to maintain any consistent alliances within the *pays d'en haut* when they had little to offer and small sense of what these communities actually wanted. Frantic deployment of material gifts brought a network of relationships into existence towards the end of the war, but in British eyes Indians could not be relied on to pursue strategic objectives. The sudden cession of all British claims over the *pays d'en haut* in 1783 left the Algonquians to fall back on their own devices. In some American eyes the lingering presence of the British in forts around the Great Lakes formally ceded to the USA in 1783 would make them the *éminences grises* of the troubles to come. Local British agents undoubtedly continued to supply weapons, along with food and clothing, to their Indian clients, but the drive towards further conflict on the Ohio had enough local energy not to require such external stoking.[59] The Algonquian peoples managed to construct a form of confederation in the mid-1780s that could have been an agency of stability across the region. Its power, however, came only from agreement among the essentially disparate village and ethnic groupings that made up their world, and such agreement proved impossible to make meaningful in the face of the immediate pressure that fell on the *pays d'en haut*.

George Rogers Clark, the inveterate Indian-hater, had continued to raid villages through the war years, and as soon as peace was declared encouraged settlers to push across the Ohio. They told the Indians that peace with the British did not mean peace with them, and they would not have peace on any terms that gave a vestige of dignity to the Algonquians. Clark set down explicitly in 1783 his approach to the 'problem': given that the Indians 'have no notion of being dependant on Either the British or Americans', this attitude must be changed by force. 'We shall be Eternally Involved in a war with some nation or other of them, until we shall be . . . reduced to the necessity of convincing them that we are always able to crush them at our pleasure.' Therefore, such a crushing blow should be struck now, in the aftermath of the war's depredations: 'A greater Opportunity can never offer to Reduce them to Obedience than the present moment.'[60]

This sentiment continued to fester through the decade, as thousands of settlers rafted down the Ohio or trekked across the mountains into Kentucky. Finding land there already too dear for their pockets, they spilled northwards across the river – as early as 1785 over 2200 households had reportedly settled on lands declared off-limits by the federal government. Military observers described many of them as 'banditti whose actions are a disgrace to human nature', and Arthur Saint Clair, first Governor of the Northwest Territory, reported in January 1788 that while 'we hear much of the Injuries and depredations that are committed by the Indians upon the Whites . . . at least equal if not greater Injuries are done to the Indians by the frontier settlers of which we hear very little'.[61] The two confederacies, American and Indian, signed a series of treaties in 1784–6 whereby lands north of the Ohio were ceded to the Americans for formal settlement.[62] But neither the Indian nor settler populations were interested in respecting the deals done by leaderships who had no real power in a region dominated by village communities and roving war bands.[63] In September 1786 a Cherokee raiding party crossed another line when it publicly butchered two settler women, a mother and daughter, throwing them hamstrung into a fire to die. A Kentuckian revenge raid hit a completely different group of Shawnees, burning their village and seizing the chief as he held up the text of his treaty with the Americans as a talisman. He was cast into a fire with 'gunpowder set around him in small bags'.[64]

With only 350 men on the Ohio, the US Army could not restrain 'the deep rooted prejudices, and malignity of heart, and conduct' that Secretary of War Knox reported in the summer of 1787 as Congress debated the Northwest Ordinance. The 'flames of a merciless war' were already lit.[65] George Rogers Clark was leading full-blown expeditions across the river 'to kill and scalp as many as he may conquer', as press reports had it, and he was not the only Kentuckian leader to muster men for such missions.[66] Clark's largest mission in 1786 ironically ended in failure, and ultimately in personal disgrace, as his undisciplined and disgruntled men turned for home, and he became embroiled in disputes that eventually saw him broken by legal entanglements. Clark's was an individual failure, but his version of frontier life was sadly prevailing. Inflamed by the strong liquor readily provided by settlers and traders, Indian society was losing even the fragile stability that still remained. Villages and settlements could be peaceful one season, and racked by murders and revenge slayings the next. By July 1788 American regular soldiers were the targets of raids that enflamed opinions further, and made yet another treaty signed that year, ratifying American settlement up to the Muskingum tributary of the Ohio, already worthless.[67]

The summer of 1789 saw a further escalation, as Kentuckian raiders killed the followers of Indians who were seeking to maintain friendly relations, and defied federal authority that tried to rein them in: militia refused to serve in efforts to round up the raiders, and the distinction in Indian minds between 'Big Knives' and 'real' Americans faded further. Three hundred warriors raided an army supply convoy and then withdrew with their whole tribe closer to the Mississippi, from where they raided into settler territory. Many French long-term residents of the *pays d'en haut* now sought official American protection, and those who held slaves, fearing the Northwest Ordinance would free them, also took them across the Mississippi into Spanish territory. The common middle ground was torn apart. The Indian Confederacy that had signed away the lands north of the Ohio no longer truly existed: its temporary pacific unity was displaced by the leadership of tribes closer to the immediate conflict, who looked to war as the only solution. On the American side the same decision had been taken.

Washington's government had no choice but to assert control north of the Ohio. They believed that they had a series of binding treaties granting them those lands. More importantly, the lands had already been sold. Naked greed played a prominent part in the political machinations of this decade, in which debts and their solutions plagued the United States, and their leading citizens schemed to get rich on those very solutions. Arthur Saint Clair, the Governor dispatched to the Northwest Territory, had been the president of the old Confederation Congress that had written into the 1787 ordinance the requirement to honour previous land-grants and sales. He had been manipulated into this plum position partly at least by the good works of the Reverend Dr Manasseh Cutler, the flamboyant head of the Ohio Company. In July 1787 Cutler had schemed for his enterprise a grant of five million acres at the junction of the Ohio and Muskingum rivers: as he wrote, 'one million and a half for the Ohio Company and the remainder for a private speculation, in which many of the principal characters of America are concerned'. His next sentence was telling: 'Without connecting this speculation, similar terms and advantages would not have been obtained.' Cutler blessed the Constitutional Convention with his presence the same month, and lobbied hard to keep such grants protected under the new Constitution.[68] A year before the Americans forced the Muskingum boundary into one last treaty, then, they had already sold those lands, and the finances of the United States depended, at least in part, on sustaining the value of such existing and future sales. In passing, we may note that, while claiming to pay a dollar an acre for the land, Cutler's deal, funded with depreciated bonds from the war years, and riddled with political backhanders, yielded closer to nine cents an acre for the government, for lands that the Company would later sell for $1.25 an acre, cash down (including to Frenchmen lured over in 1790 by the Scioto scheme).[69] The whole thing was a flagrant swindle, but the good faith of the United States had been committed. The lands could not remain in the hands of the Indians.

Those Indians were made the villains of the piece by a persistent language of blame. 'Constant hostilities' on the part of the Indians, as Saint Clair reported in person to Washington in the summer of 1789, were leading to a 'habit of retaliation' among Kentuckians: moving through the federal territories north of the river to do so, they risked leaving the government's power 'prostrate'. The Governor sought congressional approval to raise militias, in conjunction with regular troops, to 'carry war into the Indian settlements'.

Though he hoped to use this as a mere threat, to 'obviate the necessity of employing force' against the Indians, it was a new step forward. The President passed the matter to Congress, which duly authorised a militia levy on 29 September 1789.[70] Slow attempts at diplomacy through the harsh winter months brought news by the spring of Indian intransigence. The peace proposed by the Americans was, they asserted, a plan 'to take away by degrees' all their lands; contradictory messages from different authorities showed clearly, one war leader said, 'that they intend to deceive us'. The American leaders in the West, Saint Clair and General Josiah Harmar, conferred on 15 July 1790 on plans for 'punishing' the recalcitrant tribes. Meanwhile, in New York, representatives of the civil population had been pressing demands on Congress and government alike for decisive action. Flooded with stories of murderous incidents and widespread depredations on property, Secretary of War Knox abandoned his previous diplomatic view of Indian relations – Harmar was now in receipt of 'a standing order', issued the previous month, 'to extirpate, utterly, if possible, the [Indian] banditti' alleged to be victimising the frontier.[71]

Political pressures had forced Knox to revise a view he committed to paper in December 1788, that such a war on the Ohio would be 'embarrassing beyond conception' for lack of funds to support it, 'must languish' because of that lack and 'might be protracted to such a length as to produce extreme distress and disgrace'.[72] No such pessimism was to be heard in the West, especially not once the new Constitution was in operation, and the laws to raise the necessary revenues had been, at last, put in place. In 1789 Harmar had written that 'I live in hopes to have ample revenge' on the Indians; his correspondence routinely denounced them as 'savages' and 'merciless villains'; he expected a 'general war'. The feeling was widespread – one subordinate officer reported with satisfaction to Harmar that summer that he had turned away a delegation of Indians seeking peace, but 'would have deceived them by making peace with them' if it had not meant giving them goods he did not care to waste. 'It certainly was high time' that they were brought down by war.[73]

Henry Hay's world of intermingled French, Americans and Indians at Kekionga was doomed. The village – 'that nest of villainy' – became the strategic goal of an offensive launched in 1790, ostensibly to protect white settlers from continued 'outrages'.[74] The results were a fiasco – in October over 120 US troops were killed as they advanced on the village, and a year later, under the personal command of Governor (and Major General) Saint Clair, a larger force of some 920 officers and men was almost wiped out, in the battle of the Wabash.[75] Two-thirds of the troops and all their two hundred camp-followers were slaughtered; only twenty-four soldiers escaped unwounded. They had faced some two thousand Indians and had fled in panic when their defensive perimeter broke. The United States Army was almost wiped out by the 'banditti' they had so joyfully marched to slaughter. All of Knox's fearful prophecies came to pass. It would take another three years to build a new army, the Legion of the United States, led by the fiery General 'Mad Anthony' Wayne. These three thousand men eventually routed the main Indian force at the battle of Fallen Timbers in August 1794. Even this decisive victory killed no more than a few dozen of the some fifteen hundred warriors, but, disheartened, most of the leaders agreed to a peace treaty decisively yielding the Ohio lands in 1795.[76] Warfare and dispossession would mark the United States' Indian policies across the continent from now on.

How epochal the shift was to be is marked in the career of a young lawyer, based in 1789 at Nashville on the Mississippi, in what would shortly become Tennessee. So fragile was the attachment of this man and some of his colleagues to the United States and all it stood for that they swore oaths of allegiance to the King of Spain to gain free passage for their goods down the river. Spanish America, under the influence of universalising Catholicism, was noted for its racial tolerance, whereby even former slaves could rise to positions of responsibility and multiplying forms of *mestizo* racial blending took place – a set of features that, in many Anglo-Saxon eyes, tainted it irredeemably. The lawyer, Andrew Jackson, would later become the scourge of Spanish holdings on the continent, invading and conquering Florida in 1818, and ultimately the architect, as President of the United States from 1829, of the genocidal expulsion of Indians from all lands east of the Mississippi.[77]

As late as the seventeenth century it had been normal for Europeans to perceive American Indian chiefs as kings. This did not mean relations were harmonious, any more than relations between European kings were, but the name is a marker that Europeans were prepared to think of such figures as equivalent in respect, if not power, to their own leaders.[78] New England settlers fought a bloody war against local tribes in the 1670s, which ended with several hundred Indians enslaved and whole tribes broken up, which may mark the beginning of the breakdown of this respect, but they still called their enemies' leader 'King Philip'.[79] The great Shawnee war leader Tecumseh, a young warrior in 1789, later encapsulated the new vision of his era, which he would spend his life fighting against: 'They do not think the red man sufficiently good to live.'[80] The Enlightenment's language of 'noble savages', coupled with a century of mass slavery, and perhaps the uneasy conscience provoked by treating fellow men thus, had produced a turn seen most starkly on the Ohio, but no longer absent elsewhere. In India a more advanced state of military technology, and far greater material wealth, still compelled a modicum of respect from British leaders towards their native foes – Tipu Sultan in 1791 was treated harshly, especially in the matter of his sons, but not beyond the bounds of relations between sovereigns. Worse was to come, however, and renewed wars across the decade ahead would show that, to the British, Indians were no longer fit for other than subjection. European culture marked others down for subjugation and death, even as it wrestled to establish whether all its own members were 'sufficiently good' for freedom, equality and rights.

# 'No, sire, it is a revolution'

## *From the Estates-General to the Bastille,*
## *France, May–July 1789*

As if all the crises besetting France in the spring of 1789 were not enough, another minor, if highly symbolic, crisis was touched off mere days before the opening of the Estates-General, when instructions were sent out from Versailles detailing what the deputies of the three orders should wear. Clothing was emblematic of social, political and cultural divisions in quite overt ways. In New York both Washington and Adams had fretted over their costumes for the inauguration, before settling on near-identical sober brown. In London, meanwhile, Fox's Whigs had since the previous decade called themselves the Buff and Blue, borrowing Washington's own wartime uniform colours for their party garb. In the winter of 1788–9 Pitt's supporters founded a Constitution Club in preparation for a renewed election fight – membership requirements included the purchase of a party uniform, topped off with a vivid orange cloak (invoking William of Orange and 1689), which Pitt himself was seen wearing in the Commons at least once.[1] It was not just in the steamy heat of India that jackets and breeches, buttons and bows, marked out identities, and transgressions, indelibly.

Thus, when Royal Grand Master of Ceremonies the marquis de Brézé issued his instructions to the Estates-General, he was making an explicitly political statement. Clergy were to wear the variously coloured and adorned garb of their profession, which marked its own hierarchy from cardinals' red caps via the purple cloaks of bishops to the humble cassocks of the parish priests. Representatives of the Second Estate – the nobility – were to adorn themselves in suits of black augmented with 'magnificent' gold braiding on every part, and solid gold buttons too (though these were optional). They were also enjoined to wear lace cravats and hats with high feather plumes. The Third Estate, by contrast, were to wear unadorned black from head to foot, plain muslin cravats and three-cornered hats on which decorative braids and buttons were specifically banned. The message being conveyed could not be clearer.[2] One Third Estate deputy bemoaned the order to wear a 'dog-eared hat' while his noble colleague from the same constituency was permitted a 'superb *panache*'. The required distinction, he noted acidly in a letter home, 'painfully taught me that I have, for thirty years, lived in ignorance of the divisions that prejudice has fixed between men'. The comte de Mirabeau, who, despite his personal nobility, was ordered into the dowdy garb of the Third since he had chosen to be elected by them, drew more immediate political conclusions. In the first edition of a new newspaper, fashioned as an ongoing *Letter to His Constituents*, he printed a comment that 'this unfortunate distinction of orders' was 'the original sin of our nation . . . of which it is absolutely necessary that we be purified if we expect to regenerate ourselves'. Moreover, he called on deputies to reject the notion that they were 'from such or such an order' and affirm that they were 'true representatives of the universality of the kingdom'.[3]

Reinforcing the distinction of orders by dress thus seemed to stir a resentful rage among deputies, a governmental misstep merely illustrating the blindness of the denizens of Versailles to the profound conflicts rising around them. But it is informative to observe two other points about the reaction to these instructions. In the first place, some nobles were not best pleased with them either. One went as far as to publish a pamphlet condemning the 'lavish ostentation' involved. Another, Garron de la Brévière, baulked at the cost of the outfit. In a letter he hesitated over paying out: 'I will see what the others do . . . In general, it is thought that we might well have been spared this expense.'[4] Moreover, among the Third Estate deputies themselves, dissenting reactions focused less on the invidious distinction with the nobility and more on the limitations the costume placed on their own sense of self-worth. As many as a third of them, from the opening ceremonies onwards, simply rejected the dowdy outfits and continued to wear the brightly coloured and embroidered garments of the fashionable and well-to-do. A vote a few weeks later rejected firmly a call to adopt the black outfits as a badge of commoner pride.

If many deputies actively fought against their representation as lowly, they nonetheless could not help being subjected to an intense impression of the grandeur of Versailles. Provincial Third Estate deputies expatiated in letters home on the splendour and pageantry of three days of opening ceremonies, including individual presentations to the king in the magnificent Hall of Hercules, where red marble pillars stretched up to a huge ceiling, covered with a 480-square-metre painting of the Greek hero being carried up to Olympus as a god: a reminder of the transcendent claims of kingship that Louis XVI still embodied. There was then a procession through the town of Versailles watched by several hundred thousand hushed spectators, led by the mounted royal falconers, hooded hawks on their arms, and followed by all the pomp a baroque court could produce. Even here, however, the Third continued to chafe against restrictions. As they marched across the town they had agreed almost spontaneously to shun the seating by order and *bailliage* imposed on them for the opening religious service, and arranged themselves 'more or less pell-mell' around the church.[5]

Arriving and establishing themselves at Versailles had already been a daunting procedure, which had led many to fall back on collective arrangements with the other men of their regions and provinces, first for finding lodgings in the packed town, and then for sociability. Such anchors of familiarity would prove highly necessary, for the royal state, after the final opening ceremonies on 5 May, effectively left the Estates-General to it. The minister Necker had made a three-hour speech that had contained some general suggestions on reform, hidden among much verbiage and recapitulation of the situation, and droned out so dully that few could have taken it in. When the Third Estate deputies reassembled on the morning of the 6th, the chamber that had held the royal throne and all three orders was left to them alone – with no indication either of how they should proceed to debate or what they should talk about. A mass of men, well qualified but almost entirely ignorant of the vast majority of their fellows, reverted to what they did know, and rapidly developed a series of regional caucuses. Within a couple of months these would break down as more ideological divisions appeared, but in at least two cases such divisions emerged from the different perspectives of provincial delegations themselves. The deputies from Dauphiné, in the upland south-east around Grenoble, had experienced some of the more violent confrontations of the early 'pre-revolution', but they had also forged a unity that crossed the boundaries of the three orders. Meetings at the château of Vizille had assembled nobles and commoners in pursuit of common reformist goals, and the ideas they brought to Versailles, for a 'union of orders' leading to a renunciation of privilege with the goal of a 'balanced' constitution and a new political role for the nobility in an 'upper house', would be influential through the summer.[6]

Such a spirit of compromise, however, found little accord elsewhere. The single most influential delegation proved to be that of the Third Estate of Brittany, which arrived after enduring violent conflict with the *parlement* of the province, and alongside a boycott of the whole proceedings by their intransigent noble brethren. The historic Estates of Brittany, meeting the previous year, had already brought together many who found themselves in Versailles, and after their election these men had met again in Rennes to agree on a political line before travelling to the capital. They held their first formal meeting at Versailles on 30 April, in the back room of a café, and combined provincial business with sessions to which they invited all comers among the deputies. This Breton Club also enrolled the delegates from the parish clergy who had come from the province, after the higher clergy had joined their noble fellows in boycotting the election. Their overtly political aims were clear. Firstly, they would act as a genuine political caucus, debating and deciding issues by majority vote, and binding themselves to support the outcome of their deliberations unanimously. Secondly, and underpinning this practice, they would be wholly opposed to privilege of any kind. Other deputies wrote at the time that the Bretons 'harboured an implacable hatred against the nobility' and had 'an uncontrolled passion' for their humiliation.[7]

Unsurprisingly, this attitude rapidly aborted any attempt to find common ground with the compromisers of the Dauphiné delegation, but men from other provinces, and whole delegations from Provence, Artois, Franche-Comté, Anjou and elsewhere were soon joining the Breton debates. The Breton position, which some had elaborated even before the opening ceremonies, insisted that the different orders should do nothing separately – and the Third Estate in particular should not even ratify its own members' credentials lest it be taken as a sign that they acknowledged their separate status. Merger with the other two orders was the first priority, with the further proviso that if they refused to unite, the Third could be, as some *cahiers de doléances* had hinted months earlier, a national assembly by itself. In votes over the coming weeks, no more than a tenth of the whole six hundred would support wholeheartedly such intransigence – but neither could others obtain a majority for doing anything as concrete as agreeing on rules of debate, taking minutes or electing a presiding officer. Informal discussions with representatives of the other two orders nevertheless continued in the background, and deputies stood out against 'drastic measures' and the 'vehemence and passion' of the Breton approach, 'unjustly suspicious of anyone' seeking conciliation.[8]

Such conciliation did not occur, however, and as the Estates-General continued in effective suspended animation into June, attitudes were hardening in other quarters. The clergy, though dominated numerically by curés, or ordinary priests, had a powerful contingent of bishops and other senior figures, determined to preserve their order's prerogatives. Almost a microcosm of the larger debate between nobles and Third, the clerical body also included a handful of liberal grandees, who as early as 6 May had pushed a motion to join with the Third to verify their credentials. This was defeated, but only by 133 votes to 114. During the early weeks of the sessions it seemed that a strong minority of over a hundred curés were considering joining with the Third. The conservative bishops, however, pulled out all the stops. Using every tactic from subtle hints of individual preferment to blatant warnings of a threat to religion itself, and with more and more priests growing wary of the radical voices in their own ranks, they applied pressure to bring the views of the great majority of the clergy closer together. The numbers prepared to defy the leadership steadily dropped to dozens and then a handful. The Third Estate deputies watched this process with dismay. One noted that a particular bishop 'swallowed another curé every day', while a second was more caustic about the priests' reluctance: 'these curés are pathetic'.[9]

In the nobles' chamber there were not even the early signs of openness that the clergy had displayed. When they voted on 6 May about the verification issue, the nobles rejected unity by 188 votes to 46. From their first sessions, the nobility was intransigent, and contained well-organised conservative blocs working to preserve their prerogatives. Meeting in 'clubs' no less dedicated than the Bretons, the conservatives even tried to block the admission of notably 'Patriot' delegations, such as that of Dauphiné, and later that of Paris, to their order. The liberal stars of the Society of Thirty were scorned, in the words of one marquis, as 'creatures of the minister Necker, insanely anxious to achieve popular fame'.[10] The politics of the Court injected themselves into the meetings, as wavering individuals were wined and dined among the 'greats' of the kingdom, including the comte d'Artois, arch-conservative brother of the king, and other favourites of Queen Marie-Antoinette. By 28 May, when the nobles voted again on the preservation of their separate deliberations, the majority in favour had risen to 207 versus 38.

The experience of weeks of meetings drew the nobility and the Third in ever more divergent directions. The nobles' touchy sense of personal honour was elevated to hysterical heights: honour, duty, courage and sacrifice resounded round the chamber endlessly, and on at least two occasions liberals and conservatives fought duels over words spoken in debate. With many speaking of their 'vassals' back home as if they lived in an earlier century, they remained determined to see off the challenge from the Third.[11] Meanwhile, witnessing this, and experiencing their own weeks of debate, the Third's deputies began to undergo a profound shift. Continual discussion, even if it produced no concrete outcome, began to nurture their awareness of one another's talents, and to expose many to elaborations of ideas they had not previously considered. Many likened it to a 'school of public law' or an 'academic lecture' in the justice of their claims.[12] The effects were further heightened by the continual presence of vast crowds at Versailles. More prominent deputies could not appear in public without being fêted, and even the obscure received marks of public affection. The galleries of the meeting hall were thronged every day, their occupants sometimes outnumbering the deputies, and the public, despite a generally genteel composition, soon developed an active role in debates, cheering radical propositions and deriding the dull or unpopular. Royal authority seemed unwilling to act: the garrison of Versailles played almost no role in keeping order, and the Nation and its legislators appeared to mingle freely. The effect was dramatic, and by the end of May one speaker was moved to remind the deputies 'that we deliberate here in the presence of our masters' – a shocking suggestion of popular sovereignty in a monarchy, but one that carried the day against a motion to close the galleries.[13]

With events such as the nobles' vote on 28 May seeming to preclude even royal attempts at conciliation – for the government was growing tired of the delay, and pressing, ineffectively, for remedial action – the attitudes of the Third took a decisive swing towards the 'Breton' position. One further symbolic snub may have helped: when Louis and Marie-Antoinette's eldest son died on 4 June, casting a pall over the court, Third Estate delegations were refused access to the king, when it was known he was still receiving the nobility and bishops. 'This is the proof that the nobility has the upper hand,' one embittered deputy was heard to say.[14]

In this grim atmosphere the *abbé* Sieyès, elected to the Third Estate from Paris but having only recently joined, produced a motion on 9 June that he had presented to the Breton Club the previous evening. It had an electrifying effect, and virtually unanimously the Third Estate voted on 10 June to call the other two orders to ratify their credentials in common, and announced that, whether they did or not, it would proceed to business as the sole legitimate national body. At its session on the 12th, it followed this through, joined by three curé deputies, the only ones willing to risk the wrath of their bishops. A few more curés trickled in over the following days, but the nobility stayed away *en masse*. On the 17th, after further earnest debate, roared on by huge crowds, the Third voted by 491 to 90 to declare itself the 'National Assembly'. As the deputies filed out to the applause of the thousands of spectators, 'joy and exhilaration were in every heart and on every face'.[15] Whether they cared at that moment to acknowledge it, the deputies had set a collision course with the nobility, and with the politics of the Court, that now had no peaceful resolution. Fortunately for them, as the reaction of their audience showed, they were far from alone in their determination.

As spring turned to summer across France, and the price of basic foodstuffs kept rising, there was a continuing wave of direct action that combined visceral fears of hunger with increasingly targeted politics. In Picardy, north of Paris, by the end of May many abbeys and monasteries had been stripped of their grain stocks by organised expeditions from the countryside. Seigneurs began to receive the same treatment in June, and were sometimes forced to write renunciations of their feudal rights. In the forests and fields around Paris, where many of the highest nobility maintained hunting reserves, collective assaults on these ravagers of crops had begun in the winter, and by June 1789 even the queen's own private reserves at Saint-Cloud had been attacked and pillaged. As well as killing the game, many stripped the forests of firewood – always a contentious commodity – and some farmers reportedly owned new wagons by June, purchased from other peasants at 'ludicrously low prices', as one minister phrased it, having 'once belonged to the abbey of Saint-Denis'.[16]

Attacks on grain stocks continued, and aristocratic game was hunted down by whole communities in the Champagne region. But action was also maintaining the more political charge it had developed in the winter in the south-east. Peasants around Lyon refused to pay church tithes, while the city's workers asserted that duties on goods entering the city had been suspended: by royal order, they claimed. Similarly, in the south-west tithes and taxes were contested, and in Normandy episodes of categorical refusal to pay any taxes were reported. Near Carcassonne tax offices were burned to the ground, and many elsewhere were threatened with a similar fate. Peasants and townsfolk regularly flouted demands for tolls and duties on roads and city gates. Reports from Rennes and Nantes of threatening crowds of peasants emerged in early July, and the sub-delegate of Ploërmel in central Brittany made clear the nature of some threats about the clerical tithe on 4 July:

> All the peasants around here and in my area generally . . . say quite openly that there will be no collection without bloodshed on the senseless grounds that as the request for the abolition of these tithes was included in the *cahier* of this [district], such an abolition has now come into effect.[17]

These 'senseless' beliefs had nonetheless burgeoned in the aftermath of the Estates-General elections. The lieutenant general of the *bailliage* of Saumur put it succinctly, if smugly, during the process itself:

What is really tiresome is that these assemblies . . . have generally believed themselves invested with some sovereign authority
and that when they came to an end, the peasants went home
with the idea that henceforward they were free from tithes, hunting prohibitions and the payment of feudal dues.

As another commentator noted from Provence, such views were
often interpreted as the will of the king himself, who was rumoured
to wish 'every man to be equal', and thus 'these poor misguided
people believe they are exercising their rights and obeying the
king'.[18]

Though members of the social and political elite were content to
dismiss the evolving situation as the product of a collective delusion,
a more plausible explanation would be that royal approval, sometimes rumoured to take the form of 'golden letters' commanding an
end to privilege, was a good cover story for communal decisions that
the situation had simply become intolerable. Licensed by the summoning of the Estates-General to expect improvement, and seeing
all around them the continuing signs of privileged intransigence
amid economic collapse, the common people were making their own
revolution. In a consummate irony that would colour all the other
developments of this year they were also terrifying the leaders of the
Third Estate. Towns and cities across France looked out to their
hinterlands and saw chaos. For many there was little distinction to be
made between disruption to trade and travel caused by peasant
assertions, and the rumoured effects of 'famine pacts' and aristocratic conspiracies. As the propertied classes flocked to hear readings
of letters home from their deputies at Versailles, with news of scorn
and deadlock, so many local authorities, and some unofficial gatherings, took their own action. Citizens' militias formed – the first even
before the Estates-General had met, but in an accelerating trend
through the spring. Some were simple volunteer patrols, others the
revival of moribund ancient municipal companies, others still took
more organised and innovative forms. By June the process stretched
out into the countryside, with semi-official communal militias forming from Flanders to Gascony.[19] Defences against pillage and the
feared 'brigandage' of plotters, they were also a mark of the collapse
of the state.

Even in Paris late June saw dramatic evidence of the loss of authority. Twice in a week units of the French Guards, who had shot down protesters in April without compunction, mutinied when called out for public-order duties. Other troops refused to repress crowds protesting at the arrest of ringleaders in the mutiny, and the authorities had to relent and release them from custody. By this stage the aspirations of the new National Assembly and the wishes of the Crown were set on the road to direct confrontation. After its renaming on 17 June the Third Estate had been heartened by a shift in opinion among the clergy, which on the 19th had voted, by a majority of only twelve, to unite with it to verify credentials. Many still felt that the king was behind them: that he had not challenged the Third's actions was 'proof', one deputy confided to his diary, 'that His Majesty is not unhappy with us'.[20] On 20 June, however, the Assembly found its meeting place closed, and near panic ensued. The official, and genuine, explanation was that the king wished to hold a royal session of all three orders and the chamber was being remodelled in readiness. Fearing a dissolution, however, the Third Estate deputies and some of the clergy rushed to a nearby indoor tennis court as an improvised chamber, and there pledged a solemn oath to remain united until they had fixed a constitution for France.

It was a moment of high drama, and indeed melodrama, with deputies raising a forest of hands towards Jean-Sylvain Bailly, *doyen* of the Assembly, and hundreds of spectators, infected with the same urgent belief in the danger they faced, cheering on this act of principled defiance. The deputies still ended with cries of 'Long live the king' and listened eagerly to rumours that Necker was pressing the king to approve their actions.[21] For one deputy it was evident that 'the best of kings' had been 'led astray by the arrogant aristocrats who surround him'; but at the same time the formal declaration by the deputies, that 'the National Assembly exists wherever its members come together', was an open challenge to the forces of the Crown to try to do away with them, as so many recalcitrant *parlementaires* and others had been banished to internal exile over the centuries before. Just as royal government was wherever the king went, so the deputies now suggested that the body of the Nation, and its political legitimacy, would follow them, regardless of royal actions. For the 'aristocrats' who did indeed surround Louis XVI such a challenge could no longer go unanswered.

When the royal session took place on the 23rd it was bitterly anticlimactic: the deputies had already been angered by being left huddled outside in the rain while the first two orders were seated, and now they were anxious and dispirited. One unsympathetic noble wrote that 'it seemed like they were waiting for an execution'.[22] Louis' speech attempted to quash all the proceedings of previous weeks, and ordered the Estates-General to function as three separate chambers. He also put forward what he had failed so conspicuously to offer in May: a concrete programme of reforms. But as these amounted to little more than cleaning up government and introducing more equality to taxation, they quite failed to rise to the situation. When the king left, stunned deputies remained in their seats, until the Master of Ceremonies attempted to shoo them into the separate chamber made ready for them. At this Mirabeau found his voice, denouncing the officer as having no place in their august deliberations, and confronting his demand imperiously: 'I say to you that if you have been charged with removing us from here, you must ask for orders to employ force, for we shall only quit our places by the power of bayonets!'[23] By a massive majority the deputies affirmed all their previous resolutions, and declared themselves inviolable. Such defiance concealed terrible anxiety, and one deputy would later recall 'that terrible evening when it seemed like everyone was in mourning'.[24]

In the short term the deputies seemed to have scored a triumph, as over the next two days most of the clergy and several dozen nobles joined the National Assembly, and on the 27th the king ordered all three orders to unite. Many of the remaining nobles accepted this move only with great bitterness, and after a circular letter from the comte d'Artois asserting a real danger to the king's safety if they did not act as he requested. An observer recorded that some entered the National Assembly 'still enflamed with fury, others overwhelmed with sadness and embarrassed even to sit down'.[25] This apparent capitulation concealed the real shift in royal strategy, however. Troops were already more in evidence around the palace, and the galleries had been closed to spectators. Harkening to the voices of the queen and other ultra-conservatives at Court, Louis had ordered forces to begin gathering around the capital. The enemies of change were indeed, as the deputies feared, preparing to crush the Third Estate, even as the country continued to fall apart around them.

*

Louis-Auguste le Tonnelier, baron de Breteuil, embodied the contradictions of the French monarchy and its quest to uphold the
values of tradition, hierarchy and religion. Fifty-nine in 1789, he had
a long and distinguished career behind him: after brief service in the
Royal Guards he became a diplomat in 1758, and served at major
European Courts including those of Russia, Austria and Sweden. In
1783 he became Minister for the Royal Household – an apparently
decorative title that concealed the responsibilities of a modern
interior ministry. There he showed the influence of Enlightenment
humanitarianism at the heart of government. Within a month of
taking office he had closed the infamous state prison of Vincennes,
where the comte de Mirabeau and the philosopher Diderot, among
many others, had once been locked up for offending propriety.
Breteuil also limited the use of *lettres de cachet*, the sealed royal orders
that had made such imprisonment possible, and moved in more practical terms to replace Paris's pestilential old hospitals and cemeteries
with new and more salubrious institutions, while embracing the
values of religious toleration with moves to improve the civil status
of France's Protestants: a minority of over a million who for a century
had been denied the sanction of the law for their marriages and
inheritances.[26]

Breteuil did all this while reflecting in his personal life the values
of a Court society. He had been married at twenty-two to the beautiful daughter of a wealthy financier – a marriage that seemed happy,
despite rumours that Breteuil had bedded his future mother-in-law
to secure this lucrative match. But when his wife died in childbirth
(along with the baby) thirteen years later, he took up a string of mistresses. He seems to have been an unusually successful womaniser.
One Dutch lover left him her fortune when she died in 1781 (which
he used to buy and renovate a huge Norman château) and another,
Catherina van Nyvenheim, returned with him from a diplomatic
posting to The Hague and was married off to the senile duc de
Brancas to provide her with a respectable entry to the Court. The son
she then produced was widely assumed to be Breteuil's. Meanwhile
Breteuil advanced the career of his one legitimate daughter by marrying her to the comte de Goyon-Matignon, who was inconsiderate
enough to die in a carriage accident, leaving her widowed and preg-
nant at sixteen. She found consolation by taking as her lover a young
clergyman named Charles d'Agoult, whom Breteuil welcomed into

his household and in 1787 would persuade Louis XVI to appoint as Bishop of Pamiers.[27]

Breteuil it had been, among others, who politicked behind the scenes to ruin Calonne's original reform plans in that year, playing his factional cards so daringly that he had already fled Versailles, fearing his own downfall, when the queen's favour saved him. When Breteuil did leave office, during the political storms of the summer of 1788, ostentatiously refusing to sign a batch of the hated *lettres de cachet*, he might have seemed to be striking a liberal note, but beneath the surface he was more alarmed at the threat to royal power posed by ongoing reforms – 'treacherous ideas', he was later to dub them.[28] Withdrawing to his château, he kept in contact with Court politics, while cultivating the view that preparations for the Estates-General were 'unleashing passions which will lead to far more permanent and incurable ills' than the ones that had prompted the crisis.[29] As the events of the spring and summer began to unfold, he waited for a call.

Forces around King Louis XVI were increasingly persuading him to regret his openness to reform. While Queen Marie-Antoinette herself had flirted in late 1788 with support for Third Estate claims, largely out of hatred for the conservative nobles who had defeated her favourite, Brienne, the reality of those claims had chilled her. She joined forces with her brother-in-law, the convinced reactionary Artois, who saw the Third Estate's self-definition as a National Assembly as a rebellion that 'had imperatively to be crushed, without hesitations or half-measures which would only be seen as proof of the government's failure of nerve'.[30] Artois and his allies launched an offensive to capture the king's mind that reveals how very personal the politics of the era remained.

After the Third Estate's self-designation as the National Assembly on 17 June, the minister Necker had drafted a plan which would see the king essentially capitulate to this move, but the royal council meeting which was on the brink of approving it was halted in unprecedented fashion by the personal intervention of the queen herself – a whispered message from a page calling the king away mere seconds before declaring the matter closed. The following day, she and Artois launched a devastating assault. Confronting the king in his apartments, Marie-Antoinette berated him for failing to see that the throne was being 'overturned by men of faction'; her impassioned delivery was seconded by a delegation from the Paris *parlement*, come to pledge aid to the Crown if only it would dissolve the Assembly; leading churchmen followed, begging Louis 'in the name of Saint Louis and the piety of his august ancestors to defend religion'. The attack was consummated by the appearance of the duchesse de Polignac, Marie-Antoinette's bosom companion, bearing in her arms the king's surviving son and leading his daughter by the hand, imploring him 'to hesitate no longer and to confound the plans of his family's enemies'.[31] In tears, Louis agreed, and the declaration he made on 23 June was the product of a thoroughly aristocratic vision of constitutional monarchy, in which the survival and pre-eminence of the privileged order remained essential to its being.

While this declaration ended with a ringing threat, voiced by the king in person, to 'effect the good of my people alone' if the Estates would not co-operate, Louis almost at once undermined this by casually refusing to act against the deputies who impudently refused to shift from the hall: 'Oh well, let them stay,' he was reported to have said when informed.[32] The situation became yet more obscure, and dangerous, when Necker was summoned to the palace that evening and was followed by an anxious and angry crowd of several thousand who feared that he had been dismissed. This terrifying human wave surged inside, right up to the doors of the royal apartments, seeming to put the royal family at their mercy. Panic ensued, and Marie-Antoinette begged the minister not to resign, fearing for her life if such a report escaped. Necker also had an hour-long private interview with the king, in which Louis was clearly heard to lose his temper about the 'sacrifices' he was making and the harvest of popularity Necker seemed to be reaping from them.[33] When Necker refused to leave the building discreetly, but marched out to be carried in triumph back to his lodgings by the crowd, there to meet many of the Third Estate deputies, he solidified his enemies' perception that his popularity mattered more to him than the welfare of the Crown.

It was now that Breteuil re-entered the scene. Through his political allies, including the Polignac family, he had been kept in touch with all the Court's efforts to oppose the Assembly, and in the week after 23 June he was emboldened to write directly to the king offering his services. On 2 July he received a reply asking him to explore means, through his well-known contacts with Parisian bankers, to raise significant sums of money for the royal cause. Events now moved fast. On the 5th a meeting at Versailles, under Artois' auspices, agreed details of a loan package of 100 million *livres*. On the 8th Breteuil himself came to Paris, and learned that both of the king's brothers were pressing the monarch to see him directly. On the afternoon of 11 July Necker was informed by letter that he had been dismissed, and was ordered to leave the country at once. Shunning the publicity he had courted the previous month, he left for Brussels without even changing his clothes. The next day the appointment of a new set of ministers, headed by Breteuil, was made public. As head of the royal finance council he was effective prime minister, but his arrival unleashed a catastrophic confrontation that would see his rule go down in history as the 'Ministry of the Hundred Hours'.[34]

Breteuil's plan seems essentially to have been one of carrot and stick. In a climate of looming political collapse he reached out behind the scenes to moderate leaders of the Assembly, hoping to open negotiations. Meanwhile royal troops gathered around Paris and Versailles, threatening a forceful resolution. Reports would later emerge that at least some of these moves were successful. The duc d'Orléans, widely viewed as the leader of radical discontent – not least by the queen, who had raged that he was planning on 'seizing the Crown' – was said to have had a secret meeting with Breteuil, and repented of his opposition, while the comte de Clermont-Tonnerre, Breteuil's cousin, argued in the Assembly against a motion calling for Necker's reinstatement. Meanwhile Jean-Sylvain Bailly, *doyen* of the Assembly and an old friend of Breteuil, wrote asking him to work with the Assembly for the common good.[35]

But if events had moved fast in bringing Breteuil to power, they were now moving even faster towards casting him from it. The military build-up around Paris had been obvious for weeks to the population of the great city, and seemed to have only one meaning – a *coup d'état* against the population that might otherwise defend the National Assembly. In fact, ironically, the elderly War Minister, the maréchal de Broglie, confined his orders exclusively to defensive preparations. On 11 July he reported 'reason to fear a violent insurrection at daybreak tomorrow', in the face of which 'we cannot defend the whole of Paris', and ordered troops to concentrate on protecting a brief list of key points.[36]

This extreme timidity was invisible to the Parisians, and to the deputies of the National Assembly. On 8 July Mirabeau had vehemently denounced the 'warlike preparations of the Court', warned that they might provoke 'excesses' and sponsored a motion begging the king to withdraw them. The king replied on the 10th that the troops were there 'to ensure and even to protect the freedom which must reign in the deliberations' of the Assembly, but that if they worried the Assembly he might consent to move it, and the Court, *en masse* to another town. This seemed more of a threat than an offer, risking dividing the deputies from their popular defenders.[37] The actions of the Crown seemed particularly ill placed, as the newly united deputies of the three Estates were learning to work in something approaching harmony. As early as 1 July a Third Estate deputy wrote of his pleasure at seeing the nobility vote as individuals in a debate: 'a substantial portion of this order fully intends to reconcile itself to public opinion and work for the success of the Estates'. Some nobles were pleasantly surprised by the welcome they received, and the manners of the commoners with whom they now had to rub shoulders. The marquis de Ferrières, a wry observer of his own order's foibles, noted that commoners heard him speak in committee 'with a great deal of decency', and decided that 'I would much prefer that a bourgeois imagine himself my equal than to see a great aristocrat think I'm his inferior.' Other commoners seemed flattered by the nobles' condescension, praising 'the finest names in the kingdom' who lent a new 'air of seriousness' to the Assembly.[38] While some of the more recalcitrant nobles withdrew from the Assembly, others went back to their constituencies specifically to be freed from the restrictive mandates they had been given to defend their order's privileges. The situation was fluid, but seemed hopeful.

In Paris, however, the general mood was one of dread. Pamphlets had circulated since early summer, allegedly 'exposing' the 'grand conspiracy of the aristocrats' to destroy the nation. Reports from all sides spoke of rioting peasants and mobilising troops, and those troops themselves spoke of drastic action. The English traveller Arthur Young met a young officer en route for Paris on 9 July who told him fifty thousand men were being gathered because the Third Estate 'were running mad' and needed 'wholesome correction'.[39] As bread prices in the capital climbed towards – and beyond – unprecedented levels, the public space was dominated by turbulent crowds and grumbling queues. The mutiny of the French Guards at the end of June, and the authorities' inability to assert control, set the tone – a feeling that the capital had already turned against authority, and that only troops brought in from elsewhere might pose an effective threat. Thus great efforts were made to win over the first detachments: common soldiers were fêted with free drinks, and hailed by crowds as they pledged to leave the National Assembly in peace. Officers, by contrast, were hissed in public, and left in no doubt of popular hostility. The mutinous spirit of the French Guards even extended as far as Versailles, where a group of them brawled successfully with cavalrymen on 6 July. Four days later there was a mass breakout from the artillery barracks at the Invalides, where eighty soldiers scaled the walls and rushed to the Palais-Royal, a pleasure garden at the heart of the city where thousands gathered daily to gossip and agitate, there to be toasted as heroes.[40]

Those soldiers who did not rally to the Patriot cause were looked on with even more fear as a result. The Royal Allemand cavalry regiment, for example, made up largely of German-speaking Alsatians, remained loyal to its aristocratic commander, the prince de Lambesc. As word of Necker's dismissal leaked into the city on 12 July, the cavalrymen found themselves at the heart of an iconic confrontation. Disorder broke out all over Paris as the news spread. Necker was regarded, however exaggeratedly, as almost single-handedly responsible for fending off mass starvation the previous winter, and as the man holding the 'aristocratic plot' in check in the political realm as well. His dismissal thus meant food prices would soar higher, and the National Assembly be taken prisoner to a town far from a capital crushed by mercenary troops. Orators at the Palais-Royal rallied crowds to the need for 'defending our homes against the fury of a threatening army', and protesting crowds spread around the city's boulevards, closing the theatres and carrying before them busts of Necker and the duc d'Orléans.[41]

In the gardens of the Tuileries palace, where polite Parisian society gathered to stroll on this summer Sunday, an angry confrontation developed through the day between crowds and troops, and by early evening there was a stand-off on the nearby Place Louis XV, with detachments from several cavalry regiments confronting a mass of people of every social class. Shots and stones had been exchanged, so far without casualties, when the Royal Allemand regiment was brought in by the garrison commander in an effort to clear the square. Witnesses on either side differ dramatically over what happened next. The officers generally noted their moderation and caution, and the violence they received from the crowd, who had barricaded the square with chairs from the Tuileries gardens. From dozens of civilian witnesses to an inquiry held the next year, however, came reports of a rapid deployment – a charge – and escalating accounts of injuries and deaths inflicted. Lambesc himself unquestionably hit a man with his sabre, concerned that a group were trying to cut off the horsemen's retreat. Despite the fact that this man lived to testify a year later, his brutal death became a fixture in the instant iconography of 'Lambesc's Charge'.[42] As evening drew in, news was running through central Paris that the prince de Lambesc 'was massacring everybody in the Place Louis XV'. In the Palais-Royal 'Everyone shouted "To arms!"' as this report was repeated.[43]

As darkness fell, the city rose in a wave of spontaneous revolt. The royal commanders tried to bring troops across the river into the centre of the city, but came under fire from French Guards at various points and decided 'that they were no longer in a position to resist the rebels, who were bringing up vastly superior forces'. The troops were withdrawn from the city and were back in their encampments by 5 a.m. on the 13th.[44] In truth, no one knew what was going on in Paris that night. The most determined elements of the crowds took advantage of the royal withdrawal to attack the hated customs barriers that added a third to the price of food. Forty out of fifty-four were burned to the ground, and in several places breaches were made in the wall that connected them. At dawn the monastery of Saint-Lazare was attacked by a large crowd, convinced of the building's role as a centre of food hoarding: fifty-three cartloads of grain were taken and sold at the central markets by groups including neighbourhood leaders and French Guards. They also released the delinquents held in the monastery's prison, and crowds went on to open the La Force prison – though not other jails that held convicted felons, and indeed the inmates of the Châtelet prison were shot at by French Guards when they attempted a breakout.[45]

The fear of disorder ran almost as high as the dread of royalist assault. Drums, cannon and alarm bells rang at 5 a.m. on 13 July to summon the city's assembly into emergency session. This body was made up of the delegates who had chosen the city's deputies for the

Estates-General, and had remained in existence as an expression of the Parisians' concerns for the political future – as had the gatherings of the sixty neighbourhood districts that had delegated its members. When the city assembly met it voted for the formation of a militia – at first of twelve thousand but raised within the day to forty-eight thousand, eight hundred men from each district. The men of this nascent force were to seek out arms and ammunition at key sites across the city, their quest building towards an epochal confrontation. But it is instructive to see how the spontaneous clash of fears and determination played out at a local, and indeed individual, level.

Pierre Maréchal de Saint-Firmin was a former army officer who became a captain in the Parisian National Guard, as the new militia was soon named. He set down his account of the events of 12–14 July a few months later. On the 12th, he noted, he had been 'occupied solely in disarming the men whose murky cohorts were terrifying the capital'. In this role he had 'thrown himself into this frightful league under the pretext of following them', taken a musket he was given, and then 'deserted' to conceal it, and others, at his house. But his account of the 13th changes tack dramatically. Suddenly 'the collection of these arms served to go to the Invalides and collect the cannon, which we took to the City Hall'. There 'we spent all night under arms', before getting word on the morning of the 14th 'that troops were appearing at the gates of Paris . . . To march on the enemy I formed a body of two hundred men all with military service.' As they approached the eastern suburbs Saint-Firmin noted that 'Alarm was general, one saw groups fleeing on all sides, thinking all was lost. The windows were garnished with stones, tiles and cobbles.' He formed a barricade of dung carts, and 'behind each wagon were citizens armed with sickles, scythes and pitchforks, the pews of the churches were flung in front to hinder the cavalry horses'. Saint-Firmin had three cannon at his disposal 'advantageously placed' and loaded. He took his troops on a patrol, and 'after a very tiring course' discovered that the feared attackers were 'two patrols from the countryside, marching with drums beating'. Feeding his tired troops at his own expense, he headed back to the City Hall for new orders, but trod on a broken bottle and had to go home to have the wound bandaged. Thus he was separated from his troops when 'the general alarm sounded', and he remained on alert in the centre of the city while events ran their dramatic course elsewhere.[46]

Particularly telling in Saint-Firmin's narrative is the point where the actors of the 12th – the 'murky cohorts' of a 'frightful league' – become without comment an inclusive 'we' that is conducting a military campaign. As the great city was rocked by escalating rumours of massive assaults, the population seems to have bound itself together, momentarily forgetting the habitual fears that divided the propertied from the poor. On the morning of the 14th a huge crowd surged over the Invalides, a barracks complex for retired soldiers on the Left Bank, seizing thirty thousand muskets held there. The soldier-pensioners, who had been stationed by their governor behind loaded cannon, refused to fire, and five thousand troops encamped only a few hundred yards away remained in their tents – they 'would refuse to march', one commander reported, if any officers had dared give the order.[47] This dramatic reinforcement of the military leadership's helplessness was stark evidence that the Crown had lost control of the situation decisively. But as so often, it would take more vividly symbolic events to bring that message home to all involved.

The Bastille was a medieval fortress, a cluster of tall towers looming over the humbler dwellings of eastern Paris, and casting a wide penumbra of legend and fear. It was to the Bastille that the shadowy police agents of the Crown had swept those they wished to question in seclusion, and thus in the popular mind it was a haunt of torture and the worst excesses of power. No matter that by 1789 no such practices remained, or that a mere handful of undistinguished lunatics and bankrupts graced its cells: the Bastille's fall to the forces of revolution marked the indisputable overthrow of that arbitrary power, and of all that the 'aristocratic plot' allegedly wished to defend. But it would never have fallen at all without mistakes, misunderstandings and plain incompetence.

The governor of the fortress, Bertrand-René Jourdan de Launey, had no practical military experience, having inherited his post from his father thirteen years before. Now in his fiftieth year, he was timorous and indecisive. In the preceding weeks, for example, he had had the fortifications patched up, and cartloads of scrap iron and stones hauled to the top to cast down on attackers, but he had failed to stockpile any rations inside the walls, which also lacked a water supply. The garrison was mostly made up of the same kind of pensioners who had surrendered the Invalides, supported by a platoon of

Swiss troops sent in a week before. After witnessing the disturbances of the 12th, de Launey ordered all of them inside the high walls, abandoning defensible positions in outer buildings. Thirty thousand pounds of gunpowder in 250 large barrels were also shifted inside from the nearby royal Arsenal. Having at first left these in the court-yard, de Launey ordered his already weary soldiers to transfer them to the cellars on the 13th, as the first crowds began to gather out-side.[48] The soldiers got little sleep that night, as random shots from the Parisians brought repeated alarms and calls to the battlements. It was the gunpowder that brought a much larger crowd to the Bastille on the morning of the 14th. While the Invalides had fallen swiftly, yielding up its arms, the Bastille's supplies seemed safely locked away.

The city's elders began to try to mediate this crisis as the morning drew on. Two delegations, one from the central assembly and one from the local district, visited the Bastille and were shown round by de Launey. The fears of those outside about cannon pointing from the walls were met by withdrawing them – though this itself sent a further wave of dread through the crowds that they were being taken in to be loaded. When the governor offered the first delegation a meal, their extended absence from view provoked a clamour that they had been locked up, stoking tension even more. The second delegation was reassured, and de Launey even personally had the garrison swear to them that 'they would not fire nor use their arms unless they were attacked'. Exhortations to open the fortress, how-ever, met strong resistance from the Swiss – such dishonour was not to be countenanced.[49] The pensioners of the garrison seemed less decisive, though. Prospects for a peaceful resolution seemed fair, and after reporting to the local district the delegates were setting off to proclaim the governor's pacific promise to the still-growing crowds when an explosion announced that combat had been engaged.

The crowd, pushing forward in ever larger numbers, had begun to press against the outer gates, from where the troops had been with-drawn on the 12th. Pensioners on the inner towers had waved their hats and gestured to them, attempting to make them go back, know-ing that the Swiss officers would order fire from the towers if the gates were breached. But the crowds, viewing these antics perhaps as encouragements rather than warnings, had pressed on. The perilous situation – with repeated alarms of troops marching on the city –

pushed individuals to heroic recklessness. Two men leapt over the outer wall via the roofs of shops built up against it, and others followed their example. They grabbed axes and sledgehammers from the guardhouse, and smashed the drawbridge mechanism. One man was killed as the bridge slammed down, but the crowd rushed in, battering down the next set of gates. At the walls of the inner fortress there was a brief parlay between officers on the walls and the crowd surging below. Heedless of warnings – because most of them never heard them – the crowd rushed closer to the inner drawbridge, until the fatal order was given, and a volley of musketry was loosed, accompanied by a single cannon shot that boomed across the neighbourhood. For most of the assailants this came as an act of betrayal. Few had seen the men scramble over the wall to let down the first drawbridge, and most took it as an invitation from the governor to enter. Now they were being fired upon without warning, as far as they knew. The cry went up, 'Treachery!'[50]

From early afternoon a true siege was joined. The crowds scattered to cover in the many buildings of the outer courtyards – including the governor's own house. The most ardent attackers, with arms scavenged from across the city, were in the kitchen block nearest the towers, and began sniping at the defenders. Others, showing striking initiative, took two cartloads of straw from a nearby brewery stables, set them alight and ran them, billowing smoke, towards the inner gates, blocking the defenders' sights. At this moment a third official delegation, this one again from the city assembly, arrived. Their mission was almost comically redundant, for they had been deputed to ask whether the governor of the Bastille 'is willing to accept in that fortress the troops of the Parisian militia, who will guard it in conjunction with the troops at present stationed there'. The delegates found themselves in the midst of a battle – despite their waving of white handkerchiefs, and attempts to alert all parties to their importance, 'further implied by our dress and our confident bearing in the face of danger', but 'the firing never ceased'. Approaching from another side, they persuaded 'a great number of citizens in arms' to stop shooting, only to see several fall to shots from the Bastille: 'The attackers ... therefore resumed their fire with as much courage as indignation. Our remonstrances, our prayers could no longer halt them.'[51]

A fourth delegation approached a little later, this one reinforced by a drummer and a formal white flag. At this more imposing spectacle most of the besiegers ceased fire, and so too did the pensioners on the walls – some even held up their muskets reversed, as if to signal surrender. But the governor himself, perhaps fear-stricken by events, yelled to his soldiers that this was just another trick to get inside the fortress, and ordered another volley, which struck down three men near the officials. A second 'treachery' almost cost the delegation their lives at the hands of enraged besiegers, who thought they had been led into a trap, but the men pleaded their own virtue and this crisis was defused.

Now, however, the larger crisis approached resolution, for running at the double down the rue Saint-Antoine from the City Hall came sixty men of the French Guards, and another three or four hundred militiamen, dragging with them five cannon. The military men, led by a middle-aged second lieutenant and a former Swiss Guard named Hulin, first tried bombarding the towers from a distance, but these light field-pieces could not scratch the centuries-old stonework. The inner gates would have to be breached, and a daring throw of the dice was called for. The lieutenant, Élie, led a group in a dash to clear away the carts of straw that still smouldered in front of the gates, losing two men to fire from the towers in the process. Then, under continued fire, Hulin and the soldiers dismantled two of the cannon and hand-carried them, barrels, carriages, wheels and all, across the shattered outer gates and reassembled them in the open space before the inner moat.

Three cannon manned by the Swiss troops were primed to fire behind the raised drawbridge: if it were lowered they could blast away the attackers' pieces, but only at the expense of exposing the garrison to an onslaught. The pensioners certainly thought the game was up, and clamoured for the governor to surrender on terms before the gates fell. De Launey shared their fears that they would all be 'slaughtered by the people', but for a moment entertained the manic scheme of blowing up all the gunpowder – death before dishonour. Some pensioners later claimed to have actually driven him back from the store rooms at bayonet point. De Launey tried to use the threat of an explosion to secure formal terms from the besiegers, having a note passed through a crack in the gates – where Élie collected it, balanced precariously across the moat on a plank. It demanded guarantees of safety, or else 'we shall blow up the garrison and the whole neighbourhood'.[52] While the crowd outside yelled for the drawbridges to be let down at once, the Swiss officers thought de Launey would have to carry out his threat, only to see the pensioners, perhaps on their own initiative, dropping the drawbridge. The Bastille had fallen.

The attackers had suffered over eighty dead, with over a dozen others mortally wounded, and nearly a hundred other injuries, some of which were crippling. The garrison was almost unharmed, and for the most part would remain so, even though some – ignorant of the effective surrender – fired on the crowd as it entered the inner court-yard. Men, and some women, surged through the fortress, ransacking offices and apartments, releasing in triumph the few prisoners, and taking charge of the gunpowder. The ordinary soldiers of the garrison were generally treated well. De Launey, however, had been marked for death. Though leaders of the besiegers, including both Hulin and Élie, tried to shepherd him into custody at the City Hall, their progress was halted time and again by surges from a crowd that demanded instant justice for the governor's earlier 'treachery'. He was beaten and kicked, becoming progressively weaker with each wave of attacks, until outside the City Hall itself he fell into the hands of a group set on finishing the job. Writhing in their grip, and yelling, 'Let me die!', he kicked a man in the groin. As this man fell, shouting, 'I'm done for', someone else plunged a blade into de Launey's belly, the signal for a flurry of stabs and shots that left his body bleeding in the gutter. The kicked man, an unemployed cook named Desnot, was offered the honour of decapitating him, which he did with a pocket knife. Crowd justice, like royal justice, ended with the display of the victim's head on a pole.[53]

Perhaps this killing liberated a stronger impulse to vengeance, for three officers of the garrison who had not yet been brought to safety were also killed, as were three of the pensioners, apparently at random. Less random, and indeed a token of the wider revolutionary import of the moment, was the shooting dead of Jacques de Fles-selles, the royal administrator of the city. He had been unable to furnish demanding crowds with arms the previous day, and had fatally shown them some chests that proved to be empty. This 'treachery' had been cried about the city throughout the 14th, and shortly after de Launey's death de Flesselles left the City Hall to try to explain himself. Struck down by a pistol shot, he too was decapi-tated and his head paraded as a sign of victory and justice.

That the Parisians were victorious was evident as news of the taking of the Bastille reached the Crown's commanders. An immediate military evacuation of the city was ordered, and the troops who had sat passively all day on the Champ de Mars abandoned their tents and marched in torrential rain out of the capital, past still-burning customs barriers, to seek shelter in the parks and villages of the plain between Paris and Versailles. En route, subject to the patriotic pleadings of locals, dozens deserted, and the next day the maréchal de Broglie had to confess his conviction that the troops 'would not fight against their fellow citizens'.[54]

Meanwhile, at Versailles, the National Assembly had lived through three days of total uncertainty. At the news of Necker's dismissal they had set themselves *en permanence*, taking up station in their hall by shifts to guard against any moves to dissolve the Assembly. Rumours of everything from a military assault to a popular march on Versailles had the deputies pacing the aisles, straining for the sound of cannon. Some wrote letters, fearing they might be their last, depicting their 'frightful state . . . all to be assassinated or, at the very least, to be carried off'.[55] Remarkably, on the 13th many formerly reticent nobles were driven by the crisis to swear allegiance to their fellow deputies, 'to share . . . a common voice and a common heart', and at 3 a.m. on the 14th a commoner recorded in his diary his wonder at the sight of these men 'once so favoured by the blind chance of birth . . . [who] sleep now or walk about the hall, mixed together with the commoners'.[56] On the evening of the 14th, after another day of dread, the Assembly heard an account of the events at the Bastille, and de Launey's fate, and sent a delegation to inform the king. The latter insisted he was in charge of the situation, replying that he had instructed the city's administrator, de Flesselles (already dead) to take charge of the militia, and ordered the troops withdrawn from the city. The magnitude of what was happening seems to have escaped the king. Another delegation who gave more news of what Louis called 'misfortunes' was told that 'it is impossible to believe that these are the results of my orders to the troops'.[57] The duc de La Rochefoucauld-Liancourt, a noted philanthropist and member of the Assembly, gained a clearer picture of the situation later that night, and woke the king to inform him. The exchange that ensued, while private, entered circulation and became legendary almost at once: 'But, this is a revolt?' Louis stammered. 'No, sire,' replied the duke, 'it is a revolution.'[58]

If the duke did indeed use those words, he certainly did not mean by them anything more than a great and significant political upheaval – for that was the common sense of the term 'revolution' in human affairs. It would take many more turbulent days before this great event was understood as the overturning of a whole order. Indeed the deputies of the National Assembly themselves were at first horrified by news of the violence, their minutes recording it as 'disastrous', producing 'the most mournful impression. All discussion ceased.' The following morning deputies were consumed with the fear that the conflict had been engineered by the king's new set of ministers, to persuade him to unleash repression. The marquis de Sillery, making this link, spoke of the events of the last three days as 'massacres' and 'bloody executions' that 'have carried the people to an excess of fury that is very difficult to stop'.[59] It was the king himself who burst this pessimistic bubble, appearing in the Assembly at only a few moments' notice. With only his brothers and a few soldiers as entourage, he proceeded to take the deputies' breath away by announcing a full withdrawal of his troops to their provincial barracks, accepting the deputies' declarations of the previous month, and their very existence as a 'National Assembly', and pledging himself to co-operation for the common good. In a hysteria of relief the deputies cheered, wept, stood on the benches, threw their hats in the air and in several cases fainted. One even had a fatal stroke, 'dying for joy', as a witness put it.[60]

The surviving deputies formed a guard of honour *en masse*, surrounding Louis as he walked back from the hall to his palace, encircled by vast crowds on the first truly sunny day in weeks. A royal band struck up a jaunty air as they arrived, the popular song that went, 'Where are you better than at home with your family?' The deputies' mood would have been shattered if they had known what the king's actual family were pressing him to do. A stormy royal council session that evening ended with Louis taking the advice of his hardliners by preparing to follow his troops eastwards to launch what would be a civil war on Paris. Only the repeated advice of the maréchal de Broglie, that no troops could be relied upon against the city, forced a change of heart in the early hours of the 16th. The result was a mass exodus of the conservative leadership of the Court, led by the king's brother Artois. He told a confidant, to whom he gave the charge of escorting his children to safety, that the king 'is

being taken to Paris tomorrow, he will be held captive there, and
only my liberty can guarantee his own'.[61] As he fled towards the
frontier, he is unlikely to have reflected on the fact that his intransigence was largely responsible for the crisis.

Artois' hatred of Necker had very probably led to his dismissal on
the 11th, which had triggered panic. Breteuil's original plan had
called for Necker to be retained in office but penned in by conservative colleagues until a more consolidated military response was
ready and the Assembly could be properly intimidated into co-
operation. What transpired, therefore, was already a half-cocked
scheme even before Paris erupted.[62] The decision to abandon
confrontation meant the end of Breteuil's 'Ministry of the Hundred
Hours' – if the king was to put himself into the hands of the revolutionaries, those he had appointed to defy them would not be
safe. Several ministers fled along with other aristocrats on the 16th,
even before their resignations were announced to an overjoyed
Assembly, along with news of the recall of Necker. Breteuil himself
slipped out of France disguised as a Benedictine monk.[63]

The sixteenth of July brought joy to the National Assembly for
several reasons. Besides learning of the ministry's fall, and rumours of
the flight of the aristocrats, deputies were delighted to be joined by
the last group of nobles who had held out against deliberation in
common, and further reassured by news from Paris. Some deputies
had journeyed there on the 15th, and returned now to report on scenes
of jubilation. Instead of carnage they saw 'all the most vivid signs
of affection . . . Citizens congratulated and embraced one another.
All eyes were wet with tears, intoxicated sentiment was everywhere.'
There were 'regrets' over what one speaker now euphemistically
called the 'terrible moments' of the last few days, but Paris is now
'worthy of liberty; she has earned it by her courage and energy'.[64]
News such as this may have prompted the last nobles to come on
board, and combined with that of the recall of Necker, and of the
king's planned trip to Paris on the 17th, began to create the new,
profound meaning of 'revolution' these days would carry into the
future.

---

# 'For all men, and for all countries'

## *Declaring rights in America and France*

R ights – their definition, their codification, their declaration for all
time – are at the heart of the history of 1789. But the experience
of formulating the two great declarations that frame this year, and the
concepts of rights that emerged within them, are more contrasting,
and in their underlying conceptions more contradictory, than is
conventionally allowed. One was dictated by history; the other by
rationality. One limited sovereignty; the other encoded it. One was,
in its ultimate concerns, essentially pre-modern; the other set out
the first clear statement of political modernity. Both documents
shared a rich heritage, and a certain family resemblance, but like
any siblings, they were also completely individual.

The attempt to make the American Constitution stand up without a Bill of Rights was probably always futile. Though the 1787
Convention had wrangled itself to a stop over the point, it was not
one that the people of the new Republic were likely to abandon.
Not least because, in their political hearts, they were Englishmen,
and as such they knew that a political structure designed to preserve
liberty must enumerate the rights that made up that freedom. In
1789 'freeborn Englishmen' across the globe were celebrating the
centenary of just such an enumeration, the first self-named 'Bill of
Rights' issued by the rebellious Parliament as an indictment of
the fugitive James II, and as a negotiating platform for the accession
of William III and Mary as joint, Protestant, sovereigns. Begun on

22 January 1689, accepted by the new monarchs in the spring and signed into law on 16 December, the Bill declared explicit limits to executive power to make and carry out law, raise taxes and maintain an army. It also insisted on regular judicial process, including duly empanelled jury trials, freedom of elections to Parliament and freedom of debates within Parliament. It further declared, against the threat of wild Irish and Highland Catholic militias that James's plots had conjured up, 'that the subjects which are Protestants may have arms for their defence suitable to their conditions and as allowed by law'.[1]

With the coming of independence one of the prime concerns of the new states was to frame their political existence securely, and legitimately, in terms of right and justice as they understood them. This often turned out to be a contentious and sometimes long-winded process, and even those that acted fastest, such as Virginia, which published a 'Declaration of Rights' on 12 June 1776, had passed through acrimony to do so. Virginia's declaration was largely the work of George Mason, gentleman, scholar, opponent of slavery (and slave owner) and student of the philosophy of John Locke. It was the latter that gave form to his resonant first article:

> That all men are by nature equally free and independent, and have certain inherent rights, of which, when they enter into a state of society, they cannot, by any compact, deprive or divest their posterity; namely, the enjoyment of life and liberty, with the means of acquiring and possessing property, and pursuing and obtaining happiness and safety.[2]

Passing through the mind of Thomas Jefferson and under the editing pen of Benjamin Franklin, this passage would shortly ring out in the Declaration of Independence itself, but to secure the original's acceptance in Virginia had taken four days of dispute. To declare men equally free seemed to some slave owners a 'pretext of civil convulsion', and they were not reassured until it was explained that slaves were not to be 'constituent members' of the society in question and thus such maxims were inapplicable to them.[3]

Other rights given in the Virginia Declaration were less contentious, because they were less general – indeed part and parcel of a very specifically English traditional definition of justice. Before the mid-seventeenth century, English courts, like those elsewhere in Europe, had been in large part the instruments of executive whim. In particular, characters odious to power could be taken up and pursued, their affairs ransacked and their answers compelled – under torture in some cases – until an actionable cause presented itself. By strict law this was unjustified, and the matter was brought to a head in 1637 when John Lilburne, an outspoken radical publisher, was brought before the notoriously inquisitional Star Chamber court. He declared: 'I see that you go about this examination to ensnare me . . . I shall answer no more . . . I think by the law of the land, that I may stand upon my just defence, and not answer to your interrogatories.'4 The matter was formalised in statute a few years later. This, and a series of other points embedded in the maxims of English Common Law – that 'law of the land' decided by generations of cases and precedents, rather than by individual statutes – took their place in Virginia's eighth article:

> That in all capital or criminal prosecutions a man hath a right to demand the cause and nature of his accusation, to be confronted with the accusers and witnesses, to call for evidence in his favour, and to a speedy trial by an impartial jury of his vicinage, without whose unanimous consent he cannot be found guilty, nor can he be compelled to give evidence against himself; that no man be deprived of his liberty except by the law of the land or the judgement of his peers.

As well as drawing on philosophy and common-law tradition, Mason and his colleagues also drew directly on the 1689 Bill of Rights, with their ninth article taken verbatim: 'That excessive bail ought not to be required, nor excessive fines imposed; nor cruel and unusual punishments inflicted.' The Virginians also paid attention to more recent struggles, denouncing in their tenth article 'general warrants' allowing for search or seizures of places, persons or property not specifically named, for offences 'not particularly described and supported by evidence'. These had been a *cause célèbre* of the 1760s – John Wilkes had spent time in the Tower of London for defying one, and the Navigation Acts that hindered American trade had licensed their use by Revenue men.5

Though the Virginia Declaration provided a template for many

others – seven states' final declarations bore the mark of its language – there were many variations and reservations at work.
Pennsylvania's declaration echoed Virginia's in many particulars, but
also accompanied a constitution that was very far from the balanced
preservation of gentry society seen in the latter, and a political scene
where shenanigans of various kinds would make its nobler provisions
moot for years. One such provision extended religious tolerance
beyond the purely Christian to other sects, a measure taken further
by Maryland, which exempted such sectaries from oaths of office and
allegiance. However, Maryland also declared religious worship to be
a duty (Pennsylvania had called it a natural right), licensed taxation
'for the support of the Christian religion' and restricted formal freedom of speech to legislative debates.[6] Neighbouring Delaware took
the matter of such declarations in new directions, barring the clergy
from holding civic office (while upholding the virtue of religion in
general) and stating boldly that 'no person hereafter imported into
this state from Africa ought to be held in slavery under any pretence
whatever'.[7]

Some states – New Jersey, Georgia and New York – formulated
constitutions that enumerated 'rights' as part of their general structure, not as a separate charter, though these documents generally
included much of the substance of such declarations. Though this
approach was relatively uncontroversial in these places, the attempt
to do likewise in Massachusetts, the fount of revolution, saw the
work of the state convention thrown out in 1778 by a five-to-one
majority of town meetings. Feeble assurances of jury trial and religious freedom had not been enough to answer fears that men's
'natural rights' might be undermined if they were not seen to be
declared in advance of any ordering of political society. The following year a new committee was set to drafting a declaration, much of
the work falling to John Adams. Perhaps as a result, the version
approved in 1780, in no fewer than thirty articles, was rather prolix,
taking almost all the language of Virginia, for example, and then
more than doubling it. Including by now standard declarations of
inalienable popular sovereignty, judicial due process and the defence
of natural rights including freedom of the press, it also noted: 'Every
subject has a right to be secure from all unreasonable searches and
seizures of his person, his houses, his papers, and all his possessions'
(Article 14); 'The people have a right to keep and to bear arms for

the common defence' (Article 17); and 'In time of peace, no soldier ought to be quartered in any house without the consent of the owner; and in time of war, such quarters ought not be made but by the civil magistrate, in a manner ordained by the legislature' (Article 27).[8]

Such measures spoke both to the recent history of the colony under the British and the future federal text. As elsewhere, however, religion proved a sticking point for this charter. The draft gestured towards both a power for localities to maintain churches and a salaried Protestant clergy, and a general religious toleration. In the town-meeting debates that followed such plans were denounced as everything from a licence for ungodliness to a Tory plot to re-establish the Church of England. Six towns called for a formal obligation for Sabbath rest to be included in the declaration; and one denounced freedom of the press as a licence to 'Dishonour god by printing herasy [sic]'.[9] Such was the ardour occasioned by the debate, and the new proposals it generated, that it is highly likely that only organised fraud, and perhaps even the blatant suppression of extant 'no' votes, produced a supposed two-thirds majority for approval of the text announced on 15 June 1780.[10] The four years it had taken the states to agree their declarations boded ill for Congress, as it contemplated renewing the debate in the summer of 1789.

Less than a year earlier Alexander Hamilton, writing as 'Publius' in number eighty-four of the *Federalist Papers*, had been starkly opposed to a bill of rights for the USA: such items were 'not only unnecessary in the proposed Constitution but would even be dangerous . . . why declare that things shall not be done which there is no power to do?'[11] Declared rights, he implied, opened the path to assumption of powers not mentioned, merely because they were not specifically banned. Hamilton's argument, from the man who had advocated the rule of a king in all but name, was both disingenuous and convoluted. In the very same article he had praised a series of limitations in the Constitution: on the suspension of *habeas corpus*, and on various other unjust legal proceedings, its prohibition on the creation of an order of nobility and its limitations on the definition of treason. None of these was necessary, according to his own argument, yet he promoted them as virtues of the text. Others eyed them more coldly. Robert Yates, who had left the Convention in disgust at its direction, wrote as 'Brutus' in a text published as the *Antifederalist no. 84*:

Does this Constitution any where grant the power of suspending the habeas corpus, to make ex post facto laws, pass bills of attainder, or grant titles of nobility? It certainly does not in express terms. The only answer that can be given is, that these are implied in the general powers granted.[12]

Those who refused to specify other items that would be safeguarded against such implied powers, Yates declared, 'are wilfully endeavoring to deceive, and to lead you into an absolute state of vassalage'.

Hamilton's sophistry had little effect against such cold suspicion and the heritage of state declarations. With the large states all having already pleaded for enumeration of rights during the ratification process, the demands for a Bill built up. This was despite the views of those such as James Madison, who wrote to Jefferson in October 1788 that such declarations seemed rarely to withstand the force of political majorities: 'In Virginia I have seen the bill of rights violated in every instance where it has been exposed to a popular current.'[13] It is certainly the case that a steady stream of lawsuits concerning religious toleration, press freedom, and intrusive searches, among other causes, seemed to show an oppressive mentality at work in the 1780s at odds with the states' fine words, but such cases could equally be seen as the strongest argument for setting down principles and allowing courts the chance to protect the vulnerable – for evidently no one else would.[14]

It was the abiding alarm at the power of the state, and a determination to resist it, that made the Bill of Rights a core issue in 1789. Antifederalism was still a powerful force – it had obliged the ratification of the Constitution to carry a heavy freight of expected amendments, and on 20 November 1788 the Virginia General Assembly had formally passed a call for a new convention to rewrite the text, an idea also circulating in several other states. With two, Rhode Island and North Carolina, still hesitating over whether even to join the new union, the stakes were high.[15] At the heart of the struggle would be the figure of James Madison, who had nursed the original 1787 Convention into existence, and whose slender frame would now carry the burden of securing its legacy. Despite his inner conviction that the new Constitution did not require a Bill of Rights to be just, he was now convinced that amendments to that end were essential, to 'give the government its due popularity and stability', as he wrote to Jefferson late in 1788.[16]

To be in a position to offer amendments, Madison had to get into Congress, which proved difficult. The arch-Antifederalist Patrick Henry commanded a majority in the Virginia Assembly, which denied Madison one of the state's two Senate seats on 8 November 1788. The tone of debate was summed up by Henry's denunciation of Madison as a man who could not be trusted with his constituents' interests and whose election would provoke 'rivulets of blood throughout the land' from an enraged citizenry. To try to block Madison from the House of Representatives, Henry then gerrymandered an electoral district that had produced a two-thirds majority against ratification earlier in the year, and forced it on him by imposing a residency requirement for candidates – this district, which had his home at one corner, was the only one Madison could stand in. Federalists were as outraged in Madison's defence as his opponents were against him. One charged of Henry that 'the man who leads a *mob* majority ... is the most cruelly oppressive of all possible Tyrants'; others noted 'palpable untruths' in the call for a second convention that accompanied these manipulations.[17]

Madison was mortified at the thought that a man of his talents and reputation should have to go begging for votes – he wrote to Washington that he had 'an extreme distaste to steps having an electioneering appearance' – and the fact that the poll was on 2 February 1789, sending him trekking round rural backwaters in the depths of winter, was even more vexing.[18] But he went, and he succeeded, even against the war-hero candidate the Antifederalists put up against him, winning by 1308 to 972 among an electorate of solid, fifty-acre-property owners (over half of whom, nonetheless, did not trouble to turn out).

The first months of the new Congress saw little opportunity to press the matter of rights and amendments. The House of Representatives, after waiting a month to reach a quorum, spent April frustrated at the Senate's ongoing wrangles about protocol, with staunch Federalist members fuming that government revenue was running away – until tariffs were established by law, goods were entering the country untaxed, while the national debt swelled. Madison, whose time had been taken up in these early weeks as one of the inner circle of Washington's advisers on forms for the new government, announced to the House on 4 May that he intended to bring forward a package of amendments, but he did not finally speak on the matter, the House being diverted by other business, until 8 June.[19] By then he had already succeeded in arguing the House out of considering petitions from Virginia and New York for a second convention – there was, he said, nothing to consider, for if two-thirds of states made such a demand, a convention was automatic, and if they did not, then there was no power in Congress to make one happen.

As Madison spoke on 8 June, in favour of amendments as a 'declaration of the rights of the people' and necessary to allay fear that 'we are not sincere in our desire to . . . secure those rights', others vehemently objected. A series of Federalist speakers claimed that 'taking up the subject of amendments' would be disruptive, indeed alarming to a public who wanted good government, not further constitutional wrangling.[20] Madison seemed to be being beaten down – his weak voice never flourished in a debating chamber that, unlike the Senate, welcomed a public gallery of frequently noisy observers. But he rallied, held the floor, saw off demands to send the matter into a committee and proposed a list of some nineteen amendments. What he offered was a distillation of core issues from the two hundred separate amendments suggested during the ratification process, within which there were some seventy-five distinct concrete proposals. Long debate would refine these further into twelve points (only ten of which were to be ratified) – but much of that debate had far more to do with fears about the motivations of different parties than with the substance of the proposals' wording.

Even among some who were friendly to Madison's goals there was apprehension. Governor Edmund Randolph, who had refused to sign the Constitution but then dramatically changed his mind to support ratification, wrote to Madison before Congress opened that 'I feel great distrust of some of those who will certainly be influential agents in the government' and that without rapid work on amendments a Hamiltonian vigorous government might become established unshakeably, to the detriment of liberty.[21] Those more openly opposed to the new order were even more emphatic, and suspicious. A friend in Congress wrote to Patrick Henry after Madison's speech that the object of his plan was 'unquestionably to break the spirit of the Antifederalist party by divisions'.[22] On the other hand, a friend wrote to Madison in May from North Carolina that 'the true antis in the State do not wish to hear' that amendments had been successful, and another in June confirmed that there was Antifederalist anger that 'your motion on that great and delicate subject directly contradicts' their prophecy that Federalists would never allow amendments to be debated.[23]

But if Madison's move disconcerted the Antifederalists, it did not please the true Federalists either. The House plunged after 8 June into an arduous and essentially repetitive debate, in which all the issues thrashed out at ratification conventions, and some that went as far back as Philadelphia in 1787, were revisited, with little sign of movement on either side. Representative Jackson of Georgia spoke for the irritation of Federalism: foreign nations will 'treat us with the contempt we have hitherto borne by reason of the imbecility of our government' if it is not swiftly strengthened, 'and how long it will remain in such a situation, if we enter upon amendments, God only knows. Our instability will make us objects of scorn.'[24] Thrust aside again by the pressure of other business, amendments were brought back on 21 July, when debate became entangled for hours about whether to discuss them on the floor or in a committee. The latter view prevailed, and Madison was appointed as one of eleven to consider the matter and report back in a week. Federalist scorn continued to rise. One letter writer commented that Madison was 'haunted with the ghost of Patrick Henry . . . he has not the strength of nerves which will allow him to set at defiance popular and factious clamours'.[25] On the other side of the factional divide, Henry himself was noting the growth of the President's powers as the new government took shape: 'see how rapidly power grows, how slowly the means of curbing it'. Madison's amendments, for him, were moves to 'lull suspicion' and offer 'guileful bait' to get Rhode Island and North Carolina inside the Federalist system.[26]

It was not until 13 August, delayed yet again by more pressing business, that the House set to examining the revised proposals of the committee fully. Debate raged for eleven days. Once again first principles were revisited, to the fury of some. Representative Tucker of South Carolina tried to put forward a plan to allow the people to 'instruct' their representatives: to issue binding mandates, in effect. This, opponents yelled, was 'liable to great abuses' and would likely 'be exercised in times of public disturbance' in the name of 'the prejudices of faction': it was frankly 'dangerous'.[27] Tucker also tried to limit congressional power to only those items 'expressly' mentioned in the Constitution, and even attempted, at the very end of the debate, to limit federal powers of raising revenue to the emergency situation of state requisitions not being forthcoming – which would have destroyed the independent initiative of the government.[28]

While much opposition came from overt Antifederalists, who persistently found themselves in a minority of no more than a third of the House, other interventions were sometimes disconcerting for other reasons. Samuel Livermore objected to the clause prohibiting 'cruel and unusual punishments'; did this mean, he asked, that cutting the ears off a criminal, a sentence he regarded as sometimes necessary for good order, would be prevented?[29] In the sweltering heat of late August such comments must have struck a particularly irritating note. Debate was noticeably bad-tempered throughout, and at the end saw a dramatic change of heart. Throughout the summer the House had agreed with Madison that amendments should mean just that – textual changes to the Constitution itself. Some had quailed that this in effect threatened to create an endless cycle of change: 'we may go on from year to year, making new ones, and . . . the people will never know what the constitution is'.[30] There was no doubt that this did not lend itself to immediate clarity – Madison's draft was full of 'delete from . . .' and 'insert at . . .' that only intimate familiarity with the original document could untangle. But only a vote on the last day of debate agreed a proposal to word the amendments as a separate text, creating the 'Bill of Rights' as a distinct entity for the first time.

The final language of the House's draft passed to the Senate on 24 August 1789, where debate was secret, but apparently little less acrimonious. The Federalist plutocrat Robert Morris publicly dismissed the 'nonsense they call Amendments', others called them 'milk-and-water' and Senator Maclay's diary recorded many opponents speaking 'contemptuously' of the text. A motley series of new suggestions did come up, including reinforcement of the 'separate and distinct' nature of the three branches of government, and restrictions on the term in office of any president to eight years in sixteen. All these were rejected, but the Senate made twenty-six changes to the House's version.[31] One item that passed into oblivion was a proposal Madison had held dear to his heart. In his original draft he had proposed that the Constitution should ban individual states from

Opening of the Estates-General, 5 May 1789, with the Third Estate's dowdy uniforms in contrast to the splendour of their surroundings, and their fellow deputies of the clergy and nobility. *(Bridgeman Art Library)*

The Palais-Royal in its heyday of high-society gossip, before the pre-revolutionary crisis filled it with waves of alarm and agitation. *(Corbis)*

Mutiny on the *Bounty*: the iconic moment of Bligh's forced departure in his packed open boat, April 1789. *(Bridgeman Art Library)*

John Adams, the prickly New Englander whose attachment to protocol blasted his hopes of influence for the Vice-Presidency. *(TopFoto)*

Thomas Jefferson, slave-owning polymath and advocate of Franco-American amity. *(Getty Images)*

The Gnadenhutten Massacre, imagined here for a later, more sympathetic audience than the original victims received. *(Ohio Historical Society)*

Edmund Burke, a deep thinker whose views on the real meaning of freedom took him from radicalism to a founding role in modern conservatism. *(Bridgeman Art Library)*

The Trial of Warren Hastings. The massive interest in this 'trial of the century' is vividly on display. *(Bridgeman Art Library)*

Richard Brinsley Sheridan, who shared the labour of prosecuting Hastings with Burke, before breaking dramatically with him over events in France.
*(The Art Archive)*

Cornwallis and the sons of Tipu Sultan. A contemporary image celebrating the Governor-General's victory, depicting the hostage-taking as an act almost of paternal care. *(Bridgeman Art Library)*

The Tennis Court Oath, a sketch for a monumental and unfinished painting, as the storms of the French Revolution consigned many of the participants in this moment of unity to the outer darkness. *(Bridgeman Art Library)*

The siege of the Bastille, July 1789, after the fall of the outer drawbridge, and before the heroic advance of the Parisians' cannon. *(Bridgeman Art Library)*

The infamous 'orgy' or banquet of 1 October 1789, which persuaded Parisians that counter-revolution was looming at Versailles. *(akg-images)*

A contemporary image of the March on Versailles of 5 October 1789, well-dressed women mingling with the lined faces of the poor. *(Corbis)*

The Slave Revolt on Saint-Domingue. Images such as this spread vivid terror of the carnage across a whole hemisphere. *(Bridgeman Art Library)*

Irish rebels in 1798, the early Victorian illustrator Cruikshank maintaining a tradition of depicting them as subhuman. *(Getty Images)*

violating 'equal rights of conscience, or the freedom of the press, or the trial by jury in criminal cases'. It was the only significant restriction on state, as opposed to federal, powers put forward, and the Senators, chosen by state politicians rather than the common electorate, had no stomach for it.[32] The Senate's version was agreed on 14 September, and it took the rest of the month to agree and vote on a final form of words.

Twelve amendments were sent forward to the states over George Washington's signature, but the first two, concerning the future size of the House of Representatives and the salaries of Congressmen, met a variety of objections from the states and fell away. Despite the rejection of all the amendments by Georgia and Connecticut, the Bill of Rights seemed on course for adoption, until it met Patrick Henry and his supporters in Virginia. Henry remained convinced that the text 'will tend to injure rather than serve the Cause of Liberty', and served as a sop to justify the 'exorbitancy of Power granted away by the Constitution from the People'.[33] Henry's powerbase in Virginia seemed to be weakening, however, and after nearly a month of intermittent discussions the lower house of its legislature, where he sat, seemed on the verge of passing the amendments. He was so vexed that he abandoned his seat and went home on 12 November. The amendments passed, and went to the state senate, where Henry's supporters found surer ground for their intransigent opposition. Rejecting a third of the amendments, and refusing negotiation with the lower house, the Virginia senate succeeded in delaying ratification for two entire years. But even this intransigence could not outlast a general political sentiment towards completion, and the Virginia Senators eventually fell into line on the ten surviving amendments: Washington finally notified Congress of ratification on 31 December 1791, and Jefferson, in his by then established role as Secretary of State, was able to communicate the final text officially to state governors two months later.

The language of the Bill of Rights remained resonant with the struggles of the foregoing century: the Third Amendment, with its prohibition of peacetime quartering of troops on the population, answered what was little more than a ghost of British tyranny. The Eighth carried the pithy language of the 1689 Bill into the future: 'Excessive bail shall not be required, nor excessive fines imposed, nor cruel and unusual punishments inflicted.' The Sixth and

Seventh guaranteed rights at trial 'according to the rules of the common law' that were hallmarks of English freedoms. The Fifth retained the British institution of indictment by grand jury, and guaranteed other rights of due process, and against double jeopardy, self-incrimination and unjust confiscations, that formed basic parts of the 'freeborn' challenge to absolutism in that British context. So too did the Fourth, insisting upon warrants 'particularly describing the place to be searched, and the persons or things to be seized' against the administrative tendency to 'unreasonable searches and seizures'. The Second Amendment, of course, drew on the shadow of the 1689 Bill, and on a recent past of colonial warfare and patriot resistance, to assert: 'A well regulated militia, being necessary to the security of a free state, the right of the people to keep and bear arms, shall not be infringed.' The First Amendment addressed directly the concerns about Federalist tyranny, with its crystal-clear language: 'Congress shall make no law respecting an establishment of religion, or prohibiting the free exercise thereof; or abridging the freedom of speech, or of the press; or the right of the people peaceably to assemble, and to petition the government for a redress of grievances.'

Here the crucial word for the draftsmen of 1789 was 'Congress'. States still had establishments of religion, of various kinds, though they would phase them out over coming decades, and there was nothing in the Bill of Rights which prohibited states from arbitrary acts – those were matters for their own charters and constitutions. It would be a century before the Supreme Court began to contemplate applying the Bill of Rights as a general remedy against authority. In 1789 the key amendments in political terms were the Ninth and Tenth. The former was vague, but reassuring to the moderate wing of Antifederalist opinion: 'The enumeration in the Constitution, of certain rights, shall not be construed to deny or disparage others retained by the people.' The latter was more sharply drawn, and would have been even more so if Carolina's Tucker had inserted 'expressly' where he wanted it, as the fourth word: 'The powers not delegated to the United States by the Constitution, nor prohibited by it to the states, are reserved to the states respectively, or to the people.' The Bill of Rights, in these terms, laid the ghost of a Hamiltonian King of America. It was able to do so – and, for the future, to become a talismanic text – because it represented nothing so much as a consolidation of 150 years of British thought on political freedom; or, more precisely, on civic rights in a liberal state. The American text closed a discussion, in terms that almost all the participants already implicitly understood, at a point when a new political edifice merely awaited its capstone. The French Declaration of the Rights of Man and the Citizen, however, burst forth at a moment when their political edifice still lay in ruins around them, and posed difficult and poorly understood questions about its rebuilding, in terms that many found incomprehensible or objectionable. Little wonder it had a much stormier history ahead of it.

As the French National Assembly and the press digested and disseminated their new epoch-making notion of what had occurred at the Bastille and afterwards, smoothly assimilating the violence of 14 July into a narrative of triumphant virtue, they simultaneously faced the difficulty of accommodating further popular violence into their world view. It was not only obvious enemies who were under attack. An official from one central neighbourhood gave his own account of the city on the night of 15 July:

> I had orders [from the district] to inspect the exterior of Paris, the Arsenal, the Bastille etc., etc. To carry this out at night I was on horseback: on the quai de la Feraille, my horse was stabbed twice with a pike . . . they took from me my sword, a pistol and my hat. Returning . . . I passed down the rue Croix des Petits Champs, where a large number of Guards took aim at me, incited by many women yelling out of their windows, 'He's a traitor, kill him' . . . Arriving behind [the church of] St-Roch, I was beaten with musket-butts and knocked from my horse.[34]

It was one thing for gun-toting workers and artisans to save the capital from military assault, as all continued to believe was the case, another for crowds to lynch a woman found in man's clothing outside the City Hall on the 15th. Damned as a suspected spy, she was saved by the personal intervention of the deputy Jean-Sylvain Bailly, who had been elected mayor of Paris (alongside Lafayette, triumphantly appointed as Commanding General of the Parisian National Guard, but as yet unable to impose much restraint on those supposedly under his command). It was another thing still for soldiers to be beaten by a mob at Versailles itself, where two were rescued by a cohort of over forty deputies on the 18th, or for rioters to lynch a baker in the nearby town of Poissy the same day. Deputies rushed there, and the man, found with the noose around his neck, was reprieved only when the Bishop of Chartres begged on bended knee for his life.[35] Events were demonstrating that, if the deputies thought they had won a form of sovereignty from the king by their persistence, the crowds thought that they had taken another form – the sovereign right to punish – into their own hands when they defeated the 'attack' on Paris. And there seemed to be plenty of targets for the application of that eminent and bloody right.

The king visibly capitulated to Paris, addressed there by the new Mayor Bailly on the 17th with a speech comparing him to Henri IV, who two centuries earlier 'had reconquered his people; here it is the people who have reconquered their king'. Bailly meant these words as joyous reconciliation, but they would have sent a chill down the monarch's spine.[36] Some in the Assembly were baulking at the trail of violence that the victory had unleashed; and on the 20th, shortly after hearing the tale of events at Poissy, the conservative comte de Lally-Tollendal tried to have the Assembly pass a motion against all political violence. Those more welcoming of change rallied to defend at least some popular actions. One noted that if they repudiated 'all armed men indiscriminately . . . what citizens will arm themselves in time to save the fatherland' if despotism revived? An obscure provincial named Maximilien Robespierre raised the wider implications of political power and authority: 'Is there anything more legitimate than to rise up against a horrible conspiracy formed to destroy the nation?'[37] Lally's motion fell, but only two days later the Assembly faced another wrenching example of the powers their revolution had unleashed.

Two government officials, Bertier de Sauvigny and his father-in-law, Foulon de Doué, were arrested by Parisians in the suburbs – whether by a mob or a militia it remained genuinely hard to tell. Brought to the City Hall, Foulon was in the custody of the new administration, including Mayor Bailly, when those outside began to clamour for an immediate trial. Both men were held to be part of the 'horrible conspiracy' of the supposed 'famine pact' that had driven food prices through the roof. The popular assumption of punitive sovereignty was on full display, and the municipal officials were obliged to construct the apparatus of a trial – judges, secretaries, a prosecutor – on the steps of the City Hall. The havering reluctance of the officials to proceed to a sentence (and a blundering attempt by General Lafayette to assert his authority by personal bluster) eventually drove the crowd to seize Foulon, hang him from a lamp-post and butcher his body. His head, the mouth mockingly stuffed with grass, was held up before the horrified Bertier, to taunts of 'Kiss Papa!', before he too was brutally slain and paraded in triumph. Foulon's heart was sent in to Bailly and his councilmen: 'We all looked away,' the mayor's diary recorded. 'It was a day of atrocities and mourning.'[38]

The reflections of the deputies in the days that followed were profoundly troubled. One, Antoine Barnave, later to become a noted moderate, earned temporary infamy for declaiming, 'This blood that was shed, was it then so pure?' But most rejected the travesty of their vision of justice offered by mob rule. Some thrust the blame on *étrangers* – foreigners or unspecified outsiders – and 'homeless vagabonds'; others feared that a 'people of cannibals' had been unchained. Clermont-Tonnerre, Breteuil's pro-revolutionary cousin, 'feared we might all become barbarous . . . I asked myself, painfully, if we were even worthy of being free.'[39] Others, more trenchantly, agreed that the time had come to end such 'bloody and revolting scenes', especially as they debased the memory of the events of the previous week. A relatively conservative commoner, Pierre-Victor Malouet, made a clear distinction: 'Resistance to oppression is legitimate and honours a nation; licence debases it.' New 'excesses' must now be prevented.[40]

Lurking in the minds of many deputies, especially the more radical of the commoners, remained the fear that disorder was the weapon of the 'aristocrats' – that label being increasingly used to brand those who opposed the Patriot course of embracing change. As the National Assembly pondered its new ascendancy in the weeks following 14 July, it had to listen to a rising torrent of reports from the provinces of the revolutionary consequences of the events at Paris. News of Necker's fall had prompted responses in many towns and cities fundamentally similar to that of Paris. Old municipal bodies were ousted, militias were formed, garrisons suborned to new loyalties and, with the subsequent news of the Bastille and the king's capitulation, the consolidation of a new regime, with fulsome expressions of loyalty to the National Assembly, seemed achieved.

From the countryside, however, came a grimmer picture. Continued unrest against feudal seigneurs blurred into political hostility to 'aristocrats', and further into renewed fears that the 'famine pact' was entering a new and deadly stage. With the crops ripening and shortage everywhere, rumours of 'brigands' paid by the enemies of change to attack farms and burn supplies flourished with almost supernatural speed. As such reports rebounded around the country in what would become known as the 'Great Fear', a massive armament of rural communities was the prime response, often leading to further outbreaks of violence against suspected 'aristocrats' – and each outbreak of real violence prompted rumours of many more.

The wildfire nature of these episodes meant that news of them reached the capital almost simultaneously, reinforcing the impression that such a widespread outbreak could not be spontaneous: 'one cannot believe,' wrote one, 'that warnings were sounded everywhere at the same time'. Thus the urban interpretation of the Great Fear was that it was itself the product of an aristocratic plot to make the country ungovernable. Deputies lived in 'a state of mortal anxiety' for news from their homes, while noting that all the trouble could be blamed on 'plots hatched in hell'. Along with the aristocratic enemy, some blamed 'Guineas from Mr Pitt', an early appearance of an abiding Anglophobic reaction.[41]

Meanwhile there was an almost complete collapse of governmental power. Necker, though recalled to office, had to be tracked down with almost a week's head start on his journey into exile, and did not return until 29th July. He could not form a new ministry until 4 August. In the meantime the Assembly itself did not know quite what to do. With the initial euphoria fading, resentful hostility between nobles and commoners began to simmer. Efforts to get started on the business of a new constitution were hesitant. A committee reported on 27 July that only a few outlines of clear agreement could be gleaned from all the many *cahiers* of the three orders. Beyond dispensing with the privileges of the nobility and clergy over tax, and requiring the state itself to be more open in its fiscal affairs, all else was uncertainty and division. Wider legal privileges, and seigneurial rights, clouded the issue. Were the French to become all citizens in a new polity, or were the nobility to remain a caste apart, even if folded into a new political fraternity?[42]

The radicals of the Breton Club now came again to the fore. Their plan was to tackle both the stalemate in the Assembly and the troubling rural unrest by launching a move to surrender the rights of seigneurs: a first gesture of renunciation that it was hoped would break the logjam, and calm the peasantry with a concrete gain. Others had had similar ideas, including various of the noble deputies most involved with charitable and philanthropic works, and it was one of these, the duc d'Aiguillon, who agreed to put the motion forward, on the evening of 4 August. Before he could do so, another noble, the vicomte de Noailles, leapt to his feet with a similar proposal. D'Aiguillon followed up with a flustered version of his planned speech, but seemed nonetheless to have captured the mood of the Assembly. A flurry of speakers came forward, invoking horror stories of feudal oppression and making emotive appeals. One in particular roused 'noble enthusiasm' on all sides with a stirring call to follow 'English America' in the renunciation of 'feudalism'.[43]

Not all the enthusiasm was perhaps without self-interest, or thoughts of self-preservation. One of the next speeches was made by the duc du Châtelet, a relatively hardline noble who had been a nominal commander of troops in Paris until resigning on 16 July, and who was, in the words of the watching marquis de Ferrières, 'tormented with anxiety and wild fears' at possible popular revenge. Du Châtelet not merely supported the general proposition of a sacrifice, but on the spot cast aside his own privileges (though he did not forget to assume a 'just compensation' would be offered). In any case for the next two hours a running list of noble and clerical privileges were cast onto a growing bonfire of distinctions, as what one observer could only call 'a kind of magic' took hold.[44] Noble rights to their seigneurial incomes were joined by their rights to hold courts, and hunt over fields and crops; the clergy gave up their fees for services, and their own seigneurial status, while du Châtelet returned to the fray by demanding an end to the church tithe (perhaps because a bishop had just surrendered hunting rights). The end of privileges of all kinds over taxation, and indeed the abolition of the most iniquitous taxes themselves, was embraced with fervour.

In the third hour of speeches the commoners joined in, casting down the privileges of geographical, municipal and corporate groups. In a telling moment the moderates of Dauphiné and the radicals of Brittany made a joint call for an end to provincial privilege, and such theatricality was part and parcel of what one noble deputy recalled as

a 'combat of generosity' between the orders. By two in the morning
there seemed little left to give up in this 'bountiful example of mag-
nanimity and disinterestedness'.[45] Motions had even been put
forward for religious equality for Protestants, the abolition of noble
status in itself and the suppression of colonial slavery. Such pure
universalism, however, did not survive even the first codification in
the official minute, which listed sixteen areas of renunciation, and
was voted by acclamation before the exhausted deputies retired for
the night. Men from all sides of the emerging political spectrum,
including many who would later become extreme 'aristocrats', had
for a few hours been joined in a great project. As one moderate noble
put it, 'Let us abandon all distinctions; let us only regret that we have
nothing else left to sacrifice; let us consider that henceforth the title
of "Frenchman" will be distinction enough for every generous soul.'
A commoner deputy wrote home that 'in the future, only wealth,
talent and virtue will distinguish one man from another . . . We are a
nation of brothers. The king is our father and France is our mother.'[46]
Events were soon to prove, however, that this was anything but a
happy family.

Thomas Jefferson's enthusiasm for declarations of rights transcended
national boundaries in more than mere location. As early as 12
January 1789 he sent to Madison a projected French declaration of
rights drafted by Lafayette, the latter evidently eager to fill the space
he had left in his hallway beside Jefferson's declaration for such a
document. The text included some strikingly prescriptive suggestions – equal inheritance among siblings, for example, paired with
the restriction of the franchise to landed property, the right to divorce
coupled with compulsory militia service for all citizens. While many
of these fell by the wayside, this early draft included much that was
to be made public six months later. On 11 July, in the calm before
the storm, the noble champion of liberty proposed a declaration to
the National Assembly.[47] It was a concise statement of positions
already familiar from previous American texts, opening with the con-
tention: 'Nature has made men free and equal; distinctions necessary
to the social order are founded only on general utility.' As it went on,
men were born with 'inalienable and imprescriptible rights' including freedom of opinion, property, 'communication of his thoughts by
all possible means' and what Lafayette put into French as *la recherche*

*du bien-être*, the famous 'pursuit of happiness' that Jefferson had borrowed from Mason's Virginia text.[48] Assertions of the necessity for the separation of powers, and for free consent to legislation and taxation, followed. But already a distinctly French flavour had begun to creep in. Some points were perhaps little more than flourishes – to make 'the care of his honour', as well as his life and property, an individual's right, for example – but others cut deeper. American texts habitually referred to 'the people' as the source of sovereign power: it 'is vested in, and consequently derived from' them, according to the Virginia text. Lafayette's text, in both its January and July drafts, placed such power significantly elsewhere: 'The principle of all sovereignty resides in the nation. No body or individual may have an authority that does not emanate expressly from it.'[49]

The Americans had an easy time defining who was in charge – they were, and they were the people, in a series of republics freed from a tyrannical monarch. France, however, still had its monarch. A summary on 27 July of the digested contents of the *cahiers*, the registers of grievances that had come up with the deputies in the spring, revealed that the first two political principles laid down were 'The French government is a monarchical government' and 'The person of the king is sacred and inviolable'. Though this left many questions open – and they listed them, beginning with 'Does the king have legislative power, limited by the constitutional laws of the kingdom?' – it denied plausibility even to the British model of a Bill of Rights set against royal excess. The nation could not be the same as 'the people', set against kings, for the nation was still monarchist in 1789.[50] The man who hastened to reply to Lafayette's proposal on 11 July, the moderate conservative comte de Lally-Tollendal, had raised the stakes higher still:

> It is frightful to say, it is still more frightful to think; but we all know it only too well, calumny surrounds us, it spies on our actions to disfigure them, and on our speech to corrupt it . . . how they will say . . . that on the rights of nature, which will be no more, to hear them, than the right of force, we wish to establish the undermining of all authority.[51]

A declaration of rights alone, to hear Lally, was tantamount to a surrender to anarchy – or to the shadowy forces of reaction who would exploit anarchy to their own ends. Everything that had followed in the weeks after 11 July only impressed such dreadful possibilities more firmly on deputies' minds.

A debate that began on 1 August and ran on into the eve of the great abolition of feudalism on the 4th reiterated these fears. Many speakers articulated the notion that America, and the Americans, were emerging from a state of nature, and that by contrast 'the positive law of a great people that has been united for the past fifteen centuries' demanded attention to realities – such as the existence of rich and poor – not abstract rights. The moderate Malouet spoke of American 'man in the bosom of nature . . . in his original sovereignty', but also, contradictorily, depicted the United States as 'a society already prepared for democracy by its customs, manners, and geography . . . entirely composed of property-holders already accustomed to equality'. The real fear underlying such rather absurd claims emerged as Malouet went on: France was no such place, and its oppressed masses could not be trusted to take the message of rights in the way it was intended: 'announcing in an absolute manner to suffering men, deprived of knowledge and means, that they are equal in rights to the most powerful and most fortunate' could 'destroy necessary bonds' and bring 'universal disruption'.[52]

Others, however, preferred to dwell on positive possibilities. The duc de Montmorency-Laval, who had fought alongside Lafayette for the American cause, pressed France to surpass that precedent: 'they have given a great example to the new hemisphere; let us give it to the universe'.[53] Many were familiar with the American example, even if their language repeatedly placed those scions of English common-law tradition in some more utopian mould. The first French-language collection of the various constitutions of the former colonies had been published in 1783, and its translator, the duc de La Rochefoucauld d'Enville, sat in the Assembly. Jean-Nicolas Démeunier, who had published an *Essay on the United States* in 1786, and Dupont de Nemours, who in 1788 had produced a study on *The Principles of Confederated Republics*, were also present, along with many who had been avid readers of such works.[54] Démeunier seconded Montmorency-Laval in debate, and added that the work of producing a constitution could be judged by the public only in light of principles that should guide such a work – and those were universal rights, which could only uphold a just social order.

As debate moved on, the need for a declaration seemed to become settled, because discussion shifted to a subsidiary issue – whether such a text should also embrace the duties of man in society. A heated debate on 4 August was dominated by concerns of the clergy, always alert to moral failings, that 'egoism and pride' awakened by the 'flattering expression of *rights*' would be harmful without corrective attention to duties. They succeeded in getting a formal roll-call vote, but lost to those who preferred the more optimistic language of rights alone, and the session ended with a near-unanimous vote that such a declaration would preface their new constitution.[55]

After this decision, and the ecstatic session that followed with its abandonment of privileges – clearing the decks, in effect, for a more 'universal' notion of citizenship and rights – the deputies of the National Assembly came violently down to earth on 7 August. Minister Necker presented a sombre account of the state of the country – 'a frightful picture of disorder and public calamity', one group wrote home that evening. The deputies were the only real authority left in France, where 'the executive authority was impotent, the laws had no force, and the courts had ceased functioning'. Rioters even burst onto the streets of Versailles twice in mid-August. Several deputies' letters recorded the feeling that they sat 'in the midst of a pile of ruins'. Confronted by the mammoth work of reconstruction, one wrote: 'I confess the task frightens us.'[56] Moreover, both the clergy and the nobility were visibly regretting what had been done on the 4th. The property and rights of the Church had been pledged as sacred only weeks before, but tithes had been cast away, and many among the clergy saw them as a desperate sacrifice to save the bigger prize, the lands of the Church, its very material substance. A renewed threat to these could not be discounted, and anxieties grew. With many nobles also regretting their renunciations – 'We are now no more than the first peasants on the land,' one wrote to his wife – conservative forces in the Assembly grew stronger, even as Patriots still seemed bewildered over the first steps to take.[57] The heavy stress on the need for 'feudal' dues to be redeemed by hefty cash payments, at the core of the codification of the 4 August changes, voted a week later, partly assuaged some of this resentment, but opposition in principle persisted, and soon focused on the debates about the declaration of rights.

The Patriots, eager to have such a declaration, were themselves divided. The appeal of short, simple, apparently self-evident statements, on the American model, was clear to many; but, for some, this was no way to build a new constitution. Paradoxically, given the widespread rhetoric about the Americans' achievement being possible only because of their 'new' conditions, some influential figures argued that a really new constitution could not be built on such disjointed statements as the former colonists offered, with their gaps, overlaps and contradictions. The marquis de Condorcet, leader of France's scientific elite, and the economist Dupont de Nemours both wrote in 1789 criticising the Anglo-American tradition of balanced powers and specific declared rights. Such crude shopping lists of limitations on government offered no real defence against tyranny, because, they argued, they did not set out clearly the real principle of a free government, which should be based on universal rights. These, articulated as a set of interlocked principles, would, when disseminated widely, make tyrannical rule literally impossible – for no informed people would agree to breaking any of the links in the chain of well-ordered administration.

The *abbé* Sieyès left a similar analysis among his papers – rather than representing a bargain between the people and power, a proper declaration would emphasise that 'there is *only one* power, *only one* authority'.[58] He went on to offer an elaborated draft to the Assembly, in which the declaration took the form of a philosophical treatise, establishing each principle unshakeably and logically before moving on to the next. It was a work praised for being 'as profound as it is rare' in debate on 27 July, but as one deputy delicately put it, 'perhaps in its very perfection' were its limitations, since only a truly philosophical citizen might understand its subtleties. Thus the drafts that continued to dominate discussion in the following month were largely based on the more 'Anglo-Saxon' model.[59] Sieyès' ideas would infiltrate the final text, however, as they had already been present even in Lafayette's draft of 11 July. Alongside them, partly as a result of growing conservative strength, was a series of restrictions on freedom that came from very practical concerns and went to the heart of what 'rights' could and should mean.

The process of coming to a form of words was laborious and at the same time highly pressurised. A 'committee of five', among whom were Mirabeau and Démeunier, was appointed to produce a draft declaration in mid-August, drawing on all the discussion that had gone before. With over twenty published versions to work from, the committee nonetheless managed to produce a draft that satisfied no one. Mirabeau's own speech, introducing this version to the Assembly on 17 August, observed that 'an exposition of this kind, when it is destined for an old and almost failing political body, is necessarily subordinate to many local circumstances and can only ever attain a relative perfection'.[60]

Many felt it fell far short of even that, demanding that such a declaration must be better, and should instead ring out 'for all men, and for all countries'. Mirabeau sarcastically retorted in his newspaper, the *Courrier de Provence* (the third new title in two years from his presses), that he 'hadn't thought of declaring the rights of the [African] Cafres, nor those of the Eskimos, let alone those of the Danes or the Russians', but this fell on deaf ears.[61] In an ensuing debate the comte de Lally-Tollendal, who had been so fearful of precipitate declarations in July, now called for a stark choice – either a short, clear text adopted now, or an abandonment of the whole project until after a constitution was written: 'the people is waiting, wanting, suffering' and they should not 'leave it any longer prey to the torments of fear, the scourge of anarchy . . . let it sooner receive the effects and later know the causes' behind its new rights.[62]

What is perhaps most remarkable is that the deputies did not give up at this point. The most radical among them had been slipping in influence since the traumatic events of late July. The Breton Club, which had pioneered defiance of royal authority, was drifting back towards being a purely regional gathering by the end of August. Others were emerging on what we can now define as the 'left' – for since 22 July the seating in their chamber had been rearranged as a 'racetrack' oval of tiered benches, with the President's chair in the centre of one long side, and the radicals seated themselves at the end to the President's left. Liberal nobles such as Adrien Duport (formerly of the Society of Thirty) and the brothers Charles and Alexandre Lameth joined the most talented of the radical Third Estate orators there, but they were evidently a small minority, and faced a far larger and better-organised conservative bloc.[63] A combination of pressure from their constituents and concern to shape the unfolding political process led many of the most conservative noble and clerical deputies, who in some cases had fled in terror in July, to rejoin the Assembly in August. Some, such as the advocate of *parlementaire* power Duval d'Éprémesnil, spoke grandiosely of returning 'to the bosom of the Assembly, to live or die for the *patrie*'; others simply gathered their strength for the contest ahead.[64]

Meanwhile, within the former Third Estate itself, more conservative forces were also rallying. At the heart of a new movement eventually to be known as the *monarchiens* was the Dauphiné delegation, which had been in favour of conciliation between the orders since the Estates-General first met. Under the leadership of Jean Joseph Mounier, a Grenoble judge who had been at the forefront of early struggles with the local *parlement*, and later reconciliations with the nobility, this group reached out via other eminent men – Malouet, the Archbishop of Bordeaux Champion de Cicé, and Lally-Tollendal and Clermont-Tonnerre from the nobility – to form a bloc for practical, cautious action. By late August they could claim perhaps two to three hundred supporters. Their plans had been clear as early as 21 July, when the comte de Virieu, a close associate of Mounier, wrote: 'it is important to be sensible, deliberate, moderate, cool . . . otherwise we will destroy and tear and break everything, and whatever we build will not stand'.[65] The *monarchiens* worked in an organised fashion to command the centre ground – by the end of August, for example, distributing slips of paper with names of those to vote into the chair and secretaryship of the Assembly. They also worked not to lose contact with a firming bloc on the 'right', where the more intransigent nobles and clerics sat as far as they could from the radicals.

In this context it would not have been surprising if the declaration of rights had been postponed indefinitely – many nobles had archly remarked in their correspondence that they would see such truths proclaimed as men's subjection to paternal social authority, and homage owed to God.[66] Instead, perhaps impelled by the idea that a work that had already taken up so much time could not be allowed to lapse in humiliating failure, the Assembly seized on a particularly laconic, even anodyne, draft from one of the standing committees into which the deputies had been grouped for detailed discussion. And from 21 to 26 August, almost exactly as the House of Representatives in New York was drafting its Bill of Rights, they hammered out a declaration in seventeen articles.

It began with a preamble, taken essentially from the draft of Mirabeau's 'committee of five', that declared 'ignorance, disregard, or

contempt for the rights of man' to be 'the sole causes of public misfortunes and the corruption of government'. Hinting back towards
Sieyès' idea of a didactic, philosophical exposition, the preamble
went on to declare that this text existed 'so that the acts of the legislative power and those of the executive may be the more respected,
since it will be possible at each moment to compare them against the
goal of every political institution' – indicating there clearly that this
was to be treated as a universal document. The 'simple and incontestable principles' that the declaration claimed to lay out were also,
however, a vision – a somewhat contradictory vision – of a polity
with very particular characteristics.[67]

Some of these came so clearly from the situation in which France
found itself in 1789 that to call them universal was to be wilfully
blind. Assertions that 'A common tax is indispensable' and 'must be
shared equally among all the citizens' (Article 13); that 'All citizens
have the right to ascertain, personally or through their representatives, the necessity of the public tax' (Article 14); and that 'Society
has the right to demand that every public agent give an account of
his administration' (Article 15) spoke directly to the fiscal crisis over
privilege and supposed maladministration that had brought the
country to revolution. Other clauses spoke vividly of what it was
that the deputies thought they were moving away from. 'Social distinctions can be based only on public utility' (Article 1); 'No body, no
individual can exercise authority' unless it comes from the Nation
(Article 3); 'All citizens . . . are equally admissible to all public dignities, positions and employments, according to their ability, and on
the basis of no other distinction than that of their virtues and talents'
(Article 6); and the 'Public force' – the military – 'is instituted for the
benefit of all, and not for the personal advantage of those to whom it
is entrusted' (Article 12). The prominence of these criteria made
sense only as a flight from an aristocratic world where seigneurs did
exercise power in their own names, where nobles claimed great
offices as their property and military officers held their commissions
for social advancement and Court status.

Much, of course, in the declaration looked forward to a new
world of equality. It asserted that 'men are born and remain free and
equal in rights' (Article 1) – and 'remain' was inserted specifically
against the criticism that 'in the lands where there are slaves, one
can still claim that men are born free'.[68] It defined the 'natural and

imprescriptible rights of man', for the defence of which 'every political association' existed, as 'liberty, property, security and resistance
to oppression' (Article 2) – a rather more hard-edged formulation
than Jefferson's (and Lafayette's) pursuit of happiness. Liberty was
defined as 'being able to do anything that does not injure another',
its 'only limits' being the mutual guarantee of others' ability to
enjoy their 'natural rights' (Article 4). More practically, nodding
both to the American declarations and to the former history of
abuses, the declaration forbade arbitrary arrest, limited punishments to those laid down by law as 'strictly and evidently necessary'
(Article 8), enforced a presumption of innocence and ensured that
'every citizen may freely speak, write and print' to safeguard 'the
free expression of thought and opinions' as 'one of the most precious rights of man' (Article 11).

But that article, like many others, was qualified: freedom existed
'subject to accountability for abuse . . . in the cases determined by
law'. It was 'only by law' that the limits on mutual freedom in Article
4 could be determined, and the law, naturally, which laid down
penalties and determined modalities of arrest and trial. 'The public
order established by law' according to Article 10 had to be protected
against 'trouble' from 'opinions', including religious ones – a qualifi-
cation that some outraged radicals thought licensed 'a civil and
religious Inquisition', while a priest wrote that it had been a battle
fought 'to prevent open religious practice for all faiths'.[69] Since there
was as yet no 'public order established by law', the point remained
moot. What the declaration did insist on was the absolute nature of
law itself, and the sovereignty from which it derived. It vested the
'principle' of that sovereignty 'essentially in the Nation' (Article 3) –
not the people, a point that had made a difference from the
American precedents since Lafayette's first draft. Law, moreover, 'is
the expression of the general will' (Article 6). Though this article also
insisted that the law be equal for all, and that 'all citizens have the
right to participate personally, or through their representatives, in its
formation', its very wording emphasised the supremacy of an unqualified, undivided, sovereign body.

The 'general will' was a concept taken from Rousseau's *Social
Contract* of 1762, a powerfully ambiguous but wildly influential text,
much read in the years running up to 1789, which espoused the idea
that a political community must have an essential unity – to be found

through each participating individual meditating on the nature of the 'general will' before taking political decisions. Since Rousseau also spoke quite explicitly against legislation and government by representatives, and his book overall was somewhere between a utopian fantasy and a pessimistic diatribe on the impossibility of good government for people afflicted with corrupt modern morals, its influence was problematic, to say the least.[70]

The ambiguity of this construction, in a declaration of rights often supposed to be highly individualist, was emphasised in Article 7. While affirming that only the law and its prescribed forms could allow someone to be 'accused, arrested or detained', and that those who 'solicit, expedite, execute or effect the execution of arbitrary orders must be punished' – a sideswipe at royal *lettres de cachet* in no uncertain terms – the article went on: 'but every citizen summoned or seized by virtue of the law must obey at once; he makes himself guilty by resistance'. Such a formulation, in effect a duty inserted among supposed rights, was highly authoritarian, especially alongside a specific omission. Several proposed drafts had included 'the right to bear arms'. Sieyès had suggested 'the right to repel violence with violence', and as late as Mirabeau's committee draft the right to bear arms 'for the defence of themselves and the common defence' had been included (lifted in this phrasing from the Pennsylvania constitution).[71] No such clause persisted into the final version. Clearly, for the French framers, the right of 'resistance to oppression' could never include that of defence against the state itself.

# 13

# 'Your houses will answer for your opinions'

## *The French Revolution imperilled*

Whatever its deeper limitations, the Declaration of the Rights of Man and the Citizen was greeted with unbounded joy by the patriotic population of Paris, and by all France as word spread. Since the upheavals of midsummer, city and country alike had clung avidly to every scrap of news from Versailles. The fears that had produced so many punitive expeditions and near riots among the peasantry had been assuaged, somewhat, by the abolition of feudalism, and now the text of a new foundation for national politics – one that set the ending of privilege and humiliating distinctions in stone – seemed to presage an age of liberty for all. Across the capital, in hundreds of taverns and cafés, tens of thousands of Parisians met every day to digest the political news and to speculate on their new future. The press had broken the final chains of absolutist restraint, and in the weeks after the fall of the Bastille new journals had erupted into life, each one claiming to be both the most patriotic, and the most authoritative, of observers. Jacques-Pierre Brissot had launched a prospectus for a newspaper, the *French Patriot*, as early as March, an 'impartial, free and national journal', pledged to bring 'harmony of opinion' that could only be 'the fruit of a gradual instruction'.[1] In cafés, reading rooms, bookshops, billiard halls and across the open spaces of a bustling city, the works of Brissot and his many competitors were snatched up hot from the presses as the great crises of the summer unfolded.

Brissot's paper did not produce its first regular edition until 28 July 1789, and the very first item it chose to report indicated the sort of news that was rapidly to become the bread and butter of this journalism. It cited a deputy of the National Assembly's claim that a *parlementaire* from Besançon had blown up a party of Patriots. Expressing no scepticism over the report at all, the *French Patriot* denounced the 'atrocious action' and reported as fact that

This infamous aristocrat had drawn a great number of Citizens to his château for a festival. After the meal, the guests were led into a wood. A mine had been laid under the ground. Servants in on the plot with their master lit the fuse. The explosion took place; several people were killed and buried under the piles of earth and stones; others were grievously injured. The monster who had imagined this infernal manoeuvre was already in flight, and no one knows where he has taken refuge.[2]

There had indeed been an explosion at a château in the region, most probably the fruit of overzealous torch-bearing searchers probing too closely a stock of gunpowder, but in the atmosphere of the summer of 1789 only a vile plot by an aristocrat could account for such an incident. By the end of the summer, following the Great Fear, and confirmed reports that the comte d'Artois and his ilk were gathering across the frontiers, aristocratic plotting seemed to threaten everywhere, even in the heart of the National Assembly itself.

Those who were most active in canvassing these fears in Paris gathered in the Palais-Royal. Originally built by Cardinal Richelieu a century and a half before, this oblong of territory in central Paris had been given to the family of the ducs d'Orléans by Louis XIV. As their privileged private property, the open space at its centre, and the cafés that sprang up around it, had sheltered a zone of free speech. Here the police might spy clandestinely, but could not openly arrest those who gathered to eat, drink and gossip scandalously – let alone those who frequented the gambling dens and brothels secreted in the luxury apartments on its outskirts. The latest duke, when he came into his inheritance in the early 1780s, had sought to capitalise on the commercial potential of the Palais-Royal. In a huge development two whole new streets were laid out inside the original enclosure, and surrounding a remodelled, narrower garden were colonnaded walkways with dozens of boutiques and hundreds of new apartments available for rent. Eager to recoup the massive costs involved, the duke allowed the site to become even more of a commercial free-for-all. Unfinished construction on one side was taken over by a market place of hastily erected wooden stalls, where the goings-on were so wild that it was soon nicknamed the 'Tartars' Camp'. Free speech nonetheless remained the hallmark of the Palais-Royal, and in the run-up to 14 July huge crowds had gathered there, taking in news and gossip, generating their own interpretations and agitating for action.[3]

The fall of the Bastille changed nothing about this situation, and though the new revolutionary militia of the National Guard could not be excluded from the Palais-Royal by defunct ideas of privilege, they had to tread warily against a real threat of riot. Even some among the crowds themselves thought things were getting out of hand, and pamphlets circulated in July and August calling for controls on the wild rumours that seemed to come to life spontaneously in the ferment – one even proposed a 'scrutative assembly' of known Patriots to vet every report before allowing it public credence.[4] Such concerns were layered with ironies, for it was a fixed assumption on the less radical sides of politics that the duc d'Orléans was managing popular agitation to support a bid for the throne. His courting of popularity, his known preference for a liberal politics akin to that of British Whigs and his evident support for radicals within both the National Assembly and the press all added to an underlying perception that a royal duke, with massive wealth at his disposal, could not be so openly in opposition to his cousin the king without some deeper, self-interested motive.[5]

Beliefs of this kind even stretched to Thomas Jefferson. In an official dispatch to Secretary of State Jay on 27 August 1789, Jefferson reported that a 'faction . . . of the most desperate views' was gaining strength 'in the assembly as well as out of it. They wish to dethrone the reigning branch and transfer the crown to the Duke d'Orléans.' The grouping was made up of 'persons of wicked and desperate fortune, who have nothing at heart but to pillage from the wreck of their country'.[6] Reports that the duke was borrowing large sums of money were allied to news that he had allegedly been in contact with Pitt's government to seek support, and the French government 'even apprehend that that court will support his designs by war'. Jefferson's concerns had global ramifications, reporting rumours that both the French Court and the Orléanist faction had plans to sell the French Caribbean colonies to Britain for cash – and Jefferson thought the latter story, at least, true. On the other hand, he also noted that 'The emancipation of their islands is an idea prevailing in the minds of several members of the national assembly, particularly those most enlightened and most liberal in their views. Such a step by this country would lead to other emancipations or revolutions in the same quarter.'[7]

Such rumours swirled in the summer of 1789, and the British reformer Jeremy Bentham even wrote a letter to Mirabeau urging him to promote such a liberation, on good utilitarian grounds.[8] Meanwhile, in a letter to James Madison, Jefferson named Mirabeau as the 'chief' Orléanist, whose actions might bring 'temporary war', but that 'The king, the mass of the substantial people of the whole country, the army, and the influential part of the clergy, form a firm phalanx which must prevail.'[9]

Jefferson's optimism perhaps came in part from an event he had himself hosted only days earlier. On 25 August Lafayette had written, begging him to employ his good offices and help reconcile opposing political groups in the Assembly 'to prevent a total dissolution and a civil war'. Though this was scarcely a promising context, Jefferson's dinner party on the 26th, hours after the passage of the Declaration of Rights, seemed to offer a fresh start.[10] On one side were a trio of moderate leaders, including Mounier, and on the other the former *parlementaire* Adrien Duport, the radical barrister Antoine Barnave and a cavalry officer and nobleman who had emerged with a surprisingly radical stance on popular sovereignty, Alexandre de Lameth.[11] The meeting reflected an ideological deadlock that had not yet burst onto the floor of the National Assembly, but had hamstrung the efforts of a Constitutional Committee of deputies. The men appointed had failed to solve the basic issues of constitutional structure, notably two core matters that had divided the Americans for so long two years before: the structure of the legislature and the powers of the executive.

The French were again, as the Americans had been, pinned by the vision of the British model. Mounier's *monarchiens* believed firmly, on practical grounds and following the example of Montesquieu in theory, that a balanced two-chamber legislature, with a royal sanction on legislation (and thus the possibility of veto), was the solution that could take France into the future. Others, however, recalling the long decades of condemnation of British political corruption, wanted the power of the executive kept out of legislation, and also followed the logic of the Declaration of Rights in seeking an undivided national legislative body. When privilege had been renounced, and all citizens declared to have an equal right to take part in law-making, what grounds could there be for giving half the legislature to the nobility, as the British did? The *abbé* Sieyès was one who was firmly of such a view, and along with one of the original Breton radicals, Isaac-Réné Le Chapelier, he had been blocking progress in the Constitutional Committee against a *monarchien* majority.[12]

The *monarchiens'* position was based on the hope of returning discreetly to the optimism that had reigned before the upheavals of July, and of recognising, as Mounier put it in debate, that 'The National Assembly is charged by its constituents to make the authority of the king respected' and 'must regulate, and not destroy' that authority.[13] Against such claims, however, stood what were taken to be the self-evident facts of aristocratic conspiracy at Court, and a belief among the more radical deputies, and Parisians, that such plotting remained an active threat. The rise of the *monarchiens* in the Assembly itself had been read by some as an 'alliance between the Clergy, the Nobility and a part of the Commons, which together constitute a new aristocracy'. The radical deputy from Arras, Maximilien Robespierre, stated bluntly in a letter of 5 September that 'the majority of the National Assembly is the avowed enemy of liberty'.[14] Others agreed, and saw the notion of allowing a royal veto as a direct challenge to the gains of the revolution – pass the veto, and the king had the right to nullify the abolition of privilege, and the Declaration of Rights itself, which still lay, officially unpromulgated, on his desk in Versailles.

The deputies began a hesitant and directionless debate on these critical issues on 28 August. Mounier's opening assertion that the matters could be resolved swiftly on the basis of six articles containing 'simple principles . . . susceptible of very little discussion, since they are found in everybody's *cahiers*' proved that he was, in this sense at least, living in the past.[15] Just how strikingly matters had progressed beyond those documents' respectful tones was made clear days later, when the voice of the Palais-Royal made itself heard at Versailles. On 31 August, moments after the comte de Clermont-Tonnerre, stepping down after a two-week presidency of the Assembly, had congratulated the deputies on consecrating 'the eternal principles on which rest the liberty and dignity of man', the new president, the Bishop of Langres, had to report bad news from Paris. Lafayette, as commander of the National Guard, had been obliged to suppress a 'riotous gathering' in the Palais-Royal, where a crowd had seemed bent on marching on Versailles. The *monarchien* comte de Lally-Tollendal added details he called 'heart-rending'. He had seen a motion passed by the gathering in the Palais-Royal, which sought to condemn a list of deputies as 'traitors and aristocrats', and threatened to eject them from the National Assembly and subject them to punishment, in the name of preventing a royal veto coming into existence.[16] Perhaps most tellingly, the text opened with a direct reference to the Declaration of Rights, and its eleventh article on freedom of expression, as an authority for the Parisians' actions.

Two anonymous letters that also reached the Assembly made even grimmer reading. One, from 'the patriotic Assembly of the Palais-Royal', warned that if 'the aristocratic party', including 'one hundred and twenty ignorant or corrupted members of the commons', continued to 'trouble harmony' by demanding an absolute royal veto, 'fifteen thousand men are ready to *enlighten* their châteaux and their houses' – the double meaning of 'enlighten' was lost on no one. The second letter reinforced this threat – the absolute veto 'that we regard as destructive of liberty' was not to be passed, or else 'two thousand letters' were ready to be sent to the provinces detailing deputies' conduct, and 'your houses will answer for your opinions, and we hope that the old lessons will begin again. Think of them, and save yourselves.'[17]

Deputies listened to these readings in 'grim silence', and then burst out with denunciations: some said the menaces should be scorned; others retorted with counter-accusations against 'aristocrats'. Mounier, betraying alarm beneath bravado, called for a reward of 300,000 *livres* for those who gave up the instigators of the threats, while asserting that 'the Assembly must not quit Versailles; it must brave the perils, and if it must perish, the good citizens of Paris and the provinces will avenge it'. Stronger spirits began to prevail, however. Clermont-Tonnerre asked if mere 'popular effervescence' was

enough to intimidate an Assembly that had defied 'armed despotism'. A third deputy read from a letter he had received from an
anonymous priest, accusing him of being 'associated with the horrible conspiracy formed against the King and the monarchy': the
deputy ironised on his fate – if he was left off one proscription list, he
was sure to find himself on another from the opposite flank.[18] In
the end the Assembly, ever conscious of its collective dignity and
its historic role, passed over the menaces of the Palais-Royal to turn
to the veto question on its own terms.

The National Assembly seems to have debated this issue, in sessions that dragged on over two weeks, in a curious mixture of
partisan hostility and philosophical exaltation. Newspapers such as
the newly founded *Moniteur*, which offered near-verbatim accounts
of debate, frequently had to report hostile exchanges between what
were openly called 'the two parties existing in the Assembly', and
some of these degenerated into extended shouting matches.[19] The
comte de Virieu, a leading *monarchien*, raged in his letters about the
'scoundrels' and 'madmen' on the radical side, sharing Jefferson's
evaluation of 'this heinous party of conspirators' trying to bring the
country to ruin.[20] The radicals continued to fear that the *monarchiens*
were selling out to an 'aristocracy' for whom nothing less than the
destruction of everything gained since 14 July – or indeed since early
June, and the foundation of the National Assembly itself – would
suffice. Yet at the same time many deputies rejoiced in the freedom
to debate first principles. The Protestant pastor Rabaut de Saint-
Étienne declaimed, 'what an assembly, messieurs, where one can
risk such discussions without fear'. 'What times we live in,' he added
a little later, 'since we can freely speak and hear these great truths!'[21]
Others wrote home exuberantly of hearing orations that were astonishing in 'their eloquence, their insights, their wisdom', and thought
that 'Never have such important subjects been discussed in France,
never has a more noble career been opened up to journalists and
orators.'[22]

Such exaltation, however, merely exacerbated the deputies' problems. Clermont-Tonnerre denounced the tendency to insist that
'everything is new for us. We are proceeding to a regeneration; we
have created new words to express new ideas.'[23] A vaguely Rousseauist attitude, which defined the political constitution as a problem
that could be solved only by going back to the first principles of a

united, sovereign nation, seemed to permeate many on the left of the Assembly, even if they did not always quote Rousseau openly in their support. Since Rousseau's *Social Contract* could even be read as depicting the impossibility of reforming long-established societies, such vagueness is unsurprising, but a view of the Revolution as a fresh start, a 'regeneration' as Clermont-Tonnerre noted, was sufficiently well formed to allow speakers to scorn the historically based arguments of the *monarchiens*.[24]

When Mounier and his fellows invoked Montesquieu, or Blackstone, the great authority on English law, and even John Adams, who had written a critical examination of republican constitutions only a few years before, they urged Frenchmen to 'consult the lessons of experience and not disdain the examples of history'. 'Not a year ago,' Mounier noted, 'we spoke enviously of the liberty of the English'; now, he said, 'we dare to look with contempt' on their constitution, 'pronounce rashly that the English are not free' and 'blindly invoke' Rousseau in our support.[25] On the other side, however, equally strong arguments against historical precedent were put forward – it was 'an arsenal where everyone finds all kinds of weapons', said the radical priest Henri Grégoire, where 'the multiplicity of facts often demonstrates the violation of principles'. Rabaut de Saint-Étienne also stood out for principle over experience: 'one will always commit dangerous and stupid errors in departing from the necessary principles upon which legislation depends'.[26] Such determination to rely on principle did not stop speakers including Grégoire and Rabaut raising their own historical points, when they were apposite. Grégoire offered, for example, a whole lesson in the evils exposed by recent British constitutional history – the protests of John Wilkes, oppression of America and Ireland, religious intolerance, corruption and bribery, and the defects of the suffrage depicted in the Commonwealthmen's writings (he cited James Burgh's *Political Disquisitions* directly on this).[27]

Jean-Baptiste Salle, an otherwise undistinguished doctor from Nancy, showed the near-rapturous heights to which those in favour of the 'regeneration' position could rise: 'Nature, which is never extinguished, reawakens in great circumstances. New passions come to set souls afire: The maxims of egoism which isolate mankind yield within a short time to those unfamiliar and delicious fervours that bring it together.' This was how, he went on, the

French, 'having been sunk in slavery for centuries', could rise again under the influence of 'those great passions which are naturally held in reserve in every heart'.[28] This kind of belief pushed aside not only arguments for a royal veto, but also those for a bicameral legislature. Lally-Tollendal had pronounced, in opening these debates, that only a balanced structure could regulate the passionate pursuit of power that was 'a general and incontestable truth' of human nature. A single-chamber legislature risked leaving the constitution 'abandoned to inconstancy, caprice, and all the human passions'. Without 'fixed laws' such a chamber would cause the people to 'relapse into servitude, into the most shameful of all servitudes, that which sacrifices the multitude to the unstable passions of a small number of men'.[29] Rabaut de Saint-Étienne and his fellows retorted with repeated invocation of the principle they had agreed to the previous month: 'sovereignty resides in the nation' and thus its representatives must be supreme. Rabaut denounced the balance of powers in the British constitution as a sham, 'a forced invention, a pact, an imaginary contract, not to make legislation better, but to accommodate those who disagreed'.[30] Under new, regenerated circumstances, virtuous representatives of the nation did not have to be feared, or their powers divided, to keep them on the right path. In this context the pleas of Brissot in his newspaper, to look to the new American example, where a presidential veto could be overturned by a two-thirds legislative vote, fell on deaf ears.[31]

With the veto still hovering undecided above them, a detour into debate on the nature of the legislature produced a strikingly decisive result on 10 September. By 849 to 89, with 122 abstentions, the *monarchiens*' plan for an upper house with lifetime appointments was voted down in favour of a single chamber, regularly elected. Almost no one outside the *monarchien* core, besides a few isolated clergy and nobles, supported the bicameral solution. One reason for the huge majority may have been the powerful effect of Rousseauist rhetoric of unity on the members of the former Third Estate; another, on the part of some 'aristocrats', was a determination to create a structure that would be as weak and unstable as possible, to provoke collapse. Still another motive, expressed quite clearly by some among the provincial nobility, was to do down the great courtiers of the high nobility, whom they believed had been agitating, since the days of the

Society of Thirty, to secure their seats at the table of power. The marquis de Ferrières wrote bluntly that 'the Senate of Mounier and Our Seigneurs will not be. Thus this fruit of their cabals, this secret motive of the union of the orders, they shall not have, and this is justice.'[32]

If such votes came close to mere personal or factional spite, principled argument remained the meat of debate. Mirabeau, for example, while condemned by Jefferson as an agitator of disorder, spoke out decisively for an absolute royal veto power. He managed to do so while also presenting the monarch as a sort of Rousseauist national representative: 'The prince is the perpetual representative of the people, as the deputies are its representatives elected at certain times.' A purely negative royal role in legislation, to resist the calls of partiality or factional control, was 'the inexpugnable rampart of political liberty' and should be as absolute a veto as possible. For one who supposedly sought to bring down the whole edifice of monarchy, albeit in favour of the king's cousin, Mirabeau was remarkably ardent in reconciling strong royal powers with the rhetoric of the national cause: 'It is not for his particular advantage that the monarch intervenes in legislation, but for the very interest of the people.'[33]

On the other side of the debate, against the veto, it rapidly became clear to leading radicals such as Grégoire and Rabaut that there was only a small minority in favour of denying the king any veto. Their attention thus focused on embedding such a power in a context of national, rather than royal, sovereignty. This meant making the veto 'suspensive' – an acknowledgement, as both speakers noted, that elected assemblies 'can err' and their decisions might need to be held up: 'This suspensive veto', Grégoire stated, 'is only an appeal to the people, and the people, assured that it will be able to pronounce definitively, will not be embittered by it.'[34] We can read in these words, nonetheless, the underlying fear of strife – what would the 'embittered' people do? – and Rabaut presented the other side of similar fears. Use of a suspensive veto, he said, needed to be followed by a direct submission to referendum on the contentious item, 'Otherwise, from session to session, from refusal to refusal, the prince would have the right to stop everything; the National Assembly would become a chimerical phantom; and the king would become a despot.'[35]

Such language exposed the collision course the National Assembly was set upon: with many of its members (and thousands more outside) convinced that the king was surrounded by those bent upon subjugating the people, the Assembly yet had no choice but to go forward with the construction of a new order around the very institution that seemed to threaten to destroy it. And for the zealous advocates of popular sovereignty, if contented by their apparent victory over the unicameral legislature, further defeat loomed the next day, when a marathon twelve-hour session finally brought the veto issue to a vote. A quarter of the Assembly – almost entirely nobles and clergy – continued to favour an absolute veto, and with around another quarter absent, the opponents of the veto found themselves a small minority. The centre of gravity lay with the supporters of a suspensive veto, which won in a final vote by 673 to 325.[36]

This result seemed to favour the line of those such as Grégoire and Rabaut on the veto as an 'appeal to the people', and produced a mass resignation of *monarchiens* from the Constitutional Committee. But ten days later, amid general exultation at news that the king had at last agreed to promulgate the decrees abolishing privilege (but not the Declaration of Rights), the *monarchien* Clermont-Tonnerre, from the chair of the Assembly, used his position to rush through a motion on the actual nature of the suspensive veto. With this approved by 728 to 224, it would now require no fewer than three consecutive legislatures (each of two years' duration, as decided the day after the veto vote) to pass an identical measure before a 'suspensive' veto could be overridden. A moderate deputy noted coolly in his diary that this measure 'has all the advantages of an absolute veto without any of the inconveniences', while a radical lamented that 'yesterday, through shrewdness, cunning and cabal . . . our enemies the royalists won the day'.[37] It is intriguing to note that, amid such strife, in a letter of 13 September Jefferson had recorded the outcome of his dinner party three weeks before: a deal 'giving the king a suspended veto while the legislature will be a single body elected by the people'.[38]

Whether we take this as evidence of subterranean machinations, or merely the rewriting of history in hindsight by an interested party, the atmosphere of defeat and crisis persisted. Some among the original group of Bretons who had done so much to make the Third

Estate into the National Assembly in the spring were now debating whether it was worth remaining there at all. On 18 September, even before the installation of the veto, one of them, Constantin-François Chasseboeuf de Volney, bemoaned before the Assembly 'what terrible consequences threaten the continuation of a state so violent and precarious' as France found herself in, and placed the blame squarely on the Assembly itself. He demanded immediate elections, 'to substitute a truly national representation for a vice-ridden and contradictory representation, where private and personal interests, set in equal balance with the general interest, have the power to oppose such a powerful force against the public will'. Though the press reported that this was 'universally' applauded, the president of the session swiftly closed discussion, despite radical voices calling for a vote.[39] The writers of the American Constitution, of course, had faced stalemates, walkouts and despair, but they had done so in a select group, working in secret, and with an overwhelming presumption that a viable outcome would be reached. The French were arguing in the full glare of publicity, with accusations not merely of party but also of subversive and treasonous faction running rampant, and with the entire population of one of the world's largest cities breathing down their necks. And that pressure was only going to get worse.

Underpinning the whole revolutionary process in Paris was fear: fear of hunger as food prices rose to exorbitant levels; fear of unemployment as rich employers and customers fled their town-houses and defaulted on their bills; fear above all that what had been tried once, a military suppression of the city's hard-won freedoms, would be tried again. With the fear came both anxiety and assertion. For decades before 1789, under what the French were now starting to call the Old Regime, many of these same fears had held sway, provoking a perpetual tension, a quest for information, the pullulating political gossip of a city riddled with police spies and the echoes of Court factions. But Parisians had also been capable of action, and in every generation some spark had produced bold evidence of their unwillingness to be totally cowed. In 1750 it had been reports of police agents kidnapping children from the streets that had provoked murderous riots – and the parade of one dead policeman past the house of his master, the lieutenant general, to add a political

point about blame. The Flour War of 1775 had passed through the city like a whirlwind, as city-dwellers joined their country cousins in denouncing by force the abusive withdrawal of royal protection from their food prices. The political hurricane that had climaxed in late July 1789 left the Old Regime as so much wreckage in its wake, but as Parisians took up the new rituals of attention to the press and the news from Versailles, the old habits of oppositional assertion continued with a new stridency.

Workers demonstrated by their thousands through August. Groups from tailors and shoemakers to bakers and apothecaries, all constrained by Old Regime work practices and rules of subordination, demanded new economic freedoms to go with their political ones. Wig-makers, in high demand for the daily setting of aristocratic headpieces, extorted new rules for relations with their guild masters with a mass demonstration of four thousand on the Champs-Élysées. Domestic servants, feared as the dependent lackeys of the rich, were less successful, still being excluded by their status from participation in the city's politics, despite threats to bring forty thousand onto the streets in their support. Overt fear of the poor led to Lafayette's National Guard being used to break up the 'public workshops' where over twenty thousand jobless men had been given work at municipal expense as unskilled labourers. Dispersed to the provinces, such men earned little sympathy from the more settled classes of the city, being seen as little better than brigands and prey for aristocratic subversion.

Consumers also protested, meanwhile, a series of riots and near riots forcing the revolutionary authorities to lower bread prices by decree on 8 August, only for the National Assembly to reinstate Turgot's mistake, a free market in grain and flour, on the 29th. Coming as a late-summer drought hindered distribution of still-slender supplies, this merely stoked the rising opposition between the city's people and a set of authorities that, for radicals of all stripes, were dangerously close to falling under the aristocratic spell. Some, such as those at the Palais-Royal on 30 August, began to foment direct political action against the Assembly. Others bolstered their collective assertion of rights with massive parades to the church of Saint-Geneviève, the city's patron saint. Organised by neighbourhood and trade, these processions by their sheer scale presented 'something horrifying' to at least one educated observer, gatherings

that were ostensibly about thanksgiving for the liberation of July becoming a troubling demonstration of popular power.[40] As food troubles ground on into September, crowds became bolder. By the time Volney uttered his call for the Assembly's replacement, Parisian crowds were concluding a three-day bout of protests, from commandeering convoys of grain carts and forcing local authorities to sell them at a 'just price', to clamouring at the doors of the City Hall itself for action against hoarders and speculators in grain.

Food and politics were inseparable, not least because popular starvation, all the radical press and pamphlets cried, was a weapon of the resurgent aristocrats, for whom the work of stalemating the National Assembly and wearing down the capital's Patriots went hand in hand. The combination of these concerns was stirred into violent life by the arrival at Versailles on 1 October of a new regiment of troops, summoned in September to reinforce the royal guards. The Régiment de Flandres was welcomed by its fellows in the royal Gardes du Corps with a banquet, held in the opera house attached to the palace. The king, the queen and their four-year-old son and heir were there – unusual in itself and reinforced in its strangeness when Marie-Antoinette carried the child between the tables, showing him off (or reminding them what they were there to defend). The troops gradually succumbed to more and more fervent expressions of loyalty. Cries of 'We only acknowledge our king! We do not belong to the nation!' rang out. In scenes reported by the revolutionary press as verging on the orgiastic, officers clambered up to the royal box to offer compliments to the queen, and others trampled on the tricolour 'national' cockades they tore from their hats. In an even more sinister transfer of loyalty, some reports said that the men replaced the cockades with the white of the royal house of Bourbon, and, shockingly, the black of Marie-Antoinette's Habsburg Austria.[41]

News of this horrifying event pushed Parisian politics to a new pitch of frenzy. While club orators called for Lafayette to stir the National Guard into action, by 4 October reports spoke of women in the Palais-Royal demanding a popular march on the palace at Versailles. On the 5th women from across the city converged on the City Hall, apparently determined to solve both the bread crisis and the larger political deadlock by getting decisive municipal action, or installing a new municipality. To male observers it was a spectacular and unprecedented sight – women apparently of every social

class (though predominantly the doughty and foul-mouthed stall-holders of the markets, and other hardy members of the working population) spent the morning flocking through the streets, and the groups that converged on the City Hall were reportedly armed with everything from crowbars and pikes to axes and muskets.[42] Building on their long tradition of safeguarding their households' subsistence with protest, but suddenly elevated to a new height of national significance, the several thousand women, and unknown numbers of male supporters, spent two hours searching the City Hall, from where the political leadership had fled, before gathering again, to the sound of the alarm bell ringing from its steeple, around 11 a.m. Threats to hang Mayor Bailly and General Lafayette were too much for the male Patriot leaders who had rushed to the scene, and various of them persuaded the women that a march to Versailles, to take up matters with the king himself, would be a more profitable course.

Around six to seven thousand women undertook the twelve-mile march, arriving in the early evening to thrust their way into the deliberations of the National Assembly. A small delegation was initially greeted cordially, and their linked demands, for bread and the punishment of the royalist outrages of 1 October, were seconded when a group were chosen to be presented to the king himself. On a day when the left of the Assembly had been outraged to hear a letter from the king, continuing to temporise over the promulgation of both the Declaration of Rights and the new constitutional decisions, the unexpected arrival of support from Paris must have seemed a welcome reminder that they were not isolated, as the radical Barnave put it, among aristocrats who 'attempt, with unbelievable bad faith, to reject everything they had previously seemed to accept'.[43]

More support from Paris continued to arrive. Upwards of twenty thousand National Guards, gathered by the tolling alarm bells, had thronged the city centre, and prevailed on Lafayette to lead them to Versailles. As the women had before them, they toiled through persistent rain, and arrived to find the situation confused and dangerous. After the first delegation of women had been welcomed by the Assembly, more marchers began to push their way into the hall, remaining even after the session was officially adjourned. Some broke into a stock of refreshments kept for the deputies, and picnicked on looted wine and cold meats. As night closed in, others,

men and women alike, began to seek out their perceived enemies among the deputies. Mounier was visited at his house by a gang of men who threatened to cut off his head. Another moderate, Malouet, had to be rescued from a pike-wielding crowd by Mirabeau, who had been bizarrely lauded earlier by the women as *notre petite mère*, 'our little mother'.[44] One of the other prominent cries in the Assembly had been '*à bas la calotte!*', an insulting reference to priests' hats. A number of such men were hounded by groups of Parisians: one had a nervous breakdown; two others, trapped in a stairwell, gave each other what they feared might be a last confession; a fourth, more robustly, battered his way free of a pursuing gang with his umbrella, laying out four men before escaping. Even the more patriotic priests were subjected, as one recalled, to 'public loathing'.[45]

Amid darkness and confusion, yet more sinister designs seemed to be afoot. Notwithstanding his personal bravery in rescuing Malouet, Mirabeau (along with his supposed master, Orléans) was to be widely suspected of concocting these events for his own gain. What sort of gain that was to be emerged clearly from a number of accounts of what happened later that night, as the radical Parisians encountered the royal family in person. Contrary to radical perceptions, there was confusion and hesitancy at the heart of the Court. Weeks earlier, in light of the 30 August demonstrations, the royal council had discussed a plan, supported by leading *monarchien* deputies, to move the Court to safety at Compiègne, and transfer the Assembly to Soissons, away from Parisian influence. But Louis XVI himself vetoed the move, conscious, perhaps, of the destabilising signals such a royal flight would send out to a country still poised on a knife edge of disorder. When word arrived at Versailles on 5 October of the approaching column of Parisians, the royal council met again in an emergency session. The ministers with military backgrounds advocated an immediate retreat of the royal family, covered by loyal troops, to the château of Rambouillet; the civilian ministers demurred. With the council split down the middle, the king's casting vote for staying put was decisive – and remained so, even after the queen, returning from walking in her idyllic Petit Trianon, begged him to flee. Louis was seen pacing up and down, muttering, 'A fugitive king . . . a fugitive king', haunted by the dilemma before him.[46]

Once again, as in July, the lack of real military planning by the Court is striking. Even after the king's decision to stay, the garrison of the palace was not deployed to good effect to guard him. The Régiment de Flandres played no significant role in events, and the royal Gardes du Corps were scattered, a large body going, uselessly, to the Trianon. Many of those at Versailles were not dressed or armed for actual service, and throughout the evening stood-to in the rain 'with hats that should have been carried under the arm on our heads, and ceremonial swords in our hands', as one recalled.[47] Meanwhile, that evening, a flight to Rambouillet was discussed again by ministers, and some were sitting in their carriages ready to go when the king reaffirmed his decision to stay. At midnight General Lafayette presented himself to the royal family, having made his way through a crowd of angry courtiers, to insist that they leave, not for the countryside, but for Paris. Only this move, he said, could guarantee their safety. All concerned retired to bed, the king promising to consider the move.

At 5.30 a.m., in an episode swiftly elevated to legend, a group of the formidable market women of Paris, with assorted male companions, got into the royal apartments and charged for the queen's bedroom. Cutting down at least one guard on the way, and reportedly yelling that they would tear out Marie-Antoinette's vitals, they reached the very door of her chamber before the queen, shrieking in fear, could flee to the king's apartment. Her empty bed was hacked to ribbons. Outside, shots were exchanged, and casualties suffered on both sides. Terror and confusion prevailed. One courtier later recalled how he collapsed after rushing to the queen's bedroom and finding it empty and bloodstained.[48] National Guards stood-to under Lafayette's command and drove the crowds out of the palace, but the whole building was now surrounded by an angry mob – they had come to Versailles to get something done, and a day's delay had made them no less determined. Wet, cold and enraged, with the heads of two Gardes du Corps waving on pikes above them, the crowd chanted, 'The king to Paris! The king to Paris!'

Lafayette urged the king to show himself, but when he did, they yelled for a sight of the queen. Demonstrating that, whatever her flaws, she was certainly courageous, Marie-Antoinette went alone onto the balcony, and stood, in front of dozens of levelled muskets, for two minutes. Miraculously, this seemed to appease the collective rage, but there was no avoiding a decision on the crowd's central demand. The king reappeared and announced that he would indeed lead his family to Paris. Wild cheering erupted, and later that day the royal family's carriage was accompanied to the city by a veritable carnival of popular triumph. Chants that they were bringing back 'the baker, his wife and the baker's boy' reflected a near-mystic sense that the royal presence would guarantee bread for the people. But this episode inevitably embittered yet further, if such a thing were possible, the royal family's relations with the revolutionaries. The queen never forgave Lafayette for allowing her to come so close to death, a death that she and many aristocrats thought was the aim of the 'Orléanist' conspiracy. Even Lafayette himself blamed Orléans for the events, and in a tense, face-to-face confrontation shortly after the royal arrival in Paris, prompted the duke to flee to London in fear of political reprisals.[49]

On every side the 'October Days' confirmed predetermined impressions of the political scene. Radicals in the Assembly, noting the king's growing intransigence and aristocratic resurgence in the previous weeks, thought that 'once again we owe our salvation to the Parisians', and it was a 'second revolution' that had 'humiliated the aristocracy' so 'it will never rise again'. The *monarchiens*, on the other hand, were devastated: the 'vilest riff-raff of Paris' had invaded the political process, which was now so contaminated that no good could come of it. While urging the entire right to abandon the Assembly, several *monarchien* leaders, including Mounier, withdrew in person, and their agenda vanished from the political scene. Those in the middle ground between these positions were deeply troubled, writing of the 'ingratitude' of the common people, their 'natural inconstancy' and 'slavery to their passions', as well as, tellingly, of 'the ease with which they are led to disastrous opinions' – reinforcing the widespread view that all these troubles came from agitation essentially factional in origin.[50]

The royal family were settled in the Tuileries palace, unused by royal occupants for over a century – the inconveniences of this were long to rankle with the king – and the National Assembly voted to follow them on 9 October. They closed their session at Versailles on the 15th, and reopened four days later, after a great deal of inevitable upheaval, in the hall of the archbishop's palace near Notre Dame Cathedral. They would find a new, permanent home, adjacent to the

Tuileries, only in mid-November. So hastily had their temporary chamber been prepared that there was a shocking accident a few days later, when a spectators' balcony collapsed onto the deputies, seriously injuring seven. Nonetheless, the ill omen such an accident seemed to provide was overridden by a new sense of achievement. With the king 'safe' in Paris, and having signed the Declaration of Rights, the single-chamber legislature and the suspensive veto into law after the 6th, it seemed that the revolution could proceed now on an even keel. What the deputies could not know was that, even as they were planning their own move to the capital, Louis XVI was drafting and dispatching a letter to the King of Spain, his cousin and closest ruling relative, in which he unequivocally denounced all their works. The letter was a 'solemn protestation against my enforced sanction of all that has been done contrary to the royal authority since 15 July of this year', and a declaration of intent to work towards rolling back the revolution to the position Louis had been willing to accept when he commanded the royal session of 23 June: no abolition of feudalism, no change to the Church, no end to royal control of legislation and no Declaration of Rights.[51]

In the final three months of 1789 the deputies of the National Assembly wrestled to consolidate the revolution, ignorant of the royal intention to undo all their work. As they did so, however, they remained poised between a series of oppositions: euphoric perceptions of the possibility of regeneration and hard-nosed alarm at the state of the nation; energetic radicalism and determined conservative resistance; and perhaps above all, between a repeated emphasis on unified national sovereignty and a growing suspicion of mob rule. The Assembly had been settled in Paris only two days when on 21 October fresh food riots broke out and one baker was gruesomely lynched in the very heart of the city. Rather than simply bemoaning such events, or reinterpreting them as a struggle for freedom, as they had done in the summer, the deputies now hastened to pass a statute providing for the declaration of martial law, under which ringleaders of the riots were tried and executed within days by the Parisian authorities under Lafayette's vigorous leadership. The shadow of these events, and those of the 6th, helped to produce crushing majorities in favour of restricting the franchise in debates over the following week. Election was to be an orderly affair, based on voters who paid at least some tax choosing 'electors' (who paid more) to form local assemblies, there to choose representatives, whose eligibility for national office depended on their paying an even higher amount in tax. The 'electors', meanwhile, would form the cadre to choose a wide range of civil officials, including judges and municipal prosecutors as well as local mayors and town councils.[52]

Yet, if such arrangements pushed the unruly mob out of politics (or so the deputies hoped), they were accompanied by a grievous assault on the already traumatised nobility. A series of debates through the autumn led in mid-December to decisions that effectively wiped clean the map of France, and thus erased much of the nobility's sense of collective existence. Ancient provinces, and the identities that went with them, were to be extinguished – even their borders were smothered by the creation of an entirely new map of local jurisdictions: the *départements* that endure to this day. Nobles had accepted that the privileges of such bodies had to go in August, but the move to a clean slate smacked of a 'regeneration' that left literally no place for the former Second Estate. Rumours that radicals planned to move for the abolition of nobility itself had already run through Paris in November, just after two other assaults on the power of the privileged.[53] The *parlements*, who had been in their customary recess throughout most of the summer's drama, were sent on permanent vacation by a decree of 3 November. The bodies who had perhaps done the most to call the Estates-General into existence were thus propelled by it into the shadows, with a clear signal that they might not survive the Assembly's reforming zeal (and indeed, within a year, they would be erased by a new judicial system, aligned with the network of *départements*).

Meanwhile the other privileged order, the First Estate of the Catholic Church, faced up to the threat some of its representatives had feared since August – the seizure of its property to pay the state's debts, and thus the ending of its independent existence. Formally proposed in late September, and debated furiously through much of the second half of October, the final vote came on 2 November. In the concluding debate the radical Breton Le Chapelier articulated the philosophical clash at its heart: he was 'astonished' to hear expressions such as 'our adversaries, our property' emerging from some of the clerical deputies, who were 'uniting and making common cause, defending themselves as if an independent individual brought before our tribunal'. Le Chapelier stated the radical case unequivocally: the 'property' of the Church was nothing of the sort, the clergy was the 'administrator' of a stock of wealth that existed, like the prayer it funded, 'for the nation'. Moreover, and in this he went on to a direct attack, not to take over the Church's property would be to neglect the fact that 'you have wanted to destroy the orders, because their destruction was necessary to the salvation of the state'. Leaving the clergy in possession of what was, by some estimates, a tenth of the country's landed wealth would be to violate all the principles of civic equality to which the revolution was committed. As for the claim that the Church supported the poor, a key point of reference for many in the debate, Le Chapelier accused clerical institutions of making a 'caste' out of the poor with a 'sterile and dangerous charity, suited to the maintenance of idleness'. The 'Nation', by contrast, in taking over such responsibility, will set up 'workshops useful to the state, where the unfortunate will find subsistence alongside employment . . . there will be no more poor, except those who wish to be'.[54]

Mirabeau followed him with a long speech taking to task the 'puerile and frivolous objections' with which discussion had been laden.[55] Addressing arguments about the juridical and theological status of the Church and the clergy as a body, he dismissed as nonsensical the claims that were at the heart of many clerical objections. Mirabeau, like other speakers in favour of the proposal, took the 'Nation' for granted as an effectively timeless collective body, exactly the kind of existence they were no longer prepared to allow the Church. Clerical supporters, however, thought that the 'Nation' had no meaningful existence outside a necessary relationship with religion, mediated by the clergy, for whom their property was indeed a sacred trust, but one that the 'Nation' had no right to violate. The strength of feeling about this was such that the final measure, passed by 568 to 346, avoided overt confiscation by declaring church property to be merely 'at the disposal of the nation', with the latter body pledged to pay for the clergy and the 'relief of the poor'.

Another amendment had added the clause that such arrangements were to be 'under the surveillance and following the instructions of the provinces'.[56] With the majority of some provincial delegations firmly opposed to any change, many on the right hoped that this phrasing would see all but the most invidious examples of clerical property, such as the vast wealth of some abbeys, left untouched. The marquis de Ferrières, writing home, noted that 'the capitalist-speculators had seen all this wealth as so much prey they prepared to devour. The provincial deputies see differently, and will not let strangers usurp that which is the resources of the towns and countryside.'[57] The elimination of the provinces themselves, of course, was to dash such hopes, and the increasingly desperate state of the finances drove on a logic of expropriation. When, in December, bonds called *assignats* began to be issued to state creditors in place of cash, the right to redeem them for parcels of actual church land, labelled as 'national property', *biens nationaux*, was integral to their value.

Mirabeau himself, so instrumental in this debate, was to see a more personal set of hopes dashed only days later. After his triumphant assertion of the rights of the National Assembly back in June, Mirabeau's dual role as orator and newspaper editor had kept him at the centre of political life. Never uncontroversial, and occasionally, as with his failed efforts to draft a Declaration of Rights, misjudging the mood of the Assembly, he was nonetheless increasingly recognised as a political force in his own right. While Jefferson could dismiss him as the dangerous machinator of an Orléanist cabal, in practical terms he could not be kept out of the equation. One deputy wrote of him at the end of October that he was, quite simply, 'a giant among pygmies', and indeed the only one with 'the genius, the talents, and the force of character to save us from the horrible chaos into which we have plunged'.[58] Even Lafayette, sworn opponent of the 'Orléanists', was drawn into discussions with Mirabeau about the future direction of government, discussions that entailed revisiting a vexed question of the separation of powers. The king had posed this question for the Assembly in August, when he invited three deputies, including the *monarchien* archbishop Champion de Cicé, to become ministers. Accepting, they sidestepped any constitutional issues by quietly ceasing to attend the Assembly, a move that infuriated Mirabeau. His *Courrier de Provence* thundered: 'in vain can a narrow and suspicious doctrine pretend that the independence of the legislative body would suffer from this presence, of which a neighbouring state offers an example and of which the salutary effects are proven by experience'.[59]

Given that the 'neighbouring state', Britain, had spent much of the last decade in furious arguments about the 'unconstitutional' manipulation of Parliament by the government, this was perhaps not the point best suited to the circumstances. Though Mirabeau argued again in late September that 'we need the co-operation of enlightened ministers', even he had to add a proviso: he was 'not afraid of ministerial influence, as long as it does not operate in the secrecy of the cabinet'. The fear of the power of government, which across the Atlantic had viewed John Adams's vice-presidency as a potential route to despotic domination, was only redoubled in a French context where actual government ministers had plotted to shut down the Assembly in July. This, coupled with uncertainty about Mirabeau's own distinctive qualities, would lend principled weight to what was, in other respects, a classic piece of political intrigue. For it was Champion de Cicé, currently installed as Keeper of the Seals, or Justice Minister, who worked on colleagues and acquaintances within the Assembly, as it debated a motion put forward by Mirabeau on 6 November to give ministers a 'consultative voice' in the Assembly.

Intriguingly, this motion came as part of an immense speech by Mirabeau, ranging across the financial difficulties of France, which placed great weight on the potential of the United States to relieve the current dearth of food in the country – not just by shipments of grain, which had been under way since the previous winter, but by the management of the Americans' debt. 'We have', said Mirabeau, 'in the United States a resource which seems to have been prepared for the present circumstances.' The USA owed 5,710,000 *livres* in interest payments, due on 1 January 1790 – enough to buy food for all of Paris for two months. Mirabeau looked forward to being able to call on such funds, now that 'union and concord are re-established among the States'. Not only 'the interesting and fruitful ties of liberty', but the fact that 'we have shed our blood on their soil to help them conquer' that freedom, meant that 'they will not refuse to pay their debt to us'.[60] The various proposals Mirabeau put forward to effect this relief, however, were turned aside by the immediate response to his ministerial proposal, which had at its heart the idea that a ministerial presence in the Assembly would bolster confidence and public credit.

A Breton doctor named Blin took the floor with an argument that hinged dramatically on the British example. Mirabeau's proposal, he said, opened the way to the 'venality and corruption' with which the British government managed its affairs: 'Everyone knows that the majority of the British parliament do not even take the trouble to hide the sale of their votes.' He reminded his listeners that 'the most interesting, the most useful' proposals in the House of Commons had come in past decades not from the ministry but the opposition, and had been defeated by the weight of purchased votes. The evils of this, he claimed, had been visible in British conduct in their war with America. Given the context of the discussion, the desperate hope of food and financial aid from the United States, it was ironic to blame 'the loss of these colonies' on ministerial neglect of the 'most interesting' proposals he admired: by Blin's own argument, had the British been closer to his own ideal, France would not have a new ally to look to. Blin went on to denounce the spirit of party that ministers would bring to the legislature – they would either dominate unjustly or be defeated by opposing factions, which would 'humiliate, without necessity or utility, the executive power'. Therefore he proposed that 'No member of the National Assembly may enter ministerial office during the sitting of the Assembly.'[61]

Others leapt into the debate, with America 'experts' including the duc de La Rochefoucauld d'Enville and the vicomte de Noailles seconding the hopeful prospect of transatlantic support, but also sharing fears at the British example.[62] An indecisive vote, however, meant that Mirabeau's proposal stayed on the table, and was revived the next day. Champion de Cicé, anxious to safeguard his own ministerial position against Mirabeau, alerted several deputies to the orator's supposed ambitions, and on the 7th they stepped up. The conservative comte de Montlosier warned that the proposal was 'as vicious in principle as it is dangerous in its consequences and pernicious in its effects'.[63] Another deputy alerted by Champion de Cicé, Jean-Denis Lanjuinais, was even more blunt. Reversing the usual concern about ministerial influence, he warned that ministers themselves might become 'the playthings of ambitious men'. As he elaborated, 'an eloquent genius leads you on and subjugates you, what could he not do if he became a minister?'[64] With such an obvious personal allusion, Mirabeau leapt into the debate, and wrestled to refute the fears expressed. Sensing it was a losing battle, he made a last throw by recognising that 'popular rumours about me have given fears to certain persons, and perhaps hopes to others', and offering to exclude himself, by name, from the ministry in a formal vote.[65] But Blin's original motion, reintroduced by Montlosier, was passed. The purity of the National Assembly was to be secured against the contamination of ministerial office – in other words, a standing opposition was created between 'virtuous' popular representatives and the agents of the king, automatically suspected of intriguing against the rights of the Nation.

Thomas Jefferson, and his optimism, had left the country by the time the conflicts of the autumn erupted. Though he remained convinced in his last dispatch home to Secretary of State Jay (whom he was to replace) that 'England will give money to produce and to feed the fire' of Orléanist mischief, he was also certain that such interference would not prevent a settlement. Almost his last letter from Paris, to a friend in Virginia, stressed the future industrial co-operation of America and France. He had visited Milne's works at La Muette, and come away with costings for delivery of 'a compleat set of machines' within five weeks of order; he pledged to 'render every service I can to the Society for encouraging manufactures' when he returned. Another letter, giving his farewells to Necker, dwelt on their joint success in attacking the British whaling trade.[66] Rumours of popular violence troubled his last days in Paris, however, and the first confused reports of the October Days followed him onto the boat at Le Havre, where he had been waiting with his family for calmer weather. He had written earlier in September to Thomas Paine that France was on course to produce 'a good constitution, which will in its principles and merit be about a middle term between that of England and the United States'.[67] He did not spell out how he perceived this 'middle term', but a less optimistic, and perhaps more realistic, reading of what the French had committed themselves to trying was that they had offered Louis XVI the powers of a British monarch, while constructing a system of political representation more purely democratic than even the Americans had dared. The careful political arithmetic of the American constitution-makers – who had embraced a presidential veto but allowed an immediate overriding vote, who had taken the powers of the states and embedded them in the Senate, forcing negotiation for progress – were lessons the French, in their fears about aristocratic resurgence and demagogic unrest, had neglected to learn.

The consequences would haunt them over the next few years, but though it is tempting to fault the structural choices of the French as steps on the road to Terror, the reality of their situation should not be neglected. Perhaps a more mixed constitution would have been France's salvation, but it is worth noting that the epithet *deux-chambres*, designating believers in bicameralism and a 'House of Lords', soon became an insult among the nobles who had fled France to make a counter-revolution – including the king's own brothers.[68] For such *émigrés*, any such 'English' plans were an unconscionable compromise with the despised commoners, especially when, by late 1790, the demagogue Mirabeau was among those proposing such a revision of the constitution. There is no sign that the royal family ever seriously considered living with the revolution in good faith. When, in June 1791, they attempted to escape Paris for the security of the frontier garrisons – only a few miles from their *émigré* relations in the east – they made that clear for all to see. The remaining moderates in the National Assembly, now led by former 'radicals' such as Barnave, Lameth and Duport, were driven to transparent deceit, claiming this 'Flight to Varennes' showed the king had been 'kidnapped' by counter-revolutionary forces, and 'rescued' by the people.[69] The consummation of this pathetically optimistic folly, in giving constitutional power to the king the following September, was rewarded by his stonewalling veto of measures against the increasingly warlike *émigrés* in the autumn of 1791. New, even more radical political forces emerged, led by the journalist and now Assembly deputy Brissot, to press for a victorious war to cleanse the frontiers of this threat. Meanwhile the king and his ministers equally craved conflict – the latter seeking an excuse to discipline the radicals, the former in the insane belief that he would be allowed to turn the army on the people.[70]

War came in April 1792, and with it disaster – for how could an army, many of whose officers had fled to the enemy (and with the rest under suspicion by their troops), bulked out with untrained volunteers, launch immediate offensives against skilled professionals? Disaster brought a second revolution, and a bloody assault on the defenders of the Tuileries palace on 10 August (after the king had already surrendered to the custody of the Assembly) that paved the way for a massacre of suspected counter-revolutionaries in the prisons of the capital three weeks later. But less than three weeks after that the armies of the newly declared Republic put their foes to flight at the battle of Valmy, about which the poet Goethe declaimed (from the defeated Prussian camp), 'From this place and from this day forth commences a new era in the history of the world.'[71]

By the time of these events France's old enemy across the Channel had already discovered that the shadow of 1789 fell upon them as much as anyone, and even before they were dragged into war against France in the spring of 1793, Britons (and Irish) were wrestling with the ways in which that momentous year had changed politics forever.

---

# 14

# 'The greatest event it is that ever happened in the world'

## *The British and the French Revolution*

Before Thomas Jefferson left Europe for good, he heard from Britain of the great impact the French Revolution was having there. Dr Richard Price, the Dissenting cleric and political economist whose fame spread across both shores of the Atlantic, wrote to him on 3 August 1789, even before the momentous declarations of that month, to thank him for news of

> the origin, progress and completion of one of the most important revolutions that have ever taken place in the world . . . that must astonish Europe; that Shakes the foundation of despotic power; and that probably will be the commencement of a general reformation in the governments of the world.[1]

Price went on to hope that such an example would soon cause 'the friends of liberty' in Britain 'to bring about a reformation of abuses so palpable as to be incapable of being defended'. Six weeks later Thomas Paine offered Jefferson his views on the penetration of the French example:

> The Mass of [the English] so far as I can collect says that France is a much freer Country than England. The Press, the Bishops &c says the national assembly has gone too far. There is yet, in

this Country, very considerable remains of the feudal system
which people did not see till the revolution in France placed it
before their eyes.

Paine observed that 'the Multitude here' had been 'terrified with the
cry and apprehension of Arbitrary power, wooden shoes, popery and
such like stuff' – the notion that the French peasantry, suffering
under papist tyranny, were so poor that they had to wear wooden
shoes was an oft-repeated propaganda image of the century. In the
face of this, he noted, the British 'thought themselves by comparison
an extraordinarily free people, but this bug-bear now loses its force,
and they appear to me to be turning their Eyes towards the
Aristocrats of their own Nation. This is a new mode of conquering,
and I think it will have its effect.'[2] Paine was to be proved both
right and wrong: the French Revolution was to have its effect most
decisively in Britain and its empire, but in a far more bitter, long-
drawn-out and, ultimately, grimly bloody fashion than he could have
hoped. Within a few years Paine himself would be in flight from
charges of sedition, and ultimately treason, and the 'Multitude'
would be burning him in effigy in over four hundred locations up
and down the country – but others among them would be consuming over 200,000 copies of his rousing call for a British revolution,
*The Rights of Man*.[3]

The very day that the Parisians stormed the Bastille, Prime Minister
William Pitt wrote perspicaciously to his mother that events in that
country were 'coming to actual extremes', which made France 'an
object of compassion, even for a rival'. Yet this was no occasion for
alarm – the same letter reassured her, always concerned for her son's
frail frame, that the summer recess of Parliament would afford opportunities for 'a good share of holidays'.[4] Only a few days earlier the
House of Commons had voted to uphold the Corn Laws, which prevented exports of grains while they were at their current high prices,
and had thus decisively closed off one potential expression of Pitt's
compassion. Necker himself had written to Pitt asking him for a
relaxation of the statutes in late June, to ease the French provisioning situation, but the British Board of Trade reported to the Prime
Minister that stocks were low, and only Parliament could overrule
the law. The great campaigner William Wilberforce moved a motion

to do just this, on humanitarian grounds, but the Commons could not be brought to agree. Pitt's hands were tied (or, at least, he felt it was an issue not worth expending precious political capital on), and the future would prove that stocks were not sufficient to have supported much traffic to France – British merchants would be scouring the markets of Europe for supplies by the autumn. Nonetheless, the impression the episode left in France was of a nation determined to profit by their misfortune.[5]

Repeated suspicions of British interference – which ran, as we have seen, as high as the circles around Jefferson – could not have been further from the truth in the Revolution's first year. By the end of July the British ambassador in Paris, the Duke of Dorset, was at the centre of accusations of fomenting disorder so serious that he gained the government's approval to deny them publicly. The *French Patriot*, with its editor Brissot's long record of cross-Channel connections, was one of the few to take such denials seriously, and tried to educate its readers:

> One cannot conceive how the English Ministry, with its king's continued state of dementia, and the need it has of peace to preserve its authority, could desire war. One conceives even less how the English nation could demand it, when it would evidently be an act of baseness which would cover her in shame in the eyes of the universe, and when moreover it is so well demonstrated that peace is necessary to her prosperity, and that she cannot undertake a war, even a successful one, without being exposed to bankruptcy.[6]

Pitt, with his years of work to balance the books, might have objected to the conclusion, but he would have agreed with the sentiment behind it. Unfortunately Britain's quest to recover from its diplomatic isolation after the American War had already left marks of humiliation and resentment on the French that no amount of cosmopolitan wishing was to erase.

The turning point in this quest had been 1787. At the start of the year it seemed that French support for a Patriot Party of disaffected commoners in the Dutch Republic would succeed in toppling the power of the Orange Party, headed by the country's quasi-monarch, the Stadtholder. For Britain this risked putting the entire seaboard of the continent under the influence of France – with modern-day Belgium then part of her ally Austria's possessions. Pitt allied with Prussia, whom he had been eagerly courting for several years, to counter the threat, while sending £70,000 in subsidies to the Orangists at the end of May 1787. But French intervention was still dreaded. What clinched the matter was the utter collapse of French diplomatic influence that accompanied the failure of Calonne and Brienne's reforms. French politicians had to watch as their Patriot allies were ousted by Prussian troops, backed by British cash, while French armies stood by helpless, lacking the funds to risk an open-ended confrontation.[7] Though the British continued to fear that the French would fight back in other realms, and one concern about expeditions such as that of La Pérouse to the Pacific was that they might swoop on the vulnerable Dutch East Indies, the diplomatic balance of power slipped further and further from the grasp of Louis XVI's ministers. When in the same year France's nominal allies Austria and Russia launched a combined attack on the Ottoman Empire, also a friend of France, her diplomatic embarrassment grew.

British influence rose further in 1788. Energetic local diplomacy by the British ambassador to Denmark saved Sweden from the consequences of an ill-advised, opportunistic attack on Russia. The Danes were brought to an armistice, preventing a fatal pincer movement against a country both Britain and Prussia saw as vital to preserving the regional balance of power.[8] Meanwhile France had sunk ever further into diplomatic impotence. Pitt's views on the appointment of Necker in August had been notably charitable: it was 'probably the best thing that could happen for that country', as Necker would 'set himself in earnest to put their finances in real order, if the thing is possible; and will probably avail himself of the necessity of a free constitution'. Nevertheless, as Pitt was able to note the following month, 'The state of France, whatever it may produce, seems to promise more than ever a considerable respite from any dangerous projects.'[9] The subsequent madness of George III seemed for a while to strike as fatal a diplomatic blow as it had threatened to do to Pitt domestically. Pitt was helpless as reports leaked out of French efforts to draw Spain into a Quadruple Alliance alongside Austria and Russia. On the king's recovery Pitt rushed William Eden, architect of the favourable 1786 trade treaty, to Spain to explore luring that nation into alliance. It was a desperate throw, since, as Eden reported back, 'Religious Prejudices and general Bigotry' that were 'maintained here by the Influence of Princes' stood in the way, alongside a pre-existing defensive 'Family Compact' with France.[10] But the collapse of French internal authority in the spring of 1789 made the problem moot: that nation would be making no more aggressive moves on the world stage for some time.

While Eastern Europe remained turbulent, once purely domestic politics returned to an even keel Pitt's ministry found itself in an enviable position regarding the old enemy. Though there was no question of actively intervening in the French situation, it was enough to be able to sit back and watch that country's domestic politics ruin her on the world stage. Further revolutionary upheaval, this time in the Austrian Netherlands, confirmed France's powerlessness. Factions in the National Assembly and the Court pulled in different directions, French ambassadors scarcely knew in whose name they operated and it was obvious to the eyes of all Europe that France could make no meaningful threats or promises. In a further humiliating irony the following year, it would be British pressure on her ally Prussia that allowed Austria to restore authority in the Netherlands without international strife.[11] In the context of such a shocking reversal of fortunes, with the formerly isolated Britons 'incontestably in possession of the balance of Europe', as one ambassador put it in 1790, it is little wonder that many among the French, who only a few years before had regarded themselves as the rightful 'arbiters of Europe', increasingly saw 'guineas from Mr Pitt' as the explanation for their collapse into anarchy.[12]

Intriguingly, though the British government would have nothing to do with revolutionary affairs, even downgrading its Paris embassy staff to little more than an observation post after the summer of 1789, other prominent Britons were fervently concerned with the course of events in France, and were part of an international coterie that, to hostile minds, could well be interpreted as a conspiracy to destroy the power of kings. At Bowood House, a palatial country mansion in Wiltshire, philosophical radicals of all kinds had gathered since the early 1770s around William Petty, a Whig politician who had been Prime Minister briefly in 1782–3 before the Fox–North coalition. Then the Earl of Shelburne, he was elevated by Pitt to be Marquess of Lansdowne in 1784, as some compensation for leaving him out of his cabinet. Effectively retiring from public life, he could then give even more attention to the thinkers and schemers whom he had encouraged for more than a decade.[13]

Their names are a roll-call of figures from the international republic of letters and its radical connections. Richard Price was one such, and helped secure for the chemist Joseph Priestley an appointment as Bowood's librarian through the 1770s, freeing him to conduct some of his most important experiments on the nature of oxygen there. Josiah Wedgwood and Matthew Boulton both provided ornaments from their factories for Bowood's rooms, and met socially with its master, who in return supported industrial advances with parliamentary speeches and was among the first shown round Boulton and Watt's revolutionary Albion Mill.[14] Jeremy Bentham undertook some of his early speculations on utilitarian legal reform while enjoying Lansdowne's hospitality. Major John Cartwright had sought the then Earl of Shelburne's approval for his draft of *Take Your Choice* in 1776, while in the 1780s Lansdowne kept alive the spirits of the Society for Constitutional Information and the London Revolution Society. He supported the rights of religious Dissenters and had launched the political careers of several prominent radical Whigs, including Benjamin Vaughan, who combined politics with his natural-historical correspondence with Jefferson. The ferment of reforming ideas emerging from Bowood had taken to print in 1788 in the *Repository*, a journal started by Vaughan, which failed to make an impact on the public.[15] It printed a letter in February of that year bemoaning the fact that 'Ever since . . . the revolution at Christmas 1783 [Pitt's assumption of power], all men in England have been making up their minds to endure an absolute government', and warned of 'a political lethargy; from which nothing but some violent blow can awaken and rouse to action' the people.[16] Revolution the next year in France, however, seemed to offer more hope of influence, and followed up a long-standing continental connection.

Such links reached to the very top of the Whig party. The ending of the American War had restored connections in a cross-Channel aristocratic world where it was not unusual to find even a Polignac – Marie-Antoinette's notorious favourites – dining in London high society. If politics was not on the agenda at such gatherings, other links most emphatically reflected ideological sympathies. The vicomte de Noailles, who in 1789 leapt up to propose the abolition of feudalism, had corresponded with Whigs even before the American War; the marquis de Lafayette made similar connections after it, and had embraced Whig efforts to support abolition of the slave trade, 'a trafick so disgracing to Mankind', as he wrote in his not quite perfect English in 1788.[17] Charles James Fox, in particular, became a close and warm friend of the marquis. He was also attached to the duc d'Orléans, rather ironically, given the latter's increasing detestation by Lafayette. Orléans had been a fixture on the circuit of Whig sociability since the early 1780s, a well-known 'anglomaniac' with a particular passion for horse-racing, and had spent considerable time in Fox's company at Bath in early 1789, where one was convalescing from his failure to seize the reins of national power and the other was awaiting the summons to the Estates-General. By the end of July 1789 Fox was asking a mutual friend to pass on best wishes to the duke, and enquire about visiting him in a city that had just experienced upheavals he saluted unequivocally: 'How much the greatest event it is that ever happened in the world, and how much the best.'[18]

But beyond such generic enthusiasm for liberty over despotism – the latter being very much how the Whigs in general viewed almost all European politics – there was little active engagement with real events in France from the top of the party hierarchy. Indeed, from spring through to August 1789, the main preoccupation of the Foxites was to find a way of reconciling the Prince of Wales with his father, particularly in light of the queen's open horror at their jubilant plans for the regency. High-level meetings discussed the delicate language of a 'memorial' justifying the prince's behaviour, until a preliminary note delivered on 14 August brought, three weeks later, a tart reply: the king would allow that the prince's 'conduct has proceeded from errors of judgment', if and when he began to show 'that respect and affection, which parents have a right to claim'. In this light, Fox's request to the prince a month earlier, to 'take some favourable occasion of laying me at the King's feet' and bidding him 'make use of so humble an instrument as I am' if he saw fit, was, even through the grovelling language, hopelessly optimistic.[19] In disarray, rebuffed by public opinion, scorned by the Crown and still caught up in the increasingly wearying travails of the Hastings impeachment, the opposition leadership had very little constructive to say about the French Revolution.

It was from the more leisured surroundings of Bowood House, where Lansdowne's political retirement had allowed him to nurture his philosophical circles, that a more programmatic eye could be turned across the Channel. Just as the more socially eminent French reformers had taken up with Whig society in previous decades, so the more ideologically adventurous had been drawn to Bowood. Men at the highest levels of reforming endeavour, most notably Turgot, had already been in correspondence with leading lights of the Bowood set in the 1770s, and the following decade added a new dimension, with the house acquiring a reputation for sheltering those at odds with the authorities. Brissot was one of several notable publicists to pass through, and it was in the congenial surroundings of the circle that Mirabeau spent much of his time in England. While there he also came into contact with another group of refugees, on the run from a French-sponsored overturning of democratic reform in the Swiss republic of Geneva. Étienne Clavière, the banker, anti-slavery activist and promoter of transatlantic co-operation and trade, was one such who made his way in the world independently, but others had fallen on harder times. The British government had collaborated in a plan to settle many of them and their families in a 'New Geneva' near Waterford in Ireland, and George III had personally subscribed £50,000 to the project, but it had collapsed for lack of a steady flow of continental Protestants willing to be transplanted into Catholic Ireland.[20]

Lansdowne had patronised this group as its leaders straggled back into England, appointing one, Étienne Dumont, as tutor to his youngest son. In the spring of 1789 Dumont was allowed to go to Versailles, along with another prominent leader of his Genevan party, to seek the support of Necker for a restoration of their position in the city. With the minister unforthcoming, the Swiss switched their efforts to the rising political career of their Bowood acquaintance, Mirabeau. The latter already had connections with Clavière, who now became his adviser on fiscal policy, while Dumont and others researched and wrote many of his most acclaimed speeches. Dumont also edited the *Courrier de Provence*, giving both Mirabeau and the Swiss a public mouthpiece for reforming ideas. Although the avowed goal of the Swiss was ultimately French support for a return to their homeland, it should not be thought that they were insincere in their messages about utility, democracy and the public good. Notions cultivated in discussion with figures such as Bentham filtered out thus into French debates, though not always fruitfully. While the National Assembly was still wrestling with its own procedures in June 1789, a tract on parliamentary practices drafted by several British legal luminaries, translated by Dumont and published with a preface by Mirabeau, was offered as a model to the deputies by the great orator. It was greeted with the chilly comment, 'We are not Englishmen, and we do not need Englishmen.'[21] In light of such responses, Bentham put on hold his own plans to advise the French in a treatise on *Political Tactics*. It was connections such as these that added verisimilitude to the accusations of conspiracy against Mirabeau that redoubled after the October Days, notably in a vitriolic and melodramatic pamphlet by the right-wing journalist Jean-Gabriel Peltier, *Domine salvum fac regem*. Relating the already well-known rumours of Mirabeau's Orléanist caballing as fact, Peltier also denounced the true authorship of many of his most famous works. Clavière, Brissot, Dumont and others were named, while Mirabeau's noted work on the American Order of the Cincinnati was attributed to '*docteur* [Richard] Price, and it has been claimed by him'.[22] If the pamphlet went overboard with some such assertions, it was enough to scupper the chances of this international network having further influence in French politics – as the ignominious end of Mirabeau's ministerial ambitions in November made clear.

The activities of the Bowood set and its associates in the Society for Constitutional Information and other radical gatherings were, however, to produce an entirely unexpected and dramatic turn in British politics, emerging from what seemed at first a very unlikely source. Scourge of ministerial despotism, defender of the rights of oppressed Indians and Irishmen, friend and correspondent of Thomas Paine, Edmund Burke was about to perform an astonishing political transformation. As revolutionary events unfolded in France, Burke was weighed down with the Hastings impeachment. He feared that the Court was sheltering Hastings, and that the leaders of Fox's party were too timid, and too concerned to rebuild links with the monarch, to pursue the matter with appropriate vigour as the trial sessions ground on. In his own ardour for the prosecution he was becoming a pariah, writing in May 1789: 'My strength was always in those admirable Men . . . with whom I have been connected. Stripped of them, I am nothing.' By August his reflections were turning more generally melancholy: he wrote to a friend that 'Party is absolutely necessary at this time', meaning by that term the conscious adherence to a principled set of beliefs as a guide for conduct, but 'I rather fear, that there is not virtue enough in this period to support party'. By the end of the year his mood had turned to anger: 'What is the conduct of our pretended friends[?] Put an end to the trial [they say]; you have spun it out too long, the people are tired of it . . . I have done with that sort of friends. It rests only with me in what manner I am to conduct myself in this defeat produced by their desertion.'[23] He had turned sixty in January and was now emphatically ageing, with the principled Whig project of defending constitutional liberty, to which he had devoted decades, crumbling around him.

In this mood of dejection, combined with the furious work of preparing trial speeches and supporting noble parliamentary causes, including Wilberforce's unsuccessful moves against the slave trade, much of the early drama of the French Revolution passed Burke by. In August he expressed 'astonishment at the wonderful Spectacle', but saw 'something in it paradoxical and Mysterious' about the relation of violence and reform. Lurid press accounts, and the rumour-mongering correspondence of French acquaintances, heightened a sense of melodrama, and he could write in early October of France as a country 'where the Elements that compose Human Society seem all to be dissolved, and a world of Monsters' was coming into being.[24] Accounts that arrived shortly thereafter of the October Days seem to have begun to crystallise Burke's sense that all could not be well with a supposedly progressive event that relied for its impetus so much on grim violence. What alarmed him even more, as he expressed to a French correspondent at the turn of the year, was that 'some people here are willing that we should become their scholars too, and reform our state on the French model'. Burke now felt pressed to defend the underlying values of a system whose flaws he had so eloquently denounced.[25]

As he did so, he felt himself further abandoned by his Whig friends. Charles James Fox had been noted in society toasting the 'Majesty of the People' days after the attack on Versailles, and Richard Sheridan, who had caballed against Burke's position on the regency, was stirring pro-French opinion against him.[26] The actions of the radical wing of the Whig movement, as the great anniversary date of 4 November 1789 passed, had reinforced Burke's horror, and left a lasting impression. Dr Richard Price, at sixty-six even more of a political veteran than Burke, offered a sermon at the service he had been too ill to attend the previous year, preceding the annual dinner of the London Revolution Society at the London Tavern. He moved swiftly from Christian duties to civic ones, in a text devoted to 'love of our country' that imposed strict requirements for 'citizens of the world' to 'help to prepare the minds of men for the recovery of their rights and hasten the overthrow of priestcraft and tyranny'. 'Most' governments, Price noted, 'are usurpations on the rights of man', and he drew attention to the problematic slavishness of so many of the addresses that had greeted the king's recovery in the spring: unworthy of 'enlightened and manly citizens', they neglected the fact that made George 'almost the only lawful King in the world, because the only one who owes his crown to the choice of his people'.[27]

While Price praised the revolution of 1689 for affording liberty of religious conscience, the right to resist abuses and to elect representatives, he denounced the limitations on such freedoms, and the essentially corrupt nature of parliamentary representation: in a profound shift, he now looked to foreign examples to rectify this, hoping that the 'pure and equal representation' now achieved elsewhere would shame the British into reform.[28] While the United States might be one source of inspiration, Price perorated with ill-disguised joy on events in France:

> I have lived to see the rights of men better understood than ever; and nations panting for liberty, which seemed to have lost the idea of it. – I have lived to see THIRTY MILLIONS of people, indignant and resolute, spurning at slavery, and demanding liberty with an irresistible voice; their king led in triumph, and an arbitrary monarch surrendering himself to his subjects.[29]

Though Price later claimed he meant only to refer to Louis XVI's visit to Paris in July, the echo of the ignominy of October was evident, and in his closing remarks Price seemed to assert that such actions were of a piece with what should spring forth from the British tradition: 'Behold the light you have struck out, after setting America free, reflected to France, and there kindled into a blaze that lays despotism in ashes, and warms and illuminates EUROPE.'[30]

To cap all this, at the dinner that followed, a formal address to the French National Assembly was proposed, in which the assembled diners, led by Lord Stanhope, aspired to see 'the glorious example given in France' produce a 'general reformation in the governments of Europe, and to make a world free and happy'. Stanhope's long-time friend and correspondent, the duc de La Rochefoucauld-Liancourt, read this to a delighted Assembly three weeks later, which reciprocated with warmest sentiments of appreciation.[31] Burke's fear of reform being mooted on the French model had real causes, but it remained isolated as the momentous year moved into the past. When Parliament gathered for its annual debate on defence spending, the 'army estimates', in February 1790, even the Prime Minister was moved to make internationalist noises about France – when that nation settled from her 'present convulsions' into 'freedom resulting from good order and good government', she 'would stand forward as one of the most brilliant Powers in Europe; she would enjoy just that kind of liberty which I venerate'.[32]

Burke spoke up in the debate to argue that such a hope might be by now forlorn, that demagogic principles had taken hold of France, and risked transmission across the Channel. Moreover, he went on, this was driving him to a split with his party, and 'he would abandon his best friends, and join with his worst enemies . . . to resist all violent exertions of the spirit of innovation'. Though Fox made conciliatory noises about not wanting to see undiluted democracy brought to Britain, Sheridan was far more scathing, accusing Burke, in effect, of taking Pitt's shilling. Burke's retort was to declare himself henceforth 'separated in politics' from Sheridan, and to be 'concerned to find that there were persons in this country who entertained theories of government, incompatible with the safety of the state'.[33] From this point on, Burke embarked seriously on the work that was to define an era, and of which he had begun a first sketch, in correspondence with a young French aristocratic acquaintance, late in 1789: *Reflections on the Revolution in France*.

The title, and its subtitle, 'on the proceedings in certain societies in London relative to that event', was announced in the press as early as 12 February, and the work seems initially to have been planned as a rapid-fire pamphlet. A month later Thomas Paine visited a Whig bookseller and learned that it was held up: 'he believed Mr Burke was much at a loss how to go on; that he had revised some of the sheets, six, seven, and one nine times!'[34] What emerged in November was no pamphlet, but rather a vast polemic, a sustained rhetorical performance of the superiority of tradition against unformed innovation, running to over three hundred pages without chapter breaks or other divisions, one vast open letter to Burke's concerned French friend, with a single chain of argument binding together the whole.

Burke acknowledged that, 'all things taken together, the French revolution is the most astonishing that has hitherto happened in the world', but his astonishment was not favourable – the thing overall was a 'monstrous tragi-comic scene' that provoked 'alternate contempt and indignation; alternate laughter and tears; alternate scorn and horror'.[35] From these premises he laid into Richard Price's sermon, making it his prime target for a good third of the text. Ironically raising the same arguments he had used to defend the rights of the Prince of Wales to the regency against Pitt's 'ministerial despotism', Burke lamented Price's contentions about the king's crown being the gift of the people. Giving chapter and verse from statute, he showed that the Glorious Revolution of 1689 was at most 'a small and temporary deviation from the strict order of a regular hereditary succession', and that the architects of the Bill of Rights had remade that succession and bound it in law for the defence of common freedoms.[36] He railed against the challenge to historically grounded freedom that the Revolution Society's doctrines seemed to pose – would they annul habeas corpus, or the right of parliamentary consent to taxation, because they had been 'passed under those whom they treat as usurpers'?[37] Over dozens of pages Burke proved, to his own satisfaction at least, that the freedoms enjoyed by Britons were inseparable from the solid and hereditary institutions of their constitution.

Burke was caustic on the whole nature of the French project – by setting aside their former ways the French were behaving as if they had been no more than a 'gang of Maroon [i.e., runaway] slaves, suddenly broke loose from the house of bondage, and therefore to be pardoned for your abuse of the liberty to which you were not accustomed and ill fitted'.[38] In these circumstances Price's exultation at the 'king led in triumph' drove Burke to some of his most fulminating passages. He depicted the National Assembly by the end of 1789 as sitting under the dominion of the Parisian mob, who had hounded out the most respectable part of the deputies:

> There a majority, sometimes real, sometimes pretended, captive itself, compels a captive king to issue as royal edicts, at third hand, the polluted nonsense of their most licentious and giddy coffee-houses. It is notorious, that all their measures are decided before they are debated. It is beyond doubt, that under the terror of the bayonet, and the lamp-post [for lynchings], and the torch to their houses, they are obliged to adopt all the crude and desperate measures suggested by clubs composed of a monstrous medley of all conditions, tongues and nations . . . In these meetings . . . every counsel, in proportion as it is daring, and violent, and perfidious, is taken for the mark of superior genius.[39]

Before going on in the second half of the text to a detailed, not to say exhaustive, denunciation of revolutionary policies, Burke lashed out at the events of the October Days in particular. Their assault on Marie-Antoinette's inviolable royal dignity particularly appalled him, having himself seen the Queen as a dazzling young princess on a 1773 visit to Versailles:

> surely never lighted on this orb, which she scarcely seemed to touch, a more delightful vision . . . I thought ten thousand swords must have leaped from their scabbards to avenge even a look that threatened her with insult. – But the age of chivalry is gone. – That of sophisters, oeconomists, and calculators has succeeded; and the glory of Europe is extinguished for ever.[40]

He warned that France was on course to destroy entirely the upper echelons of its society, and, in a phrase that echoed down the decades to come, that, 'Along with its natural protectors and guardians, learning will be cast into the mire, and trodden down under the hoofs of a swinish multitude.'[41]

The book was an instant success, selling twelve thousand copies in a month, with French, German and Italian translations following, and pirated American and Irish editions soon after. Burke was flooded with letters of support from the pillars of propertied society.

The University of Oxford awarded him an honorary doctorate, and George III himself exclaimed at Court, 'Read it! It will do you good! – do you good! Every gentleman should read it.'[42] Among those who did and were not impressed was Charles James Fox. He thought 'the writing of that work to be in very bad taste', while Benjamin Vaughan wrote to his Bowood patron Lansdowne that he preferred to remain 'idle for a fortnight' than to devote himself to 'detecting Mr Burke's inaccuracies', which were evident to anyone with the knowledge of French affairs Vaughan claimed.[43]

Others were less reticent in coming to the defence of revolutionary sentiments. The pioneer feminist writer Mary Wollstonecraft produced *A Vindication of the Rights of Men*, in which she addressed Burke directly: 'Did the pangs you felt for insulted nobility, the anguish that rent your heart when the gorgeous robes were torn off the idol human weakness had set up, deserve to be compared' with the 'misery and vice' of poverty and oppression? The Scottish doctor, lawyer and journalist James Mackintosh produced a *Vindiciae Gallicae*, or 'vindication of the French', in which he particularly scorned Burke's argumentative style: 'he can advance a group of magnificent horrors to make a breach in our hearts, through which the most undisciplined rabble of arguments can enter in triumph'.[44] As Mackintosh's Latin title indicates, Burke's text stirred up considerable interest among the educated and leisured classes, and it would prove to be the downfall of the united front of Whig opposition that Fox and Burke, among others, had worked so hard to build up through the 1780s. But it would be the response of Burke's old friend Thomas Paine that changed the political landscape forever.

Paine had been eager to deal with Burke's arguments ever since he had learned of the text's gestation early in 1790. Prospects for controversy even reached the press, with the London *General Evening Post* reporting in March that Paine 'would answer it in *four days*' when it appeared.[45] In the event, it would take far, far longer. Through 1789 Paine had been on a curious, double-sided mental journey. On the one side, he had continued to be enamoured of his bridge project, so much so that he wrote grandiosely to Jefferson the day before the Bastille fell that he intended 'to open the way for a Bridge over the Thames' by exhibiting his design in London, and went into debt on the project to the tune of £600 to his American partner, Peter Whiteside.[46] Bridge plans continued through into 1790, assisted by further funds from his Bowood acquaintance Benjamin Vaughan, who had (with near-inevitable political irony) family money from the West Indies trade. It took much of that latter year to find a site and complete erection of a trial bridge, finally opened for inspection in September, at a shilling a time, near a well-known pub called the Yorkshire Stingo at Lisson Green in north-west London.[47]

Bad weather, injuries on site and continual hard work and worry dogged Paine, further troubled when Whiteside went bankrupt and he was dunned by creditors for the £600 – only intervention by two other American merchants kept Paine from a debtors' prison, and helped him pay off the sum.[48] The bridge, though admired by many, including a party from the Royal Society led by Joseph Banks himself, did not produce the revolution in engineering that Paine hoped for. It was little remarked on in the press, and no concrete orders, or even expressions of interest, emerged from the show. The span ended up rusting as autumn turned to winter, before being seized by the Walker foundry against the costs incurred in manufacture. While Paine must have suffered bitter disillusionment at the end of a dream that had occupied him for half a decade, his mind was also turning elsewhere. As he wrote only a few days after the publication of Burke's *Reflections*, 'At present I am engaged on my political Bridge. I shall bring out a new work . . . soon after New Year. It will produce something one way or other.'[49]

Since his arrival in Britain Paine had already formed a series of 'political bridges', and as we have seen felt confident enough in early 1789 of his connections with the opposition Whigs to boast to Jefferson of the opportunities the king's madness might provide. He had been welcomed as a house guest of Burke, and dined with the Duke of Portland, Fox and Lansdowne. There had been jocular reference to him as the 'unofficial American ambassador', but as the plans for the regency fell apart, so the larger conceits of the Whigs, and Paine's response, soured them on him. He wrote again to Jefferson in March 1789: 'I believe I am not so much in the good graces of the Marquis of Lansdowne as I used to be – I do not answer his purpose. He was always talking of a sort of reconnection of England and America, and my coldness and reserve on this subject checked communication.'[50] Beyond the implausibility of

Lansdowne's dreams of reunion, a deeper rift was setting in between the radical Whig tradition and the ideas occupying Paine. Burke's vision of the impregnable historical virtues of the British constitution might have been turned, in the *Reflections*, to a conservative purpose, but it was not fundamentally different from that of the 'Commonwealthmen' in general, or from any of the other loose strands that underlay the thinking of the Revolution Society. They were rooted in the past, where what mattered were the peculiarly English (even Anglo-Saxon) virtues of a people and its idiosyncratic arrangements, to be defended from 'corruption' as a process of decline, not an inherent weakness. Paine was quite thoroughly new in his outlook – humanity in general had rights, and was entitled to form new constitutions as it saw fit, for the common good.

Three months spent in Paris from late November 1789 attuned Paine further to this universal message. There he met again his admirer Lafayette, and received from him the key to the Bastille, 'this early trophy of the Spoils of despotism, and the first ripe fruits of American principles transplanted into Europe'. Paine was to deliver it, with these words, to George Washington, and it remains at Mount Vernon to this day. Lafayette, meanwhile, had received the key ceremoniously from the hands of another Americophile, Jacques-Pierre Brissot, acting as representative of the Commune of Paris. Brissot, with his anti-slavery collaborators, including the marquis de Condorcet, welcomed Paine into their circles, at a moment when all seemed optimistic in France.[51] Paine was so taken up with this mood that he could write to Washington recommending 'the propriety of congratulating the King and Queen of France (for they have been our friends) and the National Assembly, on the happy example they are giving to Europe'. He enclosed a speech from the king that, Paine observed, showed 'that he prides himself on being at the head of the revolution'.[52]

Such optimism – entirely blind, of course, to the secret reality of the monarch's counter-revolutionary plotting – had been bolstered by a ceremonious visit of both Louis XVI and Marie-Antoinette to the National Assembly on 4 February, in which they had proclaimed just the sentiments Paine depicted. Even before this, he had read their conduct, and their presence in Paris, with a blithe eye. He wrote to Burke on 17 January 1790, describing a crowd 'immense, but orderly and well arranged' that greeted the king on a visit to the

City Hall: 'every one was armed with something . . . Scythes, Sickles, Carpenters Chisels and iron Spikes fixed upon Sticks'. The king passed between rows of such roughly armed men, holding their weapons above him in an arch, 'under which he had to pass, impressed perhaps with the apprehension that some one was to fall upon his head'. Paine went on, as if conscious of the consternation he might be causing: 'I mention this, to shew how natural it is that he should now feel himself tranquil.'[53] His correspondent would find such descriptions grist to his own mill of horrors, but Paine was not daunted. As his engineering efforts fell away, he was taken up more and more with revolutionary politics, travelling to Paris in the summer of 1790 to carry the American flag in ceremonies honouring the Revolution's first year.

Once Burke's text was out, Paine locked himself away in the Angel Inn, Islington, to digest and answer it. In three months of frenetic writing, incorporating to his new purpose parts of a history of the Revolution he had planned, he produced forty thousand words of bold refutation, Part One of *The Rights of Man*. Much of it was taken up with direct rebuttal of Burke, and he characterised the *Reflections* overall in a typically pithy image:

> I know a place in America called Point-no-Point; because as you proceed along the shore, gay and flowery as Mr Burke's language, it continually recedes and presents itself at a distance before you; but when you have got as far as you can go, there is no point at all. Just thus it is with Mr Burke's three hundred and fifty-six pages.[54]

Burke's meditations on the end of chivalry were mocked as 'a world of windmills, and his sorrows are, that there are no Quixotes to attack them'.[55] While Burke denied the existence of the rights of man depicted on what he called 'paltry and blurred sheets of paper', Paine insisted that such rights could be taken from the very origins of mankind itself, and their loss was due to 'upstart governments, thrusting themselves between, and presumptuously working to *un-make* man'.[56]

Pouring scorn on the defence of noble privilege and the rights of an established Church, Paine cast the decisions of the French in transatlantic context: it was 'by observing the ill effects' of such systems in Britain 'that America has been warned against it', and by experiencing such effects that the French have come to abolish such institutions, 'and, like America, have established UNIVERSAL RIGHTS OF CONSCIENCE, AND UNIVERSAL RIGHTS OF CITIZENSHIP'.[57] In an intriguing footnote Paine showed the consequences he thought would follow. As he observed, 'Manchester, Birmingham, and Sheffield, are the principal manufactures in England', thanks, he said, to their embrace of toleration for religious Dissenters: 'It was the only asylum that then offered, for the rest of Europe was worse.' Now, however, 'France and America bid all comers welcome . . . those manufactures are withdrawing, and arising in other places', and he cited directly the Milnes' enterprise at Passy. Paine foresaw a flight of Dissenters after recent failures in Britain to amend the test laws, and noted 'frequently appearing in the London Gazette, extracts from certain acts to prevent machines and persons . . . from going out of the country . . . but the remedy of force can never supply the remedy of reason'.[58]

For Paine all the revolutions of the age were linked, and he went forward into a brisk but erudite account of the intellectual antecedents of 1789. He poked fun at Burke's declamation of astonishment: 'As wise men are astonished at foolish things, and other people at wise ones, I know not on which ground to account for Mr Burke's astonishment; but certain it is, that he does not understand the French Revolution.' Beginning with Montesquieu, passing over Rousseau and Raynal, the physiocrats Quesnay and Turgot, and coming to the American Revolution, Paine illustrated the development of a 'school of Freedom', in which the dispatch of Franklin to Versailles played a laudable part, and Lafayette's adventures forged 'another link in the great chain'.[59]

In moving towards his conclusions, Paine contrasted the vigorous principles that had come into being through these connections with the devotion to hereditary privilege displayed by Burke. He quoted a German mercenary, taken prisoner during the American War, on the value of 'American' liberty, which was 'worth the people's fighting for . . . in my country, if the prince says, Eat straw, we eat straw'. In Burke's view Britain was 'wanting capacity to take care of itself, and that its liberties must be taken care of by a king . . . If England is sunk to this, it is preparing itself to eat straw.'[60] Reviewing the politics of the 1780s, he attributed much of Pitt's popularity to the perceived evils of the Fox–North coalition: an electorate offering its votes to Pitt in rage, and then sticking by him because it 'feels itself urged along to justify by continuance its first proceedings'. On the regency, Paine claimed, 'Never was . . . a nation more completely deceived.' Fox may have exhibited odiously hereditary claims, but Pitt's arguments 'went to establish an aristocracy over the Nation, and over the small representation it has in the House of Commons'.[61] In particular, the convolutions Parliament had gone through revealed what a hollow sham much of the structure of the supposed 'constitution' was: 'Among the curiosities . . . was that of making the Great Seal into a King; the affixing of which to an act, was to be royal authority. If, therefore, Royal Authority is a Great Seal, it consequently is in itself nothing; and a good constitution would be of infinitely more value to the Nation.'[62]

In his final pages Paine became unashamedly a revolutionary. Government 'is not, and from its nature cannot be, the property of any particular man or family . . . a nation has at all times an inherent indefeasible right to abolish any form of government it finds inconvenient, and establish such as accords with its interest, disposition, and happiness'.[63] In his closing paragraphs Paine prophesied that 'hereditary governments are verging to their decline' thanks to 'the enlightened state of mankind', and that a 'European Congress' might form, to 'promote the civilisation of Nations with each other', an event 'nearer in probability, than once were the Revolutions and Alliance of France and America'.[64]

So revolutionary were Paine's words that his first publisher, Joseph Johnson, took fright and abandoned the project, even as the unbound pages were lying in his warehouse. Paine himself, with a borrowed horse and cart, and £40 loaned by an old friend, had to transport the pages to another printer for binding. The work, thus delayed, came out at three shillings a copy on 13 March 1791, missing by three weeks the birthday of George Washington, to whom Paine had diplomatically dedicated it. By the end of the month it was into its second reprinting, and by the end of May its fifth, and an astounding fifty thousand copies had already been sold – many of them in Ireland, where the cause of liberty pressed even closer than in Britain.[65] Translated almost at once into French, Dutch and German, it was yet its English that attracted much attention, and condemnation. Paine had written in a forthright, plain style that clashed violently with contemporary notions of appropriate vocabulary for political discussions. It was, one knighted reader said, 'in defiance of grammar, as if syntax were an aristocratical invention', but also, he noted, done with 'natural eloquence' and a 'kind of specious jargon, well enough calculated to impose upon the vulgar'.[66] The vulgar, the common people, were exactly its intended target, and the fears of commentators that Paine might 'seduce his illiterate and unskilled' readers, of the kind to be 'easily duped to think seditiously', reflected a real alarm at his project.[67]

Even the most forthright among the British radical elite were taken aback. The Society for Constitutional Information voted Paine its thanks 'for his most masterly book', but only after heated debate, concern over the more inflammatory passages and misgivings over Paine's underlying message – that the ancient constitution they stood sworn to restore did not, in fact, exist. Paine stepped up the pressure on such groups, and on the government, with plans to print massive cheap editions of the book. The three-shilling printings had not attracted official condemnation, largely because of the social prejudices of the authorities – at that price they felt there was little risk of the work falling into the hands of the mob, instead of 'judicious readers', as the Attorney General later recalled.[68] Paine took potential heat off himself by decamping to Paris from late April to July, where he joined a forlorn attempt by his friends Brissot and Condorcet to prevent the National Assembly reinstating Louis XVI after his attempted escape. Paine himself narrowly escaped a grim fate at the hands of a revolutionary crowd shortly after the king's departure, as he found himself hatless, and thus without the obligatory tricolour cockade, at a moment when the least sign of suspicious conduct raised cries of '*aristocrate!*' Only his friends' cries that he was '*un Américain*' saved him from a beating, or worse.

Returning with his revolutionary enthusiasm undimmed, Paine heard of the rising political temperature in Britain. At Birmingham a mob subsidised by local notables had attacked the property of prosperous Dissenters, crying out for 'Church and King', and destroyed, along with several houses, the library and laboratory of Joseph Priestley. Meanwhile a government-subsidised biography of Paine, dragging him through assorted kinds of invented and embellished dirt, was put on the streets of the capital, and Paine thought it wise

to cancel plans for a trip to Ireland – not least, perhaps, because
vaunted English liberties counted for little to the authorities across
that stretch of water. Paine instead stayed with an old friend in
London, receiving visitors ranging from Whig politicians to Mary
Wollstonecraft, from Joseph Priestley to the French ambassador.
While enjoying this leisured existence, Paine was also hard at work
on the follow-up to his text. Part Two of *The Rights of Man* was an
even more explosive grenade thrown into the heart of a country
increasingly at odds with itself.

This text was even harder to get published than the first. Paine's
previous two publishers refused at first to be involved, and the third
bailed out in February 1792 when the full manuscript was revealed
to him. He went back to his previous publishers with a written
undertaking to be named as 'author and publisher', and thus legally
indemnifying them, and they finally agreed to take the risk.[69]
Pushed out in cheaper editions, Paine's work was at once a social and
a political challenge to the foundations of the Hanoverian order. It
took as its starting point once again America, where 'the rapid
progress . . . in every species of improvement' was taken as evidence
for the harmful effects of other systems of government.[70] Unlike the
previous part, this was set out explicitly as a political treatise, with
chapters 'Of Society and Civilisation', 'Of the Origins of the Present
Old Governments' and 'Of the Old and New Systems of Government'. Monarchies, aristocracies and all the nonsenses of a feudal
past were to be pushed away, and he was bold in his prescriptions for
a future society of welfare and peace. More than bold indeed –
alarmingly specific. Government was to be a republican representative democracy, which would thus do away with all the costly
contrivances of courts, and once again America was called on to justify this: 'I presume, that no man in his sober senses, will compare
the character of any of the kings of Europe with that of General
Washington. Yet, in France, and also in England, the expense of the
civil list only, for the support of one man, is eight times greater than
the whole expense of the federal government in America.'[71]

Paine gave an account, rebutting the claims of the virtues of
England's ancient 'constitution', of what it meant for a democratic
nation to create its own institutions. American procedures for creating the Articles of Confederation were recounted (glossing over the
difficulties), but the role of public opinion in summoning the 1787

Convention was lauded and the essentially democratic procedures of ratification described at length. All this was compared with the English notion that the rulers have, apparently, the right to decide how, and by whom, they will be chosen. Paine noted coolly that 'If we begin with William of Normandy, we find that the government of England was originally a tyranny', and that what passed now for a constitution was the accumulation of the 'exertion of the nation, at different periods, to abate that tyranny, and render it less intolerable'.[72] All this would pass away under a democratic system, which would also move Europe towards universal peace, and in so doing, create further prosperity and slash the burden of taxes on populations: 'Need we any other proof of [monarchies'] wretched management, than the excess of debts and taxes with which every nation groans, and the quarrels into which they have precipitated the world?'[73]

Paine filled the later pages of the text with his carefully worked-through plans to take the revenues squandered on war and excess, and devote them to funds for the education of all children, and the payment of pensions to the aged of the labouring classes. In justifying this by common humanity, he threw out a line calling on the crowned heads of Europe – and India – to ask themselves:

> Is it better that the lives of one hundred and forty thousand aged persons be rendered comfortable, or that a million a year of public money be expended on any one individual, and him often of the most worthless or insignificant character? Let reason and justice, let honour and humanity, let even hypocrisy, sycophancy and Mr Burke, let George, let Louis, Leopold, Frederic, Catherine, Cornwallis, or Tippoo Saib, answer the question.[74]

Further proposals followed – for allowances to newly-weds and new mothers, for decent funerals for the poor, for shelters for the homeless of great cities. Then Paine would pay off gradually the army and navy – as the wars of monarchies faded into the past – and use the money to cut taxes on goods of necessity. Paine capped his system with proposals for progressive taxation. One element would be land values, including 100 per cent taxation on estates over £23,000, a measure he viewed as essential to reduce the power of landed magnates, and encourage the division of estates otherwise bound up by primogeniture. A second, perhaps even more revolutionary proposal, was to tax holdings in the National Debt progressively, and use the income from that to write off the Debt itself over time – thus, eventually, freeing the taxpaying population from what was unquestionably its most arduous burden, and one that presented the spectacle of the poor being taxed to pay interest to the rich.[75]

Paine's last concrete proposals turned again, as with his mention of Cornwallis and Tipu, to the global scene. 'An alliance between England, France and America', once the former was revolutionised, could impose a naval disarmament of Europe, followed by an ending of Spanish tyranny in Latin America. This would provide a new, liberated market for goods to replace the despotic trade with India – a 'horrid scene . . . fit only to be told of Goths and Vandals, who, destitute of principles, robbed and tortured the world they were incapable of enjoying'. Then freedom would come to all Europe, where even now 'The insulted German and the enslaved Spaniard, the Russ and the Pole, are beginning to think. The present age will hereafter merit to be called the Age of Reason, and the present generation will appear to the future as the Adam of a new world.'[76]

Paine chose to end with a biological metaphor. In February as he wrote, most buds were hard and dormant, but if he should see one swelling with life, he would not take it as a mere freak individual, but as confirmation that all buds would follow suit in time. 'What pace the political summer may keep with the natural, no human foresight can determine. It is, however, not difficult to perceive that the spring is begun.'[77]

William Pitt shared Paine's optimism as the winter of 1791–2 drew to a close; though, inevitably, for rather different reasons. Continued French diplomatic paralysis had enabled Britain successfully to see off destabilising crises in the ongoing conflicts in Eastern Europe, and also to defy Spanish attempts to exclude British traders from the Pacific coast of America. The 'Nootka Sound Crisis', which began in 1789 with the seizure of Britons' ships and possessions in what is now British Columbia, had at points in 1790–1 seemed likely to lead to all-out war, and had forced a major and costly naval rearmament. Cool-headed negotiation had won from the Spaniards almost every concession the British wanted, helped by the fact that French revolutionary politicians resolutely refused to allow their king to support his Bourbon cousin.[78] Thus when Pitt delivered his ninth budget speech on 17 February 1792 he was able to report booming tax revenues from soaring global exports, international stability and rosy prospects. Several onerous taxes, among these a widely mocked charge on female servants, were abolished, the military budget was slashed by £200,000 and Pitt concluded that 'there never was a time in the history of this country, when, from the situation of Europe, we might more reasonably expect fifteen years of peace, than we may at the present moment'.[79]

At that very moment, even before Paine's explosive work reached the streets of the capital, a group that was soon to name itself the London Corresponding Society was debating in earnest a question of heavy import: 'Have we, who are Tradesmen, Shopkeepers, and Mechanics, any right to obtain a Parliamentary Reform?' Five nights' deliberation were required for them to decide that indeed they did have such a right, and as spring beckoned, what had begun as nine men meeting in the Bell tavern grew to dozens, then hundreds (and by the summer a claim of thousands). Paying a penny a week, for the costs of the correspondence they hoped to open with other groups around the country, they started a movement that Pitt's government would soon see as a genuine revolutionary threat.[80] While the London tradesmen had waited until 1792 to form an organisation, some of their provincial cousins had been even more forward. The same Sheffield cutlers who had complained in 1787 of their rights being 'invaded' by a 'greedy, blood-sucking, bone-scraping wolf' of an employer had taken up the message of 1789 to form their own Constitutional Society by 1791, and workers in Manchester and several other provincial cities were following suit.[81]

Food prices, as a result of poor harvests and the unsettled state of Europe, were high and showed no sign of diminishing. Outbreaks of violence, accompanied by cries of 'No King . . . No Corn Bill . . . No Taxes', had already taken place in mid-1791, and by March 1792 the Sheffield society claimed almost two thousand members.[82] They presented the spectre of a movement akin to that which had arisen in France since 1790: a network of clubs dedicated to revolutionary principles, united by a common ideology and pressing (in conservative eyes) for the overturning of all order. In France such clubs had grown from Parisian roots, ironically a defensive response by politically isolated radicals from the old Breton Club at the end of 1789.[83]

Forming a new Society of Friends of the Constitution, they met in the hall of a monastery near the National Assembly, from which they took their name. The 'Jacobins' spread to a network of hundreds of towns and cities within two years, and became a decisive force in the radicalisation of the French Revolution. The threat of 'English Jacobins', especially in the shadow of Paine's thunderous pronouncements, seemed very real indeed.

On 21 May 1792, a month after revolutionary France had pitched itself into war against Austria, Pitt's government issued a Royal Proclamation against 'wicked and seditious writings', targeting Paine directly. As Pitt explained in Parliament, *The Rights of Man* 'went to the destruction of monarchy and religion, and the total subversion of the established form of government'. His fellow minister Henry Dundas waved before the Commons a petition from Sheffield workers as proof that 'great bodies of men in large manufacturing towns' were preaching pernicious and subversive doctrines. The Deputy Adjutant-General of the Army was sent that summer to tour the provinces, and report on the threat and the military's capacity to head it off. He found the 'seditious doctrines of Paine' spread 'beyond my conception'; and noted from Sheffield in particular that the local radicals were corresponding both with other groups in their locality and nationwide.[84] Booksellers and bill-stickers were targeted under the terms of the Royal Proclamation, in an effort to stem the flood, but late in 1792 alarming reports continued to arrive. Benjamin Vaughan, appalled at the coarsening of the radical tradition, declared that *The Rights of Man* was now 'as much a Standard book in this Country as Robinson Crusoe and the Pilgrim's Progress'. Another old reformer, Christopher Wyvill, wrote to William Wilberforce in horror at events in County Durham in the north, where '"No King", "Liberty" and "Equality" have been written there upon the Market Cross', and protesting miners told a local dignitary, 'You have a great estate, General: we shall soon divide it among us.'[85]

Unlike in France, however, the state stood firm and, as the Birmingham 'Priestley Riots' of Bastille Day 1791 had already shown, was able to call on a strong popular groundswell of support against contaminating foreign ideas. With news from France of the fall of the monarchy, and in September of the horrible, and much-exaggerated, massacres in the prisons of Paris, Thomas Paine fled abroad to join the newly elected Convention of the French Republic,

and was put on trial in his absence for seditious libel. Throughout
the land that winter, processions and rallies burned him, and sometimes other figures such as Joseph Priestley, in effigy. Paine was
paraded beforehand on oxen, donkeys or carts, lashed with whips,
hung on huge fifty-foot gibbets, and in one case at least doused
with bull's blood in a very blatant mock execution. In printed 'last
speeches' he supposedly confessed his 'idleness, drunkenness,
debauchery, irreligion and inhumanity', while placards round his
neck denounced him as a 'sower of sedition and libeller of our happy
and enjoyed Constitution', meeting a 'merited fate'.[86] Propertied
opinion, while sponsoring such shows, also rallied behind a new
organisation founded by the magistrate John Reeves: the Association
for the Preservation of Liberty and Property Against Republicans
and Levellers. Gathering a membership that may have outnumbered
even the spreading Corresponding Societies, and with far more influence on public affairs, the association co-operated with government
in a witch-hunt, targeting public houses that offered premises to radical groups, booksellers and printers who sold 'seditious' material
and anyone else with radical connections who could plausibly be
prosecuted, as well as sponsoring a flood of 'anti-Jacobin' propaganda
materials.[87] When France declared war on Britain in the spring of
1793, this fever of reaction reached new heights, as the opening
of global war tipped British society still further from the casual
toleration of dissent and disorder that had marked the eighteenth
century. The example of 1789 would serve, over the decade to come,
to produce drastic inversions of that year's cardinal values – across the
British Empire, but also in Terror-struck France, and, remarkably, in
the United States of America.

# CONCLUSION

# 1789/1798

Amid fulminating political controversy, the *Gazette of the United States*, a staunchly Federalist newspaper, declared on 16 August 1798 that 'it is an undoubted truth that some of the Jacobin papers are under the direction of as GREAT LIARS as ever escaped the hands of Justice in England, Ireland or Scotland'.[1] Branding the 'Republican' (or sometimes 'Democratic-Republican') opposition in its own country with the language of French revolutionary contamination, and placing responsibility for its existence at the door of radical escapees from British counter-revolutionary repression, the *Gazette* summed up in a single sentence how the international networks of aspiration in 1789 had been soured by nearly a decade of conflict and calumny. One such exile, William Duane, was about to take over the reins of such a 'Jacobin' paper, the Philadelphia *Aurora*, under tragic and politically ominous circumstances.

On 11 September 1798 Benjamin Franklin Bache, grandson of the sage of the eighteenth century, died. Though the cause of his death was a sudden epidemic of yellow fever in his home city of Philadelphia, the wider circumstances of his last months illuminate starkly how far the United States, and the world, had moved in nine short years from the promises of 1789. Born in 1769, Bache had been his grandfather's protégé. As Franklin's daughter's eldest son, his presence as he grew to adulthood had eased his grandfather's pain over the long-standing alienation from his only son, who never accepted his father's breach with the British Crown. Franklin took Bache with him on his Parisian odyssey, sending him on for two years of a 'republican' education at boarding school in Geneva before bringing him back to Paris for further study in, among other things, the printing trade. Back in Philadelphia, Franklin had continued to support Bache's pursuit of a publishing career through initial set-backs, and bequeathed him the equipment of a print shop he had set up for him on his death in 1790. Though widely noted as an awkward and even cold figure, Bache repaid his jovial grandfather's attentions by becoming an avid partisan of the free press Franklin had cherished. Bache's newspaper, the *General Advertiser*, later renamed more inspiringly as the *Aurora*, initially set out with goals of enlightened public education, echoing his grandfather's preoccupations, but by the middle years of the decade was becoming one of the most strident voices in a vigorous new American public sphere.[2]

The Federalist–Antifederalist rivalry that had inflamed the drafting of the Constitution continued apace, with Washington's cabinet officers Hamilton and Jefferson (the latter seconded by Hamilton's former ally Madison) at the head of incipient 'parties'. By 1793 their bitter dispute over the Federalists' desire to remain staunchly neutral in the by now global war of all the European powers against France caused the President to rage that '*by god* he had rather be in his grave than in his present situation', especially considering the continual Antifederalist sniping about his 'wanting to be a king'.[3] Washington left office after two terms, with the 1796 election showing the knife-edge divide: John Adams was elected President as a Federalist with 71 electoral-college votes; Jefferson, his 'Republican' rival, became Vice-President, having secured 68.[4] With Jefferson's 'Democratic-Republicans' encouraging the formation of 'societies' that looked to their enemies very much like the corrupting Jacobin clubs of France, the politics of America, at least in the larger cities, seemed to hover on the brink of revolutionary dissolution.[5] Despite Washington's famous parting advice for the country to avoid 'the baneful effects of the spirit of party' and to reject 'the insidious wiles of foreign influence', through the later years of the 1790s the United States was ravaged by just such partisanship, excited by the continued, and ever more contrasting pulls of the British and French examples.[6] Benjamin Franklin Bache placed the *Aurora* firmly, and at times scurrilously, on the Republican, pro-French side.

In 1795 the US Senate had ratified the Jay Treaty with Britain. Following terms largely laid down by the arch-Federalist Alexander

Hamilton, this normalised transatlantic relations in the interests of the mercantile class, assured the United States of its rights over the Northwest Territories, and guaranteed compensation for the hundreds of British seizures of American ships trading with France since 1793. Republican opinion, however, felt that Britain's seaborne arrogance and alleged covert aid to the hostile Algonquian Indians deserved punishment, not palliation. James Madison had been campaigning for 'a direct system of commercial hostility with Great Britain', and there had even been moves to prepare the country's defences for war.[7] This great divide merely intensified in the aftermath of the treaty, which to the French was a sign of American pro-British partisanship. Where the British had seized over three hundred American ships in 1793–4, the French in 1795–6 took almost as many, often using privateers cruising close to the American coasts from Caribbean bases.

Attempts by the Adams government to negotiate a settlement in 1797 (against Hamilton's calls for immediate war) were thrown back in the Americans' faces by the corrupt leaders of a France sinking into post-revolutionary political decline. Confronting demands for huge bribes before discussions would even begin, and a vast loan to France as a more official precondition, the American diplomats returned home. Such behaviour by the new rulers of France, while remarkable, was not isolated. In the same year Prime Minister Pitt was in receipt of a proposal to ensure peace at the cost of £2 million in personal bribes to the French leadership.[8] Jefferson, Bache and the Republicans, however, suspecting pro-British Federalist plotting, demanded to see the American agents' report. The published report discreetly presented the names of the three Frenchmen who had sought bribes as X, Y and Z, and the 'XYZ Affair' became the precursor to real conflict.

A decade after acknowledging their massive debts to France, in blood and money, and formulating a constitution, in part at least, to facilitate repayment, the United States opened an undeclared 'quasi war' against their former ally on 7 July 1798, when Congress rescinded Franklin's 1778 treaty of friendship, paving the way to a naval offensive against French privateers. Only a week later, with rival Federalist and Republican militias reportedly on the streets, Congress passed the Sedition Act, one of the grievous domestic consequences of this turn to conflict. The key provision of this made it an offence

To write, print, utter or publish, or cause it to be done, or assist in it, any false, scandalous, and malicious writing against the government of the United States, or either House of Congress, or the President, with intent to defame, or bring either into contempt or disrepute, or to excite against either the hatred of the people of the United States, or to stir up sedition, or to excite unlawful combinations against the government, or to resist it, or to aid or encourage hostile designs of foreign nations.[9]

Note that the Republican Vice-President, Jefferson, was specifically excluded from the Act's protection. Only Republican protests in Congress had secured the concession that writings had to be 'false' to qualify as an offence – the original draft had been an even more direct assault on the protections of the First Amendment. As it was, sympathetic judges and aggressive officials gave little heed to the niceties of constitutionality in the rage of factional battle. It was after his arrest, and under looming prosecution for his many offences, that Bache stayed at his desk in Philadelphia, continuing to wage a campaign of furious denunciation of Adams's government until his untimely death.

Alongside the Sedition Act, Congress also passed three separate Alien Acts, restricting the rights of foreigners to be naturalised as Americans, and allowing citizens of hostile nations, and those merely suspected of antipathies 'dangerous to the peace and safety of the United States', to be deported on presidential authority. These reflected the traumatic sense among Federalists and wider American opinion that the devastating consequences of the French Revolution were reaching far too close to home. One such consequence, an event with its own tortured connections to the promise of 1789, was the ongoing slave revolution of Saint-Domingue, to be crowned a few years later with the creation of the world's first free republic of non-white former colonial subjects, Haiti.

Saint-Domingue had echoed the currents of the revolution in France, but, tormented by the additional issues of race and slavery, had descended into violence even faster than its motherland. Wealthy white planters and merchants, the *grands blancs*, had caballed to keep power out of the hands of both the less wealthy whites, or *petits blancs*, and the free African and mixed-race *gens de couleur*, some of whom were wealthy (and slave owners) in their own right. For the *grands blancs*, revolutionary liberation meant autonomy from France, and freedom to trade with other nations; for the *petits*, it meant inclusion in a voting democracy; for the *gens de couleur*, recognition of their wealth and significance outweighing their skin. By 1790–1 all three groups had begun sporadic armed conflict, and had put weapons into the hands of slaves to bolster their ranks. This suicidal indifference to the combination of armed slaves and a pervasive rhetoric of liberty and equality indicates how distorted the perceptions of a slave-holding society can become.[10] Slaves who, on this large island, outnumbered their masters twenty to one, and who had forged a complex culture of their own by blending French and African religious and political traditions, launched an uprising in August 1791.[11] The political aims of this were astonishingly moderate. At one point slave negotiators offered to settle for extensions of slaves' rights to cultivate their own gardens and have three days free from plantation labour a week (a demand they had frequently claimed had been conceded by royal orders in the late 1780s, and concealed from the slaves subsequently). Nonetheless, violence escalated unstoppably. Hundreds of plantations were burned to the ground, and stories of atrocities were legion. In the summer of 1793 conflict between local authorities and commissioners from the newly radical French Republic helped spur a slave army's assault on Cap Français, the main centre in the north of the colony and one of the largest cities in the Western hemisphere. As the population fled in panic, the city burned, in a spectacular catastrophe that sent shockwaves round the Americas. On their own authority the Republic's agents abolished slavery, a decision ratified in France early in 1794.

Opinion in the United States in particular viewed events in the Caribbean with horror – a horror all the more vivid for having been widely anticipated in both pro- and anti-slavery polemics of previous decades. Accounts of slave forces 'spurred on by the desire of plunder, carnage, and conflagration' filled the press from the first months of the fighting, accompanied by eyewitness reports, such as one in August 1793 that condemned the 'desolation' perpetrated 'because the offspring of ourang outangs strive to become men'. All the conditions of slavery were turned against the Africans to raise readers' horror to new heights. Africans were said to be able to live from sugar-cane sap alone, and a snatched drink from the growing plant 'makes them as fat and sleek as the best provisions'. Meanwhile, so inured were they to atrocity that even mass executions 'do not seem to intimidate them, as they ... meet their fate with the greatest unconcern'.[12] By the middle years of the decade a fear of revolutionary contamination, spread by 'French negroes' escaping the fighting (or setting out on a quest for new victims) convulsed the United States. In Charleston in 1797 at least two such men were executed for a supposed incendiary plot, and similar reports had occasioned alarm as far north as New York. With their fearful echoes of fantasies of a 'Black Spartacus', these responses to the Saint-Domingue revolution helped to suppress what little progress towards emancipation the post-independence abolitionist movement had made.

By the later 1790s Saint-Domingue was a problem not just for France and America, but for Britain's global empire. The threat of spreading slave revolution made it a priority target for military repression, and in 1796 the largest amphibious assault force Britain had ever dispatched crossed the Atlantic to attempt a conquest. Thirty thousand British troops were landed, over two-thirds of whom were struck down by epidemic diseases without seeing action. In the immensely complex politics of the island, with local whites, blacks and *gens de couleur* all maintaining rival armies, alongside French, Spanish and British forces, a Spartacus did emerge, in the form of François-Dominique Toussaint Louverture, former slave, ex-overseer, fighter initially for Spain, who switched sides to France in 1792, and saw off all comers thereafter. In 1798 Louverture was able to negotiate a withdrawal of the beleaguered and disease-ravaged British forces, as he was not long after to defeat French attempts at a similar reconquest.[13] So eager still were both the British and the Americans to gain access to trade with Saint-Domingue, despite the ravages of civil war a rich market and potential goldmine of commerce, that both powers found themselves courting the man who, on the face of it, posed the greatest threat to their systems of slave-based trade. In a further irony it would be the nation to whom Louverture continued to profess at least a nominal loyalty, France, that would soon trick him into captivity, exile and death. The ruler of France would then perform an unparalleled feat of ignominy, in reinstating formally abolished slavery in all of France's overseas domains.

In 1798 Louverture's eventual nemesis was already in the ascendant in France. The revolutionised nation had descended into the legendary torments of the Terror, pursued equally by the implacable hostilities of *émigré* aristocrats and diehard Catholic clergy, and the radicals' seemingly never-ending ability to detect plots and treason among their own ranks. The men of 1789 passed away in succession. Mirabeau died of natural causes in 1791 (but shortly after was exposed as a treacherous double-dealer); Lafayette fled to captivity in Austrian hands in 1792, after failing to avert the fall of the monarchy; Brissot and all his many political associates, who had brewed the war, succumbed to the suspicion that they had plotted the people's downfall by so doing, and were guillotined in 1793. New generations of political activists had time to rise and fall in the frenzied months that followed, and the death of the Terror's high priest Robespierre in July 1794, while it halted the mass slaughter, scarcely interrupted the broader factional contest.[14] For two years there was a desperate effort to achieve a stable middle ground, with a new constitution created in 1795 presenting France with a bicameral legislature and a five-man Executive Directory – to avoid the tyrannies of monarchism or mob rule. But the disruptive forces pressing on it were too great, and by 1797 the 'moderates' of the Directory were reduced to illegal annulments of election results and sweeps of suspects to keep extremists from seizing power. After a second round of similar actions in 1798, Madame de Staël, daughter of Necker and former proposed wife of William Pitt, who had found a more exhilarating role as *salon* hostess in the turmoils of France, wrote caustically: 'Under the current circumstances, the balance of powers in our constitution is upheld by an annual revolution, alternating between royalists and terrorists. One year we kill the former, one year we deport the latter.'[15]

Amid such chaos the Republic was increasingly kept afloat by its military victories, for the one area where the Terror represented an unabashed triumph was in the organisation and equipping of massive armies. Internal counter-revolutionary rebellion was crushed by the beginning of 1794, while Spain, Prussia and the Netherlands were brought forcibly to terms by 1795, the latter including its transformation into the 'Batavian Republic' on the French model. This expansionist rush was driven to new heights in 1796 as the young general Napoléon Bonaparte continued a meteoric rise by ravaging northern Italy, driving the might of Austrian arms to capitulation and producing an epoch-making forced peace with the arch-counter-revolutionary empire in 1797. Bonaparte, of course, had a truly grandiose sense of his own significance, and while retained initially as leader of a projected invasion of Britain, he persuaded the Directory to equip a more far-flung expedition, which sailed Egypt on 19 May 1798, barely a week after another of France's accelerating succession of *coups d'état* against the electorate.

Egypt called to Bonaparte's sense of himself not only as a military genius and man of destiny – recreating the conquests of Alexander and Caesar – but to his self-image as a patron of science and the arts. While the Terror had assailed members of the former scientific elite, guillotining, for example, the chemist Lavoisier and driving Condorcet, counterpart of the indefatigable Joseph Banks, to suicide in prison, the Directory had tried to retrieve the significance of learning from something that looked very much like the hoofs of a swinish multitude. With Bonaparte's expedition (and with his express encouragement) sailed dozens of scholars, who on their arrival formed the Institut de l'Égypte, paralleling the Institut de France, newly formed as an umbrella academy of sciences in Paris. Occupying a palace on the outskirts of Cairo, these savants were soon producing two newspapers detailing their findings, and the advance of Enlightenment in Egypt generally. So voluminous would their conclusions be that their *Description of Egypt* would take a decade to begin publication, and another twenty years to complete, including illustrations in mammoth tomes a metre high.[16]

While the Institut de l'Égypte pursued the most expansive visions of the imperial Enlightenment, seeming to want to embrace a total knowledge of the Egyptian past and simultaneously to envision a new modernity to be created out of European contact, the even wider global political aspirations of Bonaparte's venture were shattered almost before they began. By the time his scholars took up residence in their palace, Bonaparte's links with France had been brutally severed. At the battle of the Nile a British fleet under the rising star Horatio Nelson had audaciously surrounded and effectively annihilated the naval force that had escorted the French army across the Mediterranean. Bonaparte abandoned his army the following year, returned to Paris and began his ascent towards total power with a *coup d'état* on 9 November 1799 (fomented by, though soon eclipsing, the man whose writings had sparked much of the fervour of 1789, Sieyès). Though Bonaparte's troops had rampaged into the Holy Land in the intervening months, they had been deprived of new equipment and reinforcements, and their greatest goal of all, to strike at the linchpin of British global power in India, was also rendered futile by events on the subcontinent itself.

Although British policy in India had languished somewhat with the departure of the forthright Cornwallis in 1793, another remarkable figure arrived in early 1798, set upon a further development of Cornwallis's goal of imperial consolidation. Richard Wellesley, Earl of Mornington, had risen as a contemporary, friend and ally of William Pitt, and seems like him to have developed through the mid-1790s an increasingly expansive sense of the potential for British power. After four years' service in London on the Board of Control of the East India Company, he sailed for Calcutta already forming plans to break French influence in southern India. There extensive networks of French mercenaries, traders and other agents had compensated for the impotence of 'official' France by making themselves indispensable, for example to the otherwise ineffectual forces of the Nizam of Hyderabad and, more troublingly still, as part of an ongoing French relationship with Tipu Sultan of Mysore. The latter, smarting understandably from his humiliating defeat by Cornwallis, had nurtured French connections to the extent of joining a Jacobin club formed among the French traders of his capital, and supposedly being greeted by them as 'Citizen Tippoo Sultan'. This horrifying evidence of the contaminating potential of French ideas was widely circulated by the British, and was added to in early 1798 by word that the French Directory was now seeking a renewed alliance with Tipu, as a second strand in its assault on Britain in the East.

With a force and self-assurance even greater than that shown by Cornwallis, Wellesley mobilised British power to snuff out this threat once and for all. Hyderabad was obliged to disperse its French troops, and a campaign into the next year ended with Tipu's defiant death on the ramparts of his besieged fortress-capital, Seringapatam. Appointed governor of the captured city, after service in the conquering army, was Wellesley's brother Arthur, who here, and in later years of service in new wars of conquest across central India, learned the many valuable lessons that would later make him the 'Iron Duke', the man who finally extinguished Napoleon's threat to the monarchic order of Europe.

If the campaigns of this year marked an imperial prelude to Wellington's future glory, his brother's predecessor Cornwallis still had another chapter to write in his career of imperial and revolutionary confrontations. After the opening of war with France in 1793, the anti-Jacobin hysteria of British propertied opinion had taken on an even darker hue. Against the background of bloody and alarmingly unsuccessful warfare by expeditionary forces in Flanders, the pursuit of the Corresponding Societies led in May 1794 (as the French Terror was reaching its peak) to arrests of its leading members, and the passage of an Act of Parliament 'To Empower His Majesty to Secure and Detain such Persons as His Majesty shall Suspect are Conspiring against His Person and Government'. This, the suspension of habeas corpus and licensing of detention without trial, was explicitly justified in the wording of the Act by the existence of 'a traitorous and detestable Conspiracy . . . for subverting the existing Laws and Constitution, and for introducing the System of Anarchy and Confusion which has so fatally prevailed in *France*'.[17] When Whig opposition members tried to protest that even the government admitted the 'ostensible object' of the radicals was 'parliamentary reform', a minister retorted that it was 'perfectly puerile to impute to them innocent intentions' and their real goal was 'plain as the sun . . . the wildest anarchy'.[18] With reports of hundreds of arrest warrants awaiting execution, the government pressed ahead with charges of high treason against three of the London Corresponding Society's leaders in the autumn of 1794.

With deepest irony, an Old Bailey jury, convinced in part by arguments that the medieval language of treason did not apply to the actions of the reformers – many of whom, ostensibly at least, went little further than mainstream Whigs had done in the early 1780s – struck a blow for British liberty with acquittals. Arguably, martyrdom would have served the radical cause better: it would certainly have given popular anger a sharper focus when the following years, times of wartime hardship verging on famine, brought renewed assaults on the rights of 'freeborn Englishmen' to oppose their government. Revived radical activity in late 1795 was responded to with a new legislative offensive, in the Seditious Meetings and Treasonable Practices Acts. These banned radical gatherings and threatened transportation for a wide range of disrespectful political utterances. Such legislation merely reinforced the continuing witch-hunt of radicals, led by zealous local magistrates and the members of the Association for the Preservation of Liberty and Property, and accompanied by a determined and remarkably ruthless use of informers and *agents provocateurs* by the government against known activists.

For dozens of radicals the unhealthy atmosphere of Britain led them to flee for America, and many became embroiled in the more extreme end of 'Democratic-Republican' activism, among them William Duane, Benjamin Bache's partner and successor.[19] Duane himself was yet another living example of the imperial entanglements of the age. Born in upstate New York but educated in Ireland, he began his career as a journalist there before taking his trade to Calcutta in the 1780s, where he needled the authorities to the extent that they deported him and confiscated his property. Vain attempts at redress accompanied by further journalism made London too hot for him, and he sailed for Philadelphia in 1795. Others of established fame had already departed. Joseph Priestley, never comfortable in his homeland after the 1791 riots, left in early 1794, to be welcomed to New York with an address from the city's teachers, among others, hoping that he would 'find in this land of virtuous simplicity a happy recess from the intriguing politics and vitiating refinements of the European world'.[20] For those with neither the resources nor the inclination to flee, the effect of this extended period of struggle was increasingly to make radical activism a matter of underground conspiracy, and to shift the emphasis thus from peaceful means towards the very insurrections the government and its propertied supporters feared.

The greatest dread of the British government focused on Ireland, and when in 1797 there were traumatic mutinies in the Royal Navy, the reported shadowy involvement of an organisation known as the United Irishmen helped generate a brutal response to the more republican assertions of some sailors. The United Irishmen had existed throughout the decade, founded among Dublin intellectuals initially as a focus for Catholic–Protestant political reconciliation, quickly taking on democratic overtones, and then sliding ever faster, in the face of betrayals, persecution and exile, towards schemes for a French-led liberating invasion of Ireland. By 1796 Theobald Wolfe Tone, a key figure in the surviving scattered leadership of the United Irishmen, had been granted a French military commission, and in that year and the next was involved in abortive plans to land armies on the vulnerable flank of imperial Britain. Despite the United Irishmen's avowed non-sectarian goals, their plots merely redoubled tensions in an arena already riven by sectarian paramilitary violence, with Catholic 'Defenders' at odds with a Protestant 'Orange Order' founded in 1795. The 1796 invasion scare in particular, with a French fleet hovering off Bantry Bay, and only the weather preventing a landing in force, brought matters to a new pitch of repressive violence. The 1797 Insurrection Act gave sweeping powers to suppress unrest and made participation in oath-bound societies, as most 'secret' and radical organisations were, a capital offence in itself. Hundreds were arrested, and magistrates and troops did not hesitate to go beyond even the wide bounds of these laws, burning the houses of suspected radicals. By early 1798 there were reports that some communities were fleeing into their fields at night for fear of being massacred as they slept.[21]

Facing the real prospect of total destruction, and with some local cohorts already breaking out into spontaneous uprisings, the leadership of the United Irishmen committed itself to revolutionary insurrection in late May 1798. Riddled with informers, much of the organisation fell prey to immediate government assaults, while those areas that did flare into rebellion saw savage fighting and atrocities on both sides. Rebels shot loyalist prisoners by the dozen at Vinegar Hill, at Scullabogue Barn up to a hundred were piked and burned to death, while on Wexford Bridge individual prisoners were piked from front and rear and hoisted off their feet still writhing in a grotesque parody of crucifixion.[22] These killings often came in the panicked aftermath of nearby defeats, and the government response was a far wider campaign of indiscriminate brutality. Tens of thousands of troops were deployed, both regulars and local militias, the latter often the most savage in practice. Surrendered rebels were regularly shot *en masse*. The pillage and arson of whole communities, rapes and outright massacres reflected a revolutionary crisis exacerbated by religious fanaticisms. Reporting rebel 'outrages', the British press claimed that the Catholic peasants had taken the oath 'By the blessed Virgin Mary, that I will burn, destroy and murder all heretics, up to my knees in blood. So help me God.'[23] This is the same attitude to Catholic fanaticism displayed by the French republican soldiers who had burned and slaughtered their way across the fields of the counter-revolutionary Vendée region of western France in

1793–4. These French republicans now landed a token force of troops in support of the Catholic Irish in late 1798, prolonging the fight for several more months and producing more massacres as all the fears of the ruling Protestant Ascendancy were given yet more proof of their reality. As many as thirty thousand may have died in what was often no more than uncontrolled savagery, licensed by religious bigotry and a quasi-racial contempt for the priest-ridden peasantry.

Over all this presided Lord Cornwallis, who had been appointed Viceroy and Commander-in-Chief in Ireland as the rebellion broke out. The evident sectarianism of sentiments on both sides horrified him, and he came to believe that Catholic emancipation, coupled with the abolition of the independent Protestant-dominated Irish Parliament, was the way to a lasting settlement. His influence brought clemency to the longer-term repression, though hundreds were executed and hundreds more sentenced to deportation. Many of these latter were warehoused in the former New Geneva settlement, whose failure had sent its exiles via Bowood to revolutionary Paris.[24] Cornwallis saw out the situation in Ireland until its sectarian parliament was indeed abolished three years later, but left his post when emancipation failed to follow (he would do one last sterling service, helping to negotiate a short-lived peace with Bonaparte's France in 1802).[25] Ireland was now to be worse off than ever for the next thirty years, living under continued religious discrimination and newly imposed direct colonial rule disguised as 'Union' with Great Britain.

Our whirlwind tour of events in 1798 brings us, then, to some starkly negative conclusions. It seems that the darker side of all the turmoils of 1789 is the one that has triumphed. Antifederalist fears of American despotism, anti-French alarms at universal anarchy, revolutionary alarms at the rise of military strongmen, radical alarms at the unscrupulous power of the establishment to crush 'English liberty' in the name of order – all can find their justification. Slavery remains, and its hold is even tightened by the terror of revolutionary emancipation; imperialism grows apace, with India now 'British' beyond any real prospect of reversal. Even in the intellectual realm the century of Enlightenment ends on a gloomy note. It was in 1798 that Thomas Malthus produced his *Essay on the Principle of*

*Population*, refuting the easy optimism of the philosophers of progress with a starkly material vision of populations condemned to outgrow their food supplies if they cannot master their procreative urges; and war, famine and disaster as the natural consequence of such profligacy. Where Adam Smith had discoursed on *The Wealth of Nations* in the year of the Declaration of Independence, and Condorcet had sketched his *Historical Picture of the Progress of the Human Mind* even under the threat of the guillotine, Malthus now licensed a view of the inevitability of suffering and relapse that would be taken to justify starvation wages in industrial Manchester, and real starvation in periodic Indian famines. Little wonder that Malthus is widely (though not quite accurately) credited with drawing upon economics the label of the 'Dismal Science'.[26]

Indisputably, the changes brought to the world by 1789 were not the ones that the most eager advocates of international co-operation for revolutionary renewal had wished for. The United States of America, 'conceived in liberty, and dedicated to the proposition that all men are created equal', as a great man later put it, saw each of its first presidents launch their own war. Washington's was against the Algonquians; Adams's, as we have just seen, against the former partner in liberation, the French. Jefferson, who brought the Republicans to power in 1800, ending the Federalist era and repealing the Alien and Sedition Acts, sent the US Navy 'to the shores of Tripoli' against the Barbary pirates who hindered trade so much. His successor James Madison, last of the constitutional architects to reach the highest office, took the process full circle. His War of 1812 saw naval triumphs against Britain, but also a futile invasion of Canada, and the burning in reprisal of the new capital, Washington, DC. Acquisition of a new national anthem, amid defiance of 'the rockets' red glare', was probably little compensation to the shell-shocked inhabitants. The final elimination of British influence with the Algonquian peoples and further consolidation of American power around the lower Mississippi were more concrete gains, however. Throughout this time, and into the decades beyond, the expansion of the United States across 'the frontier' westwards brought new lands under the yoke of slavery, at the cost of continual warfare against Indian populations.

The French legacy of 1789, meanwhile, was of bitter conflict, of a nation so ravaged by civil war that only a military dictator could bring a semblance of peace, and only then at the cost of a further generation of wars bred of unscrupulous conquest and megalomaniac ambition. Nonetheless, neither the Napoleonic Empire nor the restored monarchy that, from 1815, tried to turn back the clock could extinguish the commitment to individual rights and civic equality that the Revolution had engendered. The persistent clashes of republicans, Bonapartists and several stripes of monarchist sent France reeling from one upheaval to another across the following decades, but each shift was a step closer to a genuine nation of rights-bearing citizenship, achieved (for men at least) in the 1870s with the Third Republic.

France, meanwhile, never abandoned the fight that had brought it to the straits of 1789 in the first place – to contest global dominance with the British Empire. On that score the years after 1789 had been its lowest ebb, and while French armies rampaged across Europe, laying claim to territories and client states that the other powers would never allow to endure, British forces pursued a far more successful policy of aggrandisement elsewhere. The history of British power in South Africa began with the seizure of the Cape Colony from the French-subjugated Dutch. Taking Malta in the course of thwarting Bonaparte in Egypt began a 150-year history of control in the central Mediterranean, while possession of the Ionian Islands (and a long military partnership with Sicily and Naples) boosted classical allusions, making the British feel even more like the Romans, as is visible, for example, in the 'Regency' styles of the 1810s. Expulsion of the French from Egypt brought renewed influence in the Levant, while temporary seizure of the Dutch East Indies paved the way to the imperial significance of Singapore and consolidated trade links between India and China.

When France returned to the imperial fray, beginning with its invasion of Algiers in 1830, it was always running to catch up, missing out, in some cases by months, on putting legal claims on vast swaths of Australia and New Zealand, and settling for Tahiti; ultimately fighting its way into Indochina, and across the Sahara, sometimes as if only to make the point that there were regions of the world where the tricolour could fly instead of the Union Flag. France had, at least, abolished slavery, for a second time, after another of its revolutions in 1848. But there, as so often, it was behind Britain, which had finally ended the practice, a thorough anachronism in an industrialising world, in the 1830s. In decades to come, however, neither country would shrink from forms of colonial indentured labour that were distinct from slavery in little more than name. Imperialism, inevitably, though it seemed indispensable to great-power status in the nineteenth century, continued to be an uneasy bedfellow of a revolutionary claim to equal rights.

What, then, of Britain, the nation that did not pursue a revolutionary solution to its problems in 1789? Perhaps the truth is that, quietly, and not a little ruthlessly, in fact it did. Britain in the 1780s had been enduring a crisis, not of the material rigour of that afflicting France, or the essential challenge of identity facing the United States, but a crisis of purpose nonetheless. The American War had riven the political class, while the ability of the Fox–North coalition seemingly to abandon the principles behind that rift on scenting power merely compounded the offence. Merchants and manufacturers were at odds over the direction of the economy, defeating Pitt's plan to bring more justice to Ireland, and shattering their own nascent organisations over the 1786 treaty with France. An aristocratic political culture confronted the gaps in its own ideology of the 'Revolution Settlement' in the face of a king's madness, and party-political rivalries reached new heights of acrimony. While Major Cartwright celebrated the centenary of 1689 with his new building, and hoped to take the country back to older times of Anglo-Saxon virtue, his Revolution Mill was instead the sign of a whole new direction for society.

The Industrial Revolution is too trite an historical cliché merely to invoke as if 1789 were its culmination. A full accounting would have to take in decades of experiments with hand- and water-powered machines, go back further to the first blast furnaces at Coalbrookdale and run forwards to the railway age of the 1830s. But as we have clearly shown, the cotton industry, with its global repercussions, took a startling leap forward at this pivotal point, and would carry British manufacturing to global export dominance (assisted by the blockades of war) in the next generation. The paradox of the revolution that British affairs underwent around 1789 is that, while one pillar of ascending greatness rested on the power of industry and the mercantile middle classes, the other became cemented into a new vision of aristocratic imperial duty, a decisive step away from the 'trade' that had formerly dominated imperial enterprises.

British colonialism by the 1780s was synonymous, even to the political class, with grasping greed and ill-gotten gains: the persecution of Warren Hastings, who personally was the very opposite of the upstart self-enriching 'nabob', revealed the power of such hostile imagery at work. When this is coupled with the shameful knowledge, increasingly insisted upon by abolitionists, of the tyrannies of slavery, and with recollections of the futile efforts to suppress what many had seen as justified grievances of the American colonists, it might appear to contemporaries that little of moral worth emerged from the quest for power abroad. The shadow of the French Revolution changed all that. Well might radicals mock Burke and his rants against the 'swinish multitude', and well might self-pitying French noble exiles turn out to be unwelcome guests after a few years (so much so that Britain gladly dumped several thousand on the coast of Brittany in 1795, an invading army doomed to surrender and mass execution). Still, the fight against the Revolution, in the demonic coloration that Burke, the *émigrés* and supporters of hierarchy and subordination gave it, was a true crusade.

Some aspects of this crusade did little more than ring the changes on past propaganda – all-purpose praise of 'English liberty' worked as well against Jacobin or Bonapartist tyranny as it had for a century against 'popery'. But in its widest global manifestations the emergence of a new sense of Britain's place in the world was a conscious challenge to the messages of both the French and the American revolutions. The rising tide of British imperial dominance was a specifically aristocratic one, and it was on that very aristocratic nature that its assertion of moral superiority, and guardianship of liberty, were pinned. A politician such as William Pitt, a general such as Cornwallis, almost freakish in his personal probity in the 1780s, became a forerunner of a new sense of the obligations of power, to which younger contemporaries such as the Wellesley brothers responded. It was Charles James Fox – who lived on, in debt and opposition, until dying as a member of the short-lived and ironically named 'Ministry of All the Talents' in 1806 – who had become, in his sympathy for French radicals and his personal profligacy, an anachronism in the new century. A quarter-century of warfare and imperial expansion required of the British aristocracy and gentry a far higher toll of commitment (and loss) than previous generations had borne. While the wealthy were as much inclined to private debauchery as they had ever been, with the set around the Prince of Wales, regent from 1811, never advancing much beyond Jefferson's caustic judgement of 1789, in public life a much higher tone began to prevail. Willingness, for example, to enforce the post-1807 ban on transatlantic slave shipments with a naval patrol, at grievous cost in lives lost to sickness and with no demonstrable economic gain, marked a conception of global power as a moral responsibility.[27]

This is not to say that the eye of history must look favourably on this transformation, though eighteenth-century aristocratic ways were so squalid that almost any improvement is to be welcomed. British *noblesse oblige* did, after all, contribute immeasurably to the restoration of assorted absolute monarchs, including a number of frank reactionaries, in post-Napoleonic Europe; and ruling Indians for their own good could be almost indistinguishable from exploiting them for gain, especially as the essentially commercial ends of the East India Company continued to prevail into the 1850s. Disinterested rule also required an even firmer sense than before that the rulers were there by right, and the ruled due no more than their position indicated. If this was pre-eminently the case in the empire, the effects of such views were felt at home, too. The Duke of Wellington, as Prime Minister in 1829, could use his massive moral authority to drive through, at long last, the civil emancipation of Roman Catholics as a matter of justice (as the Test and Corporation Acts against Dissenters had been ended the previous year), but he let his government fall the next year rather than contemplate reforming the franchise to grant the upstart middle classes a proportionate political voice. Unquestionably, however, the transformation in British imperialism that followed 1789 was globally significant.

But in the very last analysis, Britain, throughout the modern era, remained the exception it had been before 1789. It was prized then by radicals on both sides of the Atlantic for its astonishing liberties, in an age of absolutism where even the demi-gods of the Enlightenment looked to 'despots' like Frederick the Great and Joseph II to impose their schemes of improvement. The shift of emphasis at this epoch, from Britain as tempestuous home of historic liberties to Britain as the heart of a fundamentally conservative vision of individual responsibility, maintained the island's tradition of swimming against the tide of Europe – and, from now on, America too. The process of constitution-making that in 1789 the United States brought to a conclusion, and the French so optimistically began, was startling in its novelty then, but became, over the course of two centuries of struggle, the only acceptable way to found the rights of citizens. Written constitutions, with liberal guarantees of rights (to greater or lesser degrees), spread like measles across Europe and the post-colonial states of Latin America from the 1820s onwards. There were flaring outbursts, sometimes accompanied by revolutionary violence, sometimes by just the threat of upheaval, in the 1830s and 1840s. By the 1860s, no other logical method of proceeding could be seen, even when creating new nations, such as Italy, out of the crumbling ruins of Habsburg and Bourbon absolutism. Even the German Empire, forged by the arch-conservative Otto von Bismarck at the point of Prussian bayonets in 1871, yielded to the spirit of the age in having a constitution, a national assembly and manhood suffrage. Tsarist Russia, in the aftermath of revolutionary unrest in 1905, issued its own written constitution or 'Fundamental Laws' in 1906, including basic human rights, even if one such law codified the autocratic power of the Tsar to hold 'The initiative in all branches of legislation . . . without his approval no law can come into existence'.[28] To go to a further extreme, even Stalin, at the height of his own Terror in 1936, bestowed on the Soviet Union a written constitution replete with the formal guarantees of liberal citizenship: Article 125 was specific, rights 'guaranteed by law' included 'freedom of speech; freedom of the press; freedom of assembly, including the holding of mass meetings; freedom of street processions and demonstrations'.[29]

As this example proves, written constitutions and declarations of rights can be mere pieces of paper, but it is the quest to ensure that they are not that has defined the modern age. Even Britain has been dragged, yelling and cursing sometimes, in the same direction. In 1948, following the work of, among others, an American, a Frenchman and an English-speaking Canadian from Francophone Montréal, the UN Universal Declaration of Human Rights was born.[30] In signing up to this, Britain finally entered the universe of 1789. The European Convention on Human Rights, signed in 1950, further bound the formerly unwritten codes of British constitutionality into an international language of rights, even if it took until 1998 for the Human Rights Act to cement this connection fully.[31] Sixteen eighty-nine, 1789, 1798, 1998 – what was begun in Britain,

with the Bill of Rights and its fears of 'cruel and unusual punishments', returns there in the end. One Briton who welcomed
revolution in 1789, Jeremy Bentham, nonetheless famously proclaimed talk of 'natural and imprescriptible rights' as 'nonsense upon
stilts'.[32] There are many, on both sides of the Atlantic and further
afield, who have shared, and continue to share, that view. But it is
upon such nonsense, and notwithstanding its abuse, that the functioning of political modernity has been erected. We may hotly debate
the impact of rights-talk on crime and social dysfunction, and argue
ferociously about its applicability in war and other forms of conflict,
but such fury of argument merely proves that we are still, fundamentally, in the world of 1789.

# NOTES

### Introduction

1. Colin Jones, *The Great Nation: France from Louis XIV to Napoleon*, London: Allen Lane, 2002, p. 404.
2. John Keane, *Tom Paine: A Political Life*, London: Bloomsbury, 1995, p. 276.
3. Ibid., p. 275.
4. Ibid., p. 276.

### 1: 'He snatched lightning from the heavens': Benjamin Franklin, the Enlightenment and France's crisis of the 1780s

1. John Ferling, *A Leap in the Dark: The Struggle to Create the American Republic*, Oxford: Oxford University Press, 2003, p. 281.
2. Walter Isaacson, *Benjamin Franklin: An American Life*, New York: Simon & Schuster, 2003, p. 157.
3. James Van Horn Melton, *The Rise of the Public in Enlightenment Europe*, Cambridge: Cambridge University Press, 2001, pp. 240–1.
4. Thomas Munck, *The Enlightenment: A Comparative Social History, 1721–1794*, London: Arnold, 2000, pp. 106–8.
5. Ibid., pp. 109–11.
6. Isaacson, *Benjamin Franklin*, pp. 96, 100.
7. Ibid., p. 105.
8. Ibid., pp. 170–4.
9. Ibid., pp. 264–5.
10. Ibid., pp. 158–62.
11. Ibid., pp. 299–300, 305–7.
12. Ibid., pp. 145, chapters 13–15.
13. See Ruth Ralston, 'Franklin and Louis XVI: A Niderviller Group', *The Metropolitan Museum of Art Bulletin*, 20, 11, 1925, pp. 271–3.
14. Michael Kwass, *Privilege and the Politics of Taxation in Eighteenth-Century France: Liberté, Égalité, Fiscalité*, Cambridge: Cambridge University Press, 2000.
15. Jones, *Great Nation*, p. 332.
16. Colin Jones, *The Longman Companion to the French Revolution*, London: Longman, 1988, p. 230.
17. Jones, *Great Nation*, pp. 294–5.
18. John Hardman, *French Politics, 1774–1789: From the Accession of Louis XVI to the Bastille*, London: Longman, 1995, p. 73.
19. Ibid., p. 153.
20. Ibid., p. 152.

21. *Mémoires secrets*, vol. 34, 1787, pp. 132–3.
22. Ibid., p. 166.
23. Jones, *Great Nation*, p. 382.
24. Peter M. Jones, *Reform and Revolution in France: The Politics of Transition, 1774–1791*, Cambridge: Cambridge University Press, 1995, pp. 115–16.
25. John Hardman, *The French Revolution Sourcebook*, London: Arnold, 1999, p. 39.
26. Ibid., p. 41.
27. Hardman, *French Politics*, pp. 80–1.
28. Ibid., p. 83.

## 2: 'The best model the world has ever produced': Governing America and Britain in the traumatic 1780s

1. Stanley Elkins and Eric McKitrick, *The Age of Federalism: The Early American Republic, 1788–1800*, New York: Oxford University Press, 1993, pp. 80–1.
2. Ibid., pp. 94–9.
3. Calvin H. Johnson, *Righteous Anger at the Wicked States: The Meaning of the Founders' Constitution*, Cambridge: Cambridge University Press, 2005, pp. 1–2.
4. Ibid., pp. 1–17; Catherine Drinker Bowen, *Miracle at Philadelphia: The Story of the Constitutional Convention, May to September 1787*, Boston: Little, Brown, 1986 [first published 1966], pp. 4–5.
5. Ibid., pp. 9–10.
6. Johnson, *Righteous Anger*, pp. 16, 22–3.
7. Elkins and McKitrick, *Age of Federalism*, p. 43.
8. Merrill Jensen, *The New Nation: A History of the United States during the Confederation, 1781–1789*, New York: Vintage Books, 1965 [first published 1950], p. 310.
9. Ferling, *Leap in the Dark*, p. 279.
10. Francis Jennings, *The Creation of America, Through Revolution to Empire*, Cambridge: Cambridge University Press, 2000, pp. 299–300.
11. Jensen, *New Nation*, pp. 313ff. on paper money and debt in general.
12. Ibid., p. 310.
13. See the account at <http://www.calliope.org/shays/shays2.html>, accessed on 3 August 2006.
14. Bowen, *Miracle*, p. 45.
15. Ibid., p. 55.
16. Charles Secondat, baron de Montesquieu, *The Spirit of the Laws*, Book XI, chapter 6, p. 160 of Hafner Library of Classics edn.: New York, 1949.
17. Ibid., pp. 161–2.
18. Bowen, *Miracle*, pp. 60–1.
19. J.C.D. Clark, *The Language of Liberty, 1660–1832: Political Discourse and Social Dynamics in the Anglo-American World*, Cambridge: Cambridge University Press, 1994, pp. 130–1.
20. Bowen, *Miracle*, pp. 126–7.
21. Ibid., p. 140.
22. Ibid., pp. 82–3.
23. Ibid., pp. 100–1.
24. Ibid., p. 108.
25. Ibid., pp. 112–13.
26. Wilfred Prest, *Albion Ascendant: English History 1660–1815*, Oxford: Oxford University Press, 1998, p. 214.
27. Clark, *Language of Liberty*, p. 45.
28. Paul Langford, *A Polite and Commercial People: England 1727–1783*, Oxford: Oxford University Press, 1992, p. 539.

29. Ibid., p. 543.
30. Prest, *Albion Ascendant*, pp. 215–16.
31. Albert Goodwin, *The Friends of Liberty: The English Democratic Movement in the Age of the French Revolution*, London: Hutchinson, 1979, p. 62.
32. Langford, *Polite and Commercial People*, p. 548.
33. Christopher Hibbert, *George III: A Personal History*, London: Penguin, 1999, p. 217.
34. Prest, *Albion Ascendant*, p. 209.
35. Hibbert, *George III*, pp. 220–4.
36. Prest, *Albion Ascendant*, p. 217.
37. Edmond Dziembowski, 'The English Political Model in Eighteenth-Century France', *Historical Research*, 74, 2001, pp. 151–71; p. 168.
38. See Langford, *Polite and Commercial People*, pp. 644–5.
39. Ibid., p. 646.
40. Roy Porter, *English Society in the Eighteenth Century*, Harmondsworth: Penguin, 1990, pp. 54ff.
41. Prest, *Albion Ascendant*, p. 257.
42. Porter, *English Society*, p. 112.
43. Ibid., p. 113.
44. William Hague, *William Pitt the Younger*, London: Harper Perennial, 2005, p. 142.
45. Ibid., p. 145.
46. Ibid., p. 154.
47. G.M. Ditchfield, *George III: An Essay in Monarchy*, Basingstoke: Palgrave Macmillan, 2002, p. 73.
48. Hague, *Pitt*, pp. 159–60.
49. Ibid., p. 165.

3: 'Vibrating between a monarchy and a corrupt oppressive aristocracy':
The woes of France and America, 1787–8

1. William Howard Adams, *The Paris Years of Thomas Jefferson*, New Haven: Yale University Press, 1997, pp. 10–13.
2. Ibid., p. 271.
3. Jean Égret, *La Pré-révolution française*, Paris: Presses Universitaires de France, 1962, p. 59.
4. Ibid.
5. Ibid., pp. 60–1, citing the *Correspondance secrète*.
6. Ibid., p. 99.
7. Ibid., p. 150.
8. Ibid., p. 151.
9. Ibid., p. 148.
10. Ibid., p. 162.
11. Ibid., p. 163.
12. Ibid., p. 165.
13. Ibid., p. 170.
14. Ibid., p. 171.
15. Ibid., p. 176.
16. Ibid., pp. 190–1.
17. Ibid., p. 201.
18. Ibid., p. 253.
19. Ibid., p. 306.
20. Bowen, *Miracle*, p. 188.
21. Ibid., p. 189.

22. Ibid., p. 191.
23. Ibid., p. 171.
24. Ibid., p. 170.
25. Ibid., pp. 177–8.
26. Ibid., p. 179.
27. Full text at <http://en.wikisource.org/wiki/The_Northwest_Ordinance>.
28. Bowen, *Miracle*, pp. 202–3.
29. Ibid., p. 201.
30. United States Constitution, Article 1, Section 9.
31. Ibid., Article 4, Section 2.
32. Ibid., Article 1, Section 2.
33. Bowen, *Miracle*, p. 198.
34. Ibid., p. 256.
35. Ibid., p. 260.
36. Ibid., p. 262.
37. Robert A. Rutland, *The Ordeal of the Constitution: The Antifederalists and the Ratification Struggle of 1787–1788*, Boston, Mass.: Northeastern University Press, 1983, pp. 51–8.
38. Johnson, *Righteous Anger*, pp. 141–2.
39. Rutland, *Ordeal of the Constitution*, pp. 95ff.
40. Bowen, *Miracle*, p. 283.
41. Ibid., p. 286.
42. Ibid., p. 288.
43. Rutland, *Ordeal of the Constitution*, p. 107.
44. Ibid., pp. 227ff.
45. Bowen, *Miracle*, pp. 297–8.
46. Clark, *Language of Liberty*, p. 59.
47. Bowen, *Miracle*, p. 298.
48. Ibid., p. 301.
49. Ibid., p. 306.
50. Clark, *Language of Liberty*, p. 137.
51. Jones, *Great Nation*, pp. 312–13.
52. Hague, *Pitt*, pp. 134–5.
53. Égret, *Pré-révolution française*, p. 316.
54. Ibid., pp. 318–19.
55. Ibid., p. 320.
56. Simon Burrows, 'The Innocence of Jacques-Pierre Brissot', *Historical Journal*, 46, 2003, pp. 843–71; especially pp. 852–3.
57. Ibid., especially pp. 865–7.
58. Thomas Jefferson, *Papers*, ed. J.P. Boyd, Princeton: Princeton University Press, 1958, vol. 14, p. 530, letter of 9 Feb. 1789 to William Short.
59. Égret, *Pré-révolution française*, p. 332.
60. Ibid., p. 334.
61. Daniel L. Wick, 'A Conspiracy of Well-intentioned Men: The Society of Thirty and the French Revolution', Ph.D. thesis, University of California, Berkeley, 1977, pp. 43–4.
62. Ibid., pp. 142–5.
63. William Doyle, *The Oxford History of the French Revolution*, second edn, Oxford: Oxford University Press, 2002, p. 90.
64. Jones, *Reform and Revolution*, pp. 142ff.
65. Doyle, *Oxford History*, p. 91.

## 4: 'The seeds of decay and corruption':
## Britain, empire and the king's madness, 1784–8

1. Penderel Moon, *Warren Hastings and British India*, London: Hodder & Stoughton, 1947, pp. 73ff.
2. Ibid., p. 78.
3. Ibid., p. 82.
4. Ibid., pp. 304–5.
5. Hague, *Pitt*, p. 172.
6. David Johnson, 'Britannia Roused: Political Caricature and the Fall of the Fox–North Coalition', *History Today*, June 2001, pp. 22–8.
7. Ditchfield, *George III*, p. 139.
8. Hague, *Pitt*, p. 180.
9. Moon, *Warren Hastings*, pp. 306–7.
10. Jennifer Mori, *William Pitt and the French Revolution, 1785–1795*, Edinburgh: Keele University Press, 1997, pp. 17ff.
11. Hague, *Pitt*, p. 192.
12. Ibid., pp. 191, 193.
13. Mori, *Pitt*, p. 26.
14. Jenny Uglow, *The Lunar Men: The Friends who Made the Future*, London: Faber & Faber, 2002, pp. 395–6.
15. Ibid., pp. 396–7.
16. Ibid., p. 393.
17. Ibid., p. 401.
18. Hague, *Pitt*, p. 230.
19. Moon, *Warren Hastings*, p. 309.
20. For a discussion of how far Hastings's fortune was made up of technically illegal 'presents', and how far his earnings had been dissipated by imprudence and generosity, see P.J. Marshall, 'The Personal Fortune of Warren Hastings', *Economic History Review*, New Series, 17, 1964, pp. 284–300.
21. Conor Cruise O'Brien, 'Edmund Burke: A Biographical Note', in Edmund Burke, *Reflections on the Revolution in France*, ed. and introduction by Conor Cruise O'Brien, London: Penguin, 1968, p. 78.
22. Nicholas B. Dirks, *The Scandal of Empire: India and the Creation of Imperial Britain*, Cambridge, Mass.: Belknap Press, 2006, pp. 66–75.
23. Ibid., pp. 78–9.
24. Ibid., pp. 94–9.
25. Ibid., pp. 100–1.
26. Hague, *Pitt*, pp. 232–3.
27. Dirks, *Scandal of Empire*, p. 105.
28. Goodwin, *Friends of Liberty*, pp. 76–8.
29. Hague, *Pitt*, pp. 238–9.
30. Goodwin, *Friends of Liberty*, pp. 33–6.
31. Ibid., pp. 50–1.
32. Clark, *Language of Liberty*, p. 33.
33. Goodwin, *Friends of Liberty*, pp. 54–5.
34. Clark, *Language of Liberty*, p. 124.
35. Goodwin, *Friends of Liberty*, p. 56.
36. Jeremy Bernstein, *Dawning of the Raj: The Life and Trials of Warren Hastings*, Chicago: Ivan R. Dee, 2000, pp. 223ff.; Dirks, *Scandal of Empire*, pp. 87–8.
37. Ibid., p. 89.
38. Ibid., pp. 106–7; Bernstein, *Dawning*, pp. 232–3.

39. Dirks, *Scandal of Empire*, pp. 110–11.
40. Bernstein, *Dawning*, pp. 236–7.
41. Dirks, *Scandal of Empire*, p. 113.
42. Goodwin, *Friends of Liberty*, p. 86.
43. Ibid., p. 85.
44. Ibid., p. 87.
45. Hibbert, *George III*, p. 258.
46. Ibid., p. 261.
47. Hague, *Pitt*, p. 252.
48. Ibid., p. 255.
49. Hibbert, *George III*, p. 270.
50. L.G. Mitchell, *Charles James Fox and the Disintegration of the Whig Party, 1782–1794*, Oxford: Oxford University Press, 1971, pp. 118–21.
51. The detail of the constitutional position can be followed in Erskine May, *The Constitutional History of England since the Accession of George the Third, 1760–1860*, eleventh edn, London: Longman, 1896, chapter 3, pp. 175–95.
52. Mitchell, *Charles James Fox*, pp. 123–4.
53. Ibid., pp. 128–9.
54. Ibid., p. 132.
55. Ibid., p. 127.
56. Ibid., p. 130.
57. Hibbert, *George III*, p. 272.
58. Hague, *Pitt*, p. 258.
59. Ibid., p. 259.
60. Ibid.
61. Ibid., pp. 260–1.
62. Ibid., p. 261.
63. Ibid., p. 262.

## 5: 'The base laws of servitude': Empire, slavery and race in the 1780s

1. Inga Clendinnen, *Dancing with Strangers: The True History of the Meeting of the British First Fleet and the Aboriginal Australians, 1788*, Edinburgh: Canongate, 2005, pp. 97ff.
2. Robin Blackburn, *The Overthrow of Colonial Slavery, 1776–1848*, London: Verso, 1988, p. 142.
3. Hague, *Pitt*, p. 299.
4. Robin Blackburn, *The Making of New World Slavery: From the Baroque to the Modern, 1492–1800*, London: Verso, 1997, p. 377.
5. Blackburn, *Overthrow*, p. 3.
6. Blackburn, *Making*, pp. 386–7.
7. Ibid., pp. 392–3.
8. David Brion Davis, *The Problem of Slavery in the Age of Revolution*, Oxford: Oxford University Press, 1999, pp. 405–6.
9. Blackburn, *Overthrow*, p. 20.
10. Blackburn, *Making*, pp. 384–5, 388.
11. See Farley Grubb, 'Babes in Bondage? Debt Shifting by German Immigrants in Early America', *Journal of Interdisciplinary History*, 37, 2006, pp. 1–34, and articles cited therein, pp. 1–3.
12. Blackburn, *Overthrow*, p. 163; Blackburn, *Making*, pp. 440–1.
13. Ibid., pp. 433–4.
14. Ibid., pp. 436–7.

15. Carolyn E. Fick, 'The Saint Domingue Slave Insurrection of 1791: A Socio-political and Cultural Analysis', *Journal of Caribbean History*, 25, 1991, pp. 1–40; especially pp. 2–6.

16. Blackburn, *Overthrow*, p. 124.

17. Trevor Burnard, *Mastery, Tyranny and Desire: Thomas Thistlewood and His Slaves in the Anglo-Jamaican World*, Chapel Hill: University of North Carolina Press, 2003. See review at <http://www.thenation.com/doc.mhtml?i=20041129&s=berlin>.

18. Davis, *Problem of Slavery*, p. 9.

19. Jill Lepore, 'Goodbye, Columbus', *New Yorker*, 8 May 2006.

20. Sue Peabody, *'There Are No Slaves in France': The Political Culture of Race and Slavery in the Ancien Regime*, Oxford: Oxford University Press, 1996; see, for example, p. 89 for the French rendition, *'nul n'est esclave en France'*.

21. Blackburn, *Overthrow*, p. 100.

22. Peabody, *'No Slaves in France'*, p. 119.

23. Ibid., pp. 122–8.

24. Dorinda Outram, *The Enlightenment*, Cambridge: Cambridge University Press, 1995, p. 66.

25. See Robert Whelan, 'Wild in Woods: The Myth of the Noble Eco-savage', <http://www.iea.org.uk/files/upld-publication46pdf?.pdf>, pp. 3–4.

26. John Locke, *Two Treatises on Government*, ed. P. Laslett, Cambridge: Cambridge University Press, 1967, p. 319.

27. Outram, *Enlightenment*, p. 73.

28. Ibid., p. 63.

29. See, for example, <http://www.discover.com/issues/feb-06/features/mega death-in-mexico/>, and Charles C. Mann, *1491: New Revelations of the Americas before Columbus*, New York: Knopf, 2005.

30. Alan Taylor, *The Divided Ground: Indians, Settlers and the Northern Borderland of the American Revolution*, New York: Knopf, 2006, pp. 144–5.

31. Ibid., pp. 148–50.

32. Ibid., p. 164.

33. Ibid., chapter 6.

34. Ibid., p. 200.

35. Johnson, *Righteous Anger*, p. 19.

36. Robert C. Davis, 'Counting European Slaves on the Barbary Coast', *Past and Present*, 172, 2001, pp. 87–124.

37. Jefferson, *Papers*, vol. 15, pp. 284, 454.

38. Linda Colley, 'Going Native, Telling Tales: Captivity, Collaborations and Empire', *Past and Present*, 168, 2000, pp. 170–93.

39. Sudipta Sen, *Distant Sovereignty: National Imperialism and the Origins of British India*, London: Routledge, 2002, pp. xii–xiii.

40. William Dalrymple, *White Mughals: Love and Betrayal in Eighteenth-Century India*, London: HarperCollins, 2002, p. 33.

41. Ibid., pp. 34–5.

42. Sen, *Distant Sovereignty*, pp. 129–30.

43. Dalrymple, *White Mughals*, pp. 30–1.

44. Ibid., pp. 42–4.

45. Ibid., p. 40.

46. Ibid., p. 41.

47. Ibid.

48. Sen, *Distant Sovereignty*, p. 123.

49. Ibid., pp. 128, 131.

50. Ibid., p. 132.

51. Dalrymple, *White Mughals*, p. 46.

52. Sen, *Distant Sovereignty*, pp. 130, 136.
53. Durba Ghosh, 'Making and Unmaking Loyal Subjects: Pensioning Widows and Educating Orphans in Early Colonial India', *Journal of Imperial and Commonwealth History*, 31, 2003, pp. 1–28.
54. Sen, *Distant Sovereignty*, pp. 18–19, 98.
55. Ibid., pp. 100–1.
56. Ibid., p. 13.
57. Franklin Wickwire and Mary Wickwire, *Cornwallis: The Imperial Years*, Chapel Hill: University of North Carolina Press, 1980, p. 18.
58. Ibid., p. 42.
59. Ibid., p. 82.
60. Ibid., p. 92.
61. Ibid., p. 95.
62. Jon E. Wilson, '"A Thousand Countries to Go to": Peasants and Rulers in Late Eighteenth-Century Bengal', *Past and Present*, 189, 2005, pp. 81–109.
63. Wickwire and Wickwire, *Cornwallis*, p. 71.
64. Ibid., p. 72.
65. Wilson, 'A Thousand Countries', p. 90.
66. Ibid., p. 87.
67. Ibid., p. 84.
68. Ibid., p. 106.
69. Jean-Marie Lafont, 'French Military Intervention in India Compared to the French Intervention in North America (1776–1785)', in Aniruddha Ray (ed.), *Tipu Sultan and His Age*, Kolkata: The Asiatic Society, 2002, pp. 63–116; pp. 72–3.
70. Wickwire and Wickwire, *Cornwallis*, pp. 119–121.
71. Ibid., p. 122; Lafont, 'French Military Intervention', pp. 83–8.
72. Wickwire and Wickwire, *Cornwallis*, pp. 122–4.
73. Aniruddha Ray, 'Contemporary French Reports on Tipu Sultan', in Ray (ed.), *Tipu Sultan*, pp. 131–54; pp. 137–8.
74. Ibid., p. 145.
75. Wickwire and Wickwire, *Cornwallis*, pp. 125–7.
76. Clendinnen, *Dancing*, p. 26.
77. Ibid., p. 30.
78. Ibid., pp. 241–2.
79. Ibid., pp. 52–3.
80. Ibid., p. 55.
81. Ibid., p. 261.

6: 'That offspring of tyranny, baseness and pride':
Abolitionism, political economy and the people's rights

1. Full text at <http://docsouth.unc.edu/neh/equiano1/equiano1.html>, accessed 23 August 2007, subscription-list pp. vi–xiv.
2. Clark, *Language of Liberty*, p. 20.
3. Richard S. Newman, *The Transformation of American Abolitionism: Fighting Slavery in the Early Republic*, Chapel Hill: University of North Carolina Press, 2002, pp. 16–18.
4. Ibid., pp. 20–1, 35–6.
5. Ibid., pp. 33–4.
6. Isaacson, *Benjamin Franklin*, pp. 464–5.
7. Marcel Dorigny, 'La Société des Amis des Noirs: antiesclavagisme et lobby colonial à la fin du siècle des lumières (1788–1792)', in Marcel Dorigny and Bernard

Gainot (eds), *La Société des Amis des Noirs, 1788–1799: contribution à l'histoire de l'abolition de l'esclavage*, Paris: Editions UNESCO, 1998, pp. 18–19.

8. Isaacson, *Benjamin Franklin*, p. 465.
9. Mori, *Pitt*, pp. 31, 44.
10. Ibid., p. 32.
11. Ibid., pp. 33–4, 44.
12. Dorigny, 'La Société', p. 22.
13. Ibid., p. 65.
14. Adams, *Paris Years*, pp. 270–1.
15. Dorigny, 'La Société', p. 66.
16. Ibid., pp. 32–3.
17. Mori, *Pitt*, p. 41.
18. Dorigny, 'La Société', pp. 34, 37–9.
19. Hague, *Pitt*, p. 303.
20. Peter Linebaugh, *The London Hanged: Crime and Civil Society in the Eighteenth Century*, London: Penguin, 1991, pp. 343–4.
21. Linebaugh, *London Hanged*, pp. 344–5.
22. Ibid., p. 347.
23. Uglow, *Lunar Men*, p. 416.
24. Linebaugh, *London Hanged*, pp. 375–6.
25. John Rule, *The Vital Century: England's Developing Economy, 1714–1815*, Harlow: Longman, 1992, pp. 182–3.
26. Ibid., pp. 186–7.
27. Ibid., p. 183.
28. Bowen, *Miracle*, p. 156.
29. Edward Countryman, *The American Revolution*, London: Penguin, 1985, pp. 214ff.; citation p. 225.
30. Ibid., p. 225.
31. Bowen, *Miracle*, p. 46.
32. Michael Sonenscher, *Work and Wages: Natural Law, Politics and the Eighteenth-Century French Trades*, Cambridge: Cambridge University Press, 1989.
33. Michael Sonenscher, 'Journeymen, the Courts and the French Trades, 1781–1791', *Past and Present*, 114, 1987, pp. 77–109.
34. Steven L. Kaplan, 'Social Classification and Representation in the Corporate World of Eighteenth-Century France: Turgot's "Carnival"', in Steven L. Kaplan and Cynthia J. Koepp (eds), *Work in France: Representations, Meaning, Organization and Practice*, Ithaca: Cornell University Press, 1986, pp. 176–228.
35. Steven L. Kaplan, *La Fin des corporations*, Paris: Fayard, 2001.
36. E.P. Thompson, 'The Moral Economy of the English Crowd in the Eighteenth Century', in E.P. Thompson, *Customs in Common*, London: Penguin, 1993, pp. 185–258; pp. 193–6.
37. Ibid., p. 189.
38. Cited in Cynthia Bouton, *The Flour War: Gender, Class, and Community in Late Ancien Régime French Society*, University Park: Pennsylvania State University Press, 1993, p. 83.
39. Thompson, 'Moral Economy', p. 213.
40. Ibid., p. 214.
41. Hibbert, *George III*, p. 119.
42. Ibid., pp. 132–3.
43. Alan Williams, *The Police of Paris, 1718–1789*, Baton Rouge: Louisiana State University Press, 1979.
44. Arlette Farge, *Subversive Words: Public Opinion in Eighteenth-Century France*, Cambridge: Polity Press, 1994, especially chapters 5 and 6.

45. Jeremy Gregory and John Stevenson, *The Longman Companion to Britain in the Eighteenth Century: 1688–1820*, London: Longman, 2000, p. 227.
46. Linebaugh, *London Hanged*, p. 363.
47. Simon Devereaux, 'The Abolition of the Burning of Women in England Reconsidered', *Crime, History and Societies*, 9, 2005, pp. 73–98; p. 78.
48. Ibid., p. 83; John Rule, *Albion's People: English Society, 1714–1815*, Harlow: Longman, 1992, pp. 240–1.
49. Ibid., p. 243.
50. See Michael Ignatieff, *A Just Measure of Pain: The Penitentiary in the Industrial Revolution, 1750–1850*, New York: Pantheon Books, 1978.
51. Cited in David Andress, *The French Revolution and the People*, London: Hambledon & London, 2004, p. 76.
52. Kaplan, *Fin des corporations*, pp. 299–300.
53. <http://www.geol.binghamton.edu/faculty/naslund/Franklin1789.html>, accessed 2 August 2006. See also <http://volcano.und.nodak.edu/vwdocs/volc_images/europe_west_asia/laki.html>.
54. Andress, *French Revolution and the People*, pp. 27–8.
55. Ibid., pp. 26–7.

## 7: 'Constant effort and continuous emulation': The revolutions of cotton and steam

1. Clark, *Language of Liberty*, p. 124.
2. Goodwin, *Friends of Liberty*, p. 57.
3. Ibid., p. 63.
4. Richard L. Hills, *Power in the Industrial Revolution*, Manchester: Manchester University Press, 1970, p. 218.
5. Ibid., p. 219.
6. Sen, *Distant Sovereignty*, pp. 105, 114.
7. Michael M. Edwards, *The Growth of the British Cotton Trade, 1780–1815*, Manchester: Manchester University Press, 1967, pp. 44–5.
8. Hills, *Power*, pp. 12–13.
9. Ibid., pp. 16–17.
10. Ibid., pp. 58–9.
11. Ibid., pp. 116ff.
12. Edwards, *Growth*, p. 80.
13. Ibid., p. 82.
14. Ibid., p. 84.
15. Angela Lakwete, *Inventing the Cotton Gin: Machine and Myth in Antebellum America*, Baltimore: Johns Hopkins University Press, 2003, p. 37.
16. Edwards, *Growth*, pp. 78–83.
17. Ibid., p. 86.
18. Ibid., p. 87.
19. Lakwete, *Inventing the Cotton Gin*, pp. 35–6.
20. Edwards, *Growth*, p. 65.
21. Jefferson, *Papers*, vol. 14, pp. 546–8.
22. Ibid., p. 546.
23. J.R. Harris, *Industrial Espionage and Technology Transfer: Britain and France in the Eighteenth Century*, Aldershot: Ashgate, 1998, p. 311.
24. Ibid., p. 317; see also Uglow, *Lunar Men*, p. 376.
25. Edwards, *Growth*, p. 65.
26. Harris, *Industrial Espionage*, p. 362.
27. Ibid., pp. 364–9.

28. Ibid., pp. 370–6.
29. Ibid., pp. 379–80, 382.
30. Ibid., pp. 404–8, 425ff, 435, 444.
31. Ibid., pp. 409, 412.
32. Ibid., pp. 384–7.
33. Serge Chassagne, *Le Coton et ses patrons: France, 1760–1840*, Paris: Ed. EHESS, 1991, p. 194.
34. Ibid., pp. 194–6, 219.
35. Ibid., p. 215.
36. Ibid., pp. 188–9.
37. Ibid., p. 218.
38. Ibid., pp. 147–8.
39. Hills, *Power*, pp. 89–91, 95–7.
40. Ibid., pp. 134–5.
41. Ibid., pp. 137–8, 142–3.
42. Ibid., p. 144.
43. Ibid., pp. 159, 161.
44. Ibid., p. 214.
45. Ibid., p. 219.
46. Ibid., pp. 219–21.
47. Edwards, *Growth*, p. 183.
48. Ibid., pp. 187–8.
49. Ibid., p. 189.
50. Ibid., pp. 200, 203.
51. Ibid., p. 254.
52. Ibid., pp. 250–1.
53. Ibid., p. 96.
54. Lakwete, *Inventing the Cotton Gin*, pp. 2–3.
55. Ibid., pp. 11–15.
56. Ibid., pp. 26–9.
57. Ibid., pp. 40–4.
58. Ibid., pp. 53–8, and chapter 8 for the full-blown emergence of Whitney's legend in the nineteenth century.

## 8: 'This general agitation of public insanity': France and Britain in the spring of 1789

1. Emmanuel Joseph Sieyès, *What Is the Third Estate?*, trans. M. Blondel, ed. S.E. Finer, intro. P. Campbell, London: Pall Mall Press, 1963, pp. 4, 51–2.
2. Égret, *Pré-revolution française*, p. 345.
3. Ibid., p. 346.
4. Timothy Tackett, *Becoming a Revolutionary: The Deputies of the French National Assembly and the Emergence of a Revolutionary Culture (1789–1790)*, Princeton: Princeton University Press, 1996, pp. 90–2.
5. Ibid., p. 113.
6. Ibid., p. 114.
7. Ibid., pp. 114–15.
8. Ibid., p. 115.
9. Sieyès, *What Is the Third Estate?*, p. 174.
10. Andress, *French Revolution and the People*, p. 92.
11. Tackett, *Becoming a Revolutionary*, pp. 28–35.
12. John Markoff, *The Abolition of Feudalism: Peasants, Lords and Legislators in the French Revolution*, University Park: Pennsylvania State University Press, 1996, pp. 30–1.

13. Tackett, *Becoming a Revolutionary*, pp. 35–8.
14. Ibid., p. 44.
15. Gilbert Shapiro and John Markoff, *Revolutionary Demands: A Content Analysis of the Cahiers de doléances of 1789*, Stanford: Stanford University Press, 1998, pp. 318–19.
16. Ibid., pp. 319–20.
17. David Andress, *French Society in Revolution*, Manchester: Manchester University Press, 1999, p. 168.
18. Ibid., p. 169.
19. Markoff, *Abolition*, pp. 30–2.
20. Andress, *French Society*, p. 168.
21. Andress, *French Revolution and the People*, p. 94.
22. Ibid., p. 91.
23. Georges Lefebvre, *The Great Fear of 1789*, London: New Left Books, 1973, p. 41.
24. Andress, *French Revolution and the People*, pp. 96–7.
25. Ibid., pp. 98–101.
26. Adams, *Paris Years*, p. 179.
27. Ibid., pp. 52–5.
28. Ibid., p. 261.
29. Ibid., p. 267.
30. Ibid., p. 265.
31. Jefferson, *Papers*, vol. 14, pp. 330, 420.
32. Ibid., p. 676.
33. Ibid., pp. 671, 673.
34. Adams, *Paris Years*, pp. 7–9.
35. Jefferson, *Papers*, vol. 14, p. 330.
36. Adams, *Paris Years*, pp. 275–6.
37. Jefferson, *Papers*, vol. 14, p. 363.
38. Ibid., pp. 372–7.
39. Ibid., p. 429.
40. Ibid., pp. 429, 431.
41. Ibid., p. 454.
42. Ibid., p. 531.
43. Hibbert, *George III*, pp. 288–90; and 181–2 for Miss Burney's character.
44. Ditchfield, *George III*, pp. 18–21.
45. Hibbert, *George III*, p. 290.
46. Ibid., pp. 284–5.
47. Ibid., p. 283.
48. John W. Derry, *The Regency Crisis and the Whigs*, Cambridge: Cambridge University Press, 1963, p. 128.
49. Ibid., pp. 129–30.
50. Hague, *Pitt*, pp. 263–4.
51. Derry, *Regency Crisis*, p. 130.
52. Hibbert, *George III*, p. 292.
53. Derry, *Regency Crisis*, p. 154.
54. Ibid., pp. 155–6.
55. Ibid., pp. 159, 161.
56. Ibid., p. 162.
57. Ibid., pp. 164, 166.
58. Ibid., p. 186; Hibbert, *George III*, p. 293.
59. Hague, *Pitt*, pp. 265–6.
60. Derry, *Regency Crisis*, p. 126.

61. Mitchell, *Charles James Fox*, p. 146.
62. Derry, *Regency Crisis*, p. 189.
63. Ibid., pp. 189–90.
64. Jefferson, *Papers*, vol. 14, p. 565.
65. Ibid., p. 566.
66. Ibid., p. 567.
67. Hague, *Pitt*, pp. 266–7.

## 9: 'Highly fraught with disinterested benevolence': Empire, reason, race and profit in the Pacific

1. Caroline Alexander, *The Bounty: The True Story of the Mutiny on the Bounty*, London: HarperCollins, 2003, pp. 127, 141.
2. John Gascoigne, *Science in the Service of Empire: Joseph Banks, the British State, and the Uses of Science in the Age of Revolution*, Cambridge: Cambridge University Press, 1998.
3. Neil Chambers (ed.), *The Letters of Sir Joseph Banks: A Selection, 1768–1820*, London: Imperial College Press, 2000, pp. 84–5.
4. Ibid., p. 86.
5. Ibid., pp. 90–3.
6. Gascoigne, *Science*, p. 154.
7. Ibid., pp. 157–8.
8. John Dunmore, *Where Fate Beckons: The Life of Jean-François de La Pérouse*, Auckland: Exisle, 2006, pp. 232–3.
9. Gascoigne, *Science*, pp. 174–5.
10. Ibid., p. 173.
11. Jefferson, *Papers*, vol. 15, p. 237.
12. Ibid., pp. 193–4, 266.
13. Ibid., vol. 14, pp. 698–9.
14. Ibid., p. 674.
15. Ibid., pp. 636–7.
16. Ibid., vol. 15, p. 101.
17. Ibid., vol. 14, p. 304.
18. Ibid., p. 621; vol. 15, p. 77.
19. Ibid., p. 100.
20. Adams, *Paris Years*, p. 273.
21. Jefferson, *Papers*, vol. 14, p. 416.
22. Ibid., p. 328.
23. Ibid., p. 331; see pp. 246–69 for Jefferson's reports and replies by French agencies.
24. Granville Allen Mawer, *Ahab's Trade: The Saga of South Seas Whaling*, St Leonard's: Allen & Unwin, 1999, pp. 79–80.
25. Jefferson, *Papers*, vol. 14, p. 250.
26. Mawer, *Ahab's Trade*, pp. 46–50.
27. Ibid., pp. 77–9, 81–3.
28. Greg Dening, *Mr Bligh's Bad Language: Passion, Power and Theatre on the Bounty*, Cambridge: Cambridge University Press, 1993, p. 181.
29. Dunmore, *Where Fate Beckons*, pp. 242–3.
30. Dening, *Mr Bligh's Bad Language*, pp. 86–7.
31. Alexander, *The Bounty*, pp. 49ff.
32. Ibid., pp. 43ff.
33. Scott Ashley, 'How Navigators Think: The Death of Captain Cook Revisited', *Past and Present*, 194, 2007, pp. 107–37; especially pp. 110–11, 118, 121–7.
34. Ibid., pp. 132–3.

35. Alexander, *The Bounty*; for example, pp. 97–8.
36. Dening, *Mr Bligh's Bad Language*, p. 74.
37. Alexander, *The Bounty*, p. 100.
38. Ibid., pp. 102–4.
39. Ibid., p. 112.
40. Ibid., pp. 116–17.
41. Ibid., pp. 57–63; Dening, *Mr Bligh's Bad Language*, pp. 70–1.
42. Ibid., pp. 69–70.
43. Alexander, *The Bounty*, p. 119.
44. Dening, *Mr Bligh's Bad Language*, pp. 85–6.
45. Alexander, *The Bounty*, p. 127.
46. Ibid., pp. 143–4.
47. Dening, *Mr Bligh's Bad Language*, pp. 89–91.
48. Ibid., p. 94; Alexander, *The Bounty*, pp. 368–9.
49. Ibid., pp. 352–4.
50. Dening, *Mr Bligh's Bad Language*, pp. 214–17.
51. Alexander, *The Bounty*, pp. 6–10; Dening, *Mr Bligh's Bad Language*, pp. 214–15.
52. Alexander, *The Bounty*, p. 337.
53. Ibid., pp. 377–8.
54. Ibid., pp. 384–5.
55. Ibid., pp. 385–6.
56. Ibid., p. 388.
57. Ibid., p. 66.
58. Ibid., p. 359.

## 10: 'Deep rooted prejudices, and malignity of heart, and conduct': President Washington and the war in the West

1. Joseph J. Ellis, *His Excellency George Washington*, New York: Knopf, 2004, pp. 184–5.
2. Elkins and McKitrick, *Age of Federalism*, pp. 34–5.
3. Ibid., pp. 36–9.
4. Ibid., pp. 40–2.
5. Francis Jennings, *The Creation of America: Through Revolution to Empire*, Cambridge: Cambridge University Press, 2000, p. 276 for Washington's manipulation of land surveys and Virginia statutes in the late 1760s.
6. Elkins and McKitrick, *Age of Federalism*, p. 43.
7. Elizabeth W. Marvick, 'Family Imagery and Revolutionary Spirit: Washington's Creative Leadership', in Mark J. Rozell, William D. Pederson and Frank J. Williams (eds), *George Washington and the Origins of the American Presidency*, Westport, Conn.: Praeger, 2000, pp. 77–91; p. 81.
8. Ibid., p. 82.
9. Ibid., pp. 83–5.
10. Ibid., p. 86.
11. Ibid., p. 89, letter of January 1784.
12. Ellis, *His Excellency*, p. 182.
13. David McCullough, *John Adams*, New York: Simon & Schuster, 2000, pp. 393–4.
14. Joseph J. Ellis, *Passionate Sage: The Character and Legacy of John Adams*, New York: W.W. Norton, 1993, pp. 38–43; McCullough, *John Adams*, p. 392.
15. Ellis, *Passionate Sage*, p. 43.
16. McCullough, *John Adams*, p. 399.
17. Ibid., pp. 400–1; see, for example, <www.loc.gov/rr/program/bib/ourdocs/

NewNation.html> at the Library of Congress, with an illustration of Federal Hall on the right, accessed 6 November 2006.

18. McCullough, *John Adams*, p. 402.
19. See Ellis, *His Excellency*, pp. 185–6; McCullough, *John Adams*, pp. 403–4.
20. Ibid., p. 405.
21. Elkins and McKitrick, *Age of Federalism*, p. 47.
22. Ellis, *His Excellency*, p. 193.
23. McCullough, *John Adams*, p. 408.
24. Ellis, *His Excellency*, p. 193.
25. Malcolm L. Cross, 'Washington, Hamilton and the Establishment of the Dignified and Efficient Presidency', in Rozell *et al.*, *George Washington*, pp. 95–116; p. 104.
26. Elkins and McKitrick, *Age of Federalism*, p. 49.
27. Ibid., pp. 49–50; Ellis, *His Excellency*, pp. 193–4.
28. Cross, 'Washington, Hamilton', pp. 104–5.
29. Ibid., p. 105.
30. Elkins and McKitrick, *Age of Federalism*, p. 51.
31. Ibid., p. 51.
32. Cross, 'Washington, Hamilton', p. 108.
33. Elkins and McKitrick, *Age of Federalism*, p. 52.
34. Cross, 'Washington, Hamilton', p. 109.
35. Ibid., p. 106.
36. Ibid.
37. Elkins and McKitrick, *Age of Federalism*, p. 55.
38. Jack D. Warren, Jr., 'In the Shadow of Washington: John Adams as Vice-President', in Richard A. Ryerson (ed.), *John Adams and the Founding of the Republic*, Boston: Massachusetts Historical Society, 2001, pp. 117–41; especially p. 119.
39. Ibid., pp. 126–7.
40. Ellis, *His Excellency*, p. 212.
41. Ibid., p. 213.
42. Wiley Sword, *President Washington's Indian War: The Struggle for the Old Northwest, 1790–1795*, Norman: University of Oklahoma Press, 1985, pp. 3–4.
43. Ibid., pp. 4–5.
44. Richard White, *The Middle Ground: Indians, Empires and Republics in the Great Lakes Region, 1650–1815*, Cambridge: Cambridge University Press, 1991, pp. 449–50.
45. Ibid., p. 451.
46. Ibid., p. 452.
47. Ibid., pp. 1–11.
48. Ibid., pp. 41–3.
49. Ibid., p. 487 n. 27.
50. Ibid., p. 470 n. 1.
51. Ibid., pp. 201–2.
52. Ibid., p. 223.
53. Ibid., p. 231.
54. See, for example, ibid., pp. 4–5.
55. Ibid., p. 368.
56. For a discussion of the culture and practices of 'Indian-hating', 1775–82, centred on the Gnadenhutten events, but disfigured by assertions of deliberate government-sponsored genocide, see Barbara Alice Mann, *George Washington's War on Native America*, Westport, Conn.: Praeger, 2005.
57. White, *Middle Ground*, pp. 389–91.
58. Ibid., p. 395.
59. Sword, *President Washington's Indian War*, pp. 122–3.
60. White, *Middle Ground*, p. 412.

61. Ibid., pp. 418–19.
62. Sword, *President Washington's Indian War*, chapter 6.
63. Ibid., chapter 5.
64. White, *Middle Ground*, p. 440.
65. Ibid., p. 416.
66. Ibid., p. 419.
67. Ibid., pp. 443–6.
68. Bowen, *Miracle*, pp. 173, 181.
69. Sword, *President Washington's Indian War*, p. 49.
70. Ibid., pp. 83–4.
71. Ibid., pp. 85–7.
72. Ibid., pp. 67–8.
73. Ibid., pp. 87–8.
74. Ibid., p. 101.
75. Ibid., chapters 12, 15.
76. Allan D. Gaff, *Bayonets in the Wilderness: Anthony Wayne's Legion in the Old Northwest*, Norman: University of Oklahoma Press, 2004.
77. Eliga H. Gould, 'Entangled Histories, Entangled Worlds: The English-Speaking Atlantic as a Spanish Periphery', *American Historical Review*, 112, 2007, pp. 764–86; especially pp. 782–4.
78. See David Cannadine, *Ornamentalism: How the British Saw Their Empire*, London: Penguin, 2002, chapter 1.
79. Jill Lepore, *The Name of War; King Philip's War and the Origins of American Identity*, New York: Vintage Books, 1999.
80. Sword, *President Washington's Indian War*, p. 7.

## 11: 'No, sire, it is a revolution': From the Estates-General to the Bastille, France, May–July 1789

1. Mori, *Pitt*, pp. 79–80.
2. Michael Kwass, 'Economies of Consumption: Political Economy and Noble Display in Eighteenth-Century France', in Jay M. Smith (ed.), *The French Nobility in the Eighteenth Century: Reassessments and New Approaches*, University Park: Pennsylvania State University Press, 2006, pp. 19–41.
3. Ibid., pp. 20–1.
4. Ibid., pp. 38–9.
5. Tackett, *Becoming a Revolutionary*, pp. 121–2.
6. Ibid., p. 125.
7. Ibid., p. 126.
8. Ibid., p. 128.
9. Ibid., p. 132.
10. Ibid., p. 134.
11. Ibid., pp. 134–8.
12. Ibid., p. 140.
13. Ibid., pp. 141–2.
14. Ibid., p. 144.
15. Ibid., p. 148.
16. Andress, *French Revolution and the People*, pp. 101–2.
17. Lefebvre, *Great Fear*, p. 40.
18. Ibid., p. 39.
19. Andress, *French Revolution and the People*, pp. 103–4.
20. Tackett, *Becoming a Revolutionary*, p. 151.
21. Ibid., p. 152.

22. Ibid., p. 154.
23. Arthur Young, *Travels in France*, at < http://oll.libertyfund.org/Texts/Econlib/Young0451/TravelsInFrance/0445_Bk.html>.
24. Tackett, *Becoming a Revolutionary*, p. 154.
25. Ibid., p. 156.
26. Munro Price, *The Road from Versailles: Louis XVI, Marie Antoinette and the Fall of the French Monarchy*, New York: St Martin's Press, 2002, pp. 49–50.
27. Ibid., pp. 44–8.
28. Ibid., p. 53.
29. Ibid., p. 54.
30. Ibid., p. 61.
31. Ibid., pp. 63–4.
32. Ibid., pp. 67–8.
33. Ibid., p. 69.
34. Ibid., p. 75.
35. Ibid., pp. 63, 79–80.
36. Ibid., p. 77.
37. Jacques Godechot, *The Taking of the Bastille*, London: Faber & Faber, 1970, pp. 181–2.
38. Tackett, *Becoming a Revolutionary*, pp. 160–1.
39. Godechot, *Taking of the Bastille*, pp. 172–3.
40. Ibid., pp. 183–4.
41. Ibid., p. 188.
42. Paul G. Spagnoli, 'The Revolution Begins: Lambesc's Charge, 12 July 1789', *French Historical Studies*, 17, 1991, pp. 466–97; especially pp. 482–4.
43. Ibid., p. 485.
44. Godechot, *Taking of the Bastille*, p. 191.
45. Ibid., pp. 192–6.
46. Bibliothèque nationale de France, Ms. n.a.f. 2670, fol. 88.
47. Godechot, *Taking of the Bastille*, pp. 216–17.
48. Ibid., p. 220.
49. Ibid., pp. 221, 226–7.
50. Ibid., p. 229.
51. Ibid., pp. 232–3.
52. Ibid., pp. 240–1.
53. Ibid., pp. 243–4.
54. Ibid., p. 253.
55. Tackett, *Becoming a Revolutionary*, pp. 162–3.
56. Ibid., p. 163.
57. Godechot, *Taking of the Bastille*, pp. 250–1.
58. Ibid., p. 251.
59. William H. Sewell, Jr., 'Historical Events as Transformations of Structures: Inventing Revolution at the Bastille', *Theory and Society*, 25, 1996, pp. 841–81; especially p. 854.
60. Tackett, *Becoming a Revolutionary*, p. 164.
61. Price, *Road from Versailles*, p. 94.
62. Ibid., pp. 85–7.
63. Ibid., p. 100.
64. Sewell, 'Historical Events', pp. 854–5.

## 12: 'For all men, and for all countries': Declaring rights in America and France

1. Full text at <http://www.yale.edu/lawweb/avalon/england.htm>.
2. Full text at <http://www.gunstonhall.org/documents/vdr.html>.

3. Robert A. Rutland, *The Birth of the Bill of Rights, 1776–1791*, New York: Collier Books, 1962, p. 45.
4. Ibid., pp. 17–18.
5. Ibid., p. 21.
6. Ibid., pp. 52–60.
7. Ibid., p. 63.
8. Full text at < http://www.nhinet.org/ccs/docs/ma-1780.htm>.
9. Rutland, *Birth of the Bill of Rights*, pp. 78–9.
10. Ibid., p. 80.
11. James Madison, Alexander Hamilton and John Jay, *The Federalist Papers*, London: Penguin, 1987, p. 476.
12. Full text at <http://www.wepin.com/articles/afp/afp84.html>.
13. Rutland, *Birth of the Bill of Rights*, p. 87.
14. See ibid., pp. 88–102, for examples.
15. Richard Labunski, *James Madison and the Struggle for the Bill of Rights*, Oxford: Oxford University Press, 2006, p. 132.
16. Ibid., p. 162.
17. Ibid., pp. 136, 139–41, 143.
18. Ibid., p. 145.
19. Ibid., pp. 185–92.
20. Ibid., pp. 192–3, 194.
21. Rutland, *Birth of the Bill of Rights*, p. 194.
22. Ibid., p. 208.
23. Ibid., p. 203.
24. Labunski, *James Madison*, p. 204.
25. Ibid., pp. 207–8.
26. Ibid., pp. 210–12.
27. Ibid., pp. 224–5.
28. Ibid., pp. 230–2.
29. Rutland, *Birth of the Bill of Rights*, p. 212.
30. Labunski, *James Madison*, pp. 218–20.
31. Ibid., pp. 235–7.
32. Ibid., pp. 203, 237.
33. Ibid., p. 243.
34. Bibliothèque nationale de France, Ms. n.a.f. 2665 f. 259.
35. Tackett, *Becoming a Revolutionary*, p. 167.
36. Sewell, 'Historical Events', p. 856.
37. Ibid., p. 857.
38. Tackett, *Becoming a Revolutionary*, p. 168.
39. Ibid., p. 169.
40. Sewell, 'Historical Events', p. 859.
41. Tackett, *Becoming a Revolutionary*, p. 170.
42. Michael P. Fitzsimmons, *The Night the Old Regime Ended: August 4, 1789, and the French Revolution*, University Park: Pennsylvania State University Press, 2003, pp. 8–11.
43. Ibid., pp. 13–14; Tackett, *Becoming a Revolutionary*, p. 172.
44. Ibid.
45. Fitzsimmons, *The Night*, p. 14.
46. Tackett, *Becoming a Revolutionary*, pp. 173, 175.
47. Keith Michael Baker, *Inventing the French Revolution: Essays on French Political Culture in the Eighteenth Century*, Cambridge: Cambridge University Press, 1990, p. 262.
48. *Archives parlementaires*, vol. 8, p. 222.

49. Jefferson, *Papers*, vol. 14, pp. 438–9. The earlier draft is more concise, 'All sovereignty resides essentially in the nation', but the substance is identical.
50. *Archives parlementaires*, vol. 8, pp. 284–5.
51. Ibid., p. 222.
52. Baker, *Inventing the French Revolution*, p. 265.
53. Ibid., p. 266.
54. Marcel Gauchet, *La Révolution des droits de l'homme*, Paris: Gallimard, 1989, pp. 52–4.
55. Baker, *Inventing the French Revolution*, p. 267.
56. Tackett, *Becoming a Revolutionary*, pp. 176–7.
57. Ibid., pp. 180–1.
58. Keith Michael Baker, 'The Idea of a Declaration of Rights', in Dale Van Kley (ed.), *The French Idea of Freedom: The Old Regime and the Declaration of Rights of 1789*, Stanford: Stanford University Press, 1994, pp. 154–96; especially pp. 159, 165–6.
59. Ibid., pp. 176–7.
60. Ibid., p. 184.
61. Gauchet, *La Révolution*, p. 94.
62. Baker, 'The Idea', p. 188.
63. Tackett, *Becoming a Revolutionary*, pp. 178–9.
64. Ibid., p. 180.
65. Ibid., p. 186.
66. Ibid., p. 183.
67. See Van Kley (ed.), *French Idea of Freedom*, pp. 1–3, for an English text largely used here; Gauchet, *La Révolution*, pp. i–ii, for the French original, from which in some cases I have taken a more literal translation than Van Kley offers.
68. Ibid., pp. 153–4.
69. Tackett, *Becoming a Revolutionary*, p. 184.
70. On this general point, see James Swenson, *On Jean-Jacques Rousseau, Considered as One of the First Authors of the Revolution*, Stanford: Stanford University Press, 2000.
71. Gauchet, *La Révolution*, p. 155.

## 13: 'Your houses will answer for your opinions': The French Revolution imperilled

1. J.-P. Brissot (ed.), *Le Patriote françois*, intro. by J.-P. Bertaud, Frankfurt: Keip Verlag, 1989; prospectus, pp. 2, 4.
2. *Patriote françois*, 1, 28 July 1789, p. 2.
3. Darrin M. McMahon, 'The Birthplace of the Revolution: Public Space and Political Community in the Palais-Royal of Louis-Philippe-Joseph d'Orléans, 1781–1789', *French History*, 10, 1996, pp. 1–29; Robert M. Isherwood, *Farce and Fantasy: Popular Entertainment in Eighteenth-Century Paris*, Oxford: Oxford University Press, 1986.
4. David Andress, 'Neighbourhood Policing in Paris from Old Regime to Revolution: The Exercise of Authority by the District de St-Roch, 1789–1791', *French Historical Studies*, 29, 2006, pp. 231–60.
5. George A. Kelly, 'The Machine of the duc d'Orléans and the New Politics', *Journal of Modern History*, 51, 1979, pp. 667–84.
6. Jefferson, *Papers*, vol. 15, p. 359.
7. Ibid., p. 360.
8. Jennifer Pitts, *A Turn to Empire: The Rise of Imperial Liberalism in Britain and France*, Princeton: Princeton University Press, 2005, pp. 107–8.
9. Jefferson, *Papers*, vol. 15, p. 366.
10. Ibid., p. 354.

11. Tackett, *Becoming a Revolutionary*, p. 189.
12. Baker, *Inventing the French Revolution*, p. 271.
13. Ibid., p. 276.
14. Tackett, *Becoming a Revolutionary*, p. 188.
15. Baker, *Inventing the French Revolution*, p. 271.
16. *Archives parlementaires*, vol. 8 , p. 512.
17. Ibid., p. 513.
18. Ibid., pp. 513–14.
19. Tackett, *Becoming a Revolutionary*, p. 190.
20. Ibid., p. 189.
21. Baker, *Inventing the French Revolution*, p. 272.
22. Tackett, *Becoming a Revolutionary*, p. 191.
23. Baker, *Inventing the French Revolution*, p. 272.
24. Swenson, *On Jean-Jacques Rousseau*, especially chapter 4.
25. Baker, *Inventing the French Revolution*, pp. 277–8.
26. Ibid., pp. 278–9.
27. Ibid., p. 279.
28. Ibid., p. 280.
29. Ibid., pp. 281–2.
30. Ibid., pp. 285–6.
31. Marcel Gauchet, *La Révolution des pouvoirs: la souveraineté, le peuple et la représentation, 1789–1799*, Paris: Gallimard, 1995, p. 72.
32. Tackett, *Becoming a Revolutionary*, pp. 192–3; marquis de Ferrières, *Correspondance inédite (1789, 1790, 1791)*, ed. Henri Carré, Paris: Armand Colin, 1932, pp. 148–50.
33. Baker, *Inventing the French Revolution*, p. 288.
34. Ibid., p. 289.
35. Ibid.
36. Tackett, *Becoming a Revolutionary*, p. 193.
37. Ibid., pp. 194–5.
38. Adams, *Paris Years*, p. 292.
39. *Archives parlementaires*, vol. 9, p. 36.
40. Andress, *French Revolution and the People*, pp. 119–20.
41. Price, *Road from Versailles*, pp. 104–5.
42. George Rudé, *The Crowd in the French Revolution*, Oxford: Oxford University Press, 1959, p. 74.
43. Tackett, *Becoming a Revolutionary*, p. 196.
44. Rudé, *Crowd*, p. 76.
45. Tackett, *Becoming a Revolutionary*, pp. 197–8.
46. Price, *Road from Versailles*, p. 105.
47. Ibid., p. 106.
48. Tackett, *Becoming a Revolutionary*, p. 198.
49. Barry M. Shapiro, *Revolutionary Justice in Paris, 1789–1790*, Cambridge: Cambridge University Press, 1993, includes a lengthy discussion of the efforts to 'pin' the October Days on radicals by judicial investigation.
50. Tackett, *Becoming a Revolutionary*, pp. 198–9.
51. Price, *Road from Versailles*, p. 109.
52. Patrice Gueniffey, *Le Nombre et la raison: la Révolution française et les élections*, Paris: Ed. EHESS, 1993.
53. Fitzsimmons, *The Night*, p. 118.
54. *Archives parlementaires*, vol. 9, p. 639.
55. Ibid., p. 640, and see ff.
56. See also Tackett, *Becoming a Revolutionary*, p. 204.
57. Ferrières, *Correspondance*, p. 187.

58. *Journal d'Adrien Duquesnoy*, 2 vols, ed. Robert de Crèvecoeur, Paris, 1828, vol. 1, p. 493, cited in Barry Shapiro, 'Conspiratorial Thinking in the Constituent Assembly: Mirabeau and the Exclusion of Deputies from the Ministry', in Peter R. Campbell, Thomas Kaiser and Marisa Linton (eds.), *Conspiracy in the French Revolution*, Manchester: Manchester University Press, 2007, pp. 42–62; p. 45.

59. *Courrier de Provence*, 11–14 September, cited in ibid., p. 44.

60. *Archives parlementaires*, vol. 9, p. 708.

61. Ibid., pp. 712–13.

62. Ibid., p. 714.

63. Ibid., p. 715.

64. Cited in Shapiro, 'Conspiratorial Thinking', p. 46.

65. *Archives parlementaires*, vol. 9, p. 718.

66. Jefferson, *Papers*, vol. 15, pp. 460, 477, 481.

67. Ibid., p. 424.

68. Price, *Road from Versailles*, p. 217.

69. Timothy Tackett, *When the King Took Flight*, Cambridge, Mass.: Harvard University Press, 2003.

70. Price, *Road from Versailles*, chapters 11, 12.

71. David Andress, *The Terror: Civil War in the French Revolution*, London: Little, Brown, 2005, p. 115.

### 14: 'The greatest event it is that ever happened in the world': The British and the French Revolution

1. Jefferson, *Papers*, vol. 15, p. 329.

2. Ibid., p. 449.

3. Frank O'Gorman, 'The Paine Burnings of 1792–1793', *Past and Present*, 193, 2006, pp. 111–55; especially pp. 116, 120.

4. Hague, *Pitt*, p. 267.

5. Mori, *Pitt*, pp. 66–7.

6. *Patriote françois*, 2, 29 July 1789, p. 3.

7. Mori, *Pitt*, pp. 57–8.

8. Hague, *Pitt*, pp. 274–5.

9. Mori, *Pitt*, pp. 62–3.

10. Ibid., p. 64.

11. Ibid., pp. 68–71.

12. Hague, *Pitt*, p. 276. On the French as 'arbiters of Europe', see Bailey Stone, *Reinterpreting the French Revolution: A Global Historical Perspective*, Cambridge: Cambridge University Press, 2002, especially chapter 1; citation at p. 50.

13. Goodwin, *Friends of Liberty*, pp. 100–1.

14. Uglow, *Lunar Men*, pp. 195, 198–9, 212, 399.

15. Goodwin, *Friends of Liberty*, pp. 102–3.

16. *The Repository*, 4, 16 February 1788, p. 225.

17. Mitchell, *Charles James Fox*, pp. 153–4.

18. F. O'Gorman, *The Whig Party and the French Revolution*, London: Macmillan, 1967, p. 45.

19. Ibid., p. 38.

20. Goodwin, *Friends of Liberty*, p. 104.

21. Ibid., p. 105.

22. J.-G. Peltier, *Domine salvum fac regem*, Paris, 1789, p. 27.

23. O'Gorman, *Whig Party*, pp. 41–2.

24. Ibid., p. 43.

25. Ibid.
26. Mitchell, *Charles James Fox*, p. 155.
27. Goodwin, *Friends of Liberty*, pp. 107–8.
28. Ibid., p. 109.
29. Ibid.
30. Ibid., p. 110.
31. Ibid., p. 111.
32. Hague, *Pitt*, p. 272.
33. O'Gorman, *Whig Party*, pp. 46–7.
34. Keane, *Tom Paine*, p. 288.
35. Burke, *Reflections*, pp. 92–3.
36. Ibid., pp. 101, 103.
37. Ibid., pp. 107–8.
38. Ibid., p. 123.
39. Ibid., p. 160.
40. Ibid., pp. 169–70.
41. Ibid., p. 173.
42. Keane, *Tom Paine*, pp. 289–90.
43. Mitchell, *Charles James Fox*, p. 158.
44. Ian Haywood, *Bloody Romanticism: Spectacular Violence and the Politics of Representation, 1776–1832*, Basingstoke: Macmillan, 2006, pp. 67, 69.
45. Keane, *Tom Paine*, p. 288.
46. W.E. Woodward, *Tom Paine: America's Godfather, 1737–1809*, Westport, Conn.: Greenwood Press, 1945, p. 167.
47. Keane, *Tom Paine*, p. 279.
48. Woodward, *Tom Paine*, p. 183.
49. Keane, *Tom Paine*, p. 282.
50. Woodward, *Tom Paine*, pp. 169–70.
51. Ibid., p. 182.
52. Keane, *Tom Paine*, p. 284.
53. Ibid., pp. 283–4.
54. Thomas Paine, *The Rights of Man*, Part 1, collected in Michael Foot and Isaac Kramnick (eds.), *The Thomas Paine Reader*, London: Penguin, 1987, p. 211.
55. Ibid.
56. Ibid., pp. 214, 216.
57. Ibid., p. 233.
58. Ibid., p. 234.
59. Ibid., pp. 238–40.
60. Ibid., pp. 246–7.
61. Ibid., pp. 253–4.
62. Ibid., p. 255.
63. Ibid., p. 259.
64. Ibid., p. 262.
65. Keane, *Tom Paine*, pp. 305–7.
66. Ibid., p. 306.
67. Ibid., p. 307.
68. Ibid., pp. 308–9.
69. Ibid., pp. 325–7.
70. Paine, *Rights of Man*, p. 264.
71. Ibid., p. 284.
72. Ibid., p. 292.
73. Ibid., pp. 306–7.
74. Ibid., p. 337.

75. Ibid., pp. 329–55.
76. Ibid., p. 359.
77. Ibid., pp. 363–4.
78. Hague, *Pitt*, pp. 277–82.
79. Ibid., pp. 305–6.
80. E.P. Thompson, *The Making of the English Working Class*, 2nd edn, London: Penguin, 1968, pp. 19–20.
81. Goodwin, *Friends of Liberty*, pp. 158–9.
82. Ibid., p. 168.
83. Tackett, *Becoming a Revolutionary*, pp. 206–7.
84. Keane, *Tom Paine*, pp. 334–5.
85. Thompson, *The Making*, p. 112, 118.
86. O'Gorman, 'Paine Burnings', pp. 127–31.
87. Goodwin, *Friends of Liberty*, pp. 264–5.

## Conclusion: 1789/1798

1. Richard N. Rosenfeld, *American Aurora: A Democratic-Republican Returns. The Suppressed History of Our Nation's Beginnings and the Heroic Newspaper that Tried to Report It*, New York: St Martin's Press, 1997, p. 216.
2. Jeffery A. Smith, 'World Revolution and American Reform', in *Franklin and Bache: Envisioning the Enlightened Republic*, New York: Oxford University Press, 1990, pp. 111–33; James Tagg, 'A Democratic Society, 1794–1795', in *Benjamin Franklin Bache and the Philadelphia Aurora*, University Park: University of Pennsylvania Press, 1991, pp. 205–38.
3. Elkins and McKitrick, *Age of Federalism*, p. 361.
4. Ibid., p. 519.
5. See Francis D. Cogliano, 'Review Article: America and the French Revolution', *History*, 1999, pp. 658–65; pp. 659–60.
6. Washington's 'Farewell Address' at <http://www.yale.edu/lawweb/avalon/wash ing.htm>, accessed 3 September 2007.
7. Elkins and McKitrick, *Age of Federalism*, p. 405.
8. Hague, *Pitt*, p. 414.
9. Full text at <http://www.constitution.org/rf/sedition_1798.htm>, accessed 3 September 2007.
10. Franklin W. Knight, 'The Haitian Revolution', *American Historical Review*, 105, 2000, pp. 103–15; especially pp. 110ff.
11. Fick, 'The Saint Domingue Slave Insurrection of 1791', pp. 1–40.
12. Ashli White, 'The Politics of "French Negroes" in the United States', *Historical Reflections*, 29, 2003, pp. 103–21; especially pp. 106–7.
13. David Geggus, *Slavery, War and Revolution: The British Occupation of Saint Domingue 1793–1798*, Oxford: Clarendon Press, 1982.
14. See Andress, *The Terror*.
15. Gauchet, *Révolution des pouvoirs*, p. 201.
16. Steven Englund, *Napoleon: A Political Life*, Cambridge, Mass.: Harvard University Press, 2004, pp. 126, 132–3.
17. Alfred Cobban (ed.), *The Debate on the French Revolution, 1789–1800*, London: Adam & Charles Black, 1960, p. 333.
18. Ibid., pp. 336–8.
19. Michael Durey, *Transatlantic Radicals and the Early American Republic*, Lawrence: University Press of Kansas, 1997.
20. Stuart Andrews, *The Rediscovery of America: Transatlantic Crosscurrent in an Age of Revolution*, Basingstoke: Macmillan, 1998, p. 85.

21. Roy Foster, *Modern Ireland, 1600–1972*, London: Penguin, 1989, p. 276.
22. Haywood, *Bloody Romanticism*, pp. 110–15.
23. Ibid., p. 112.
24. Foster, *Modern Ireland*, pp. 280–1.
25. Englund, *Napoleon*, p. 177.
26. See Robert Dixon, 'The Origin of the Term "Dismal Science" to Describe Economics', <http://www.economics.unimelb.edu.au/TLdevelopment/econo chat/Dixonecon00.html>, accessed 4 September 2007.
27. On this general area, see the excellent survey by C.A. Bayly, *Imperial Meridian: The British Empire and the World, 1780–1830*, London: Longman, 1989.
28. < http://www.shsu.edu/~his_ncp/Const.html>, Articles 8 and 9, accessed 10 September 2007.
29. Full text at <http://www.departments.bucknell.edu/russian/const/1936toc. html>, accessed 7 September 2007.
30. See the brief history of the declaration at <http://www.udhr.org/history/default.htm>. The Frenchman was René Cassin, the Canadian John Humphrey. The American was, of course, Eleanor Roosevelt.
31. See <http://www.hri.org/docs/ECHR50.html>. The subsequent European Charter of Fundamental Rights (2000) took the process even further. See <http://www.europarl.europa.eu/charter/default_en.htm>.
32. Jeremy Bentham, *Rights, Representation, and Reform – Nonsense upon Stilts and Other Writings on the French Revolution*, ed. Philip Schofield, Catherine Pease-Watkin and Cyprian Blamires, Oxford: Clarendon Press, 2002.

# INDEX